# Rivalry and Revenge

What explains violence against civilians in civil wars? Why do groups kill civilians in areas where they have full military control and their rivals have no military presence? This innovative book connects pre-war politics to patterns of violence during civil war. It argues that both local political rivalry and local revenge account for violence against civilians. Armed groups perpetrate direct violence jointly with local civilians, who collaborate when violence can help them gain or consolidate local political control. As civil war continues, revenge motives also come into play, leading to spirals of violence at a local level.

In an important contribution to the study of the Spanish Civil War, Balcells combines statistical analyses with ethnographic and qualitative research to provide new insights to scholars and academic researchers with an interest in civil war, politics, and conflict processes. *Rivalry and Revenge* is theoretically and empirically rich, and it offers a theory and method generalizable to a wide set of cases.

Laia Balcells is Assistant Professor of Political Science at Duke University.

# Cambridge Studies in Comparative Politics

## General Editors

Kathleen Thelen *Massachusetts Institute of Technology*
Erik Wibbels *Duke University*

## Associate Editors

Catherine Boone *London School of Economics*
Thad Dunning *University of California, Berkeley*
Anna Grzymala-Busse *Stanford University*
Torben Iversen *Harvard University*
Stathis Kalyvas *Yale University*
Margaret Levi *Stanford University*
Helen Milner *Princeton University*
Frances Rosenbluth *Yale University*
Susan Stokes *Yale University*
Tariq Thachil *Vanderbilt University*

## Series Founder

Peter Lange *Duke University*

## Other Books in the Series

*Continued after the index*

# Rivalry and Revenge

*The Politics of Violence during Civil War*

**LAIA BALCELLS**
*Duke University*

CAMBRIDGE
UNIVERSITY PRESS

# CAMBRIDGE
## UNIVERSITY PRESS

University Printing House, Cambridge CB2 8BS, United Kingdom

One Liberty Plaza, 20th Floor, New York, NY 10006, USA

477 Williamstown Road, Port Melbourne, VIC 3207, Australia

4843/24, 2nd Floor, Ansari Road, Daryaganj, Delhi - 110002, India

79 Anson Road, #06-04/06, Singapore 079906

Cambridge University Press is part of the University of Cambridge.

It furthers the University's mission by disseminating knowledge in the pursuit of education, learning and research at the highest international levels of excellence.

www.cambridge.org
Information on this title: www.cambridge.org/9781107548213
DOI: 10.1017/9781316392737

First published 2017
First paperback edition 2017

*A catalogue record for this publication is available from the British Library*

*Library of Congress Cataloging in Publication data*
NAMES: Balcells, Laia, author.
TITLE: Rivalry and revenge : the politics of violence during civil war / Laia Balcells, Duke University.
DESCRIPTION: Cambridge :New York, NY:Cambridge University Press, 2017. |
    Includes bibliographical references.
IDENTIFIERS: LCCN 2016047817 | ISBN 9781107118690 (hbk)
SUBJECTS: LCSH: Civil war. | Political violence. | Civilians in war. |
    Spain–History–Civil War, 1936-1939. | Côte d'Ivoire–History–Civil
    War, 2002-2007.
CLASSIFICATION: LCC JC328.5 .B35 2017 | DDC 303.6/4–dc23
LC record available at https://lccn.loc.gov/2016047817

ISBN 978-1-107-11869-0 Hardback
ISBN 978-1-107-54821-3 Paperback

*To all the victims of civil wars*

# Contents

# Figures

# Acknowledgments

This book has its origins in a PhD dissertation I defended at Yale University in 2010. At that time, the project benefited enormously from the advice provided by the members of my PhD committee: Stathis N. Kalyvas, Elisabeth J. Wood, and David Mayhew. I am very grateful for the intellectual imprint that Stathis, Libby, and Prof. Mayhew have left on me, beyond the dissertation and this book.

The research in this book has benefited from generous help offered by many different people. Albert Sesé, Anna Palacios, Josep Ventura, and Mercè Tafalla assisted me in the arduous process of data digitalization; Nacho Campanero provided crucial help with the mapping of the data. Giulia Piccolino, Albert Caramés, and Monica Palmieri were critical research assistants in Côte d'Ivoire.

Over the course of several months of fieldwork in Spain, I met a number of historians who were happy to walk me through archives, share data, or provide insider's insights on the Spanish conflict. I thank them for not having pushed me away from their discipline, but rather pulled me in. These are scholars such as Joan Villarroya, Josep Maria Roig Rosich, José Luis Ledesma, Jordi Gaitx, and Antonio Calzado. Many relatives, friends, and acquaintances, and their families, provided me with contacts for potential interviews, as well as logistical support during fieldwork in Spain: thank you, Rosó Ventura, Carles Fernández, Arsènia Clavera, Lucita Díaz, Anna Fernández, Roger Robert, Gemma Torres, Helena Simón, Albert Piñeira, Alvaro Martínez, Lluis Orriols, Pedro Riera, Gema García-Albacete, Elna Roig, Aina Roig, Mireia Calafell, Dídac Queralt, Maria José Hierro, Mikel Ochoa, Gemma Sala, Remo Fernández, Lourdes Monedero, Imelda Tejero, Joan Cucurella, Héctor Cebolla, Anna del Arroyo, and Elisa Chuliá. In different localities I visited, I found support from strangers who helped me find testimonies of the war: Jaume Teixidó, Toni Orensanz, Pere Audí, and Angela Jackson are some of them. Above all, I am particularly grateful to all my interviewees, who took the time to meet with me and recount their experiences: chatting with them helped me to learn a great deal about the civil war in Spain, and it also made me realize that what it takes for knowledge to be built is not merely scholarship, but also vital experience.

Several graduate school friends read parts of the manuscript in its different stages. In particular, I am grateful to Ana Arjona, Abbey Steele, Dominika Koter, Harris Mylonas, José Fernández-Albertos, Victor Lapuente, Andrés Santana, Alberto Penadés, Jonah Schulhofer-Wohl, and Ryan Sheely for their constructive feedback over these years. As I was turning the dissertation into a book, I received very helpful comments from Anna Grzymala-Busse, Roger Petersen, Alexander Downes, Erik Wibbels, Pablo Beramendi, Margaret Levi, Karen Remmer, Carles Boix, Michael Ward, Eduardo González Calleja, Thad Dunning, Sabine Flamand, Santiago Sánchez-Pages, Josep Maria Colomer, Michael Munger, Margaret Foster, Jordan Roberts, Katie Webster, Georg Vanberg, Scott Straus, Aila Matanock, Justine Davis, Giulia Piccolino, Yvan Guichaoua, Matthew Mitchell, Alvaro Laparra, Andreas Wimmer, Costantino Pischedda, Rachel Stein, David Carter, Andreu Arenas, Page Fortna, Deborah Avant, Jake Shapiro, and two anonymous Cambridge University Press reviewers.

In addition, the book manuscript has benefited from feedback in several great venues, including the Harvard University International Relations speaker series, the Princeton International Relations Faculty Colloquium, the University of Denver Sié Center Series, the Northwestern University Security Studies Working Group, the University of Virginia Lansing Lee/Bankard seminars, the Columbia University International Politics Seminar, the European Political Science Association 2013 Conference, and research seminars at University of California (Berkeley), University of Washington (Seattle), George Washington University, New York University, University of Michigan, Universidad Católica de Chile, ICS-Lisbon University, Institut d'Anàlisi Econòmica-CSIC, Binghamton University, Brown University, and Uppsala University.

Earlier versions of selected parts of Chapters 2 and 4 were previously published in my 2010 article, "Rivalry and Revenge. Violence against Civilians in Conventional Civil Wars." *International Studies Quarterly* 54(2): 291–313. 2010 by Wiley, DOI: 10.1111/j.1468-2478.2010.00588.x; and in my 2011 article, "Continuation of Politics by Two Means: Direct and Indirect Violence in Civil War." *Journal of Conflict Resolution* 55(3): 397–422. 2011 by SAGE Publications, Inc., all rights reserved. Earlier versions of some materials in Chapter 5 were published in my 2011 article, "La muerte está en el aire: los bombardeos en Cataluña, 1936–1939." *Revista Española de Investigaciones Sociológicas* 136: 193–214. 2011 by CIS, doi:10.5477/cis/reis.136.25. Related versions of some elements in Chapter 7 were published in: Laia Balcells, Abel Escribà-Folch, and Lesley Daniels. 2016. "The determinants of low-intensity intergroup violence: the case of Northern Ireland." *Journal of Peace Research* 53: 33–48. 2016 by SAGE Publications, Inc., all rights reserved, doi: 10.1177/0022343315610399; and in Laia Balcells and Stathis Kalyvas. 2014. "Does Warfare Matter? Severity, Duration, and Outcomes of Civil Wars."

*Journal of Conflict Resolution* 58(8): 1390–1418. 2014 by SAGE Publications, Inc., all rights reserved. I thank the publishers of these journals for their permission to draw from this work. I also thank Abel Escribà-Folch, Lesley-Ann Daniels, and Stathis Kalyvas for letting me use some of the materials of our co-authored research in Chapter 7 of the book.

Several institutions have provided funding for the research in this book, for which I am very thankful: the Harry Frank Guggenheim Foundation, the Niehaus Center for Globalization and Governance (NCGG) at Princeton University, Duke University, Yale University (Leylan Fellowship; John Enders Fellowship; Macmillan Center; Leitner Program in Political Economy, and Graduate School of Arts and Sciences), the Catalan Government through the Catalan Institute of Peace (ICIP) research grant (2011RICIP18), and the Spanish Centro de Investigaciones Sociológicas (CIS) through the *Ayuda a la finalización de tesis doctorales*.

My family and friends deserve to be thanked for their invaluable support during several years of research and writing. I am particularly grateful to my parents, my brothers, and my partner for their encouragement to complete this project. Special thanks are due to my grandparents, who were the first to tell me about a civil war they had to endure when they were just kids. The stories of my great-grandparents, who fought for the Republic, are among many civil war stories I have heard and read over the years. The book is dedicated to all the people who are behind these stories; that is, to all the victims of civil wars.

# Conventions

a) Throughout the manuscript, I make reference to several oral sources. Between 2007 and 2009, I conducted over nine months of fieldwork in Spain, which involved archival and bibliographical research, and semi-structured interviews to survivors of the civil war in different provinces throughout the country. Following an institutional review board (IRB) protocol for the protection of human subjects, I refer to these interviews anonymously in this book (an anonymized list of interviewees is provided in Table A.4.12 of the Appendix). This research was approved by Yale University's FAS Human Subjects Committee under IRB protocol number 0704002514.

b) Names of locations (e.g., municipalities, counties, and regions) are included in English. When there is no translation, the name in the original language is included.

c) All quotations from written and oral sources in Catalan, French, or Spanish have been translated into English by the author.

# Preface

When I was a kid, my brothers and I used to spend some weeks of each summer with our grandparents in a small town on the Catalan coast. One summer, my grandmother's uncle from Santander, el Tio Manolo, came to spend a few days with us. El Tio was a bachelor in his seventies, highly energetic, cheerful, and witty. He could spend hours talking, recounting the story of his life, which was marked by a civil war and a dictatorship. Tio Manolo was conscripted by the Republican army when he was 17 years old – he was a member of the so-called "baby bottle's draft." He survived the battlefield, but he lost his brother (our great-grandfather), an officer of the Republican army, in a battle with the Italians in the province of Burgos in August 1937. After the end of the war, the Francoists imprisoned Tio Manolo and he was condemned to death several times; he used to tell us that he was alive by pure chance because, for some unknown reason, the prison guards never called his name at the time of execution. He spent at least seven years in prison camps. When he was released, he was almost 30, and in his adult life had known little more than violence, torture, and hunger. He was a true survivor and a paradigm of resilience; no wonder we were fascinated by him.

The story of Tio Manolo and his brother was one of combatants who fought for the Republic and lost. In addition to our uncle's stories, our grandmother would often tell us about her grandfather, who adopted her when the coup split her family in the summer of 1936. El Abuelo was a Catalan landowner and thus a conservative, and for a while he had to hide in the Pyrenees mountains, threatened by anarchist militiamen who intended to kill him. He became the mayor of his small locality after the civil war ended. When Tio Manolo arrived in his village at the end of the war, fleeing from the Francoists, he tried to help him. El Abuelo could not influence Tio Manolo's detention, but we believe that his local political power allowed him to intervene in his favor and probably help him evade execution. He might have had some agency within the apparent chaos and arbitrariness of Francoist repression.

When Tio Manolo was on the battlefield, he had switched to the Nationalist side for a while in order to try to save his life. Yet, close to the end of the war, he decided to defect back to the Republican side, even though it was clear that they were going to lose the war. When El Abuelo asked him why he had done such an irrational move, he responded, "they knew I was not one of them." Apparently, within Francoists ranks, they called him "el Rojo" (the red). Tio Manolo thus had a strong leftist identity, which was visible to others. He could mask his ideology for a while, but this falsification was not sustainable for a long time. Also, his ultimate commitment was to the Republican army.

The stories of my ancestors speak to different theoretical themes I develop in this book: the role of local political elites and civilian agency in the perpetration of violence during civil war and its immediate aftermath; the importance of political mobilization and political identities in a civil war context – even when these identities are not based on ascriptive traits; the role of emotions in explaining wartime behavior. In a way, the story of my family made me realize from an early age that civil wars are deeply complex phenomena, and spurred my interest and passion in the study of civil wars at the micro level. It is at the micro level, after all, where the different life stories transpire, where gray areas exist, where the most human and the most inhuman facets of conflict unfold.

At the end of that summer, I told Tio Manolo that one day I would write a book about his life. I never did so, but I ended up writing this book, which speaks about the war he fought, and its victims.

PART I

I

# Violence Against Civilians During Civil Wars

## 1.1 PUZZLE AND STATE OF THE ART

Between mid-July 1936 and February 1939, for nearly the entire duration of the Spanish Civil War, La Cerdanya, a region in northern Catalonia bordering France, was under the control of the Republican (also called Loyalist) army. Between July 1936 and May 1937, anarchist militiamen patrolled the area, under the leadership of Antonio Martín, nicknamed *Cojo de Málaga*. In Puigcerdà, the county town, the anarchists executed over 30 individuals, while some kilometers away, in the second largest village of the county, Bellver de Cerdanya, significantly fewer were executed: three. In Das, a tiny village of 200 inhabitants located a few kilometers from Puigcerdà, the militia executed four citizens; over the same period, in Llívia, a village of a similar size, located at a similar distance from Puigcerdà, not a single civilian was assassinated. Why did the anarchist militiamen kill civilians behind the frontlines, and why did they carry out executions in some places and not others? The two most prominent explanations of civil war violence point to factors such as the degree of military contestation and the organizational characteristics of groups. These explanations are insufficient to explain the violence that was carried out by the anarchists in La Cerdanya: during this period there was no combat in this area and the Nationalist (also called Francoist or rebel) army had no presence in this area, so this violence was not the result of military competition between armed forces. At the same time, the militias patrolling this area were all composed of the same men and led by the same person, so the (undisciplined) nature of the armed organization cannot really account for this variation either.

When the Franco-led coup failed and the civil war broke out between rebels and loyalists, anarchists and communists – who were on the loyalist side – were eager to seize the moment and start "the Revolution" in Spain. For some of these left-wing militants, eliminating counterrevolutionaries was a necessary measure to accomplish the ultimate goal of the revolution. But, most importantly, eliminating them was regarded as a crucial measure in a civil war in which both sides were highly mobilized and right-wingers could easily develop into a military threat. A parallel process, and one that was overall more brutal, took place in territories controlled by the rebels: right-wing militiamen and soldiers persecuted those suspected of supporting the Republican government and/or left-wing (e.g., communist, anarchist) organizations. Leftists in rearguard territories represented not only a political but also a military threat, and hence it was thought that they had to be eliminated in order to promote the counterrevolutionary cause.

The anarchist militiamen patrolling territories behind the war frontlines sought the elimination of right-wingers. However, they did not kill them all, and they did not kill right-wingers in the same proportion throughout the territory because they found diverging levels of collaboration across localities, which constrained or enhanced their capacity to carry out assassinations. For example, in Puigcerdà, where the anarchists managed to establish political control of the locality at the beginning of the civil war, local political elites and other citizens were cooperative with the militiamen: they informed on the location of the right-wingers and did not try to prevent their execution. Members of the local council even arrested some of these individuals, who were later executed by the militia. In Bellver de Cerdanya, in contrast, the local political authorities confronted the anarchists and they limited the capacity of the militias to undertake violent actions against the inhabitants of this locality. Similar dynamics took place at the other side of the frontline, namely, in rebel-controlled territory: local political elites collaborated to varying degrees with the military and paramilitary forces that patrolled the areas in search of leftists. Local priests, landlords, and members of the Falange, among others, were crucial collaborators of right-wing armed forces in those zones, but their degree of collaboration varied across localities: in some places they were more bloody than in others.

Although the agents of violence were the armed militiamen and soldiers, the actions of local civilians significantly influenced the level of violence exercised across Spanish municipalities during the civil war. I argue that these local actions were highly determined by local political dynamics, which would have an impact on how strongly local political elites would want to see the political enemies in their localities eliminated. In particular, greater levels of political competition between the Left and the Right at the local level led to greater levels of collaboration with the militias, and thus to greater levels of violence. For example, local competition was much greater in Puigcerdà – where the Left had won the national elections held in February 1936 with a narrow margin – than in Bellver de Cerdanya – where the Left was much more hegemonic. In other words, local political elites had more incentives to use violence against political enemies in the former village than in the latter.

Civil wars are not static phenomena, and endogenous dynamics are likely to emerge during the course of the conflict. In areas that were conquered by an armed group (for example, the Francoists), the actions of local civilians were largely influenced by preceding events and by the rival group's behavior up to then: local civilians were then willing to collaborate with Francoist authorities to settle scores with those having perpetrated violence against their peers. Due to revenge, local collaboration was higher (and thus levels of violence were overall greater) in places where an armed group had been more violent in the recent past. Revenge dynamics played a critical role in non-initial phases of the civil war. In a nutshell, in this book I posit that violence against civilians during internal war can be explained by dynamics of *rivalry* and *revenge*.

## 1.2   SUMMARY OF THE ARGUMENT

Why do armed groups kill noncombatants in the rearguard territories like the one described above? In other words, why do groups target civilians in areas that they control militarily, where they do not face direct military threats? From the point of view of military strategy, we would not expect to see violence in these areas of full military control, and yet it very often takes place. Contrary to many explanations of violence, which focus on either military or organizational factors, I argue that *political factors* are crucial in understanding violence against civilians: on the one hand, political mobilization at the national level makes armed groups wary of noncombatants with strong ideological positions, and sparks their persecution. On the other hand, political configurations determine the extent to which there is local collaboration with armed groups in the elimination of these individuals.

Firstly, I argue that the perpetration of violence against civilians follows a process of political mobilization, which I understand as the activation of political identities such that they push individuals to political action. According to Tilly, "'Mobilization' conveniently identifies the process by which a group goes from being a passive collection of individuals to an active participant in public life" (1978: 69). I posit that armed groups are likely to perpetrate violence against civilians when there are significant levels of prewar mobilization, which leads to violence based on public identities. When there is political mobilization, supporters of the enemy are perceived as threatening because such active supporters can promote resistance movements, including armed resistance, and they can provide key information to the enemy (i.e., acting as fifth-columnists). Because of mobilization, political identities become a cue for armed groups to detect potential threats in their control areas. By contrast, armed groups do not perceive threats in their areas of control in the context of civil wars where no major political mobilization has occurred during the prewar period. Why is prewar mobilization (and not wartime mobilization) relevant? Once the war starts, mobilization can mostly be undertaken by the armed group militarily controlling a given territory, so individuals cannot easily grow as supporters of the rival. Also, individuals have rational incentives to behave as if they are supporters of the group that exerts a military controls upon them (and groups know it).[1] In addition, armed groups do not perceive threats if the territory is fully segregated and there are no enemies plausibly residing behind the armed group's frontlines. Since complete segregation is rare, what matters most is whether the rival group has managed to mobilize politically in one's territory before the conflict's outbreak.[2] In short, in this book I argue that significant prewar mobilization is a precondition for violence against civilians in areas of full military control by armed groups in conflict.[3]

Secondly, not everywhere where the locals have been mobilized is there violence: this varies with the distribution of political identities at the local level. I propose a distinction between *indirect* and *direct* violence against civilians, and I argue that the distribution of political identities relates differently with respect to each of these types. These differences emanate from their diverging form of production: indirect violence is perpetrated with heavy weapons (e.g., tanks, fighter planes) and is unilaterally carried out by the armed group, while direct violence is perpetrated with small weapons (e.g., machetes, handguns, rifles) and is produced by armed groups in collaboration with local civilians. Indeed, despite the fact that militiamen or soldiers are the ones inflicting direct violence, local civilians can either constrain or enhance their killing capacity. Direct violence is thus not only driven by the armed group's motives, but also by civilians' motives. By contrast, indirect violence is mostly driven by an armed group's tactical and strategic motives because armed groups do not generally need civilian collaboration to carry out this type of violence.

When a territory is not militarily contested by a rival armed group, I argue that local civilians, and particularly local political elites, tend to think in strategic terms about who is going to have political control over the locality in the future (i.e., after the war) and they promote direct violence in places where killings are going to have an impact on the local balance of power, in a way that benefits them. It follows that civilians push for killings of their local enemies in places where the distribution of support between groups approaches parity. Killing people is accompanied by costs, but in the margin it produces "net benefits" for the local elites in places where the groups are more or less equally supported. This is why we are likely to observe more killings in contexts of

---

[1] In other words, individuals have incentives to "falsify their preferences" (Kuran 1994).

[2] The existence of potential threats within armed groups' areas of control is one of the main differences between civil wars and interstate wars. The exceptions are countries with non-core groups that enjoy support from an external rival (Mylonas 2012) or foreign nationals in conquered areas, in the context of wars of annexation (Downes 2008).

[3] As I will show in Chapter 7, at the national level, political mobilization accounts for variation in levels of violence between different countries and hence serves to explain why some civil wars are bloodier than others. However, the main focus of the book is the subnational level.

political parity or competition.[4] Conversely, local political elites do not push for killings when their group has overwhelming support (i.e., violence is not necessary to change the already favorable *status quo*) or when their group is in a situation of minority (i.e., violence cannot change the state of affairs without being too costly). In consequence, we are likely to observe less violence in such contexts of non-parity between groups.

Where territory is militarily contested – for example, near the frontlines – the incentives of local civilians are different, though: local supporters of an armed group are more likely to collaborate in the persecution of defectors, regardless of local political configurations. Because they care about the outcome of the civil war, politically mobilized local civilians and political elites collaborate to maximize the odds of securing the territory by the armed group they sympathize with. In other words, when the territory is contested, military considerations trump political strategy.

Indirect violence follows a different logic, again, because civilians are less relevant in the production of this type of violence. And yet politics is still relevant to the understanding of indirect targeting of civilians through bombings and shellings. In addition to being instrumental in diminishing the enemy's military capacity and breaking the will to fight (Pape 1996; Arreguín-Toft 2001; Downes 2008), I argue that airstrikes and artillery shelling are also utilized to eliminate supporters of the enemy. When civilians are mobilized, armed groups tend to "indirectly" target rearguard locations with high concentrations of enemy supporters, with the purpose of eliminating them.[5]

This book puts a lot of weight on civilian agency in explaining wartime violence, and particularly, direct violence against noncombatants.[6] Indeed, while tactical and strategic considerations on the side of the armed group are relevant in explaining violence of all types, strategic considerations on the part of the civilians must also be taken into account when it comes to explaining direct violence, which is perpetrated jointly by armed groups and local civilians. Moreover, I argue that civilian collaboration with armed groups is rooted in factors that are exogenous to the war, namely prewar local political configurations, but that such collaboration is also shaped by events that are endogenous to the war such as denunciations, executions or massacres. These wartime events lead to emotions such as anger, which often lead to a desire for revenge. In other words, as the civil war unfolds, individuals seek to settle scores against those who have victimized their relatives and friends. The latter makes direct violence both more likely and more intense in places where there has been greater victimization in previous periods of the war

---

[4] Hereafter I will use the terms "parity" and "competition" interchangeably.

[5] Also, in areas of military contestation, groups might use indirect violence in order to cause displacement and carry out cleansing of territories, as this can facilitate their conquest (Downes 2008; Balcells and Steele 2016).

[6] The terms "civilian" and "noncombatant" are used interchangeably in the book.

(i.e., when the rival group had control of the territory) because armed groups find greater levels of collaboration. Revenge also makes indirect violence more likely in places where the enemy has treated one's constituents harshly: armed groups can use bombings as a means to punish these localities. Political strategy motivations are expected to have a greater relevance during the early stages of civil war and revenge motivations to gain more relevance as the war develops.[7]

### Politics in Violence

This book ultimately tries to answer the question of why civilians are victimized during armed conflict. This is an important question that has serious policy implications in a world in which civil wars leave a significant civilian death toll. In Iraq, for example, the Iraq Body Count project estimated between 151,836 and 171,640 civilian deaths from violence from 2003 up to June 2015. In Syria, the Violations Documentation Center estimated over 85,400 civilian deaths from March 2011 up to September 2015, while the Syrian Center for Policy Research has estimated a total of 400,000 deaths from violence (including civilians and combatants) up to February 2016.

The question of civilian victimization has been at the forefront of recent war studies. Although a first generation of scholars, following Clausewitz (1832/1968) and Schmitt (1976), regarded violent conflicts as the result of existing political cleavages and violence as the consequence of these divisions, recent empirical research on conflict has pointed instead to the military incentives of armed groups (Valentino et al. 2004; Kalyvas 2006; Downes 2008), the survival incentives of (self-interested) civilians (Kalyvas 2006; Berman et al. 2011) or the organizational characteristics of the groups (Mkandawire 2002; Humphreys and Weinstein 2006; Weinstein 2007). There has been a tendency to assume that, despite the influence of politics at the outbreak of a conflict, the internal dynamics of war are usually driven by factors that are not inherently political. In other words, the factors that lead to the outbreak of war have been regarded as different from the determinants of violence within war. The latter body of research has de-emphasized political variables despite the fact that civil wars are usually fought over political issues, e.g., demands for self-determination and regime or leadership change.[8]

My theory brings political variables back to the fore to explain violence perpetrated against civilians during conflict. The neglect of political variables has

---

[7] Note that this framework is consistent with the idea that the dynamics of violence in civil wars of long duration tend to lose much of their ideological bearings over time and that violence is likely to become driven mostly by non-ideological and vengeful motives.

[8] See, for instance, Gurr (1970, 2000); Horowitz (1985); Bates (1999); Hechter (2001); Sambanis (2001); Reynal-Querol (2002); Toft (2003); Montalvo and Reynal-Querol (2005); Cederman et al. (2011); Wimmer (2012).

been partly motivated by the diagnosis of a so-called "political bias" (Kalyvas 2006) in the first wave of violence studies, which conceived violence purely as the continuation of politics by other means. This neglect has been aggravated by economic approaches to conflict, which often interpret violence as the mere byproduct of greedy motivations on the part of combatants (Azam and Hoeffler 2002; Azam 2006; Hegre et al. 2007; Metelits 2010; Dube and Vargas 2013) whose political goals are heavily discounted.[9] This book includes political factors in a rationalist approach to wartime violence, in which civilian agency and the strategic goals of local political elites are crucial for explaining violent outcomes.

### A Local Level Approach

Recent research has made it increasingly clear that, both from a theoretical and an empirical perspective, the study of intentional violence against civilians requires a local-level approach.[10] This approach is the most appropriate to understand the interactions leading to violent outcomes during civil war. Whereas other administrative or judicial levels (e.g., province or region) may be relevant from an institutional perspective, the "intimate" character of violence (Kalyvas 2006) underscores the relevance of the locality, the lowest space of political interaction among individuals.[11] In the context of a local political community, civilians have leverage over the armed groups because they hold relevant information and they have bonds that allow coordinated actions with respect to the armed actors (Petersen 2001; Wood 2003; Arjona 2016).[12]

In addition, at the theoretical level, a local-level approach is consistent with a micro-level explanation of the phenomenon of violence, which takes the locus of agency to be concrete individuals and not abstract entities such as ethnic or political groups.[13] At the empirical level, measurement error and omitted variable bias can be minimized by taking the locality as the unit of analysis.

---

[9] Referring to African insurgencies, Mkandawire writes: "Regrettably, the recent focus on the means of financing rebel movements and the failure of most movements to coherently articulate, let alone achieve, their proclaimed objectives have encouraged an easy dismissal of the politics of such movements and an inclination towards economic, cultural and militaristic interpretations of the conflicts" (2002: 182–183).

[10] See, for example, Petersen (2001); Wood (2003); Gagnon (2004); Kalyvas (2006); Weinstein (2007); Fujii (2009); Condra and Shapiro (2012); Arjona (2016).

[11] In Rwanda, Jason Stearns argues that the local dimensions to the conflict (as opposed to the national and regional dimensions) resulted in perhaps the greatest bloodshed (2011: 8).

[12] According to Taylor, the community is "a space where there are direct relations between members, where people have many-sided relations, and where there is reciprocity, rough equality of material conditions, and a common set of beliefs and values" (cited in Petersen 2001: 16).

[13] As Lee Ann Fujii puts it, "Examining the social dimensions of genocide also helps to locate agency at the microlevel, rather than assuming it away or assigning it to whole groups of actors, such as 'the Hutu' or 'the masses'" (2009: 20).

## Warfare and Violence in Civil Wars

Since Fearon and Laitin's influential article (2003), the literature on civil wars has tended to equate all civil wars with insurgencies or guerrilla wars fought between a weak rebel group and a strong state. To cite some examples of this common view, Jeremy Weinstein argues that rebel groups "tend to employ guerrilla warfare as a strategy against government forces" (Weinstein 2007: 203); Lisa Hultman argues that "internal conflicts are characterized by asymmetry: the rebels are the weak contenders that challenge the central power" (2007: 208); Jean-Paul Azam states that "regimented wars are an image of the past" (2006: 53). This understanding of civil war has recently been questioned, as it has been shown that irregular wars are not the only type of contemporary civil war. If we distinguish civil wars by their "Technologies of Rebellion," we can identify three types: conventional, irregular, and symmetric non-conventional (thereafter, also SNC). Conventional civil wars have clear frontlines, attacks are waged mostly from barricades and stable positions, and major battles occur that usually determine the final outcome.[14] Irregular (or guerrilla) civil wars are wars in which the state army faces guerrilla forces that typically avoid direct confrontation and hide among the civilian population; there are no clear frontlines in an irregular war, which is generally characterized by military asymmetry between the two sides. Symmetric non-conventional civil wars are wars in which two irregular armies face each other across a frontline equivalent and they consist primarily of raids (Kalyvas 2005; Kalyvas and Balcells 2010). Although a majority (53%) of civil wars between 1944 and 2004 were irregular, a significant number of civil wars (33%) were fought conventionally, including civil wars such as those that began in Nigeria and Congo in 1967, Lebanon in 1975, and Angola in 1975. In the post-Cold War period (i.e., 1991–2004), almost 48 percent of civil wars were conventional; this includes wars such as those that began in Bosnia, Croatia, and Georgia in 1992, and Côte d'Ivoire in 2002 (Kalyvas and Balcells 2010).[15]

In conventional civil wars, there is military symmetry between the two sides and there is unopposed control in the areas behind the frontlines; except for zones that are extremely close to the frontline, control over the population by

---

[14] In an "ideal" case of conventional war, two armies go to battle in a front manner, but sometimes it is the case that one of the sides is not organized as an army for the total duration of the conflict.

[15] According to Duyvesteyn, "The concept of conventional war has without much consideration been marginalized and sometimes even neglected as a concept for analysis, in particular in wars occurring in collapsed states" (2005: 65). Duyvesteyn continues, "there seems to be strong biases toward regarding conventional war as a form of war that is Western, modern, uses high-technology weapons, and is relatively clean. There are strong prejudices at work in the preferred way of seeing this kind of war. Such prejudice does injustice to some striking conventional features of wars in the developing world that hitherto have been categorized as guerrilla struggles" (2005: 79).

armed groups is overwhelming in all the localities in their zone. By contrast, in irregular civil wars, areas of total control are much scarcer, smaller, and less stable. In irregular wars, violence against civilians is more often the result of the warfare and the competition to take territory (Mao Zedong 1978; Valentino et al. 2004; Kalyvas 2006; Vargas 2009) than in conventional wars, where this violence cannot be so connected to the military struggle and it often takes place in areas far from the battlefield. Theories of civilian victimization should take into consideration such differences between wars, and they should be careful when applying explanations that have been inspired primarily by one particular type (i.e., irregular) to all civil war settings.

This book focuses on conventional civil wars, but the implications are broader in scope. In a way, I use conventional civil wars as a theoretical device to explore the choices made by armed groups and civilians under the structure of incentives sharpened by this type of warfare. Yet, this incentive structure may also be found in the context of non-conventional civil wars, for example, in areas of civil wars where armed groups find no military contestation, where violence against civilians cannot really be explained by military strategy types of factors.

## 1.3    THEORETICAL STRATEGY

The research in this book is grounded on rationalist principles and methodological individualism. The theory builds on the assumption of self-interested individuals who hold rational beliefs and try to maximize their utility in carrying out a given set of actions (Elster 2007: 191–213). However, I do not consider individuals as seeking only wealth or power; the influence of emotions on human behavior will also be taken into account. As factors, emotion and reason are not necessarily divorced, given that emotions can be instrumentalized (Frank 1988). I will pay special attention to emotions such as anger, which are often a consequence of violent actions and conducive to a desire for revenge (Petersen 2011). Thus, I consider that experiences during conflict (and corresponding emotions) have an impact on individual preferences for violence and, consequently, on civil war dynamics.

While relying on a rationalist framework, I do not constrain myself to a narrow rational-choice explanation of the phenomenon under study for a number of reasons. First, pure rational-choice explanations tend to be less successful with regard to situations involving extremely high levels of stress (Maoz 1990) or when an agent's options are not fixed vis-à-vis the possible actions of others (Elster 1986: 19-2); both of these conditions are very plausible during wartime. As Roger Petersen explains, emotions, which are mechanisms that heighten the salience of a particular concern, challenge the assumption of stable preferences (Petersen 2011: 25). Second, in any social science, relying on analytic conditions that are too strict, carries the risk of generating misleading explanations (Green and Shapiro 1996; Elster 2007). Third, findings in behavioral economics (e.g., Sen 1977; Bowles 2004) have indicated that individuals often fail to behave according to narrow self-interest, as the neoclassical paradigm assumes.

## 1.4   CASE SELECTION AND RESEARCH DESIGN

Both the theoretical framework and the empirical analyses in this book pay special attention to the mechanisms and microfoundations leading to specific outcomes. At the theoretical level, the book is based on an individualist ratio-nalist approach, but it draws observable implications at different levels (micro, meso, and macro): the main empirical tests are at the meso level, the local com-munities (Chapters 4 and 5), but it also provides qualitative evidence at the individual level (Chapters 3 and 4), and some macro-level statistical evidence (in Chapter 7).

Empirically, this book combines micro-level evidence from two very differ-ent civil wars, which share the commonality of being fought conventionally: the civil war that took place in Spain from 1936 to 1939 and the internal conflict that took place in Côte d'Ivoire between 2002 and 2011. The weight of the two cases in the manuscript is different, though: while the Spanish Civil War is the main case study of this book, the Ivorian case constitutes an external validity check. Following a recent trend in political science (see, for example, Wilkinson 2004; Posner 2004; Kalyvas 2006; Christia 2012), the research design of this book consists on systematically exploring intra-country variation (i.e., large-$n$ sub-national data), in one or several countries, and com-bining it with additional secondary evidence from other cases to lend external validity. Also, I employ a multi-method empirical strategy, with a combination of observational statistical analyses and the analysis of evidence from histori-cal archives, oral sources, and over one hundred secondary sources including publications in general history, regional studies, and local studies.

There are several reasons for the selection of the Spanish Civil War as the main case study in this book: the Spanish, along with the American Civil War, is a paradigmatic case of conventional civil war. Analyzing an ideal case is often more helpful than analyzing one that is less paradigmatic or more "mixed." Also, using this war is meant to support my objection to the general neglect of historical cases (or so-called "old civil wars") in the study of civil war violence, which risks generating misconceptions of the phenomenon. Furthermore, the Spanish Civil War has a special importance on its own because it was an out-standing conflict in the West European interwar period and led to the first open confrontation between the antagonistic ideologies of Fascism and Repub-licanism/Democracy (Lannon 2002); in addition, it was a particularly bloody conflict, with approximately 600,000 estimated deaths, including combatants and civilians (Casanova 2014). Because it happened in the 1930s, this case allows for the use of fine-grained data at a local level; for a set of regions, the data have been revisited by several historians and are very reliable; it is less common for there to be reliable data of this type in more contemporary cases. Finally, the Spanish Civil War constitutes an empirical puzzle, as none of the existing theoretical approaches of wartime violence yields an adequate explanation for the violence against civilians that took place during this conflict.

On the one hand, the dynamics of indirect violence in the Spanish Civil War have yet to be fully explained. Some authors have explained bombings during civil war by taking into account military bargaining factors, namely factors related to the balance of power between groups in conflict, or the willingness to resolve the conflict by one of the sides (e.g., Horowitz and Reiter 2001; Wood 2010). Yet, bargaining factors can hardly account for spatial variation in violence, and sometimes they cannot even explain variation over time. For example, why did the Francoists bomb Catalan localities in 1939, when it was clear that they were winning the war and there was no ongoing political bargaining with the Republican government, which had already fled the country? Also, while desperation can sometimes explain the targeting of civilians (Downes 2008), it cannot explain these strikes as the Francoists were not desperate: they were winning the war. Other authors have argued that bombings can be understood from a purely militaristic perspective: bombing is a form of coercion and punishment (Pape 1996; Valentino 2004; Downes 2008). In the Spanish Civil War, bombings indeed served combat purposes, and they aimed at destroying military garrisons, ammunition deposits, and crucial production and communication centers (Solé i Sabaté and Villarroya 2003; Maldonado 2006a). However, many bombings were carried out in cities full of noncombatants (Balcells 1987: 34). These airstrikes cannot be explained convincingly from a militaristic perspective. Although historians have usually adduced the intention to provoke terror (Leitz 1999) in explaining these strikes, this does not explain why some towns were targeted and others were not.

On the other hand, direct violence against civilians is quite puzzling in the context of a civil war like the Spanish one. Some historians have characterized this violence as the result of political factors (Linz 1996; Casanova et al. 2001; Ledesma 2003; Gaitx 2006). Yet, the tendency has been to establish a relationship between political domination and violence: violence was assumed to be greater where there were greater proportions of political enemies. But, why did a predominantly leftist region such as Catalonia experience the highest levels of violence perpetrated by left-wing forces? This violence amounts to 3.92 per thousand of the inhabitants, which is higher than the 2.96 per thousand estimated in the much less leftist region of Valencia, which was, in fact, under Republican control for a longer period of time. In a similar vein, why was the island of Mallorca – a traditional enclave of the right (Oliver 1983) – heavily victimized by the Francoists? Estimates put the number of victims of Nationalist violence at approximately 2,000 on an island that in 1936 had slightly over 100,000 inhabitants.

Some historians have argued that violence on the Loyalist side was a by-product of the undisciplined nature of the Republican army and the insufficient level of control that the Republican authorities had over the anarchist and communist militias that emerged and established their authority at a local level (Beevor 1982; Preston 1986; Vilar 1986; Luengo 1998; Torres 2002; Rodrigo 2008). Violence was perpetrated by "uncontrolled" individuals. Some have even argued that violence was the result of spontaneous outbursts of violence (Brenan 1985: 238; Ors 1995). These explanations echo principal-agent arguments, which have been developed in the conflict studies literature by authors such as Mkandawire (2002), Weinstein (2007), Humphreys and Weinstein (2006), and Cohen (2013), among others. According to this view, violence occurs whenever rank-and-file combatants have opportunities to commit violence due to the lack of discipline within their armed groups.[16] While this might seem a plausible explanation, it is an incomplete one: on the one hand, at the beginning of the war, just after the military coup, there was a vacuum of power in most of the Republican territory and violence still diverged very significantly across localities. Following a principal-agent approach, violence should have been greater in those places where Republican authorities could not control the militias, and lower where they could rule over them. On the other hand, this approach cannot account for the violence that occurred in the few territories where the Republican government managed to maintain a higher degree of control over the militias, for example, in Valencia or Menorca.[17] Moreover, the principal-agent perspective cannot adequately account for violence carried out by the Francoist army, since it exhibited a particularly high degree of hierarchical control, leaving little opportunity for the rank-and-file to behave opportunistically (Preston 1986; Casanova et al. 2001; Calzado 2006).

From a strategic perspective, it could be argued that the decision to commit violence was motivated by the need to obtain consent from and control over civilians (Kalyvas 2006), or to influence patterns of civilian support (Valentino 2004). Yet, in the Spanish Civil War, it is not clear what could have caused variation in the levels of violence in municipalities located in the same military zone, since, from a militaristic point of view, armed groups would have had the same incentives to kill anywhere within this zone, and civilians would have had constant incentives to collaborate with a given group. A similar caveat must be made to explanations based on economic incentives of groups:

[16] Other historians such as Ruiz (2009), Thomas (1986), Payne (2004), and Ledesma (2003) have challenged this view. They have shown that anarchist militiamen were very often under the strict commands of the leadership of political and trade union organizations.

[17] In Valencia, state structures were maintained for nearly the totality of the civil war (Bosch 1983: 373); yet, the number of victims of leftist violence in this region was nonetheless significant: 4,634 (2.96 per thousand inhabitants), according to Gabarda (1996). In Menorca, the military command was strong from the early stages of the war on (Martín Jiménez 2000).

geographical variation in victimization cannot be explained by attempts to occupy more "desirable" (i.e., wealthier) territories because direct violence behind the frontlines was not connected to dynamics of military conquest. Also, because armed groups had relatively strong military capacities and relied on routinized conscription, taxation, and recruitment incentives (Azam 2006) cannot account for violence. Deserters and defectors (i.e., people that did not comply with the wartime authorities) were targeted, yet this represented only a small share of the violence perpetrated by each of the groups.

In short, existing theories cannot adequately explain patterns of lethal violence against civilians in the Spanish Civil War. And, more generally, they cannot fully explain violence in civil wars with large areas of complete military control by armed groups, where military contest, armed group indiscipline, and greedy motives do not suffice to account for variation in violence. By exploring the determinants of violence in conventional civil wars, this book contributes to filling a gap in the existing literature.

## 1.5   SCOPE CONDITIONS AND EXTERNAL VALIDITY

As I have argued above, the book extends beyond conventional civil war even if it looks into a structure of incentives sharpened by the warfare that is characteristic of this type of war. The insights reached in this book are expected to be applicable to other contexts where similar conditions obtain. In addition, the empirical focus here concerns civil wars fought along ideological and ethnic cleavages, but the theory should also extend to cases with different types of divisions (i.e., religious). Where ascriptive identities are associated with the civil war cleavage, as is the case of ethnic civil wars (Horowitz 1985), we should expect the groups to have somewhat fewer "identification problems" (and therefore lesser need for local collaboration); in principle, it is easier for armed groups to identify their enemies in these contexts. However, the fact that "ethnic defection" is common in most ethnic civil wars (Kalyvas 2008; Lyall 2009) implies that ethnic membership is not deterministic of political allegiances. Put differently, identification issues also exist in ethnic civil wars. Furthermore, I argue that political mobilization, which makes identities public and visible, implies that conditions should not vary dramatically across wars with different types of cleavages. After all, ascriptive features are just one of the defining elements of any identity, including ethnic identity (Chandra 2004). The comparison between the Ivorian and Spanish cases is particularly relevant to my attempts to illustrate this point: while the Ivorian conflict was articulated along an ethnic cleavage, and therefore identities relevant to the conflict were supposedly more visible than ideological identities, violence was much less massive than in the Spanish Civil War.

This book does not address violence in the context of genocide, which is a type of political violence that is produced unilaterally by armed groups and does not aim at achieving governance of the targeted population. While some of the observed dynamics at the local level may resemble patterns that have been described in the context of genocide – for example, in Rwanda (Straus 2006; Fujii 2009) – I focus on violence in conflicts between armed groups that are not interested in completely wiping out the population in a given territory. Groups want to eliminate those individuals who are particularly threatening (i.e., strong supporters of the enemy), but not the whole group, as in the case of a genocide. Instances of mass killing are nonetheless considered in the theory, particularly with the study of indirect violence.

## 1.6 PLAN OF THE BOOK

This book is divided into three parts. The first part (Chapters 1 and 2) introduces the theory in the book. The second part (Chapters 3, 4, and 5) focuses on the Spanish Civil War. The third part (Chapters 6, 7, and 8) focuses on the conflict in Côte d'Ivoire and on evidence from additional cases before drawing broader implications of the theory and concluding the book.

Chapter 1 has introduced the book, explaining its motivating puzzle and its theoretical and empirical strategies. Chapter 2 defines the main theoretical concepts and develops a theory of direct violence against civilians. This theory explores the puzzle of violence during conventional civil wars, and it incorporates political variables in a strategic approach to wartime violence. In addition, this theory also considers emotional factors (most of them endogenous to the war), which are considered as complementary to political factors. Chapter 2 generates a set of testable hypotheses regarding the determinants of direct violence, and it presents a number of additional observable implications.

Part II looks at the Spanish Civil War, which is the main case study in the book. Chapter 3 provides an introduction to the Spanish Civil War and outlines patterns that provide a sense of the dynamics of violence that occurred in this conflict. This chapter generates descriptive inference (King et al. 1994) and develops a number of novel insights regarding this civil war; in particular, it suggests that, despite their stark organizational and ideological differences, executions perpetrated by rebels and loyalists followed similar patterns of local interactions among armed groups, political committees, and civilians.

Chapter 4 presents a comprehensive test of the theory of direct violence against civilians with quantitative data from eight Spanish provinces comprising over 2,000 municipalities, as well as qualitative evidence from archives, secondary sources, and oral sources. To test my hypotheses, I employ various statistical techniques. The results of these tests strongly support the hypothesis that Left–Right parity (measured with prewar political competition) at the local level explains direct violence in the early phases of the war, and that wartime factors (i.e., revenge motives) gain explanatory relevance in subsequent stages. The results also indicate that political domination is not the mechanism linking political alignments and violence: in other words, we do not observe greater levels of direct violence in locations with greater proportions of enemy supporters. The consistency and robustness – across armed groups and regions – of the competition variable challenges the hypothesis according to which organizational factors account for levels of violence against civilians in conflict.

In Chapter 5, I present a set of hypotheses on the determinants of indirect violence in conventional civil wars, which derive from the theory elaborated Chapter 2. This chapter also includes a battery of tests of the determinants of indirect violence against civilians with quantitative municipal-level data from Catalonia during the Spanish Civil War. The results robustly show that bombings are more likely and more frequent in places that are politically dominated by rivals. This is different from what we observe in the case of direct violence, which is greater in parity locations; this divergence derives from the nature of the production of indirect violence, which does not require local collaboration. Furthermore, factors endogenous to the war (e.g. revenge) are also found to play a role in explaining indirect violence, even though they are not as relevant as in the case of direct violence.

Part III lends external validity to the results in the book. In Chapter 6, I test the theory with data from Côte d'Ivoire, where a civil conflict (with a three-year interruption) occurred between 2002 and 2011. As in Spain, the war in Côte d'Ivoire was conventional, although it involved much less civilian victimization. I argue that the lower levels of violence against civilians in Côte d'Ivoire are due to the lower degree of political mobilization in this country, which led armed groups to devote fewer resources to victimizing civilian supporters of their enemy group. This is particularly true of the 2002–2007 period: the absence of widespread political mobilization preceding the outbreak of war made the rearguard territories rather secure for the armed groups. However, mobilization was greater by 2010–2011, and the 2010 presidential elections in Côte d'Ivoire were followed by an intense wave of violence. I explore the dynamics of violence in this post-electoral period empirically, using again the electoral results as a proxy for the distribution of supporters of each of the blocs in conflict, across provinces. Notably, the determinants of direct violence against civilians in Côte d'Ivoire resemble those in Spain: parity at the local level between supporters of the two political blocs is a key variable in explaining this violence. The consistency in the results has further relevance given that the civil war in Côte d'Ivoire has been classified as an ethnic civil war, and not as an ideological one like the Spanish Civil War. Furthermore, the war in Côte d'Ivoire falls under the "new wars" category (Kaldor 1999), whereas the Spanish Civil War falls under the "old wars" category. The fact that patterns of violence are similar across very different types of civil wars suggests that the theory put forward in this book is on solid ground.

Chapter 7 contains secondary evidence from other cases such as Northern Ireland, Bosnia, and Colombia that is consistent with the theory laid out in this book. In addition, the chapter puts forward some macro-level implications, one of which I test with cross-national data. Using a dataset on civil wars in the contemporary world, covering the 1956–2004 period, I check differences in levels of violence against civilians across historical periods and across types of civil wars, and I explain them through the lens of my theory.

Chapter 8 reviews the main findings in the book and their significance, and it also discusses competing explanations. This chapter also traces certain implications of the book for comparative politics more generally, and outlines avenues for further research. The chapter ends with some policy implications of the book regarding human security, conflict, and violence.

# 2

# A Theory of Violence Against Civilians

"Violence is rarely a solo performance."
Charles Tilly, *From Mobilization to Revolution*

"We all know that death is the ultimate vengeance."
Susan Jacoby, *Wild Justice: The Evolution of Revenge*

## 2.1 CONCEPTUAL CONSIDERATIONS

In this chapter, I develop a theory of violence against civilians in civil wars. Prior to presenting a theoretical model and hypotheses, I address and resolve a number of conceptual issues. First, I justify the focus in this book on lethal violence vis-à-vis other forms of violence. Second, I present a new typology of wartime violence against civilians, which distinguishes between *direct* and *indirect* violence. This typology is distinct from that of selective and indiscriminate violence, which is common in the literature. I argue that the taxonomy here is more intuitive and empirically portable. Although the main focus of the book is direct violence against civilians, I also explore indirect violence in Chapter 5. Third, I justify the focus on a particular type of civil war (i.e., conventional), and elaborate on the idea that making distinctions among types of civil wars according to the technology of warfare has significant implications for understanding patterns of civilian victimization. That is because the nature of warfare, which shapes the nature of frontlines and armed groups' control of territory, has key implications for the structure of incentives that lead to violence against noncombatants. Although in this book I bind the theory to a set of conditions that predominate in the context of conventional civil wars, I argue that the same conditions and set of incentives can also be present in other contexts.

## Dependent Variable: Lethal Violence Against Civilians

This book focuses on intentional lethal violence against civilians. Intentional killing is distinct from acts of endangerment that carry no goal of killing in the first place, such as torture (Su 2011). It also differs from collateral damage, which is non-intentional. The study of battlefield violence, which predominantly involves the killing of combatants, is also beyond the scope of this book. In contrast with some other scholars (e.g., Hultman 2007; Wood 2010), I treat the assassination of combatants and civilians as two separate phenomena.[1]

*Civilian* and *combatant* are thus considered here as two mutually exclusive categories. A *civilian* is a non-combatant. A *combatant* is a soldier who is in charge of a weapon and/or who works in any job related to the military endeavor (for example, bridge and barricade construction, cooking, transportation, etc.).[2] In wars in which combatants and civilians often occupy different spaces (e.g., conventional wars), the victimization of each can be differentiated more easily than in civil wars in which combatants and civilians are mingled and therefore are hard to tell apart (e.g., guerrilla wars).

During war, victimization of civilians can take a wide range of forms: sexual violence, mutilation, torture, forced labor, displacement, marginalization, and property expropriation, to list a few. Elisabeth Wood calls this a *repertoire of violence*, "a set of practices that a group routinely engages in as it makes claims on other political or social actors" (2009: 133). Despite being just one among these forms of victimization, lethal violence is the focus of this book; the other forms of victimization will only be taken into account if they are ancillary and/or contingent to lethal violence.

The focus on lethal violence has theoretical and practical motivations. First, the book aims to make a bounded contribution to the study of civilian victimization during civil war; considering other forms of violence would demand a broader theoretical framework, and it would also require loosening a number of assumptions that I make for theory-building purposes.[3] Different forms of violence require distinct theoretical approximations. Finally, measuring non-lethal forms of violence is extremely complex, and it raises many methodological problems, which should be alleviated when studying lethal violence (Kalyvas 2006: 19–20). First, intentional death (or assassination) can more easily be recognized and distinguished from non-intentional death compared

---

[1] Violence against combatants can mostly be accounted for by military factors (see, for example, Pape 1996; Arreguín-Toft 2001; or Downes 2008).

[2] This definition is slightly broader than the one provided by Downes (2006, 2007, 2008), who only considers munition workers as combatants.

[3] A number of scholars are currently researching and making substantial contributions toward the understanding of non-lethal victimization such as displacement, sexual violence or torture (e.g., Bernard 1994; Wood 2006; Hoover-Green 2006; Vargas 2009; Steele 2009, 2010; Cohen 2013; Sullivan 2014).

to other forms of victimization, which can easily be perceived as collateral to other actions.[4] Second, measures of non-lethal violence, such as sexual violence or torture, are often fraught with underreporting (Wood 2009: 133–134).[5]

### Direct vis-à-vis Indirect Violence

I present a typology of civil war violence, which introduces a distinction between *direct* and *indirect* violence, and I identify the main dimension over which these two types diverge: the technology behind their production. Direct and indirect violence are both intentional forms of violence, but they are produced differently.[6]

I define *direct violence* as violence carried out with light weaponry (e.g., guns, knives, shotguns, machetes, rifles, etc.) in a "face-to-face" type of interaction. Direct violence often involves individual identification of victims, but it can also involve executions *en masse*. I argue that the interaction between armed groups and local civilians shapes the production of direct violence during civil war. Indeed, I argue that both of these actors (and not just armed groups) make decisions that have implications regarding the production of this type of lethal violence and therefore affecting the total levels of direct violence inflicted upon other civilians. Stathis Kalyvas (2006) has argued that the production of selective violence is a "joint process" between armed groups and civilians; I contend that the interaction of civilians and armed groups is relevant for the production of any type of violence, not only the selective type, provided that such violence implies some type of face-to-face interaction between perpetrators and victims (e.g., individual or mass executions). I argue that the key role of collaboration is not solely with regards to providing information to solve the "identification problem" that groups face during wartime. To perpetrate direct violence, armed groups must locate, arrest, and finally execute the victims; at any point during the process, local civilians can either facilitate or restrain it. For example, local civilians may denounce their neighbors, help to identify and locate them, and even arrest them, which of course enhances an armed group's capacity to target its rival's civilian supporters. Conversely, local civilians may hide potential victims, help them flee to other places, or provide

---

4 For example, distinguishing intentional from non-intentional is particularly complicated in the case of displacement (Steele 2010; Balcells and Steele 2016).

5 These methodological problems in the study of non-lethal forms of violence apply to all wars, whether historic or contemporary.

6 My classification differs from that in Valentino et al. (2004), who embrace non-intentional deaths (e.g., as a consequence of famine) as indirect violence. The typology also differs from Arreguín-Toft's (2001), who refers to warfare strategies: in his typology, "direct" denotes approaches that target an adversary's armed forces in order to destroy that adversary's "capacity to fight" whereas "indirect" denotes approaches that seek to destroy an adversary's "will to fight."

deceitful information to the groups, which limits their capacity to carry out assassinations.[7]

Civilian collaboration is particularly crucial if the armed groups do not have local knowledge or access to sources of information such as registration records or political militancy lists. Empirically, it is often the case that combatants are not local residents and that the perpetration of direct violence thereby depends very heavily on civilian collaboration.[8]

Civilian agency has been empirically observed, in one way or another, in a great number of historical and contemporary experiences, ranging from historical events such as Jewish pogroms in Poland (Kopstein and Wittenberg 2010), persecution during World War II in Europe (Hoffman 1968), the Napoleonic wars of the nineteenth century (Fraser 2008), the Soviet occupation of the Baltic states (Petersen 2001), and the civil war in Angola (Azam et al. 1994; Azam 2006) to more recent events such as riots in India (Varshney 2002) and the civil wars in El Salvador (Wood 2003), Colombia (Kaplan 2013; Arjona 2016), and Peru (Starn 1995). Some authors have named these processes involving non-cooperation with an enemy or occupier, civilian disobedience, industrial action, and ideological opposition, "civilian defense" (Roberts 1967); others have referred to "social resilience" (Krause 2011) or "civil resistance" (Chenoweth and Maria 2011). Minor forms of civilian resistance have also been observed in extreme cases, such as the well-known Rwandan genocide (Fujii 2009),[9] or during the Holocaust (Finkel 2015).

In contrast to direct violence, what I call *indirect violence* is perpetrated with heavy weaponry (e.g., bomber aircraft, naval gunfire) and does not require face-to-face interaction with victims. Because of its technology of production, indirect violence is much more unilateral on the part of the group, giving very limited agency (if any) to civilians; for example, civilians cannot veto the dropping of a bomb from a plane or the shooting of a missile from a tank.

Additionally, indirect violence may be carried out in areas in which the armed group has no military presence, for example, through aerial strikes. This makes indirect violence fundamentally different from direct violence, which can only be carried out under conditions of physical control of a territory. Put

---

[7] Civilians can also presumably be neutral to the actions of the groups (Wood 2003). However, remaining neutral may not be a simple matter in wartime contexts (Petersen 2001).

[8] The emphasis on civilian agency does not imply ignoring the fact that armed groups have asymmetric coercive power with respect to civilians. After all, combatants carry weapons while civilians do not, and armed groups can brutalize local civilians who do not show compliance. Nonetheless, most of the time, armed groups do not have incentives to carry out indiscriminate violence because this is counterproductive (Kalyvas 2006).

[9] For example, Fujii explains that some people in Rwanda were saved because neighbors/friends warned them that they were being targeted (93). Conversely, she emphasizes that neighbor cooperation with militias and violent actions were to some extent behind the genocide.

differently, military control of a given territory is a first-order condition for the perpetration of direct violence, while it is not so for indirect violence.[10]

Due to technological constraints, indirect violence cannot be as precise and selective as direct violence, but this does not imply that indirect violence cannot be inflicted selectively. Indeed, while some instances of indirect violence can be completely indiscriminate, as in the case of arbitrary aerial strikes (Lyall 2009), in some other cases, indirect violence can be somewhat selective, as it is when an aerial strike targets a specific neighborhood of a city in order to target supporters of the rival armed group (e.g., bombings of strongholds of the rival). In some instances, indirect violence can be quite selective, for example, when – relying on intelligence – a drone strike targets a high priority target. At the same time, some instances of direct violence can be quite indiscriminate, as in the case of massacres affecting all inhabitants of a village, perpetrated without singling out the victims (e.g., Mai Lai in Vietnam). Some other times direct violence might be perpetrated against groups of individuals (e.g., the Tutsis, the Serbs, the leftists), and thus victims might not be targeted because of their individual behavior (Kalyvas 2006) but because of their ethnic or political identities; although such violence is targeted at groups as a whole, it is nevertheless selective.[11] In some cases, direct violence can be extremely selective, targeting individuals due to their behavior during the war (e.g., fifth columnists transferring information to the enemy group).

We can conceive of these two forms of violence, direct and indirect, as located on two different sides of a continuum of civilian-armed group's agency in the production of violence (Figure 2.1). Overall, direct violence is much more dependent on civilian agency because there are more constraints on the perpetration of face-to-face violence than on the perpetration of indirect violence; again, indirect violence is much more unilateral on the part of the

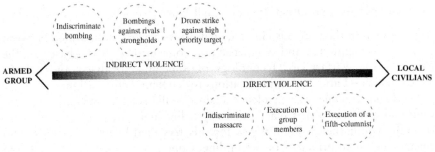

FIGURE 2.1 Civilian and Armed Group Agency in the Perpetration of Violence

[10] Armed groups can occasionally perpetrate direct violence in non-controlled territories, such as through raids and ambushes. Yet, in non-irregular civil wars, this can only happen in proximity to the frontlines, which are usually depopulated, so this type of victimization is relatively rare.

[11] Some have called this violence "collective" (Steele 2009) or "categorical" (Goodwin 2006; Straus 2015).

armed group. However, within the two types there is gradation: the greater the selectivity of violence, the greater the importance of civilian agency in its perpetration. For example, a drone strike against a high-priority target is an indirect attack that requires some local civilian collaboration (i.e., provision of information on the whereabouts of the target); it is less unilateral than an indiscriminate bombardment that requires no collaboration whatsoever. A bombing against a rival stronghold involves almost no civilian agency, but it still requires some information on the political loyalties in the locality, and that is why it is less unilateral than a fully fledged indiscriminate bombardment. Among direct violence, the execution of a fifth columnist requires more collaboration than the execution of group members, in the form of precise information. But the execution of group members requires more collaboration than an indiscriminate massacre. Local civilians can intercede against the perpetration of direct violence against group members (e.g., they can warn them so that they can flee before they are detained; they can provide deceitful information to the armed group), but their agency is more limited in the case of indiscriminate killings.

Figure 2.1 shows where the categories of direct and indirect violence stand on this continuum, and locates the different examples of (more or less selective) direct and indirect attacks in it.

In this book, I study the determinants of each of these two types of violence, direct and indirect, which I conceive of as two separate phenomena, albeit having common explanatory grounds. I consider direct violence as generally broadly reliant on civilian agency, and indirect violence as generally non-reliant on civilian agency. This chapter focuses on the determinants direct violence, as this is the most theoretically intriguing type of violence because of the complexity purveyed by the key role of civilian agency. Chapter 5 derives theoretical implications for indirect violence.

## Conventional vis-à-vis Other Types of Civil Wars

As explained in the previous chapter, civil wars can be distinguished between irregular, conventional, and symmetric non-conventional (SNC) based on the nature of the warfare or "Technology of Rebellion" (Kalyvas and Balcells 2010), which – I argue – has implications for civilian victimization.

Unlike in irregular wars, violence against civilians and combatants in conventional civil wars takes place in clearly delineated spaces. Combatants are generally young men, voluntarily or forcibly recruited by armed groups, who engage in combat primarily on a frontline. Combatants are generally killed in the course of battles, which usually include the use of artillery and airstrikes. Civilians are typically isolated from the battlefield: their everyday lives tend to be independent of the events occurring on the frontline. Combatants killed in the battlefield constitute the majority of casualties in conventional civil wars. Insofar as there are civilian assassinations, these are due to armed groups patrolling villages/towns, aerial or naval bombings, or executions or massacres taking place in the course of territorial conquest. Thus, when civilians are killed in non-battlefield areas, it is because they have been intentionally targeted, and not because they constitute collateral damage.

In irregular civil wars, the clear spatial distinction between battlefield and non-battlefield areas does not hold, as the war takes place unevenly across space; as a result, there is a much greater mingling of civilians and combatants (Guevara 1967; Mao Zedong 1978; Wood 2003), who therefore partake in the same basic process of violence.[12] Since frontlines are permeable and any action from a defector is potentially threatening the control of a locality and the safety of an armed unit, actions by defectors become relevant for war outcomes; hence control of information (in order to identify defectors among civilians) is essential for armed groups, as explained by Kalyvas (2006).[13] Another way to put it is that violence in irregular civil wars is a direct consequence of the competition for the control of territory, for which information is crucial;[14] control of information is, on the contrary, less crucial in conventional wars, where frontlines are non-porous and where the outcome of the war is mostly determined by the evolution of battles.[15] Thus, contrary to irregular wars, violence against civilians is (in conventional conflicts) unnecessary based on standard military strategy assumptions.

Although there has been a long-lasting debate on the issue, historical accounts coincide in characterizing the US Civil War, a paradigmatic case of a conventional civil war, as displaying low levels of targeting of the civilian population (Neely 2004). Violence against civilians appears to have been a rare exception rather than the rule (Hacker 2011: 328).[16] This violence concentrated in areas of conquest (e.g., Sherman's march to the South) and in areas of the country where guerrilla tactics were used: Missouri and Eastern Kansas (Edwards 1877; Fellman 1989; McPherson 1988). But, in other conflicts such as the Spanish Civil War or the civil war in Bosnia, violence against civilians was widespread in territories beyond the battlefield. If it is not militarily advantageous, why do groups in conventional civil wars decide to carry out violence behind the frontlines?

---

[12] In fact, in irregular civil wars, civilians might have greater probabilities of getting killed than combatants (Kalyvas and Kocher 2007b).

[13] Wood explains that the FMLN in El Salvador was able to maintain an insurgency that fought the government to a stalemate thanks to close and cooperative relations with civilians, who provided the FMLN with high quality intelligence (Wood 2003: 152–153).

[14] Valentino et al. (2004) argue that mass killings are carried out by groups in irregular conflicts to "dry up the sea in order that the guerrillas cannot swim." Striking the population as a way to attack the insurgents (Downes 2008) is a common counterinsurgency tactic in guerrilla wars.

[15] Only in areas close to the battlefield can civilian behavior be particularly relevant for the war because key information may be transferred to the other side. In these areas, civilians are likely be targeted for their wartime behavior (and not as much for their political identities), thereby following a pattern akin to that observed in irregular civil wars.

[16] Hacker (2011) has recently provided a new estimate of total number of deaths in the US Civil War: 752,000, who were mostly men of military age.

## 2.2  A THEORY OF DIRECT VIOLENCE

### Mobilization and Violence in Civil Wars

In conventional civil wars, armed groups' decision to perpetrate direct violence against civilians is related to political *mobilization*, and in particular to political mobilization during the prewar period. I posit that prewar political mobilization is a precondition to violence against civilians in these civil wars.

*Political mobilization* can be understood as the process by which political identities become activated such that they push people to political action (Tilly 1978). Mobilization can also be thought as "the process by which a group acquires collective control over the resources needed for action. These resources may be labor power, goods, weapons, votes and any number of other things, just so long as they are usable in acting on shared interests" (Tilly 1978: 7). Political mobilization is related to conventional and non-conventional forms of political action (Chenoweth 2015).[17] Moskalenko and McCauley (2009) define political mobilization as support for intergroup conflict and classify it in two types: "activism" (i.e., readiness to engage in legal and non-violent political action) and "radicalization" (i.e., readiness to engage in illegal and violent political action).

Political mobilization activates identities and produces deep loyalties and attachments on individuals. In the context of civil wars, mobilization is a very important dimension that armed groups take into consideration when they evaluate the context in which they are fighting. Mobilization is beneficial for armed groups when it generates deep loyalties and attachments toward their group/bloc, but it is damaging when it creates loyalties and attachments with the rival group/bloc. Mobilized individuals are key assets for armed groups in wartime contexts (Guevara 1967; Mao 1978; Slim 2008: 204). In particular, such individuals may become recruits (Bearman 1991; Humphreys and Weinstein 2008; Zeira 2012),[18] encourage economic production (Wood 2003), or hinder the enemy's actions (Petersen 2001). Because of the importance of mobilization, armed groups concentrate in political mobilization before and after a civil war outbreak.

Mobilized individuals can also coordinate and attempt to wage their own rebellion against a controlling armed group. For example, Fraser (2008) extensively explains how guerrilla warfare against the Napoleonic army germinated in Spanish society in the early nineteenth century. Also, Rowan argues that

---

[17] On political mobilization and political participation, see, among many others: Tilly (1978); Przeworski and Sprague (1986); Verba et al. (1995); McAdam et al. (2001); Beissinger (2002); Morales (2004).

[18] The mobilization of local identities (at the expense of a Southern identity) accounts for desertion in the Confederate bloc during the US Civil War; localism replaced the Confederate/Southern identity that had initially propelled men into war (Bearman 1991: 326). Humphreys and Weinstein find that in Sierra Leone "70% of CDF fighters reported joining because they supported the group's political goals" (2008: 438).

guerrilla warfare started off in Missouri after "a radical Cohort, the true Forty-Eighters, managed to convince thousands of others, ordinary German workers, shopkeepers, and farmers, to participate in armed rebellion against the legally constituted government of a state on behalf of a distant federal government" (Rowan 1983: preface). Mobilization is a necessary – albeit not sufficient – condition for collective action (Tilly 1978; Zeira 2012).

At the same time, mobilized individuals are those whom an armed group or the state may be more interested in targeting when aiming to build a "new society" or re-establish an old political order. Mobilized supporters of the enemy are dangerous during the war, and also in future periods (for example, in the postwar) because they can trigger cascades of rebellion or resistance against the new ruling group (Petersen 2001; Darden 2006). Thus, in mobilized societies, armed groups are likely to devote resources in the elimination of highly mobilized (and therefore committed) individuals for both *tactical* and *strategic* reasons (tactics refer to short-term maneuvers while strategy refers to medium and long-term schemes, Kalyvas 2006). Highly mobilized individuals constitute a threat during the war as well as in the postwar, as they are committed to a political cause that is antagonistic to the one defended by the rival armed group, and their political ideas will be threatening in the future social and political order. Examples of processes in which mobilized individuals are persecuted abound: the Bolshevik revolution of 1917, the Red guard terror in Finland (1918), the Protestant/Catholic violence in France (1562–1629), and the Cultural Revolution in China (1966–1976) are some of the most prominent ones.[19]

Armed groups are likely to devote resources to eliminating mobilized individuals by "sweeping the rear" (Downes 2008), for which they tend to use militias or irregular forces, which are complementary to regular armed forces (Arreguín-Toft 2001; Stanton 2015; Jentzsch et al. 2015). Unlike mobilized individuals, non-mobilized ones are by definition more malleable, less dangerous and are thereby less likely to be targeted by groups. For this reason, less mobilized societies are less likely victimized than more mobilized societies: groups do not need to eliminate individuals who are perceived as reconcilable.[20]

---

[19] Some might argue that high mobilization leads to the waging of "total war" (Roxborough 2009). However, I avoid using this term because it is usually associated with indiscriminate and unprovoked violence against *all* civilians of the "rival society." "Total war" implies that "the entire population and all the resources of a nation are sucked into the maw of war" (Douhet 1921, cited in Neely 2004: 439). I would not claim that prewar mobilization leads to attempts at total elimination of the enemy: even when violence is widespread, not all rival civilians are equally likely to be targeted and that not all aspects of the rival society are equally targeted.

[20] An alternative to elimination is of course "demobilization." However, armed groups can perceive demobilization as riskier, as well as much more time consuming, than straight elimination. Another alternative is displacement, but this is very difficult to undertake in civil wars with large control areas and relatively stable frontlines.

Wartime political and social mobilization is obviously paramount in civil wars. But, importantly, it is *prewar* mobilization, not *wartime* mobilization, what drives the perpetration of violence because – assuming that they are rational actors – armed groups are equally likely to mobilize civilians in their respective rearguard territories during wartime.[21] For their part, civilians have incentives to respond positively to such mobilization efforts (e.g., enlisting in recruitment lists, political organizations, etc.) following survival maximization efforts. In zones under full control by one of the armed groups, civilians do not have incentives to show allegiance to the other armed group; on the contrary, civilians have incentives to demonstrate compliance to the group controlling the territory. Even when civilians dislike the armed group controlling their territory, they have incentives to "falsify their preferences," to use Kuran's (1994) terminology. Hence, once the war begins, it is harder to infer people's preferences from their behavior.[22]

In a nutshell, I argue that conventional wars should not be the sites of mass violence against civilians in the absence of prior mobilization and that the converse should also hold. Of course, the geography of mobilization also matters: armed groups will only be concerned about their rearguards if there has been mobilization from the enemy group in this territory. However, complete segregation is extremely rare; not even in the case of secessionist civil wars, when mobilization in favor of secession is likely to be concentrated in the secessionist territory, is segregation complete.[23]

A number of considerations have to be made at this point. First, in this book, I consider prewar mobilization as exogenously given. Thus, I do not investigate the causes of variation in levels of prewar mobilization across conflicts. Political parties and social organizations (e.g., trade unions; churches, etc.), which play a major role in political mobilization (Aldrich 1995), are strategically motivated in their mobilization efforts (Przeworksi and Sprague 1989; Posner 2004). Second, I consider that identities will be relevant only insofar as they have been mobilized and are meaningful to individuals, and not intrinsically. Third, civil wars take place in the name of a "master cleavage" and armed groups are clearly identifiable with each of the sides of the political conflict. The identities that matter are those around which the conflict is articulated, which are those most highly ranked by individuals at that point in time (Gould 1995). Fourth, I do not distinguish

---

[21] Elisabeth Wood explains that, in El Salvador, the two armed parties concentrated increasingly on building political loyalties among civilians rather than only on overt military competition (Wood 2003: 160).

[22] Of course, if individuals show noncompliance, groups will identify them as enemies. Also, wartime behavior of individuals will matter in future phases of the conflict, if territory changes hands (I will come back to this point further below).

[23] Inside countries it is pretty rare for all of the supporters of one group to be in one area and all of the supporters of the rival group to be in another. This situation is more common in interstate wars, but even in that context people often get caught on the wrong side (tens of thousands of Eritreans were in Ethiopia when the war broke out in 1998, for example).

between ethnic and ideological identities because, unlike Kaufmann (1996), I do not consider that there are differences in the way different cleavages affect the dynamics of violence. In other words, political identities are not always "difficult to assess and changeable" and ethnic identities are not always "fixed and unchangeable" (Kaufmann 1996: 72). I posit instead that, if mobilized, political identities can be fixed and unchangeable; if not mobilized, ethnic identities can be difficult to assess and changeable. Fifth, I am not assuming that every member of a group is a strong or committed supporter as a result of pre-war mobilization and therefore a potential target of the rival group. However, at the same time, I am also not buying into Kalyvas's assumption that "only a minority of the population can really be described as holding tightly to one pole or the other; the majority tends to remain either weakly committed or uncommitted, part of a 'grey zone' between the two poles" (Kalyvas 2009: 602). Instead, I consider that political mobilization makes the number of committed people in a society substantive. The greater the degree of political mobilization in a given society, the larger the number of committed supporters of the groups. Sixth, I assume the degree of mobilization to be a feature at the national level, which determines the willingness of armed groups to target supporters of the enemy in the rearguard territories.

In short, prewar political mobilization is a precondition for civilian victimization in the context of conventional civil wars, where armed groups have full control of large areas of territory and fight in non-porous frontlines. As long as the country is not fully segregated, prewar mobilization is what makes groups wary of the existence of potential threats behind the frontlines. However, because of resource constraints, groups are unlikely to target everyone among the enemy population. Rational groups only devote a subset of their resources to victimize civilians because they also must devote resources to the battlefield.[24] Groups are likely to selectively target strong supporters of their rival, i.e., those who represent the most serious threat. The identification, arrest and killing of these people is made in collaboration with local civilians. I now turn to the analysis of the critical interactions between groups, local supporters and victims, which shape patterns of violence at the subnational level.

### Explaining Direct Violence

Let us imagine a hypothetical country in which a civil war erupted after a period of intense political confrontation between political parties *A* and *B*, whose platforms are now championed by respective armed groups *A* and *B*. The citizenry of this country has been mobilized along the *A–B* cleavage. The

---

[24] With respect to Rwanda, for example, Jason Stearns explains that the military lost substantial capacity by devoting significant resources to killing civilians. A military officer he interviewed argued: "The army deployed most of its forces to massacre civilians, diverting trucks, ammunition, and manpower to slaughter them. The genocide caused our resistance to crumble. It was a *cafouillage*, a real mess" (2011: 19).

two groups enjoy exclusive military control of relatively large areas from which they have excluded the rival group, and which they patrol. In addition to confronting *B* on the battlefield in attempting to increase the share of territory under its control, *A* is interested in getting rid of committed supporters of *B*, who are perceived as a potential threat. Prewar political mobilization made *B* supporters willing to organize behind the frontlines to challenge *A* or to serve as fifth columnists for *B*.

The relevant interactions in the territory controlled by *A* involve combatants of this group and the civilians living in it. The key actors in the production of violence are: 1) *armed groups* (*A*, in this area), 2) *local political elites* (who can be supporters of *A* or *B*), and 3) *local civilians* (who can also be supporters of *A* or *B*). Armed groups are the actors who have weapons and thus are the perpetrators of violence.[25] However, not all the agency of the perpetration of direct violence is in the hands of the armed groups: local civilians decide whether (or not) to collaborate with the armed group, and this has an impact on the extent to which violence can take place. In this context, all civilians are significant, but local political elites (and particularly those linked to the armed group inflicting violence) have more influence than ordinary citizens. The added leverage of local elites is a consequence of their symbolic (e.g., authoritative) or coercive (e.g., control of security) powers (Christia 2008).[26] Local political elites are crucial actors in the production of direct violence.

At the same time, local political elites and local civilians can also be victims of the violence inflicted by the opposite group. In the context of full territorial control, civilians have no incentive to show any type of allegiance toward armed groups not controlling the territory where they live, whereas they have many incentives to display open collaboration and allegiance to the controlling armed group. The armed group and their supporters are aware of this, and they do not update their prior beliefs in light of the wartime behavior of people if what they observe is allegiance amongst people they believed were supporters of the rival group. Thus, people who have demonstrated strong support for a group in the prewar period will be likely targets of its rival regardless of whether they display a different set of preferences and identities after the war has started.

## Actors' Preferences

In what follows, I list the crucial actors in the production of violence and their respective preferences, as well as their main incentives and constraints for carrying out violence against noncombatants.

[25] Tilly (2003) would call them "specialists of violence," in a division of labor in which some actors articulate political goals and others are in charge of inflicting physical violence.

[26] For example, local elites can decide whether or not to mobilize their local resources to find people who are hiding.

1) *Armed actors*: Armed actors are those with weapons and the ability to inflict violence against civilians. In addition to fighting in the battlefield, they patrol the areas under their military control and attempt to eradicate committed supporters of the rival who constitute a potential threat. They want to win the war and secure control of the territory.

Armed groups thus have incentives to engage in violence against their suspected enemies. They also face a number of constraints. On the one hand, they have resource constraints, which makes them likely to focus on getting rid of highly mobilized supporters of their rival, who represent the most serious threat. On the other hand, they are constrained by their access to local information, for which they need the collaboration of local political elites and local civilians who side with them.

Military actors benefit from killing civilians who are supporting their rival armed group because these represent a threat behind the frontlines. However, these actions can also be costly because they can face international backlash and, if these crimes are uncovered, military leaders can be prosecuted (for example, in recent times, by the International Criminal Court), and because local civilians can turn against the group as a reaction to this violence (Kocher et al. 2011; Condra and Shapiro 2012), especially if perceived as indiscriminate. Groups thus have incentives to behave with some restraint and to perpetrate selective violence instead of indiscriminate violence, whenever the former is possible.

2) *Local political elites*: Local political elites have agency in the perpetration violence because they can provide information to the armed groups regarding the presence of committed supporters in their localities. This information comes from prewar mobilization, which has politicized people and made identities visible. In addition, local political elites can use their local networks and resources to either constrain or enhance the killing capacity of armed groups –they can intercede in their actions or not. In the short term, local political elites are interested in helping their armed group secure territory. They will provide collaboration when this is militarily useful for the groups, driven by ideological motives. But political elites are also interested in maximizing the chances that they will be politically dominant in future periods.[27]

Local elites receive benefits and costs of collaborating with armed groups in the perpetration of violence. Benefits are military and political: living in a secure area, on the one hand, and achieving *political dominance*, on the other. But they also face costs of violence, as they can be persecuted by local enemies once the military power shifts, and violence can also degrade the relationship among neighbors in the locality. Local elites can predict that violence will

---

[27] The objective of political dominance prevails regardless of whether the future period is democratic or autocratic, although these considerations are likely to weight more in settings in which democratic elections are expected.

generate emotions such as anger, which can backlash against them. In short, violence is not cost-free and they take this into consideration.

3) *Civilians*: Civilians want to maximize their chances of survival. Nonetheless, if mobilized politically, civilians also have an interest in seeing their armed group winning the civil war, and securing control of the area they inhabit. Mobilized civilians also want the political party they sympathize with to dominate their locality, in present and future time.

Civilians have some agency in the perpetration of violence, but not as much as local elites, as they do not have access to power networks to enhance or limit the perpetration of violence. Finally, like political elites, civilians are likely victims of violence if they are politically mobilized and showed support for one of the armed groups before the war. They can also be the target of violence if, during the war, they behave in ways that show noncompliance or dissent. These behaviors will be rare among rational individuals, because even mobilized individuals will try to hide their conspirational activities in areas fully controlled by the rival armed group.

## Theoretical Expectations on Local Elites' Behavior

Because direct violence is produced by armed groups in collaboration with local political elites and civilians, direct violence will take place in *A*-controlled areas when armed group *A* has an interest in killing *B* supporters and local *A* supporters provide collaboration toward the identification of these *B* supporters, their arrest, and their execution. As stated above, local political elites have more agency than regular civilians, so I assume that they are the key actors at the local level.

In areas of weak military control (i.e., the group has incomplete control, and not full military control), e.g., areas close to the battlefield, local A supporters and local A political elites will collaborate with A in order to eliminate B supporters if they believe that this can help A secure the territory militarily. Politically mobilized individuals will put their lives at risk in order to provide collaboration to the armed group they sympathize with, in order to increase the probability of their military victory. It is important to note that this is different from what previous scholars have posed to occur in civil wars, where civilians are thought to collaborate solely as a function of their individual safety (e.g., Kalyvas 2006). I instead argue that political allegiances is a strong determinant of collaboration with armed groups because mobilized individuals care about who ultimately wins the civil war.[28]

But, what about areas of full military control? In contexts in which military control is secured, what are the incentives of *A* local elites to help armed

---

[28] My approach is in this sense closer to Wood's (2003) although she emphasizes the emotional "in process" benefits of these actions by activists, e.g., assertion of dignity and defiance through the act of rebelling. I consider that the actors rationality pursue a set of military and political goals.

group *A* perpetrate violence against their neighbors? I argue that local political elites have political goals and they are likely to use violence instrumentally to achieve political domination of their locality, or to secure this domination if they already have it. However, local elites will use violence if and only if it serves the goal of guaranteeing them political control at a cost that is not too high. In the language of economics, local elites will collaborate in the perpetration of violence when the marginal benefits ($\beta$) of violence are greater than the marginal costs ($k$).

Consider the set of municipalities under *A* military control. There are two political blocs, *A* and *B*, which match the master cleavage of the civil war (fought between armed groups *A* and *B*). Denote by $s_A$ and $s_B$ the shares of supporters that each bloc has at the local level, so $s_A + s_B = 1$. In areas of full military control, in which their actions have no impact on the civil war's outcome, local political elites seek political goals at the local level. Local elites payoffs depend on who attains the final political control of the municipality, which in countries with a democratic tradition is the group that has 50%+1 of support.[29]

In an area under *A*'s full military control, only *A* can contemplate having supporters of the other side (i.e., *B*) killed. Local elites do not perpetrate violence themselves, but they can make sure people get killed by denouncing them to armed group *A* (or *A* militias). By doing this, they can affect the probability of attaining final political control of the locality. However, *A*'s political elites will not have everyone killed because killings are costly. As explained above, the costs of killing range from the actual cost of carrying out the assassination to the emotional cost of having somebody in the locality assassinated and the costs of a potential backlash of the violence.[30] I assume that the marginal cost of killings is constant. The marginal benefit of killings is, however, not constant: killing *B* has a different effect on the probability of *A* attaining or consolidating power depending on the size of $s_B$ in a locality.

Figure 2.2 illustrates the distribution of $\beta$ and $k$ for group A across localities with different shares of supporters; the x axis is the size of $s_B$. The marginal benefits of killings are 0 when $s_B$ is close to 0. In this context, *A* faces little risk of losing power, and killing *B* supporters does not make a difference with regard to their capacity to retain power. $\beta$ increases as $s_B$ increases, and it reaches a peak at 0.5: here, one execution can tip the balance of power in favor of one of the two groups. When of $s_B < 0.5$, killings do not change the existing balance of power, but they have increasing marginal benefits for *A* as

---

[29] In non-democratic countries, it implies sufficient power to prevent further rebellion and to attract some social support. I will assume here that a democratic regime is expected in the postwar.

[30] Backlash can be collective or individual: for example, those who denounce or directly participate in the assassination of a neighbor can later be identified and they might be the object of vengeful actions.

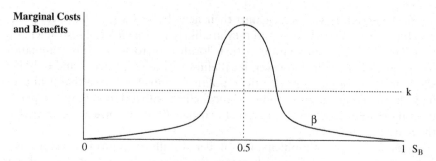

FIGURE 2.2 Marginal Returns of Violence (Perpetrated by *A*), in *A*-Controlled Areas

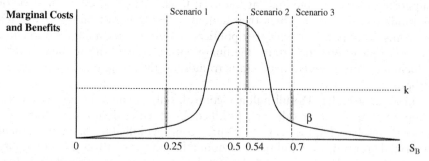

FIGURE 2.3 Marginal Returns of Violence (Perpetrated by *A*), in *A*-Controlled Areas; Three Different Scenarios

violence can help secure their political control of the locality. Closer to 0.5, *A* faces a greater threat of political turnover, so killing *B* supporters is a form of insurance in front of this threat. When $s_B \geq 0.5$, killing *B* supporters has positive returns for *A* because these killings can tip the local balance of power in *A*'s favor. However, moving away from parity situations, the marginal benefits of these killings decrease, as *A* needs to eliminate many more *B* supporters in order to attain power at the local level.

Let us imagine three different scenarios in order to illustrate the predictions of the theory, which are drawn in Figure 2.3. First, let us imagine a scenario in which *A* has 75 percent of support and B has 25 percent (thus, $s_B = 0.25$). Local *A* elites will not promote lethal violence against their local opponents because their group is already a majority in the locality and violence would not provide any political benefits. Because $k > \beta$, violence would in fact have negative net returns for *A* in this scenario, which are marked in the graph.

Another scenario is that in which $s_B = 0.7$. In this context, *A* local elites are unlikely to encourage violence against *B* supporters because violence is too costly to achieve the goal of changing the local balance of power. Here too the marginal costs of violence are greater than the marginal benefits: as marked in the graph, $k > \beta$.

A third scenario is one very close to parity, let us say $s_B = 0.54$. Hence, $B$ has 54 percent and $A$ has 46 percent of support in the locality. In this context, local political elites are much more likely to push for violence because killings can decisively alter the local political balance in favor of $A$ at a cost that is not too high: $\beta > k$. For $A$, the net marginal returns of violence are positive in this scenario, in contrast to the previous two scenarios.

This theoretical framework leads us to predict that when $A$'s supporters are either a distinct majority or a distinct minority (i.e., the margin of victory is large in either direction), local elites are likely to restrain their respective armed groups, who will therefore not perpetrate significant levels of violence against civilians. Violence is likely to increase as the distribution of support approaches parity, when it becomes more beneficial for local elites, who will encourage this violence and will collaborate with armed groups in its perpetration. Note that all of the above is true as far as local elites are not genocidal, and thus have no interest in annihilating the totality of supporters of the rival group. This assumption is consistent with Valentino et al. (2004), who argue that genocide usually emanates from strategically oriented national leaders and that local leaders are unlikely to have genocidal motivations. If the leaders were genocidal, the benefits of violence would be exponentially increasing. Also, despite the model's assumption of a rational calculation by local political elites, they are not expected to be extremely precise in their calculations. That is, it is not the case that local elites are going to be pushing for *just* one killing in situations of complete parity (i.e., 50–50 percent). But, they will push for more killings in areas around parity because violence can marginally benefit them more in these contexts. A first observable implication of the theory is the following:

*Hypothesis 2.1: Direct violence against civilians increases as the distribution of supporters of rival groups in a given locality approaches parity.*

Again, hypothesis 2.1 applies to situations in which $A$ has full military control of a territory. When control is contested, for example, in areas close to the battlefield, local collaboration is likely to be driven by military factors. Even if local political elites also have political considerations, in conditions of military contestation, military considerations trump political ones. In consequence, violence in militarily contested areas will follow dynamics closer to those in irregular civil wars.[31]

### Parity, Competition, and Polarization

So far I have argued that direct violence against noncombatants in civil wars issues from the interaction between the actions taken by armed groups

---

[31] By definition, in irregular civil wars, areas of incomplete control predominate; in conventional civil wars, areas with full military control are much more common.

and local civilians. Because violence against civilians follows prewar political mobilization, political identities exogenous to the war matter a great deal with respect to identifying and assassinating individuals. Armed groups target enemy supporters by relying on their supporters in the locality, who use violence strategically to maximize their political control of the locality. This leads violence to increase as the distribution of supporters of each of the groups approaches parity at the local level.

*Parity* between groups is conceived here as the balance of power that groups have based on their relative number of supporters. Thus, parity does not refer to the warfare capacity of groups, but simply to the relative number of people who support or sympathize with them. The distribution of supporters of the different groups can be proxied with electoral data when there are elections preceding the civil war and the macro-cleavage of the war matches the electoral one, which is not always the case. When groups are differentiated by ethnicity, language or religion, census data can also capture the number of supporters of each bloc.[32] When using electoral data, we can refer to political competition, which captures threat of political turnover (Bardhan and Yang 2004). Because I measure parity between groups with electoral data, in this book I use the terms political *competition* and *parity* interchangeably.

It is important to emphasize that parity does not mean *polarization*, even if these two concepts are extremely similar when there are two mobilized groups in a society. As conceived by Montalvo and Reynal-Querol (2005), polarization measures the extent to which the distribution of groups' supporters approaches a bipolar one. Polarization captures the same as parity when there are only two groups; when there are more than two groups, one may find high levels of parity between all or a subset of these groups in non-polarized settings. Esteban and Ray's (1994) conceptualization of polarization is slightly different, and it includes a continuous metric for the distance between groups: the greater the distance, the greater the polarization; with this measure, one can find highly polarized low-parity settings, for example if two groups represent 70 percent and 30 percent of the population, but they are very far from each other (say a secular group vs. a jihadist one). Nonetheless, it is fair to assume that in a civil war the political distance between the two sides is roughly the same in every locality, which implies that only relative sizes are relevant to understand micro dynamics of violence.

Despite their similarities, *parity* and *polarization* should be distinguished theoretically as well as empirically. Parity captures the extent to which there is competition between groups: in situations of parity, small changes can tip the balance of power in favor of one of the groups. In situations of competition, the threat of losing power is very salient (Bardhan and Yang 2004). Polarization instead captures the extent to which there is antagonism between

---

[32] As explained in chapter 7, we can use census data to measure parity between Catholics and Protestants in Northern Ireland's wards.

groups because they have similar sizes as well as distant policy positions. While some scholars have used the term "polarization" to refer to the degree of parity between groups (De la Calle 2007; Kopstein and Wittenberg 2010), I consider that the term "competition" is more appropriate because it captures more optimally the "threat of turnover" and balance of power between groups (Wilkinson 2004).

## 2.3   SUBSEQUENT TIME PERIODS

The theoretical model above assumes a one-shot static setting. Intuitively, past instances of violence will likely influence subsequent instances of violence in $t_{1+i, i=1,...,n}$. Let us imagine, for example, a second period $(t_2)$ where a territory initially controlled by $A$ is conquered by $B$. The identification and assassination of $A$ supporters in $t_2$ will be connected to both the political profile of the locality and the actions previously taken by $A$ supporters during the first period of the war $(t_1)$. An updating of beliefs about individuals is likely to have taken place during $t_1$, given the actions undertaken by individuals during that period, but it is only when territory changes hands that this updating becomes relevant. Local elites (in particular, those siding with $B$) will now collaborate with $B$ in identifying those who are believed to support $A$ because of their prewar political identities, on the one hand, and their behavior during $A$'s rule, on the other (for example, those having openly collaborated with $A$ are now identified as $A$ supporters). $B$ political elites will choose to encourage or restrain violence based on their strategic political motivations but also based on their experiences during $t_1$. It might be expected that civilians having been victimized by $A$ during the first period will have emotions that can motivate them to carry out vengeful actions. As Petersen (2011) explains, violence, victimization, and humiliation are powerful experiences that leave residues in the form of emotions (Petersen 2011: 23). These emotions create new motives for violence, revenge motives, which add to the strategic motives described in the previous subsection.

Revenge and the search for worth are emotion-based motivations that a large body of literature has found to be relevant to understanding individual behavior in intergroup relations. Revenge is a major cause of violence and the motivation for 10 to 20 percent of homicides worldwide (Pinker 2011: 529–530). Revenge can also motivate recruitment into armed organizations (Korge 2013) and terrorist groups (Silke 2003; Speckhard and Ahkmedova 2006), and it can be behind aggressive foreign policies of nations – increasing public opinion support for aggressive policies, including the use of torture (Liberman 2013; Stein 2015). The desire for revenge is often generated by emotions such as anger, shame, humiliation or resentment (Fridja 1994; Petersen 2001).

According to Roger Petersen, "emotion is a mechanism that triggers action to satisfy a pressing concern" (2002: 17). Emotions are a trigger for certain kinds of behavior, and they are often behind the outbreak of political violence and ethnic conflict (Horowitz 1985; Cederman et al. 2011; Wimmer 2012). Emotions such as fear, hatred or resentment may be present in the early stages of a conflict (for example, if the Serbs and the Croats have a history of hatred against each other, or if the Tutsis bear resentment toward the Hutus due to a reversal of power status), and they can contribute to the perpetration of violence at the local level. In the early stages of the conflict, these emotions are unable to explain subnational variation of violence because they are likely to be distributed stochastically across the territory. Yet, vengeful emotions are an important additional factor in non-initial stages, when they are directly related to events that occurred earlier in the conflict: in $t_2$, vengeful individuals are likely to be more concentrated in areas in which victimization has taken place during $t_1$.[33] Hence, dynamics of violence can be endogenous to conflict, through the channel of emotions.[34]

In a biographical account, a Marine who was deployed to Iraq in 2009 and to Afghanistan from 2010 to 2011 argues: "The emotions surrounding loss and revenge can distort reality" (Kudo 2015: SR1). Indeed, emotions can alter individual incentives in different ways, and in a civil war context they can make people denounce or kill others whom they believe are wrongdoers and thus deserve to be repaid for their crimes.[35] These vengeful motives can trump strategic motives: someone who becomes angry due to an experience of victimization and wants to repay a bad deed "will seek revenge because he wants to, even when, in purely material terms, it does not pay. His feelings of anger will offset his material incentives" (Frank 1988: 53). Thus, killings driven by revenge are not necessarily instrumental and they might not be rational. Jon Elster argues that "To get revenge is "to impose suffering on those who have made one suffer, because they have made one suffer" (Elster 1990: 862). However, vengeful motives are not necessarily irrational, or rather can be very consistent with rational motives: if a local political leader of group *A* is angry because a supporter of group *B* has killed his brother in $t_1$, he might retaliate and kill the *B* supporter in $t_2$, and in doing so he might be accomplishing two goals at once: satisfying his desire for revenge and eliminating a political enemy.

One harmful event, or a series of harmful events, can trigger emotions such as anger, humiliation, shame or resentment, which can themselves develop

---

[33] I assume that the degree of "vengefulness" of the citizens is similar across localities. Vengeful values and beliefs can vary cross-nationally (Hinton 1998; Speckhard and Ahkmedova 2006; Stein 2015), but they are unlikely to vary dramatically within a country.

[34] Petersen posits that by inflicting violence, armed forces can generate emotions such as anger and fear, which often provoke a desire for revenge. According to him, discriminate violence is more likely to lead to anger, while indiscriminate violence is likely to provoke fear (Petersen 2011: 56).

[35] For example, Cardozo et al. (2000) report that 89 percent of men and 90 percent of women in their sample in Kosovo reported having strong feelings of hatred toward Serbs; 40 percent of them experienced feelings and fantasies of taking revenge.

into grudges and the desire to hurt those who have hurt oneself in the first place. As Hinton (1998: 353) puts it, "Revenge is the moral inverse of gratitude." Revenge is also usually connected to proportionality: the biblical conception of revenge is premised on the talion principle of "an eye for an eye." However, in some cases, revenge can be disproportionate: for example, Hinton (1998) explains that in Cambodia revenge involves disproportionate retaliation against one's enemy. Also, revenge is "backward-looking" (Stein 2016): its fundamental motivation and justification lie in the original act of wrongdoing. Yet, revenge is not necessarily immediate. Some popular expressions such as "revenge is a dish best served cold" illustrate this idea. A grudge leading to revenge contains an element of latent potentiality and is frequently long-lasting (Hinton 1998). Thus, in a civil war context, individuals willing to punish those having inflicted harm on them, are likely to wait until they feel safe enough to undertake vengeful actions (for example, when their armed group controls the locality and can provide them protection). Revenge can go beyond the individual, as people can feel grudges against the whole group of perpetrators (e.g., the communists, the anarchists, the Francoists) and thus people can be repaying deeds against members of the groups who were not necessarily involved in inflicting violence in the first place. This is what Speckhard and Ahkmedova (2006) call "generalized revenge."[36]

At the meso level, a clear-cut observable implication to be derived from the above is that the more violence inflicted by $A$ in $t_1$ (against $B$'s supporters) the more violence we should expect to be carried out by $B$ in $t_2$ in a given locality. That is the case because $B$ will find greater collaboration toward the perpetration of violence in places where $A$ has inflicted more violence. This should be the case independently of prewar political configurations.

*Hypothesis 2.2:* *The greater the levels of direct violence inflicted by an armed group controlling a given locality during one time period, the greater the levels of direct violence perpetrated by a rival armed group that gains control of the same locality during the subsequent time period.*

A clear implication of this framework is that cycles of revenge (or retaliation) emerge once violence has already taken place in a locality: violence begets violence. Despite the fact that in some cases these motives can be conflated, revenge motives add to strategic motives for revenge, so violence in a locality is likely to escalate and to be greater in each round. These cycles of revenge are likely to continue until the war is over and hence opportunities

---

[36] Speckhard and Ahkmedova find that traumatized individuals in Chechnya endorsed revenge in 39 percent of the cases and "no longer regarded revenge as a duty to find and repay in kind the person who had harmed their family but instead generalized revenge became both sufficient and acceptable.... The greater the degree of traumatization and resultant PTSD, the more likely the individual was to sanction generalized revenge" (2006: 467).

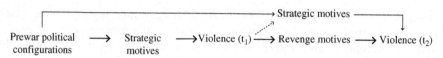

FIGURE 2.4 Local Elites Motives and Violence in Different Periods of a Civil War

to kill or to denounce to have people killed vanish.[37] Furthermore, because of endogenous dynamics, wartime factors are likely to supersede prewar identities and strategic considerations as the war develops and violent events accumulate. At an operational level, this implies that, as the civil war goes by and rounds of violence by different armed groups take place, political factors will lose relevance in favor of war-related variables. In other words, violence is likely to become progressively distilled from ideological motives as a civil war goes on.

Figure 2.4 summarizes the motives of local political elites for collaborating in the perpetration of violence against other civilians, and the endogenous dynamics of the war. Prewar political configurations shape strategic motives for violence (by, say, $A$'s supporters) in the first period $(t_1)$: as we have seen, violence is instrumental for local political elites where political parity between groups is high; violence may contribute to achieving or consolidating local political power. Emotions might also be vivid in this period, but strategic motives are those mostly behind violence in $t_1$. Violence perpetrated in $t_1$ has an impact in subsequent motives for violence, when a territory changes hands $(t_2)$. In this second period, $B$'s local elites have strategic motives for violence which are determined by prewar political configurations and also by the violence that $A$ has inflicted against $B$'s supporters (for instance, if a village has been cleansed of $B$'s supporters, there will be no competition between groups, and thus no strategic motives for violence). In this second period, $B$'s local elites are also likely to be driven by revenge motives, which are a direct consequence of the violence inflicted by $A$ in the previous period. Emotions such as anger and the related desire for revenge are likely to determine the extent to which $B$'s supporters encourage violence in $t_2$. Again, the implication is that, in the second period, independently of political configurations, we will observe higher levels of violence in places where greater levels of violence are inflicted in the first period.[38]

---

[37] The literature on social psychology has found that violent behavior leads to more violence through processes such as "desensitization through repeated exposure to the act, shifting personal definitions of violence, disengaging from moral reasoning processes, and changing other attitudes or behaviors to reduce the experience of dissonance between personal standards and the act of violence" (Littman and Paluck 2015: 20). These processes are closely intertwined with revenge, which can affect each of these processes in different ways. For example, the more desensitization, the greater the likelihood that an individual will use violence for revenge purposes; or, revenge is likely to promote disengagement from moral reasoning.

[38] Note that revenge and strategic motives in $t_2$ might be hard to disentangle. Empirically, though, there are ways to identify the causal effect of each of these factors, as I will show in Chapter 4.

## 2.4   ADDITIONAL OBSERVABLE IMPLICATIONS

In addition to the two testable hypotheses outlined above, an additional set of observable implications can be derived from the theoretical framework presented in this chapter.

First, in this chapter I have argued that in conventional civil wars, violence against noncombatants occurs because armed groups aim to clean their rearguard territories of potential enemies. Killings are likely to peak soon after the beginning of the civil war or any time a group just conquers a new piece of territory and to decrease thereafter mainly because the armed group's incentives to kill decrease as committed supporters of the rivals are eliminated. Once the strong supporters of the rival are eliminated, groups are likely to devote less resources to swap their territories in the search of fifth-columnists and similar threats.

Also, the theory of direct violence presented here should potentially be better at explaining violence in small localities than in large localities, in which there is more anonymity. In relatively smaller localities people are likely to have more information on the political ideology of their neighbours, made obvious in prewar political behavior. In larger communities, information on committed supporters of the enemy is likely to be less available because people manage to stay more anonymous. However, many of the dynamics observed in local settings might apply to neighborhoods in big cities.

Similarly, revenge dynamics may be less plausible to take place in larger locations because they make it more complicated to both identify and locate the perpetrators of violence. In larger locations, it is easier for the perpetrators to escape, and for their families to remain unidentified. In smaller localities, it is harder to keep information secret, and it is almost impossible for people to escape their kinship linkages (thus, it is easier to identify and locate relatives of violence perpetrators). This implication is consistent with the idea that both cooperative and perverse social dynamics may be more intense in smaller social settings than in larger and thereby more anonymous settings (Augusteijn 1996).

As stated above, emotions might be present in early periods of the war, especially in contexts of high political mobilization and polarization. The relative importance of emotions grows as wartime (i.e., traumatizing) events occur. But, if the prewar period has been confrontational and violent, revengeful emotions can already be present in the early phases of the civil war. This implies that we can expect violence to be more intense in places where there has been low-intensity violent conflict in the prewar period (e.g., verbal violence, strikes, riots, police violence), as local elites can use violence to settle scores and satisfy vengeful desires.

One of the main differences between conventional and irregular civil wars is the degree of fluidity or permeability of the frontlines. In irregular wars, people can flee more easily, so greater levels of displacement will be observed in areas that might be targets of the armed group. In conventional civil wars, people have far fewer options to flee: they are trapped in the rearguards. In conventional civil wars we are likely to observe greater displacement in front-line areas and in zones that are being conquered by armed groups because, when the frontline moves, displacement may be a military tool to achieve and consolidate territorial control (Balcells and Steele 2016).

## 2.5 DISCUSSION

Some aspects of the theoretical framework presented above require some additional discussion. Firstly, civilian agency regarding the perpetration of direct violence might be viewed as excessive in my theoretical framework. One might argue that the objectives of armed groups will prevail over those of defenseless noncombatants simply because armed groups are more powerful than civilians. I would not oppose the view that armed groups have more coercive power than unarmed civilians. Nevertheless, local information and social support at the local level are extremely valuable assets for armed groups (Wood 2003), particularly for militias that patrol rearguard territories with light weapons and rather selective objectives in mind. In this sense, the power of local civilians should not be underestimated. Despite the fact that there is plenty of historical and contemporary evidence illustrating the crucial role played by local civilians in various civil war processes in extremely different settings, civilians are too often perceived as lacking any sort of agency (and somewhat helpless) in the context of violent conflict.

Secondly, armed groups and political parties are imperfect entities, like any other social organization. In particular, the interests of each of the actors who constitute these groups (e.g., different factions within them) are likely to diverge to some extent. As a consequence, the outcome of the aggregation of their preferences may not be rational or even coherent. Simultaneously, groups can make tactical and strategic mistakes that can lead not only to war losses but also to seemingly "irrational" violent acts. Nonetheless, assuming the non-rationality of actors would make any theorization impossible. Thus, while I understand that this will not always be true, strictly speaking, I consider armed groups and political organizations as rational actors, which I believe is the most convenient for purposes of theorization.

An important dimension of my theoretical approach is the assumption that the perpetration of violence is constrained by the actions of local civilians who are motivated by a quest for political power. This differentiates my approach from works that emphasize armed groups' strategic considerations at the local level (e.g., Chacón et al. 2011) but do not take into account civilians' agency and/or civilians' strategic motives. Although individuals may have mixed motives to collaborate with armed groups, I argue that political considerations are likely to weigh heavily in the rationale of civilians living in a country in the throes of civil war. Civil wars often outbreak in contexts of political polarization and high political mobilization, which encourage individuals to engage politically (Montalvo and Reynal-Querol 2005; Cederman et al. 2011). During war, local politics tend to mirror macro-level politics. And, although local dynamics may not always mirror macro-level dynamics, these local dynamics have a political logic.

I also challenge approaches that have considered local dynamics of violence as completely apolitical.[39] In this sense, I concur with Petersen (2001, 2002) when he argues that there are certain circumstances (such as armed conflict or military invasion) in which people are primed by political grievances that have a significant impact on their behavior.[40] My theoretical framework does not however completely exclude private hatreds or personal motives such as greed or jealousy; after all, these elements are intrinsic to social interactions. Yet, these factors are conflated in my rivalry and revenge variables. On the one hand, in contexts of intense political mobilization, private hatreds are often blended with political or socioeconomic divisions: members of the same political party tend to be friends, and they tend to despise members of rival groups. Thus, the private and the political are likely to go together in these contexts, where friendship and kinship ties are likely to be associated with political rivalries. On the other hand, as argued above, we can expect private hatreds to be more intense in places where wartime victimization has been more severe because of the emotional residual left by previous actions: that is, private motives are conflated with revenge motives in non-initial stages of a civil war.

Finally, although I refer to situations with two groups/blocs for the sake of parsimony, the theoretical model could easily be extended to multiparty civil wars. Local elites would still be using violence strategically to change the balance of power in their favor, with the difference that the calculation would then be somewhat more complex and would include the potential for strategic alliances between groups (Christia 2012).

## 2.6   CONCLUDING REMARKS

In this book, I introduce a new typology of civil war violence against civilians, which distinguishes violence perpetrated on a face-to-face basis (*direct*) from violence perpetrated without a face-to-face interaction between perpetrator and victim (*indirect*). I argue that the determinants of direct and indirect

---

39  For example, Kalyvas (2006) argues that local cleavages are not connected to the civil war master cleavage, and that they concern private motives. Fujii, for her part, argues that in Rwanda situational factors and personal motives, such as greed and jealousy, explain violence better than ethnic hatreds and fears (2009).

40  Frésard (2004) says that that motivations for human rights violations range from the ideological to the personal, including obedience mechanisms, and that all of these motivations combine to produce the outcome of violence. I would argue that, in the context of a civil war, political motives are particularly salient.

violence are different mainly because of the disparities in their form of production: whereas the former requires some degree of collaboration between armed groups and local civilians, the latter is mostly unilateral from the perspective of the armed group. This chapter has presented a theory that seeks to explain direct violence against noncombatants in civil wars. Chapter 5 develops an ancillary set of hypotheses regarding the determinants of indirect violence.

I do not theorize in this book on the determinants of the use of indirect vis-à-vis direct violence; this is somewhat determined by the technology available to armed groups, as well as by patterns of territorial control and battlefield dynamics. When used by a single armed group, direct and indirect violence can be conceived as complements because they are both used with the goal of eliminating adversaries from a territory. However, indirect violence can be sometimes used as a substitute of direct violence, for example when an armed group does not have military control of a territory, and they resort to indirect violence because they cannot possibly inflict direct violence.[41]

Again, the theory in this book does not apply uniquely to conventional civil wars, even if the theoretical focus has been on this particular type of civil wars. I use conventional civil war as a theoretical device to suggest a set of conditions under which existing theories cannot explain violence against civilians, and in which – I argue – political identities become central, thereby challenging recent research on the dynamics of violence during conflict that has prioritized economic, organizational, and/or military factors. However, these conditions are not unique to conventional civil wars and they can exist in the context of irregular civil wars, in symmetric non-conventional civil wars, and even in the context of interstate wars.

My theory implies that prewar politics are important to understanding wartime violence; however, this does not suggest that political variables affect violence in a linear manner or that there is a mechanical extension of political conflict to the battleground. The relationship, as established here, is non-monotonic and more complex. My approach coincides with Gould's suggestion that it is generally misleading to think that conflict is a matter of overthrowing domination (2003: 38), which is somewhat latent in explanations of violence that rely on political factors.[42]

My approach to wartime violence is strategic, but it differs from existing strategic theories of violence in two key dimensions. First, I consider that individual behavior is not only conditioned by the degree of territorial control held by armed groups. Political identities matter for individual behavior and

---

[41] In addition, as I will show in Chapter 5, indirect and direct violence are sometimes interrelated: with direct violence by *A* being a trigger for indirect violence by *B*.

[42] I have defined domination in a very straightforward way, based on the number of supporters of a faction or political group at the local level. However, domination, which can be applied to any type of social relationship, can be taken as a more compound issue (see Gould's discussion of the concept, 2003: 27–66).

that is why mobilized individuals are willing to collaborate with the group they support under risky circumstances (for example, when the rival group has full military control of the area). Second, armed groups know that political identities matter and that is why they do not expect everyone to collaborate with them after achieving full military control of an area. It is because of the belief that individuals have been mobilized by their rivals in the past that armed groups patrol and attempt to eliminate dangerous suspects, based on prewar identities and behaviors. Political identities are thus at the core of my strategic explanation of civilian victimization in civil war.

In addition to political variables, I also take into consideration emotional factors that are endogenous to war. As Petersen (2011) points out, most analyses that employ static measures of violence do not take into account the powerful role of emotions that are driven by acts of violence. I have argued that violent victimization is often a trigger of violence in subsequent periods of the war because those who have been victimized carry out actions to satisfy their revengeful desires. In a nutshell, I argue that understanding the determinants of violence requires a theory that combines factors that are exogenous to the civil war (i.e., political cleavages) and factors that are endogenous to it (i.e., emotions derived from wartime victimization). The former are particularly relevant during the first stages of a civil war while the latter gain relevance as the war continues. This "rivalry and revenge" framework should apply to many civil wars, not just conventional ones.

Chapters 4 and 6 present a battery of tests of the hypotheses and observable implications developed in this chapter: in Chapter 4, I use quantitative and qualitative data from the Spanish Civil War (1936–1939); in Chapter 6, I check the external validity of the theory with evidence from the 2002–2011 civil conflict in Côte d'Ivoire.

PART II

# 3

# History of the Spanish Civil War (1936–1939)

## 3.1 INTRODUCTION

The empirical evidence in this book is largely based on the Spanish Civil War, which started on July 18, 1936 and came to an end on April 1, 1939. This chapter will introduce this civil war to the reader in a synoptic way. The goal is to historically and geographically contextualize the empirical evidence that I will analyze in Chapters 4 and 5. This chapter describes the circumstances preceding the outbreak of the civil war and the dynamics of the conflict as it developed. It also briefly outlines the specific wartime histories of different regions that I will later analyze (e.g., Aragon, Catalonia, Malaga) and it explains how these territories resemble the remaining areas of Spain, where findings should be generalizable. The chapter puts forward the idea that the micro-dynamics of violence on either side of the conflict were not fundamentally different. Indeed, the qualitative evidence from this civil war suggests that, despite the striking differences in ideology and organizational structure between loyalists and rebels, there are important commonalities in the dynamics of violence that took place in their respective rearguard territories, which were driven by local-level interactions between political elites and armed actors.

The Spanish Civil War started with a military coup carried out by a rebel military faction against a legally constituted democratic government. It lasted for almost three years and it caused around 600,000 deaths, including combatants and civilians (Casanova 2014), and over 440,000 externally displaced (Rubio 1977). According to the most current data, the total number of civilian deaths in the areas under Loyalist (i.e., Republican) control was 49,272; the total number of civilian deaths in the Rebel (i.e., Nationalist) areas is still unknown, but is estimated to be around 150,000 (Preston 2011: 22–24).[1]

---

[1] Casanova points to a total of 100,000 deaths in the zone controlled by the Rebels and 55,000 in the Loyalist zones (Casanova 2014). As I will explain below, data on total deaths during the

The Spanish civil war was a conflict between two main politico-military blocs: 1) The army of the incumbent government (Republicans or Loyalists), which also included militias of political parties (e.g., POUM – Troskist communist party, FAI – anarchist, PC – communist), trade unions (e.g., CNT – anarchist, UGT. – socialist), and the International Brigades. I include them under the label of the *Left*. 2) The rebel army (Francoists or Nationalists), which included splinter factions from the regular army, legionnaires, and various militias (e.g., *Falangists, Carlists, Requetés*). I include them under the label *Right*. I consider only these two blocs even if they had important internal divisions.[2] Thus, I do not consider the Spanish Civil War a multiparty civil war (Christia 2012): in spite of their divisions, the two main blocs (Left/Right) were clearly delineated both territorially and organizationally, and they clearly represented the two sides in the "master cleavage" of the civil war.

## 3.2  ANTECEDENTS OF THE CIVIL WAR

### The Spanish Second Republic

The Spanish Civil War was preceded by a democratic period that began with the abdication of King Alfonso XIII on April 14, 1931 and was known as the Second Republic. From 1923 to 1930, Spain was under the dictatorial rule of Miguel Primo de Rivera, who resigned and sought exile in Paris on January 28, 1930.[3] The Second Republic was characterized by a high degree of social and political polarization, and it saw sweeping legislative reforms that were accompanied by upheaval in both the political and the broader social sphere. The regime first consisted of a period of leftist government (1931–1933), which was followed by a period of right-wing government (1934–1935), and a final period of leftist (also called *Popular Front*) government, which lasted for only six months (from February to July 1936). The last government of the Republic was interrupted on July 18, 1936 by the aforementioned military coup, which ultimately failed and was followed by a civil war between the Republican loyalists and the Nationalist rebels.

Prominent historians have analyzed the civil war period in great detail and provided important insights into the relationship between the period of the Second Republic and the outbreak of the civil war. Some notable examples are

---

civil war is still incomplete and various historians are engaged in ongoing debates about the estimates (e.g., Salas 1977; Preston 1986; Martín Rubio 1987; Torres 2002; Juliá 2004). Data on refugees (e.g., Rubio 1977; Gaitx 2006) is also quite incomplete and should be used with caution.

[2] Divisions cut deeper within the Left than within the Right – with confrontations between the anarchists and the communists, and both of them in confrontation with the Republican government.

[3] The eldest son of Miguel Primo de Rivera, José Antonio Primo de Rivera was the founder of Falange Española, a fascist political party, in October 1933.

Brenan (2014/1943), Preston (1994, 2011), Beevor (1982), Malefakis (1976, 1996), Payne (1990, 2004), Tusell (1999), and Casanova (2010, 2013). It would be superfluous to reproduce their work here; instead I merely wish to review the main issues at the center of the major political debates and events during that period. This is important in getting a clear understanding of the causes and dynamics of the civil war.

*i) Land reform.* As in other European countries such as Finland, Italy, Denmark, and Czechoslovakia (Luebbert 1987), land distribution was a crucial issue in Spanish politics during the 1930s. Disputes over land distribution had their origins in earlier periods of Spanish history; for example, the nineteenth century saw intense disputes over expropriations of land owned by the Church and big landlords during the so-called *desamortizaciones* (García de Cortázar and González 1994). The distribution of land ownership was extremely unequal in certain regions of Spain, such as Extremadura and Andalusia, where the most common form of property organization (known as *latifundios*) consisted of extremely large estates owned by a small number of landowners and cultivated by low-wage peasants (Carrión 1932). This unequal distribution of property contributed to a profound structural problem in the Spanish economy, namely, the so-called agrarian unemployment (*paro agrícola*) (Vila Izquierdo 1984). The big landlords opposed Republican reforms aimed at improving the conditions of the peasants, e.g., the Law of Agrarian Reform (*Ley de Bases de la Reforma Agraria*), which was approved on September 9, 1931, and the so-called *Yunteros* reform of Cáceres and Badajoz, which was approved in 1934. As a result, there were fierce confrontations between landlords and peasants in numerous parts of the country, even in more urbanized regions such as Catalonia, where land distribution was less unequal (Balcells 1971; 1980; Riquer 1972).[4] Demands for land redistribution threatened not only big landowners but also middle class landholders. Thus, the issue of the agrarian reform was deeply polarizing (Luebbert 1987: 461). The agrarian cleavage was particularly salient during the Second Republic. According to historians, it was one of the main challenges facing the Republic (Brenan 2014/1943), a catalyst behind political violence during that period (Mintz 1982; Payne 1990)[5], and one of the main factors behind the outbreak of civil war (Malefakis 1976; Riesco 2006). Furthermore, this cleavage also had implications for the dynamics of violence during the war, as peasants and landowners were often the target of violence by one side or the other (Linz 1996).

---

4 Riquer (1972) explains that in the summer of 1933 there was an aggravation of social conflict in the Catalan countryside – the so-called *rabassaire* conflict. This forced the Lliga Regionalista (LlR) to explicitly defend the interests of the big landowners and to oppose the social reformism of Esquerra Republicana de Catalunya (ERC).

5 Stanley Payne explains that "Besides the occasional anarchist insurrections, the main sources of violence were the persistent confrontations between radicalized poor peasants and the authorities in rural districts" (Payne 1990: 274).

TABLE 3.1 *CNT Affiliation in 1936 and 1931 by Regions*

| Region | Affiliated 1936 | % Spain | Affiliated 1931 | % Spain |
|---|---|---|---|---|
| Andalusia and Extremadura | 156,150 | 31.89 | 108,725 | 19.9 |
| Catalonia | 140,952 | 28.79 | 297,481 | 54.46 |
| Valencia and Murcia | 50,972 | 10.41 | 54,548 | 9.98 |
| Castile La Mancha and Madrid | 39,200 | 8.01 | 12,988 | 2.37 |
| Aragon, Rioja, Navarre | 35,263 | 7.20 | 28,081 | 5.14 |
| Galicia | 23,865 | 4.87 | 13,418 | 2.45 |
| Asturias, Leon and Palencia | 22,731 | 4.64 | 25,960 | 4.75 |
| Canarias | 10,555 | 2.16 | 1,025 | 0.18 |
| Basque Country and Cantabria | 7,337 | 1.50 | 2,983 | 0.54 |
| Balearic Islands | 2,593 | 0.53 | . | 0.00 |
| Uncertain Location | . | . | 953 | 0.17 |
| Total | 489,618 | | 546,162 | |

*Author's Elaboration. Sources*: Cucó i Giner (1970) and Solidaridad Obrera (1936)

*ii) Class cleavage.* Also in line with what was occurring in the rest of Europe, the class cleavage was extremely salient in 1930s Spain. This cleavage was strongly connected to land distribution in the countryside, but it also involved the urban classes. It split the country ideologically into Left and Right: generally speaking, communist, anarchist, and social-democratic political parties were on the side of the peasants and workers; and fascist, liberal, and conservative parties were on the side of the agricultural and industrial landlords. Anarcho-syndicalism became very prominent in Spain (much more than in other European countries) with a significant presence in Catalonia, Andalusia, and Extremadura (see Table 3.1). However, the number of people affiliated with the anarchist trade union (Confederación Nacional del Trabajo, CNT) gradually shrunk between 1919 and 1931, perhaps due to the Russian revolution's diminishing role in shaping the workers' ideological mindset. This is perhaps also explained by the growing prevalence of a reformist ideology, reflected in the increasing rates of affiliation with the Unión General de Trabajadores (UGT), a more moderate trade union (Cucó i Giner 1970: 183–184).[6] The repression of anarchists during the Primo de Rivera dictatorship (1923–1930) also contributed to the demise of the CNT (the UGT was not persecuted) and radicalized it along revolutionary lines; in 1931, the CNT split between

[6] As of 1931, the largest share of UGT affiliates were coming from Castile, followed by Andalusia: thus, it did not have influence in the exact same regions where anarchists were prevalent. The more radical union (the CNT) prevailed in areas with a high concentration of either industrial workers or landless peasants, whereas the more moderate union (the UGT) prevailed in areas with middle-sized farms.

radical members (FAI, the *faístas*), and moderates (*treintistas*). As we will see, during the civil war, the FAI was the most violent faction.

*iii) Territorial cleavage.* During the first decades of the twentieth century, peripheral nationalism flourished politically, socially, and culturally in the Basque Country, Catalonia, and Galicia. The weakness of the Spanish state and the lack of a Spanish "scholastic revolution" created the opportunity for the consolidation of alternative national identities in territories inhabited by ethnic minorities (Balcells 2013). According to Balfour and Preston, "the cleavages were not just political and ideological but also regional because economic growth and urbanization had taken place above all in the more developed periphery of Spain, whose elites had occupied subordinate positions in the structure of political power" (1999: 4). In the Basque country and Catalonia, political forces representing regionalist interests (e.g., Partido Nacionalista Vasco, Lliga Regionalista, Esquerra Republicana de Catalunya) achieved a hegemonic presence in their respective polities during the Second Republic, and they brought regional issues to the national level, where they negotiated political decentralization. During the Second Republic autonomous Constitutions (*Estatutos de Autonomía*) were elaborated for these three peripheral regions.[7]

The territorial cleavage was also significant during the civil war, when the Francoists targeted national minorities such as Basques, Galicians, or Catalans (Sales 1957/2007; Solé i Sabaté and Villarroya 1987; Thompson 2005).[8] For example, during and after the occupation of Catalonia, there was widespread hatred against anything "Catalan," resulting in "the prohibition of the usage of the language, the printing and distribution of publications in Catalan, the destruction of libraries, museums, schools, historical monuments, cult places and other institutions" (Solé i Sabaté and Villarroya 1987: 14). Nonetheless the class cleavage was the main structuring cleavage of the civil war: an indication of this is the fact that, at the time of the coup, the different regional political parties (and their constituencies) sided with the rebels or with the government based on their position on the Left–Right political spectrum and not following their position in the territorial cleavage.[9]

*iv) Religious cleavage.* In addition to the aforementioned cleavages, there was a specifically religious cleavage, which largely overlapped with the class

---

[7] The Basque Autonomous Constitution was, however, never approved due to the outbreak of the war.

[8] In priest Gumersindo de Estella's (2003) memoirs, there are several testimonies of individuals who were executed in Zaragoza and who were targeted because of their condition of Catalans. One of them explains that a Francoist officer who had captured him said "We have to annihilate you and all Catalans!"(de Estella 2003: 76).

[9] For example, the *Lliga Regionalista* (LlR) – the main right-wing Catalanist party – and its constituency of Catalan conservatives, supported Franco despite his anti-Catalanist rhetoric and actions. The reaction of the main right-wing political parties in Valencia and the Basque Country was exceptional in that they supported the Loyalists instead of the Rebels.

cleavage. It also had strong roots in the nineteenth-century history of Spain (Montero 1961). Indeed, reforms aimed at reducing land and properties owned by the Catholic Church had been a major source of political conflict. The Second Republic's Constitution (approved on December 9, 1931) established the principle of separation of the State and the Church. Moreover, during the Second Republic, the leftist governments enacted a myriad of reforms challenging the power of the Catholic Church such as legalizing civil marriage and divorce, introducing civil funerary services, and challenging the Church's hegemony in matters of education. All these reforms led the clergy to eye the Left with suspicion. Julián Casanova describes the religious polarization during the period in the following way: "It was not that Spain was no longer Catholic ... It was that there was one Spain that was extremely Catholic, another not so much, and a third that was highly anti-Catholic. There was more Catholicism in the north than in the south, among landowners than among the dispossessed, among women than among men. The majority of Catholics were anti-socialist and supportive of the social order. The Republican and working-class Left was associated with anticlericalism. It is hardly surprising that the proclamation of the Republic led to rejoicing for some and mourning for others" (Casanova 2013: 47–48).

Before the war, political mobilization was shaped by confrontations over religious issues, particularly in the countryside (de la Cueva 1998; Delgado 2001; Casanova 2004; Ledesma 2009a). Clergymen and church properties were violently attacked – in several instances even before the outbreak of war. As we will see further below, during the war religion had a twofold impact on wartime violence: on the one hand, members of the clergy represented a large share of the victims in the Republican areas; on the other hand, priests and other religious people played a significant role in the perpetration of violence in Nationalist territories, as they were often behind the denunciations of leftists.[10] The Nationalist bloc framed the civil war as a "sacred crusade" (*Santa Cruzada*) as it argued that the fight aimed to restore the Catholic values that were under threat from the Marxists and anarchists.[11]

*v) Political polarization.* Social polarization was heightened at the political level because of the characteristics of the electoral system (Linz 1967, 1978; Linz and De Miguel 1977; Riquer 1991; Colomer 2004). The electoral system of the Second Republic consisted of a plurality rule with open lists, known as the *panachage*. Voters could cast votes for 80 percent of the candidates

---

[10] For example, Vila Izquierdo (1984: 55) explains that the priest of Badajoz (Father Lomba) was in charge of identifying individuals to be killed in an infamous massacre carried out by the Nationalists in this town.

[11] A report published by the monastery of Zaragoza described the military uprising and the civil war as follows: "On July 19, 1936, a religious–social movement began, and this had the objective of saving the Christian civilization, threatened in Spain by the Marxist mobs of the atheist Republic" (de Estella 2003: 267).

in a district (there was a cap): thus, votes would be for individual candidates, and not for closed party lists. These candidates were, however, affiliated with political parties, with which they campaigned.[12] The system encouraged the creation of large pre-electoral coalitions in order to increase the individual candidates' chances of success (Riquer 1991: 85). This contributed to the polarization in two main blocs. Furthermore, this plurality system was highly disproportional, benefiting the largest parties, and quite especially the winning coalition.

Tusell explains that, during the Second Republic, political mobilization was generalized, intensive and extensive, thanks to the role of mass parties. For example, in the province of Alicante, over 75 percent of municipalities had local offices of the right-wing party (Tusell 1991: 48). At the national level, there were three major electoral contests during the Second Republic: the 1931 elections – the so-called foundational elections (*Elecciones Constituyentes*), the 1933 elections, and the 1936 elections – also called the Popular Front elections (Tusell 1971). The 1931 elections, which took place on June 28, 1931, were "transitional elections" with the objective of establishing a new parliament tasked with drafting a new Constitution. According to Tusell, those elections were plagued with patronage practices, *caciquismo*: "there was an official candidate, partial mobilization and a clear-cut intervention on the part of the civil governors in the electoral process" (Tusell 1991: 48). Thus, "only the 1933 and 1936 elections can be considered polls that took place in conditions of normality similar to those in a country with institutions and stable democratic behavior" (Tusell 1991: 48). The 1933 elections, held on November 19, were the first national elections in which women could exercise the right to vote; the anarchists did not compete in the 1933 elections and instead undertook a campaign in favor of electoral absenteeism.

The 1936 elections were highly competitive and took place in a tense atmosphere. Two large pre-electoral coalitions competed on the Left and the Right, respectively: the *Confederación Española de Derechas Autónomas* (CEDA) and the *Frente Popular* (Popular Front). The parties they assembled were very diverse. The Popular Front, for example, had members ranging from Socialists and Republicans to Communists (the Anarchists did not compete in the elections but they endorsed the Popular Front, which promised amnesty for political prisoners, most of them anarchists). The electoral campaign was heated and there were several instances of verbal violence between candidates. Politics was portrayed a zero-sum game, with devastating consequences for the losers. The threat of the use of violence should the Left win the elections

---

[12] After legislation enacted in 1933, there would be a second round if none of the candidates in a given district obtained more than 40 percent of the vote; a minimum of 8 percent of the vote was required to participate in the second round. Thus, there were technically two rounds, but the second round was not generalized throughout the territory because it could be avoided with a minimum level of support for the winning candidate in the first round.

was present and it became especially worrisome when some right-wing candidates threatened to call on the army to safeguard the nation (Ruiz 2012:
31–32). Brenan explains that the CEDA organized an electoral campaign on
an unprecedented scale: "Monster posters displaying Gil Robles' uninspiring
features decorated the Castilian towns. The captions under them had a Fascist ring.... His election speeches were of extraordinary violence and consisted
mainly of insults to his opponents" (Brenan 2014/1943: 489).

   Thus, there was widespread political mobilization, especially surrounding
the national elections on February 16, 1936 (Jackson 1965; Tusell 1971).
"During the period preceding the elections, particularly in February 1936,
all the political parties (including the anarchists) were intensely engaged in
campaigning.... The propaganda was unprecedented in Spanish politics, especially that of the CEDA, with large posters depicting their leader Gil-Robles"
(Chaves 1995: 25). Verbal attacks were particularly intense during the electoral campaign (Alós 1978: 19). Working-class organizations, trade unions,
and local cultural associations contributed to political mobilization and they
encouraged people to go the polls (Amat et al. 2016). Mobilization had
impressive results and the level of participation in the 1936 elections was
extraordinary (the highest of the period): 71 percent of the Spanish adult
population cast a valid vote (Linz and De Miguel 1977: 37).[13]

   On February 16, 1936, the Popular Front won the national elections by a
relatively narrow margin: it obtained 60.5 percent of the Parliament's seats
(with 42.9 percent of the votes). The right-wing coalition obtained 23.7 percent of the seats (despite having obtained 30.4 percent of the votes). Again, the
electoral system was highly disproportional (Colomer 2004).

   Electoral competition and political polarization affected not only the
national party system, but also different regional party systems. For example, in Catalonia political support was polarized around two Catalan parties
(they did not compete in other parts of Spain): Esquerra Republicana de
Catalunya (ERC), on the left, and Lliga Regionalista (LlR), on the Right. Political mobilization and political polarization along the Left–Right cleavage was
also evident at the local level, as explained by this historian from Aragon: "The
1930s was a decade of intense mobilization, development and advancement of
mass leftist political parties, as well as trade unionism, which was monopo-
lized by the CNT in this zone [province of Huesca]. Out of the 67 localities,
at least in 30 of them, leftist sympathizers would meet in a Republican center or – in the absence of such a center – at a local bar. In many localities
there were two bars: one for leftists and one for rightists. [During the war]
Many café-bar owners were executed, accused of harboring the ideology of
the clients! ... In some villages, polarization was so deep that even the local

---

[13] Turnout had been 70.13 percent in 1931 (when only men over 23 years old were allowed to
  vote) and 64.94 percent in 1933, when women were allowed to vote in national elections for
  the first time (Ortega 2005).

festivities were divided: there were parties for right-wing people and parties for left-wing people" (Azpíroz 2007: 372).

The Left–Right cleavage represented by the two large preelectoral competitions that competed in the 1936 elections later matched the master cleavage of the civil war, fought between the defenders of the Republic (i.e., the Left) and those who rebelled against it (i.e., the Right). For the purposes of this book, it is important to note that, due to the high levels of political mobilization and the importance of these elections, the 1936 electoral results capture more than recent political partisanship: they are strong indicators of a deep ideological cleavage. In other words, by looking at the results of the elections in the different Spanish localities, we can determine how the ideological cleavage divided these localities.[14]

## Militarization of Politics, Coup, and Frontlines

### Militarization of Politics

The Second Republic witnessed a militarization of political life with striking resemblances to the Weimar Republic in Germany. Starting in 1933, a non-negligible number of political parties created militias or so-called "defense sections" – for example, *Joventuts d'Esquerra-Estat Català*, *Comités de Defensa de la CNT*, and *Grups d'Acció del BOC-POUM* (Pozo 2002: 8–9), on the Left. These groups engaged in activities disruptive to the public order during and after the 1936 elections. The fascist political party *La Falange*, which was founded in 1933 by José Antonio Primo de Rivera, was banned in March 1936 on account of its undemocratic practices, including protracted acts of violence.[15] The efforts of the government to preserve a context of normality for the country became futile. The criminal activities of left-wing and right-wing extremist groups made it difficult to practice "normal politics." Before the outbreak of war, political assassinations on both sides already numbered in the hundreds.[16]

A series of violent events taking place in October 1934, which have collectively been dubbed the "October Insurrection," marked the Second

---

[14] In Chapter 4, I undertake empirical analyses with the results of the 1936 elections as a proxy for the distribution of supporters of the Left and the Right at the local level. In addition, I use the difference of vote in the 1936 and 1933 elections to capture the depth of the ideological cleavage at the local level.

[15] Chaves argues that "Their activities significantly increased after the bar, in spite of the fact that they had a number of important leaders in jail" (Chaves 1995: 29). In July 1936, The Falange still had around 10,000 affiliates.

[16] The total figures vary slightly, depending on the source. Thomas estimates 1,287 assaults, 269 political murders, and 160 church burnings (Thomas 1986: 5). Payne estimates that there were around 2,000 deaths (Payne 1990: 269). González Calleja estimates a total of 2,624 fatalities due to politically motivated violence (among them, 1,550 inflicted by national security forces) (González Calleja 2014: 323).

Republic. After the conservative government revoked most of the leftist legislation passed during the first Republican government (e.g., annulment of the
Law of Agrarian Contracts, restoration of the 48-hour work week that had
been reduced to 44 hours), the main trade unions called for a "general strike."
The suspension of the Agrarian Law was a major source of discontent among
agrarian workers, but the strike was widely followed by miners in Asturias,
who made use of violence and perpetrated several atrocities such as the murder
of priests (Payne 1990: 278). The Spanish government responded with fierce
repression, making use of military troops under General Francisco Franco's
control. In fact, this has been considered General Franco's "momentum," providing him the requisite reputation and status within the Spanish military to
later stage a military coup.[17] However, repression was widespread and went
beyond Asturias: workers from all over the country were persecuted. Between
20,000 and 30,000 Republicans and Socialists were jailed, including the former Prime Minister (1931–1933) Manuel Azaña, who could not be convicted
due to the fact that there were no charges against him (Payne 2004). At least
20 people were sentenced to death.

At the same time, on October 6, 1934, the president of the Catalan
autonomous government, Lluís Companys (ERC), proclaimed the Independent
State of Catalonia (*Estat Català*).[18] Some hours later, the Spanish government
declared this proclamation void, triggering severe political repression against
the local and regional members of ERC and other Catalan nationalists. Some
of these individuals remained in prison until February 1936, when the leftist
government approved an amnesty bill. At the local level, rightist political elites
often used repression following the October insurrection as an instrument to
establish political dominance in localities. For example, a historian from Berga
(Catalonia) argues: "The events of October 6th, 1934 had a big impact in the
county. In Berga, leftist members of the local council, including the mayor, were
imprisoned. After October 6th, there was a wave of repression targeted at anyone connected to the Left. The right-wing local political elites took advantage
of this situation to regain political control of the locality. For this purpose,
they shut down the headquarters of the trade unions and left-wing political
parties" (Serra 1989: 17). As we shall see, this instrumental use of violence to
achieve or consolidate political control at the local level is similar to the one
that would take place in many localities later on, in the midst of the civil war.

The repression surrounding the October Insurrection, which affected mobilized workers and Catalan nationalists, was a harbinger of the civil war. In fact,
some have called it a "rehearsal" for the armed conflict (Díaz Nosty 1975).
These events illustrate the extent to which Spain was undergoing a period of

---

[17] For an extensive account of the October Insurrection, see Díaz Nosty (1975) and Jackson
et al. (1985).

[18] The anarchist trade union (CNT) did not back the proclamation of the independent Catalan
state.

intense social mobilization, and they contributed to a further polarization of Spanish society, both at the national and at the local level. For example, in Torrecilla de Alcañiz (in the province of Teruel), there was a riot confronting leftists and rightists six days before the military coup: "There were insults, threats, blows, and risk of imminent bloodshed ... " (Burgués 1999: 127). In Extremadura, there were frequent clashes between individuals over political differences: "Physical aggression between supporters of the Left and the Right were common in the majority of localities" (Chaves 2000: 86).[19]

In a nutshell, in 1930s Spain, long-lasting social and political animosities developed in a context of political mobilization, social polarization, and the militarization of political life. At the macro level, these dynamics have been conceived as the underpinning of the breakdown of the Second Republic (Jackson 1965; Linz 1978; Payne 1990; Brenan 2014/1943; Colomer 2004) and hence an underlying cause of the civil war.[20] As I will show later in the book, these dynamics also had implications for violence that took place during the civil war.

### Coup

On July 18, 1936, General Francisco Franco, who was stationed in the Canary Islands, and a faction of the army stationed in the Spanish protectorate of northern Morocco launched a rebellion against the government, and led a military coup that would split the army in two.[21] General Sanjurjo was the leader of the army at the time of the coup and one of the chief conspirators behind the military uprising. Other generals involved in the plot to overthrow the Republican government were Emilio Mola and Gonzalo Queipo de Llano, in addition to Francisco Franco.[22] Some historians date the coup back to July 17, the day the insurrection started in Morocco (Payne 1985: 15); others date it on July 19, when it fully reached peninsular territory, with the rebellion of the provincial garrisons (Graham 1999: 175). The date has however, commonly been placed on July 18.[23]

---

[19] The monk Hilari Raguer explains that, in his parish, he and his childhood friends used to play at "leftists and rightists" instead of "cowboys and Indians" or "cops and robbers" (Raguer 2007). This is a clear illustration of how polarized was society along the Left–Right cleavage.

[20] According to Stanley Payne, the Second Republic was "the most polarized of all modern European democratic systems" (Payne 1990: 285–286). For his part, Brenan argues that "the Civil War was the explosion in the powder magazine that had been slowly accumulating" (Brenan 2014/1943: xxviii). This explosion was however not inevitable: it was triggered by a premeditated coup that intended to remove democratically elected officials from power.

[21] The 40,000 men based in Morocco where the toughest and most efficient troops of the Spanish army, which consisted of 100,000 men at the time (Beevor 2006:49).

[22] Franco assumed leadership of the military after an agreement between the Generals on October 1, 1936 (González Calleja, personal communication).

[23] For detailed accounts of what triggered the coup and its specific dynamics, see, among others, Jackson (1965), Beevor (1982), Thomas (1986), Preston (1994), Moreno de Alborán (1998), Payne (2004), and Laparra (2013).

Stanley Payne writes: "Within approximately forty-eight hours, more than one-third of the garrisons in peninsular Spain also revolted – although scarcely 50 percent of the regular army supported this action. Instead of a rapid coup that could have been completed in a week or two, the revolt led to complete internal division and civil war" (1985: 15).[24] Indeed, shortly after the coup, the Spanish territory was split into areas of Loyalist and Rebel control. These were to become the military control areas: during the war, the frontlines mostly shifted in accordance with the victories and defeats of the armies in big battles and conquest campaigns. Figure 3.1 depicts the Loyalist (i.e., Republican) and Rebel (i.e., Nationalist) areas of control at the beginning of the war, shortly after the coup (on July 22, 1936).[25]

The coup succeeded in Galicia, Castile-Leon, Navarra, Alava, La Rioja, a large part of Aragon, a small enclave in Andalusia, Cáceres, almost all the Balearic Islands (except Menorca) and the Canary Islands (Martín Rubio 2006: 83). The coup failed in Castile-La Mancha, Valencia, Catalonia, Madrid, Menorca, the provinces of Bilbao and Guipuzcoa (in the Basque Country), Asturias (except for the city of Oviedo), Santander, Murcia, and the provinces of Malaga, Almeria, and Jaen in Andalusia.[26] The geographical distribution of the areas initially under the control of loyalists and rebels was roughly correlated with prewar political alignments, but they did not match perfectly. On the one hand, there were several territories politically dominated by the Left after the February 1936 elections, yet whose support the rebels gained in the attempted coup. This was the case of Galicia (except for a small part of the province of Lugo, which was initially controlled by the Loyalists);[27] the Andalusian cities of Sevilla, Cadiz, and Algeciras; Zaragoza City and a part of Aragon, including Huesca,[28] the city of Cáceres and part of its province;

---

[24] Despite the military split, the military junta had at their disposal the greater part of the armed forces in the country (Civil Guard, Foreign Legion, a division of Moorish troops, fourth fifths of the infantry, artillery officers), while the government had only the Republican Assault Guards and a small and poorly armed air force (Brenan 2014/1943: 517).

[25] Source: Preston (2011: 658).

[26] The rebels occupied Badajoz and Toledo in August 1936; Irún and Donostia were conquered in September 1936. Also, by November 1936 more than half of Andalusia was already under rebel control, including the cities of Huelva, Sevilla, Cadiz, Cordoba, and Badajoz.

[27] "Galicia, it should be noted, returned more Popular Front deputies than any region. It was the only Republican region that the insurgents immediately captured, and it provided the Nationalists with perhaps the most important contingent of troops, 237,385 or one-fourth of Rebel manpower" (Payne 1967: 519, cited in Seidman 2002: 120). Also, "more than two-thirds of Galicians had voted in favor of the Statute of Autonomy on June 28 of that same year, less than a month before the uprising" (Thompson 2005: 77).

[28] In the province of Zaragoza, which had held the CNT congress in May 1936, Payne argues that "the CNT [the anarchist trade union] was victim of its own disorganization, and much of the province immediately fell under rightist military control. Something similar occurred in "Red Seville," seized by General Gonzalo Queipo de Llano in an audacious coup de main, the greatest initial achievement by any of the rebel leaders" (2004: 111).

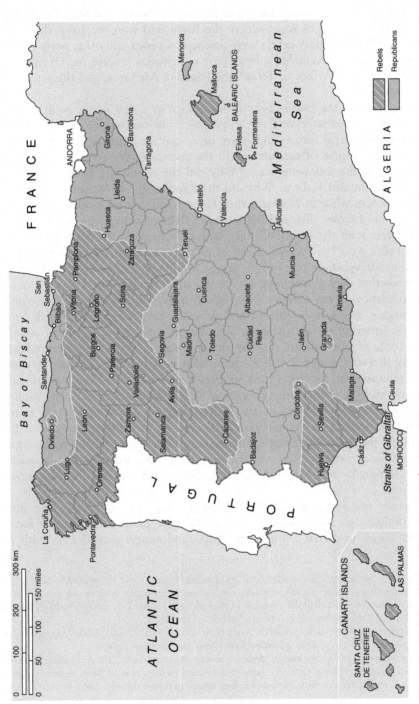

Figure 3.1  Rebel and Republican Areas, July 22, 1936

part of the province of Salamanca; and the city of Oviedo. On the other hand, there were a number of zones where the Right had won the 1936 elections and in which the military rebels were defeated: Cuenca and other parts of the region of Castile-la Mancha, a large part of Asturias (except for Oviedo), a large part of the province of Teruel, the island of Menorca, and the province of Santander.[29]

An analysis of the factors behind the success or defeat of the coup across different territories is beyond my scope here. The outcomes were the result of a combination of factors that were often quite contingent. Indeed, there was a certain degree of randomness in the success of the coup, which Vilar articulated in the following way: "Why did the rebels win in the Republican and autonomist Galicia? Why did the Republicans of Menorca win over General Bosch, while in Mallorca they failed badly against Goded? Why did Extremadura become divided into two, with Badajoz siding with the Republic and Cáceres with the rebels? Chance had a lot to do with these outcomes" (Vilar 1986: 63). The success or defeat of the coup across regions was also related to idiosyncratic traits of the regional military leaders; that is, depending on whether they were willing and/or able to undertake orders from Franco. The preferences of the military with regard to the coup were not unanimous. For instance, the Army's officials and generals were internally divided: "22 generals remained in service in the Republican zone; 17 in the rebel zone" (Pozo 2002: 58). In contrast, the majority of officers in the Navy supported the uprising (Beevor 2006: 71).[30] Preferences also varied among the lower grades of the military; yet, the lower rank soldiers were uninformed about what was going on and they often simply followed orders from on high.[31] The evolution of the events taking place immediately after the *putsch* of July 18, 1936 also had an impact on the success of the coup in the different garrisons. In Barcelona, for example, the defeat of the coup was very much a consequence of the actions of the workers and the regional government forces (*La Generalitat*) (Kaminsky 2002/1937; Pozo 2002: 46), which successfully confronted the rebels.

Overall, the geographical distribution of support and hence the initial frontlines of the conflict did not follow a pattern that could have possibly been predicted beforehand. This randomness provides us with a

---

[29] The case of Santander is discussed in detail by Gutiérrez Flores (2000: 55–56) and Solla (2005). Gutiérrez Flores argues that the rebels did not succeed in Santander because communications between Burgos and Valladolid were cut as they awaited instructions from Valladolid; leftist groups seized the opportunity to organize and defeat the rebels.

[30] In Spain, the Air Forces were part of the Army (*Aeronáutica Militar*) and the Navy (*Aeronáutica Naval*) until May 1937, when a Spanish Republican Air Force was created.

[31] Laparra (2014) analyzes the internal divisions within the Army and finds that officers who were in well-favored corps and promoted between 1931 and 1936 were more likely to remain loyal to the Republic. He also finds that subordinates tended to follow the side chosen by their senior officer.

"quasi-experimental setting' (Przeworski 2007), and makes the Spanish Civil War an appropriate case for studying dynamics of wartime violence.

### Frontlines

The Spanish Civil War involved pitched battles as well as aerial and naval attacks. The Francoist army conquered the entire Republican territory over the course of approximately three years and it formally won the war on April 1, 1939. Without entering into the details of the military history of the war, which have already been discussed by specialized historians,[32] it should be emphasized that the Nationalist army's breach of a set of stable frontlines (for example, the Ebro's frontline and the Madrid's frontline) was the crucial factor in determining the outcome of the war.[33]

Nearly all the territory studied in this book (except for the province of Malaga in Andalusia) was divided by the so-called Ebro frontline until December 1938. The Nationalists controlled the area west of this frontline, while the Republican forces roughly controlled the area to the east of it (although the control in some parts of Aragon was precarious, as the frontline moved toward the east). With the victory in the Battle of the Ebro in mid-November 1938,[34] the Francoist army began their conquest of Catalonia and Valencia. At that point, the Republican army offered little resistance, it disintegrated, and most Republican soldiers fled to France in attempts to avoid capture. Only some of them succeeded.

## 3.3   INSIDE THE WAR

### Armed Groups

#### Internal Organization

The two blocs in conflict were composed of both regular and irregular forces. Throughout most of the war, the Nationalist bloc was much better coordinated and disciplined than the Republican bloc. Therefore principal–agent problems between military leaders and rank-and-file soldiers were much less severe in the

---

[32] See, among many others, Martínez de Baños (2004b, 2006), Reverte (2003, 2006), Espinosa (2005), Solano (2006), Arcarazo et al. (2007), Maldonado (2007), and Flores et al. (2008).

[33] According to Pape (1996: 336), "the Spanish Civil War was fought in series of set-piece battles, because logistics constrained both sides from fighting more than one battle at a time. The Loyalists waged a war of attrition to protract the conflict until international support could shift decisively in their favor. By forcing the Nationalists into long battles for every gain, the Loyalists were able to remain in control of large sections of the country."

[34] The so-called Battle of the Ebro (July–December 1938) was the most important battle of the war, due to its length and deadliness. It caused a total of 90,000 battle deaths: among them, 30,000 were Francoist soldiers, while 60,000 were Republican soldiers (Source: Museum of the Battle of the Ebro, Gandesa, Terra Alta).

Nationalist bloc than in the Republican one. This fact has led several historians and political scientists to explain the violence perpetrated by each side in organizational terms (e.g., Jackson 1965; Reig Tapia 1984; Luengo 1998; Casanova et al. 2001; Preston 2006; Herreros and Criado 2009; Brenan 2014/1943): they have characterized violence on the part of Francoist forces as the result of calculated and systematic efforts to eliminate the enemy whereas they have conceived violence from the Republican side as the by-product of disorder and lack of control of the militias (I will turn to this point later in the chapter).

While, in general terms, it is true that the two armed groups were antithetical in regards to their levels of discipline and organization, some caveats have to be made as this depiction of the two blocs may be too simplistic: for example, within the Francoist army, there were irregular forces, which did not always strictly obey the orders issued by top commanders, and there was also some degree of fragmentation as well as a certain lack of discipline (Cruz 2006).[35] The Republican bloc was indeed highly fragmented (Orwell 1938; Pozo 2002; Ledesma 2003; De Guzmán 2004/1938): tensions within the leftist bloc were constant from the beginning of the war on. In May 1937, members of the Communist party engaged in an armed confrontation with members of the Trotskyist party, the *Partido Obrero de Unificación Marxista* (POUM), and the anarchosynidicalists of the FAI, in the streets of Barcelona.[36] Hundreds of leftist sympathizers from all these groups were wounded and killed. The internal division within the Loyalist bloc not only involved differences between communists and anarchists: the latter were in turn challenged by the Republican governmental authorities, who opposed their *modus operandi* (Azaña 1986). By October/November 1936 – as the various leftist organizations came to realize that the centralization of political and military power was necessary to win the war – they started to become more disciplined (Azaña 1986; Pozo 2002; De Guzmán 2004/1938; Ledesma 2009b). Military columns were turned into battalions and brigades during the winter of 1936 (Beevor 2006: 203).[37] Some months later, after the events of May 1937 in Barcelona, the anarchist political forces were expelled from the government and the Communist party emerged as the leader of the leftist bloc. They constituted the so-called Popular Army, and the organization transitioned from being loose and decentralized to being more cohesive and centralized.[38]

---

[35] In an interview, a former combatant told me that the Legion was the most disciplined faction within the Francoist bloc (Testimony 9). He recalled a soldier in the Legion being severely punished for giving tobacco to prisoners.

[36] At the heart of these confrontations was the profound anti-statism of the anarchists (Graham 1999: 195).

[37] In Catalonia, the regional government tried to establish the eastern forces as an independent Catalan army, unsuccessfully (Beevor 2006).

[38] The role of Soviet external support was non-negligible with respect to this centralization process. As Balfour and Preston (1999) explain, "Soviet military aid was accompanied by intense pressure to curb the revolutionary tendencies on the Republican side" (7).

## External Support

Foreign support played an important role in the unfolding of the Spanish civil war and it was a crucial factor behind its outcome for it tilted in favor of the Francoists (Thomas 1986; Balfour and Preston 1999; Radosh et al. 2001; Payne 2004). The Spanish Civil War was a crucial event in the interwar period and it involved a number of states. Italy and Germany sided with Franco and used the Spanish battleground as a training arena for the strategic air warfare that they would undertake in World War II (Solé i Sabaté and Villarroya 2003),[39] while the Soviet Union, Mexico, and Czechoslovakia provided material support to the Republican side.[40] The International Brigades, which were the first case of "Foreign Fighters" of the twentieth century (Hegghammer 2010), supported the Republicans. However, they were volunteers and the extent of their support was limited, especially given the fact that Western powers did not act in favor of the Republic. Balfour and Preston (1999) explain that "the British and French arms embargo and the isolationism of the United States in the 1930s deprived the Spanish Republic of the right to buy arms from the democratic powers"(6). To top it all, Salazar's Portugal made alliance with Franco, allowing the Northern and Southern rebel armies to remain connected by using Portugal as a corridor.[41] Moradiellos (1999) writes: "Without the consistent military, diplomatic and financial support given by Hitler and Mussolini, it is highly unlikely that the side led by Franco would have been able to achieve such an absolute and unconditional victory. Without the suffocating embargo imposed by the non-intervention policy and the inhibition of the Western powers, with its serious effect on military capacity and moral strength, it is highly unlikely that the Republic would have suffered an internal collapse and a military defeat of great proportions" (121).[42]

Although they were very important for the outcome of the civil war, I will not treat these external powers as independent actors in the conflict. National leaders of the Republican and Nationalist armies retained control over military decisions at all times. For example, the International Brigades were disbanded by the Republican first minister Juan Negrín in September

---

[39] Leitz (1999) explains that "Of the few comments Goring made at the Nuremberg Trials about the Spanish Civil War, he emphasized the need to test this Luftwaffe as a motive for Germany's intervention.... Luftwaffe planes and pilots were undoubtedly trained in Spain" (130).

[40] Stalin allegedly sent a telegram to the Spanish loyalist government in October 1936 saying "It is our duty to help the Spanish people. This fight is not a private affair of Spain" (Campoamor 2005: 150).

[41] The Portuguese police detained thousands of Spanish citizens who crossed the border to enter Portugal, and delivered them to the *falangists* in Badajoz (Vila Izquierdo 1984: 58).

[42] The intervention of Germany and the Soviet Union in the Spanish Civil War also had implications for the balance of power between factions within the Republican and Nationalist blocs: the small Falangist and Communist parties obtained positions of overriding influence (within the rightist and leftist bloc respectively) as a result of these interventions (Brenan 2014/1943: xxix).

1938, and their members were obliged to leave the country.[43] Also, Franco's "determination to stand up for his own interests" led him to take actions against those who were challenging his orders whenever he deemed it necessary (Leitz 1999).

## Technology and Warfare

The Spanish Civil War is, like the American Civil War, a paradigmatic case of a conventional civil war. The military tactics used in this conflict were predominantly conventional, with heavy weaponry used in combat battles determining the outcome of the war. As explained above, the frontlines remained fairly stable over time and they had little fluidity and permeability. As Kaminsky observed in 1937: "The civil war has evolved and has become a big war between two large armies, which have all the methods of destruction and the most modern techniques" (Kaminsky 2002/1937: 197).

As is common in conventional conflicts, many more combatants than civilians were killed during the Spanish Civil War. At the subnational level, the extent to which victims were either combatants or civilians depended on the dynamics of warfare on the ground. For example, in Extremadura, the province of Badajoz witnessed a greater proportion of battlefield deaths than Cáceres, which was much more of a rearguard province (the total number of people killed in the battlefield in Extremadura was 6,678; 5,760 of them died in Badajoz and 918 of them died in Cáceres) (Chaves 2004).

Another classical feature of conventional wars, also exemplified in the case of Spain, is routinized conscription. In the Spanish Civil War, young men were recruited to either the Republican or the Nationalist army simply depending on the side where they happened to reside when the frontlines were set. Although women were also highly mobilized for the "war effort" (Cenarro 2006), they were not conscripted. Volunteers fought on each side as well, together with the conscripts. Some of the conscripted men became deserters.[44]

The combination of rather exogenous frontlines (i.e., frontlines shaped by the outcome of the coup at the subnational level) and routinized conscription made recruitment somewhat independent of the ideological background or political affiliation of individuals. This caused conflicts within families and often bizarre situations, including brothers residing in different locations and fighting against each other (Fraser 2001: 151).[45]

---

[43] The reasons behind this decision were mostly geostrategic: Juan Negrín, who announced this decision in front of the League of Nations, attempted to force the withdrawal of the Italian and German fascist forces from Spain, and he sought to persuade the Western democracies to end their embargo on the Republic.

[44] McLauchlin (2014) explains that desertion was more frequent in more mountainous localities, where armed groups had less ability to find those that were hiding.

[45] Due to conscription, combatants in the armies were drawn from all over. This is the opposite of what happens in irregular civil wars, where recruitment varies across the territory and is

Groups sporadically used irregular tactics in areas close to the front-line, quite especially where the terrain was rough (e.g., in some mountains in Extremadura; in some parts of the Pyrenees). Nonetheless, the prevalent method of combat during the Spanish Civil War was trench battle with heavy artillery. It was a civil war fought frontally.[46]

## 3.4   VIOLENCE AGAINST CIVILIANS

In conventional civil wars, there is a quite clear distinction between battlefield and rearguard territories. Combatants are located in the battlefield, and noncombatants in the rearguard. Violence against civilians mostly takes place in rearguard territories. In this section, I describe the violence that took place in the rearguard territories of the Spanish Civil War. I will refer mostly to lethal violence against civilians, which is the main focus of the book.

### Leftist Violence

Leftist violence, also known as "red terror," consisted of both individual and mass executions in the Republican (i.e., Loyalist) zone. Members of the clergy represented a large share of the victims of this type of violence: a total of 6,832 clergy members were assassinated (Rodrigo 2008: 99): among them were 4,184 priests, 2,365 monks and 283 nuns.[47] Most of them were killed in July and August, 1936. As José Luis Ledesma writes, "There was not another institution or social group that suffered from such rapid and methodical violence" (Ledesma 2009a: 10). Members of the clergy, identified as strong supporters of the Nationalists, could not easily hide or disguise themselves. Thus, they became easy targets for leftist militants. In addition, as Delgado (1992) has explained, many militiamen saw killing priests as a "revolutionary obligation."

Nonetheless, religious officials were not the only targets of leftist violence: violence also targeted politicians, landlords, and people with well-known conservative political ideas (Casanova 2005: 95). At a lower scale, violence also affected deserters within the Republican Army and members of leftist parties. Intra-leftist violence was, however, not as significant as some historical

---

positively correlated with the degree of presence and proximity of an armed group (Gates 2002; Arjona and Kalyvas 2008).

[46] Interestingly, Noam Chomsky explains that a prominent Italian anarchist, Berneri, proposed that the leftists should not fight a conventional war because they would not win such a war: he argued that they should instead wage a guerrilla war (Meléndez Badillo 2009).

[47] Women were thus not the most victimized among the clergy. This pattern in religious violence makes the Spanish Civil War very different from other civil wars such as the Russian Civil War, where 3,500 (49.2 percent) nuns were killed out of a total of 7,100 clergy members.

accounts lead us to believe – in Catalonia, for example, it only represented around 2.8 percent of the leftist violence (Solé i Sabaté and Villarroya 1989).[48]

In the early phases of the conflict, leftist direct violence was perpetrated without any kind of judicial procedure.[49] Before being executed, prisoners would sometimes be interrogated in detention centers known as *checas*, which had been set up by leftist militants. Later on, when order and discipline were imposed behind the frontlines, violence was perpetrated through judicial channels (e.g., Popular Courts) (Casanova 2005: 95–96). The same process of legalizing violence took place in the Nationalist zone (Rodrigo 2008: 97–98). Yet, in both areas, what masqueraded as legal process was in fact a way of concealing a great degree of arbitrariness.

A common form of violence during the early stages of the war consisted of mass killings in prisons (the so-called *sacas*). One of the most infamous *sacas* took place in Paracuellos del Jarama and Torrejón de Ardoz (at the outskirts of Madrid) in November 1936, in which leftist armed forces executed 2,700 prisoners as the Nationalist army approached Madrid and started a siege that would last until the end of the war (Casanova 2010: 198). The following excerpt from *La Causa General* (in the Spanish National Archive) provides an example of a *saca*:[50]

On the night of October 20, 1936, a group of nearly three hundred militiamen, together with security guards of Ocaña's prison, barged into the director's office and demanded that the detainees be handed over, which he refused. They entered the holding cell area and removed 152 people who were unjustly detained and bound together in twos, and they put them in four lines.... they then executed them in Ocaña's cemetery. (Source: Causa General de Toledo-Cáceres, 10491, Pieza 3).

The Left also perpetrated indirect violence, consisting mostly of airstrikes, in rebel-controlled territories. Comparatively speaking, however, the leftists perpetrated much less indirect violence against non-combatants than the Nationalists (Abellà 1973; Solé i Sabaté and Villarroya 2003). This was partly due to the limited air force capacity of the Republican army as compared to the fascist rebels, but it was also a consequence of the ideological makeup

---

[48] Indeed, intra-leftist violence has become well-known partly as a consequence of Orwell's book "Homage to Catalonia" (1938), and Ken Loach's film, "Land and Freedom," which was inspired by it. Yet, intra-leftist violence was in fact quite marginal. The lack of cooperation within the Left had relevant political consequences, but did not have much impact on the dynamics and levels of violence.

[49] Clara Campoamor argues that the Republican government was very often against these executions, but that they did not do much to prevent them (105).

[50] *La Causa General* comes from a major judicial investigation undertaken by the Francoists after the war, which aimed at establishing responsibilities for war crimes. As explained in the Appendix, this investigation was highly biased against the Republicans, whose crimes were largely exaggerated. By contrast, the crimes committed by Nationalists were significantly underestimated. The archives of this judicial process are located in the Spanish National Archive.

of the Republican government, which was fundamentally different from that of the Rebels and their allies. The Republicans were more restrained in the perpetration of indirect violence against civilians.

In addition to lethal violence, leftist armed forces also victimized civilians in other ways. For example, some people were dispossessed of their properties (e.g., lands, industries, real estate) through collectivization campaigns that were widespread throughout the Republican rearguard.[51] Leftist soldiers and militiamen also perpetrated rapes and mutilations, mostly against members of the clergy (Gil 2006: 45), although these were not widespread practices. There was looting of Church property (including the destruction and burning of churches and altars) in hundreds of villages under Republican control.[52]

## Rightist Violence

Rightist violence against civilians, also called "blue" terror (Salomón and Ledesma 2006) or "white" terror, also took the form of both indirect and direct violence. In places controlled by the Right, people were killed face-to-face; in places not controlled by the Right, violence was indirect (i.e., through airstrikes and shellings). As in the case of leftist violence, rightist repression was both regular and irregular in character. The army and the militarized public order bodies directed the repression, which was very often carried out by *Falangists*, *Carlist* militiamen, or mercenaries working for big landlords (Calzado 17–18). Irregular assassinations (i.e., *paseos*) were relatively common, especially during the early stages of control of a territory (Linz 1996; Solé i Sabaté and Villarroya 1987).

Rightist repression went beyond executions, including social marginalization, arrests (e.g., concentration camps, prisons), deportations, and labor subordination (García Piñeiro 2002: 137–147). Indeed, during the war and the postwar periods, those who were considered opposed to the interests of the Nationalists were either sacked from their jobs, or relegated to subordinate positions (García Piñeiro 2002). Economic sanctions were also imposed on suspected leftists (Casanova and Cenarro 2014). Many women were raped and publicly humiliated (e.g., by head-shaving) by irregular and regular Francoist forces (Salomón and Ledesma 2006). A common form of victimization was torture, as were forced exile and mass displacement (Fillol 1971; Artís Gener 1976; Pujol 2003). Finally, the Francoists carried out widespread

---

[51] According to Brenan, the highest incidence of collectivization occurred in locations dominated by the anarchists: "In those places where the committees were Anarchist, there was a definite policy of collectivization which was intended to prepare the way for a thorough-going social revolution" (2014/1943: 318). Although the Catholic Church was one of the main victims of these processes, landlords and business owners were also affected.

[52] Anticlerical violence took place in many areas dominated by socialists, communists and republicans, and thus not only where anarchists ruled (Casanova 2010: 210).

cultural repression, both against national minorities (i.e., Basque, Galician, and Catalan) and against people with a liberal or leftist ideology.

Since the Nationalists were the victors, rightist violence took place in the postwar period too, up until around 1945. Following the example of respected historians (Gabarda 1982; Solé i Sabaté 2000; Casanova et al. 2001; Juliá 2004; Anderson and del Arco Blanco 2015), I argue that this early postwar violence can be conceptualized as wartime violence.[53] Indeed, in *La Causa General*, one can find hundreds of files of trials on individuals who were convicted for their behavior or ideology during the civil war and who were sentenced as late as 1945, if not later (e.g., Causa General, Caja 1049/2 Toledo; Gabarda 1993; Díaz-Balart and Friend 1997; Solé i Sabaté 2000). Postwar violence included assassinations not only of civilians but also of many former combatants, namely, members of the Republican army who were punished for their wartime service. Many nonlethal forms of violence also continued in use in the postwar period. The so-called Law of Political Responsibilities served a legal mechanism for all of the repressive processes in the postwar period. Sanctions imposed on suspected leftists included the inability to carry out professional activities, restrictions on the right to relocate, and economic sanctions.

During the war, the Right perpetrated indirect violence mainly through artillery shelling, and bombardments from the air and from the sea. Again, indirect attacks by rightist armed forces in the Republican rearguard territory were much more common than the other way around. The intervention of the German Condor Legion and Italian military forces contributed to the use of aerial attacks (Balfour and Preston 1999) against cities in the rearguard.[54] Many have argued that bombings were used as a coercive tactic, to force surrender of the Republic. Yet, as Pape interestingly points out, the use of aerial force as a form of coercion in the Spanish Civil War failed in its objectives because the Rebels did not manage to coerce the Loyalists into surrender before they were completely defeated (Pape 1996: 335). Chapter 5 analyzes the determinants of indirect violence, with an empirical exploration of airstrikes in Catalonia during the Spanish Civil War.

## Micro-Dynamics of Violence

Several historians have argued that violence did not follow the same patterns on each side of the civil war. However, and despite the fundamental differences between the respective ideologies and organizational structures of the two blocs fighting in the Spanish Civil War, a close look helps us identify some

---

[53] Francoist violent repression continued until the end of the dictatorship in 1977, but after 1945 this violence is no longer considered directly related to the civil war.

[54] The Condor Legion included volunteers from the German Air Force (Luftwaffe) and from the German Army (Wehrmacht Heer).

common patterns in the micro-dynamics of direct violence that took place in each of the sides. On both sides, violence was perpetrated by both regular and irregular forces. There were trials against defectors, but a common form of direct violence against civilians were the so-called *paseos*, in which people were detained and executed without trial. These were very frequent at the early stages of the civil war. The following excerpt illustrates the common *modus operandi* of these "rides" on the Nationalist side:

"In Plasencia, Severiano Caldera explains, unprecedented events occurred: at night, the militarized and fanatical *Falangists* would enter homes by force and violently remove men who would be put in lorries and later murdered in the outskirts of the village. Their corpses would be scattered in ditches and neighboring paths. They were not buried, they say, in order to teach everyone a lesson. Others were thrown into the river with their hands and feet tied" (Chaves 1995: 105).

On the Republican side, anarchist and communist militiamen operated in a similar way (Bosch 1983; Casanova 1985; Solé i Sabaté and Villarroya 1989; Cenarro 2002a; Ledesma 2003; Dueñas 2007). For example, the Republican politician Clara Campoamor (elected representative of the liberal party "Partido Radical") explains in her memoirs how these *paseos* occurred in Madrid when the capital city was under Republican control:

"Patrols of militiamen started to practice detentions in households, on the street, in any place where they thought they would find enemies. Militiamen, operating outside the law, would emerge as 'popular judges' and carry out executions following arrests. Very soon a tragic expression became popular in the rearguard: they would give someone 'a ride'." (Campoamor 2005: 99)

Some testimonies and historical accounts of executions have drawn parallels between the two sides. Brenan, for example (2014/1943: 322), writes the following about executions carried out by the Nationalists: "The method of execution was similar to that employed on the Republican side: the victims were taken from their houses in lorries driven by young *Falangists* and *Carlists* and shot before dawn outside the town." Bueso, for his part, writes what follows about the violence that took place in Republican areas: "A revolutionary committee had emerged in every district, which detained those who looked suspicious, many of whom disappeared after leaving in a car, escorted by armed militiamen, for a 'ride' (*paseo*). Later on, he learned from reliable sources that the *paseo* system had also been employed in the fascist zone, exactly like in the red zone, and using the same name" (Bueso 1978: 191).

On both sides we can identify three main actors intervening in the perpetration of irregular violence:

1. *Militiamen* and *Soldiers*: Militiamen, together with regular soldiers, were the main perpetrators of direct violence against civilians; they were what Tilly (2003) has called "specialists of violence." As explained above, during the Second Republic, extremist parties were associated with paramilitary

organizations such as the *Requetés* and the *Falange* (i.e., on the Right),[55] or groups of militant workers and antifascist militias (i.e., on the Left). They were, in effect, the germinal form of the armed militias that operated during the war, either in fight on the battlefield or patrolling in the rearguard territories. As Beevor put it, "In the rear areas the Falange had rapidly developed into the nationalists paramilitary force, assuming the task of 'cleaning up'" (Beevor 2006: 94).[56] In some cases, these militias were formed by citizens and volunteers (Casanova 2010: 192) and behaved quite like self-defense groups; in the Republican areas, they were often made up of peasants and low-skilled workers (Solé i Sabaté and Villarroya 1989: 78).[57]

2. *Local Committees*: called *Comités Antifascistas* (i.e., on the Left),[58] or *Comisiones Gestoras* (i.e., on the Right). During the civil war, these committees were the real centers of political decision-making (Pozo 2002: 19); they did not have any constitutional legitimacy, and yet they replaced the legally constituted local councils from the prewar period in a process initiated everywhere and simultaneously as soon as the war began. The local committees developed from the official local councils and they emerged as the local rulers. Weapons bans were usually enacted after committees were formed, and all residents were forced to turn in their weapons.[59] In December 1936, the Republican government approved a decree according to which new city councils were to be formed and the local committees were to be disbanded; however, this did not bring about any major changes to the *de facto* nature of local rule.

In areas under Republican control, the committees were often revolutionary institutions, which hoped to articulate a new society, often through campaigns to collectivize private property. They were made up of local left-wing politicians and members of trade unions. In some regions, these local committees were united under larger organizations (e.g., the "Antifascist Militias Central Committee" in Catalonia), which exhibited varying degrees of internal

---

[55] One example is the fascist militia "Black Squad," which was behind the murder of the legendary writer Federico García Lorca in Granada (Casanova 2013: 36–37).

[56] Similar paramilitary organizations emerged in Ireland in the 1912–1922 period, and they played a crucial role in the violence that occurred during the revolution and civil war (Hart 2003: 89–90). Hart argues that such militias proliferated in interwar Europe, notoriously in Germany and Italy, and that their emergence was symptomatic of political polarization and the decline of governmental legitimacy in the eyes of a majority of the population. "And in each case, the end result was the breakdown of democracy and the imposition of a new state" (Hart 2003: 90).

[57] Ruiz (2007: 103) argues that over 200 rearguard militia groups of varied sizes carried out arrests in Madrid in the summer of 1936.

[58] Other names were *Comités Revolucionarios* (Revolutionary Committees) or *Comités Antifascistas Revolucionarios* (Antifascist Revolutionary Committees). The inclusion of the word "revolutionary" in the name of the local committee usually implied that it was made up largely of anarchists or communists, as opposed to moderate leftist political parties.

[59] "The local committees regulated local political life, taking the role of the old city councils. They had sections such as Taxes, Health, Social Assistance, Defense, and so on" (Pozo 2002: 440).

cohesion and discipline.[60] In other regions, the local committees were not connected to one another and there were no overarching provincial organizations
(e.g., in Extremadura, as explained by Vila Izquierdo 1984). In Rebel areas, the
committees had a very different nature and origin: they were not created out
of a willingness to implement a revolution in a decentralized manner. Rather,
committees were a mere continuation of previous local councils, from which
leftists where excluded. The committees were composed of local right-wing
political leaders, as well as other important right-wing figures, such as the
most important landowner, the local Civil Guard commander, a *Falangist* and,
quite often, the priest (Beevor 2006).

The local committees were usually composed of unarmed civilians, but they
possessed a high degree of agency when it came to perpetrating violence. Their
interactions with the armed militias had a crucial impact on the violence that
took place on the ground. During the civil war, the committees held meetings
in order to compile lists of suspects – potential targets of the militias – but
they also arrested people, helped the militias find them, and sometimes participated in looting (e.g., the burning of churches on the Republican side). For
example, Anthony Beevor explains that "When Major Castejón's 'Column of
Death' reached Zafra on the road to Badajoz, he ordered the local authorities
to provide him with a list of 60 people to be shot" (Beevor 2006: 91). When
the militias came into the villages, the committees could be more or less cooperative with them in perpetrating violence: "In those places where the local
authorities such as the mayor, the local chiefs of the Falange, etc. opposed
them, there were no assassinations and, when they did take place, they were
minimal. The same cannot be said of places where the opposition to killings did
not exist, where the repressors acted with total leeway" (Chaves 1995: 97). It is
important to note that several historical accounts indicate that the behavior of
the local committees was determined mostly by local factors; in other words,
the supra-local organizations (i.e., governmental or military authorities) did
not play any significant role in determining the behavior of the local committees vis-à-vis the armed groups. This is consistent with the fact that there was
a lot of local variation in the behavior of local committees and consequent
violence against civilians.

On some occasions, individuals in the local committees were armed
(Gabarda 1996; Azpíroz 2007: 384) and they carried out violence themselves.
This was more often the case on the Francoist side than on the Republican side. On the Republican side, this was the case of committees that were
dominated by the CNT-FAI (thus, the anarchists). The *modus operandi* for
anarchist armed committees was that they would not carry out killings in their
own localities but they would do so in neighboring ones (Maymí Rich 2001;

---

[60] In Catalonia, the committees integrated different leftist factions, mirroring the Antifascist Militias Central Committee, which had been governing Catalonia since July 21, 1936 (Beevor 2006:
106–107).

Gutiérrez Casalá 2006); armed committees from neighboring localities would delegate tasks to one another so that they could deny responsibility for violence in their hometowns (Delgado 1993).[61] On the Nationalist side, sometimes the leaders of the local committees were authorized to use the police garrisons, as well as their weapons and munitions, not only for personal defense but also "to preserve order in the municipalities and to aid in the task of keeping the localities under insurgent control" (Chaves 1995: 35). In these cases, the line between local committees and armed militias was blurred. Yet, in the vast majority of cases, the committees were not armed, and civilians were killed by the specialists in violence, the gunmen who patrolled the territory.

3. *Civilians*: civilians were victims, but sometimes they were also key collaborators in the perpetration of violence. Indeed,local civilians could help armed groups by denouncing their neighbors, turning people in, and even arresting them.[62] Conversely, they were also able to prevent victimization by helping people escape, by hiding them, by manipulating information, and so on. Casanova explains that local civilians had an important role in the identification of the potential victims: "The neighbors, led by the Committee, used to accompany the militiamen through the streets of the village, leading them to the houses of potential targets and identifying them in order to avoid mistakes"(Casanova 2007: 43). Cenarro (2002b) argues that civilian collaboration was necessary for the perpetration of violence even when it was institutionalized through Francoist channels, for example, during the postwar (see below). In less organized instances, such as during the massacre of Badajoz, civilians (and quite particularly, local affiliates of the Falange) were also in charge of identifying the individuals who were to be killed (Vila Izquierdo 1984: 55).

Across military control zones (i.e., Republican, Nationalist), the interactions between these three actors (*militias*, *committees*, and *civilians*) had an impact on levels of violence through the following stylized process: militiamen (or soldiers) who patrolled a territory in a non-centralized way perpetrated violence against suspected enemies. When militias entered a given municipality, they would make contact with the local committee in order to get information on supporters of the enemy in the locality. Sometimes the local committee had already imprisoned these individuals. If not, members of the committee would provide the militias with a list of suspects or show the militiamen where these individuals lived. Once these individuals were arrested,

---

[61] This phenomenon bears a remarkable resemblance to the way anticlerical violence was carried out in the nineteenth century: peasants would burn the church of a neighboring village, but not their own (Beevor 2006: 86).

[62] Ruiz explains that the militias patrolling Madrid were "to a great extent reliant on ordinary *madrileños*, especially the city's concierges, for information concerning 'spies' "(Ruiz 2007: 110).

they were imprisoned and, ultimately, executed (sometimes, the execution was immediate, with a *paseo*). However, there were many occasions in which committees did not participate in identifying, imprisoning, and executing political enemies. The committees would sometimes neither provide a list of names nor help the militiamen in their search for suspects. On occasion, they would even inform potential targets in order to help them escape the militias.[63]

The interaction between civilians, local authorities, and militias/armed groups was also important in the somewhat more institutionalized acts of violence against the enemy. For example, in Catalonia and Aragon, the violence that took place during and after the Nationalist army came to occupy a given territory was much more institutionalized than earlier forms of violence on the part of leftist forces (Vila Izquierdo 1984; Solé i Sabaté 2000). When Franco's army or Nationalist militias conquered a given locality, they relied on local civilians in order to compile lists of suspects, who were subsequently imprisoned and eventually (in almost all cases) executed. Very often individuals were not killed immediately, as the Francoist apparatus followed a series of pseudo-legal procedures before carrying out executions (i.e., in Military Courts).[64] In some cases, individuals were imprisoned for months or even years before execution. In the rare cases where detainees were released, this only occurred when local authorities intervened on their behalf. Members of the local community had some agency in the process leading up to these postwar executions: for example, people could easily denounce their neighbors by saying that they were *rojos* (reds) or by claiming that they had been involved in bloody crimes during the war. Conversely, local right-wing politicians or religious authorities (that is, local leaders) could write letters demanding that detainees be pardoned, and people could help their neighbors hide or flee before they were arrested – in short, they were able to limit the perpetration of violence by the Francoists.[65]

[63] These processes are detailed in many regional and local historical accounts (see, among others, Garriga 1986; Solé i Sabaté and Pous 1988; Segura 1999; Gutiérrez Flores 2000; Crosas 2004; Campoamor 2005: 124–127; Gaitx 2006; Dueñas 2007; Casanova 2007.)

[64] On both sides, violence became somewhat legalized at some point during the war, which implies that executions followed trials or equivalent judicial procedures, even during wartime. Although it may be difficult in circumstances of war to draw a line between what is lawful and what is not (Frésard 2004: 27), it goes without saying that the judicial procedures were not objective and they involved a significant degree of arbitrariness. That was the case for rightist violence during the civil war and the postwar period, but also for the violence carried out by leftists during the war (Kaminski 2002/1937: 173). Regular or "legal" violence was more predominant in big cities than in villages, as the former adopted judicial procedures earlier than the latter (Gabarda 1996).

[65] Chaves provides a detailed account of how the intercession of local civilians had an impact on the number of executions or death penalties in Cáceres (1995: 229–230). Cenarro, for her part, explains that, in Aragon, different practices such as accusations and submitting reports or endorsement letters, were crucial for the implementation of Francoist terror (Cenarro 2002b: 71).

3.5  THE STUDY OF VIOLENCE DURING THE SPANISH CIVIL
      WAR: DATA SOURCES AND CAVEATS

There are some advantages in taking the Spanish Civil war as a case study, but it also raises some difficulties. On the one hand, because it is a well-documented civil war that took place many decades ago, the casualty figures are potentially more reliable than those from more recent civil wars, in which political and/or ideological factors are more likely to bias the data (e.g., Ball et al. 2002). On the other hand, the politics of the Francoist regime (1939–1977) made it very difficult to accurately compile victimization figures of the war, and these have only recently become available for some regions in the recent past. For ideological and propagandistic reasons, the regime ignored or covered up the violence perpetrated by the Nationalists while it investigated and made public the violent acts committed by leftists. During the civil war, many deaths on the Nationalist side, especially those killed in irregular raids, were not recorded in the civil registries (Reig Tapia 1984); and even in the cases where they were registered, the cause of death was not indicated or was misrepresented (Chaves 1995: 104). All this, together with the closure of the military archives under Franco, has made the collection of data on these killings extremely challenging.

The transition to democracy in the late 1970s led to more intellectual freedom and openness, allowing historians to engage in debates about sources and bias in the records – e.g., those provided by authors such as Salas Larrazábal (1977) or Martín Rubio (1987) – and it became increasingly more feasible to find more reliable data (Juliá 2004: 410). For example, while Salas (1977) concluded that there were 72,344 deaths in the Republican zone and 57,662 in the Francoist zone, later studies demonstrated that the Nationalist zone's figures had been significantly underestimated while the Republican zone's figures had been overestimated. Despite the gradual release of documents in the 1980s opening new opportunities for research (Ruiz 2009: 457), final figures on Francoist violence are still not available. That is especially the case for those territories under Nationalist control from the very beginning of the civil war or for areas conquered shortly after the coup. Irregular killings or *paseos* by the Nationalists were more widespread in these areas than they were in areas such as Catalonia that were occupied some months later (Linz 1996).

The passing of the Historical Memory Law in December 2007 was supposed to lead to the exhumation of bodies from mass graves, and to an increased disclosure of information by victims and/or perpetrators (although most civil war survivors have passed away). However, the conservative government led by the Partido Popular since 2011 has impeded the full implementation of this law. Thus there has not been much progress since 2007 in producing more reliable figures for the total number of deaths. If we take into account Juliá's provisional figures (Juliá 2004: 411–413), the proportion of civilian deaths by bloc is 2.14 victims of Nationalist violence for each victim of Republican violence; with Preston's (2011) figures, the proportion is almost 3 to 1. Thus, the accounts of historians such as Salas or Martín Rubio (who had attributed more violence to the Republican side than to the Francoist side) were clearly biased. In addition to this, we have to take into account the fact that more victims will be added to the Nationalist side once the exhumations of mass graves take place.

Given current data availability issues, a municipal (versus regional or national) level of analysis is the most appropriate for the study of the Spanish case. At the local level, we can rely on very fine-grained sources – at least, for a few regions in particular such as Catalonia (Solé i Sabaté and Villarroya 1986, 1989; Solé i Sabaté 2000) and Aragon (Casanova 2001; Ledesma 2009b).[66] This makes our results more reliable than if we were to undertake a regional or provincial analysis. In this book, I have focused my empirical analyses on regions for which the data is highly reliable and robust – that is, where it is not expected that the numbers will change dramatically after exhumations at mass graves): Catalonia and Aragon (for both leftist and rightist violence), and Malaga (for leftist violence). Hopefully, it will be possible in the near future to perform fine-grained analyses for the whole territory of Spain.

## 3.6   REGIONAL PATTERNS OF VIOLENCE

The provinces analyzed in this book belong to different geographical areas, and they exhibit divergent patterns of victimization by the Left and the Right. Despite the fact that I have been constrained by the lack of availability of fine-grained, reliable local data, I have attempted to select cases so as to maximize inferential leverage (King et al. 1994). By analyzing seven provinces in the northeast (Zaragoza, Huesca, Teruel, Girona, Lleida, Tarragona, Barcelona) – the provinces constituting the regions of Catalonia and Aragon – and one in the south (Malaga), which had different prewar political alignments, wartime patterns of control, distances to frontlines, and types of wartime violence, I should be able to make generalizations regarding the remaining Spanish territory as well as other civil wars. In this subsection, I contextualize these territories and I describe the patterns of violence against civilians that took place in each of them.

### Catalonia

The region of Catalonia is located in the northeastern part of the Iberian Peninsula. It is bordered by the Mediterranean Sea to the east, France and Andorra to the north, and the Spanish region of Aragon to the west. The

---

[66] The municipality is the lowest administrative level in Spain, and it has a relatively small size. In 1936, Catalonia was composed of 1,062 municipalities, extending over a territory of approximately 32,100 km². The average population of a Catalonian municipality was 1,647 inhabitants. In Aragon, 940 localities covered a territory of approximately 47,179 km²; the population of a locality was on average 1,119 inhabitants.

Pyrenees constitute a natural geographical boundary between Catalonia and France. When the Nationalist army advanced in 1938, it conquered Lleida (in the midwestern part of the region) and some counties in the west of the region, which became a combat zone for a while. One of the most affected areas was the county Terra Alta (in the southwestern part of the region), which was witness to the longest and largest battle of the war (the Battle of the Ebro, from July to November of 1938). Other counties in the Catalan Midwest (Pallars Jussà, Segrià, Noguera, Alta Ribagorça) were affected by the so-called Battle of the Segre (from April to December of 1938). Catalonia remained under Republican control for most of the war, and it was conquered by the Nationalist army in an offensive that started after the breach of the Ebro's frontline (Solé i Sabaté and Villarroya 1987; Reverte 2003). The use of aerial attacks in combination with well-organized land attacks made it a brutal occupation, leading to the surrender of this region on February 10, 1939.

Direct violence against civilians took place in Catalonia in two stages: first (from July 1936 to 1938/39), the leftist militias and the Republican army perpetrated violence against civilians living in the territories under their control; later (during and after its occupation), the Nationalist army and right-wing militias followed suit. In other words, direct violence in Catalonia can be thought of as a two-stage process: a period $t_1$, in which the Left killed civilians, and a period $t_2$, in which the Right did so. The total number of victims of leftist (direct) violence in Catalonia is 8,352 (Solé i Sabaté and Villarroya 1986: 450); the total number of victims of rightist (direct) violence in Catalonia is 3,901 (Solé i Sabaté and Villarroya 1983; Solé i Sabaté 2000).[67] Most leftist violence was "irregular," especially in the first months of the war: later on, violence was channeled through institutional means.[68]

Leftist violence in Catalonia reached its peak just after the military coup in July 1936. After November 1936, it decreased quite abruptly, only slightly increasing again in 1938 and in the first two months of 1939, right before the occupation of the region by the Francoist army. With regards to rightist violence in this region, it peaked in the months preceding or immediately following the end of the war on April 1, 1939 (Solé i Sabaté and Villarroya 1986), but killings continued for several years (Figure 3.2). These patterns are consistent with the predictions regarding the timing of violence outlined in Chapter 2: violence reaches a peak at the beginning of the conflict and whenever a group conquers a new piece of territory, as this is the period when the groups have the greatest incentives to prosecute their political enemies in order to secure

[67] This last figure includes victims of "legal" violence, and victims of the irregular violence that was perpetrated during the occupation of the territory, and amounting to approximately 513 people (Solé i Sabaté and Villarroya 1983).

[68] There was one type of violence that was "regular" throughout the whole period: the violence directed at members of the military who backed the coup or who supported the rebels. These individuals were brought to military court, where they were condemned to death.

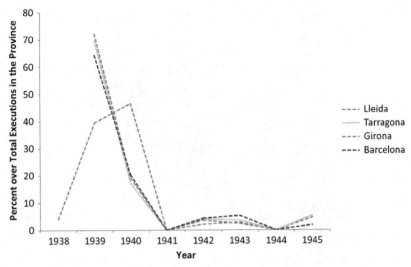

FIGURE 3.2 Executed by the Right in Catalonia, by Province

their territory. Armed groups' incentives to kill decrease as strong supporters of the rival are eliminated.

Figures 3.3 and 3.4 show the geographical distribution of leftist and right-ist executions across the municipalities of Catalonia, respectively.[69] They illustrate variation in violence at the local level (executions per thousand inhabitants) that, I claim, cannot be sufficiently explained by existing theories of wartime civilian victimization. Violence is not concentrated uniquely in zones that are close to the Aragon's frontline (i.e., in the western part), the seashore, urban centers, mountainous areas, zones near the French border.

Figure 3.5 depicts the distribution of bombings by Francoist, Italian, and German air and naval forces in Catalonia over the course of the entire civil war. These strikes were particularly concentrated in the years 1937, 1938, and 1939, until the Nationalists occupied the entire region. It can be observed that the places with the highest number of strikes were predominantly urban and costal, locations close to the French border, or locations near the Ebro frontline (to the West), where battalions or additional troops were posted during the Battle of the Ebro. Coastal positions were attacked mainly for strategic reasons (e.g., in order to impede communications, sea transportation, and the like) (Solé i Sabaté and Villarroya 1986; 2003). They were also easily targeted by naval ships or from the Balearic Islands: for example, in

[69] These maps, as well as those further below, are built from the datasets I have built from a variety of sources. More details on the datasets and the data sources are provided in the Appendix of Chapter 4. The color version of the maps are available from: www.laiabalcells.com

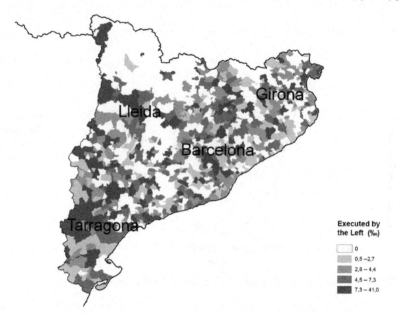

FIGURE 3.3 Executed by the Left in Catalonia

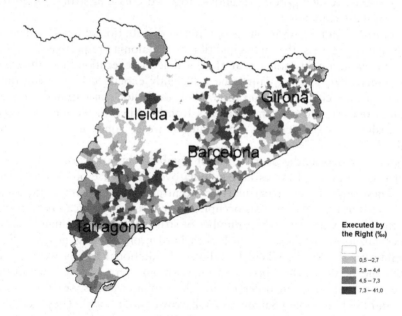

FIGURE 3.4 Executed by the Right in Catalonia

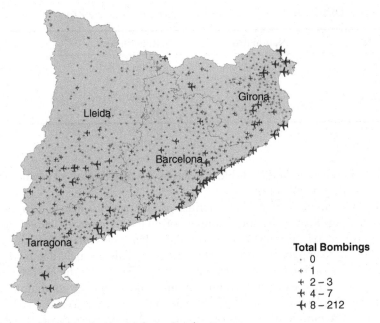

FIGURE 3.5 Bombings by the Right in Catalonia

mid-May 1938, the Italian garrisons based in Mallorca bombed Barcelona, causing 980 fatalities (Payne 2010: 481). For a while, naval strikes attempted at the conquest of Catalonia. People living in urban centers such as Barcelona and Tarragona were the most victimized (due to the high population density in these municipalities the aerial attacks had extremely lethal consequences). Nonetheless, there were also several strikes on non-coastal localities with no major military outposts or energy industries. One clear example is the bombing on the town center of Granollers (including the farmers' market) on May 31, 1938, killing 224 civilians, wounding at least 165, and destroying 80 buildings.

**Aragon**

Aragon was divided by the so-called Ebro frontline, which remained relatively stable for almost two years. A total of 366 municipalities in Aragon (38.6 percent of them) were under Francoist control during the entire war – I will label them below as Nationalist. The remaining 61.4 percent of the municipalities in the region (a total of 582) came under leftist control at some point during the war – I will label them below as Republican despite the fact that some of them were located in the "battlefield zone" (i.e., they changed hands several

TABLE 3.2 *Distribution of Localities of Aragon, in Total by Zone*

| Province | Nationalist | Republican | Total |
|---|---|---|---|
| Huesca | 77(21%) | 282(48%) | 359(38%) |
| Teruel | 34(9%) | 248(43%) | 282(30%) |
| Zaragoza | 255(70%) | 52(9%) | 307(32%) |
| Total | 366(100%) | 582(100%) | 948 (100%) |

times during the conflict).[70] Table 3.2 shows the distribution of municipalities of Aragon by control zones.[71]

The total number of civilian victims of rightist violence in Aragon was approximately 8,500; the total number of civilian victims of leftist violence was approximately 4,000 (Cenarro 2006). Violence was relatively more severe in this region compared to other areas of Spain. This is partly due to the battlefield nature of much of its territory and its proximity to the Ebro frontline, which generated greater uncertainty about control among combatants, and thereby greater incentives to eliminate enemies (Ledesma 2006c: 13).[72] As in Catalonia, the bloodiest months of violence in Aragon were those of the summer and fall of 1936 (Salomón and Ledesma 2006: 13). The patterns in Aragon are also consistent with the predictions on the timing of violence outlined in Chapter 2: violence spiked at the beginning of the conflict and whenever a group conquered a new piece of territory.

Violence in Nationalist Aragon (i.e., perpetrated by the army and rightist militias) was targeted mostly at members of leftist political parties and trade unions: "Governors, deputies, mayors, and council members committed to the Republican cause were the first to be put on the long list of those to be arrested and executed" (Cifuentes and Maluenda 2006: 41). Violence was selective, but there were also many instances of massacres or group executions, e.g., in the cemetery of Zaragoza (Heredia 2006), Teruel, or Mediana de Aragón (Ledesma 2006c: 37). Figure 3.6 depicts the distribution of rightist

---

[70] The "battlefield nature" of this region is demonstrated by the figures provided by Solano (2004) for the province of Teruel: out of the total number of victims of leftist violence in this province, 56 percent were victims of intentional violence against civilians, while 44 percent were victims of war actions. Also, the proportion of combatants among victims of direct violence is much higher than in other rearguard zones such as Catalonia.

[71] I thank historian José Luis Ledesma for his help in constructing this table. What I will hereafter refer to as "the Republican zone of Aragon" encompasses the following *partidos judiciales* (counties): Albarracin, Alcañiz, Aliaga, Barbastro, Belchite, Benabarre, Boltaña, Cariñena, Caspe, Castellote, Fraga, Hijar, Huesca, Montalbán, Mora de Rubielos, Pina, Sariñena, Tamarite, Teruel, Valderrobles.

[72] Similar processes took place in localities close to war frontlines in other parts of the country. For example, in Don Benito and Villanueva de la Serena, in Extremadura (Gutiérrez Casalá 2006: 93–94; 290–300).

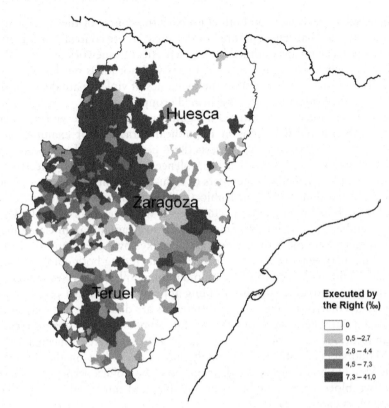

FIGURE 3.6 Executed by the Right in Aragon (1936–1939)

violence – in both the war and the early postwar period – in all the region of Aragon. We can observe that the area that was most heavily victimized by the Nationalists was the province of Zaragoza; the province of Huesca was the least victimized.

Leftist violence in Republican Aragon was very much connected to the routes taken by the brigades or armed militias on their way to the Ebro front-line, often from Valencia or Catalonia. Some of these militias had names such as *La banda negra* (The Black Squad), *Hijos de la noche* (Sons of the Night), or *Brigada de la muerte* (Death Squad). Ledesma explains that the lion's share of the villages and towns in Aragon recorded the largest number of repressive episodes as columns were passing through (Ledesma 2006b: 93). The dynamics of violence in the "battlefield" areas of Aragon differed from those in other areas behind the Republican frontlines (e.g., Catalonia, Valencia, or Murcia) or places that were always under the control of the Nationalist army (e.g., Nationalist Aragon). Some of the localities in this zone were conquered and reconquered several times by both sides over the course of the war.[73] Again, this is due to the "battlefield nature" of this area, where control was imperfect. Because the mechanisms outlined in my theoretical framework are not fully at work in battlefield zones, my empirical tests will not focus on this territory; I will analyze it mainly to show that the dynamics of violence are different from those in areas of full control by one armed group.[74]

Anticlerical violence constituted a significant share of the violence perpetrated by the anarchist militias in Republican Aragon. For example, in the religious town of Barbastro, 123 priests (87.8 percent of its clergy) were assassinated (Casanova 2004). But, direct violence by the Left also affected non-religious people, particularly members of right-wing political parties and organizations. According to Martín Rubio (1987), in the town of Teruel, almost half of those killed by the Left (42.86 percent) were members of the CEDA.

The number of bombings was much higher in Aragon than in Catalonia. In Aragon, there were more than 2,000 aerial strikes over the course of the conflict, killing between 1,000 and 1,500 people, including both combatants and civilians (Maldonado 2006b). In Catalonia, the number of strikes was around 700, but they were much deadlier (killing approximately 4,752 people) (Solé i Sabaté and Villarroya 1986). These differences are due to the fact that Aragon remained a battlefield for a long time: while some bombings were directed at civilian locations (e.g., Alcañiz), many of these strikes were connected to combat (Maldonado 2006b). Unfortunately, fine-grained data on the number of people killed in bombings or the distribution of bombings perpetrated by each of the two blocs across Aragon is unavailable, and thus I will not be able to analyze them empirically.[75]

## Malaga

The reasons for including the province of Malaga (in Andalusia) in this book are manifold. First, this region is located in the south of Spain. Historically the

---

[73] Ledesma explains the case of the town of Belchite: "Members of the police, Falangists, and soldiers executed between 100 and 200 people in Teruel and Belchite. Afterwards, the Republicans entered in Belchite in September 1937 and in Teruel in January 1938 and killed 60 and 153 people, respectively. And when the Francoist army reconquered the localities in February and March [1938] they executed dozens of people" (Ledesma 2006c: 27–28).

[74] Furthermore, from a methodological point of view, this is a difficult area to study because of the various military movements and irregularities in patterns of control. Some remarkable in-depth qualitative analysis of dynamics of violence in this territory have been done by Ledesma (2003), Casanova (2004), Casanova (2007), and Azpíroz (2007).

[75] Fine-grained data on bombings (e.g., the specific localities affected and the number of casualties) remains inadequate for most of Spanish territories. The pioneering work of Solé i Sabaté and Villarroya (1986) in Catalonia has yet to be replicated in other regions. The data on bombings I have obtained from some primary sources in the Spanish National Library (e.g., propaganda booklets counting the number of bombings in the Republican cities; Anonymous 1938, 1939) is too politicized and biased.

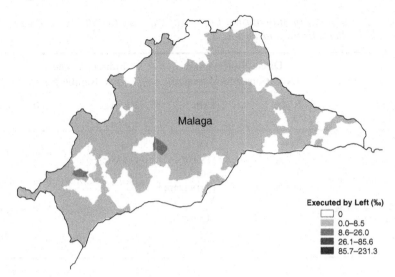

Malaga

Executed by Left (‰)
- 0
- 0.0–8.5
- 8.6–26.0
- 26.1–85.6
- 85.7–231.3

FIGURE 3.7 Executed by the Left in Malaga

geographical, economic, social, and demographic characteristics of the south have been different from those in the northeast, and these differences make this province especially useful for testing the external validity of the argument. For example, in Malaga, the agrarian conflict was intense – the *latifundios* were the predominant form of land ownership (Linz 1996) – and social and economic inequality was stark. The workers' movement throughout the 1930s was very influential, as they organized as many as 93 strikes (Nadal 1981; 1984).[76] Second, during the civil war Malaga remained under Loyalist control for a much shorter period of time than the northeastern provinces as it was conquered by Nationalist forces in February 1937. Third, Republican governmental control over Malaga was considered very precarious and conducive to wanton violence on the part of leftist militias. Indeed, the early stages of the civil war in Malaga have been described as particularly chaotic, with a lack of organization such that the defeat at the hands of Nationalist forces became inevitable (Seidman 2002: 78). In Malaga, the anarchist militias were an autonomous part of the Republican army and they even created "the independent Republic of Malaga" (Salas Larrazábal 1977).[77] Thus, the socioeconomic and political characteristics of this province before the war were quite different from

[76] The degree of affiliation with the CNT in this province was not particularly high; the UGT was the predominant trade union in the area (in 1931, affiliates in Malaga constituted 2.51 percent of the UGT affiliates in the whole of Spain).

[77] Recently, Prieto and Barranquero (2015) challenge this view and argue that the Republican state did not totally collapse in this province. In fact, they highlight the influence of local political elites in the perpetration of violence such as the socialist mayor of Antequera and the members of the ruling committee in Ronda.

TABLE 3.3 *Summary of Subnational Empirical Data on Lethal Violence Used in the Book, by Perpetrator and Period*

| Region or Province | Direct Violence (i.e., Executions and Massacres) | | Indirect Violence (i.e., Bombings) | |
| --- | --- | --- | --- | --- |
| | Right | Left | Right | Left |
| Catalonia | Yes (1938/9–45) | Yes (1936–39) | Yes (1936–39) | Marginal |
| Nationalist Aragon | Yes (1936–45) | Not perpetrated | *Not available* | *Not available* |
| Republican Aragon | Yes (1936–45) | Yes (1936–39) | *Not available* | *Not available* |
| Malaga | *Not available* | Yes (1936–37) | *Not available* | *Not available* |

those of Catalonia and Aragon, and the organizational characteristics were also different from the groups operating in the northeast.

According to data from Nadal (1984), a total of 2,607 individuals were killed in Malaga by leftist armed forces. The Nationalists allegedly killed thousands of people during and after the conquest of Malaga in February 1937. The total figures are still unknown: Rodrigo (2008) cites a total of 7,000 executions in this province between 1937 and 1940 (1,500 of whom were killed at the time of the conquest). However, some contemporary sources suggest that the total numbers were probably at least three times higher. Indirect violence took place in Malaga as early as July 27, 1936, starting with an air raid on the marketplace, which killed many civilians. Indirect violence was used in the conquest of the province, and they also targeted refugee convoys that were making their way to Almeria (see Chapter 5). In my analyses, I will only be able to use data on executions perpetrated by the Left in this province, due to a lack of fine-grained data on victimization perpetrated by right-wing armed forces.

Table 3.3 summarizes the data used in this book for each of the regions described above. Chapters 4 and 5 show the empirical results with the data from these regions, which I complement with anecdotal evidence from other regions of Spain, where the findings should be generalizable.

# 4

# Executions and Massacres During the Spanish Civil War

## 4.1 DIRECT VIOLENCE IN INITIAL PERIODS OF THE SPANISH CIVIL WAR

In this chapter, I dig into the determinants of direct violence against civilians (i.e., executions and massacres) during the Spanish Civil War, and I test the main hypotheses derived from the theoretical framework presented in Chapter 2. As in the case of any other armed conflict, we have very little first-hand information on the motives of the perpetrators of violence against civilians (Solé i Sabaté and Villarroya 1989: 70), as well as the motives of those who were key collaborators in the perpetration of this violence. There is no first-hand knowledge of their motives because they rarely made them explicit; in addition, they tried to avoid showing responsibility for these events. As Térmens writes, "Those who promoted the repression of political enemies knew that they could not make their claim public and they were worried about showing their responsibility for these events, in case the situation changed in the future" (1991: 76). Yet, guided by the theory, we can infer motives from regularities and patterns found in the data.

There is plenty of qualitative evidence from the Spanish Civil War supporting the claim that direct violence was the result of armed organizations systematically targeting their political enemies. Even if it was not always the case that those executed were affiliated with political parties or trade unions, it is certainly true that people with those affiliations were much more often targeted than other citizens. For example, in the region of Teruel, 80.23 percent of the victims of direct violence were right-wing sympathizers or members of right-wing political parties (Casanova 2007); in the city of Teruel, a vast majority of the victims of leftist violence were members of right-wing parties (Martín Rubio 1987). According to a civil war testimony, Díaz-Plaja, people were targeted in rearguard territories for political ideas "that had been expressed in the years preceding the military coup. This is something that was sometimes

87

hard to discern in big cities, but it was known to everyone in villages" (1994: 113).

The following excerpts, which are taken from the *Causa General*'s national archive, refer to assassinations that took place in the province of Toledo during the period of leftist control. They reveal that those primarily targeted (either detained or executed) were prominent right-wingers:

In the Torre de Esteban Hambrán (Toledo) in July 1936 the reds found two residents, Juan Aguadó and Casimiro Escudero, who led the Falange and the right wing militias, respectively, dragged them out of their homes and rode them around the village. They were then tied to a street light, where they were physically and verbally harassed by a mob. The same men and women who abused them then brought them to the city jail. They stayed there until the early morning of August 2nd, when they were led to the Alamin hill, along with other residents of the locality. After all sorts of abuses were committed against them, they were tied to a holm oak and assassinated (Causa General, Legajo 1049.2, Pieza 61).

The committee, formed by a distinguished group of Marxists, organized the militias into groups, which were ordered to start detaining right-wing people, who were then led to designated locations such as the municipal warehouse or prison, the chapel of Sant Antón or the local church, which had been habilitated for these purposes (Causa General, Legajo 1049.1, Pieza 61).

As the anarchist Eduardo De Guzmán makes very clear in the following passage, patrolling and cleansing the rearguard territories of political enemies was a priority for the armed groups.[1]

In Madrid, fascism has been squashed. Yet, still there is danger. There are hundreds, or even thousands, who are affiliated with the Falange Española, the TYRE, or the UME. There are people who ambush with weapons, who hold meetings and conspire to take advantage of any moment of weakness. We must remain alert and vigilant ... As much as we pay attention to the frontlines, we must not ignore Madrid. To patrol Madrid, no rifles are needed. Guns are enough. Rifles have been sent to the trenches. Hand-guns provide a useful service to the city. One thousand fellows are guarding Madrid. They chase out hidden fascists, they exterminate the *pacos*, they patrol the roads, they meticulously cleanse the city of all the enemies (De Guzmán 1938/2004: 88).

Historian Julián Casanova writes that in Aragon, "... among those assassinated [by the Nationalists], we find Republican bourgeois, political authorities, trade union leaders, workers, peasants, women and many citizens who, during the Republic, had openly shown hostility toward the defenders of a social

---

[1] In this passage, De Guzmán is making reference to the early stages of the war; at that time, killing was perceived as even more vital to securing the rear territories of potential enemies. Interestingly, this militiaman explains that rifles were not necessary in this rearguard city: "short weapons" (e.g., handguns) were sufficient. This is an example of the way warfare differs from one area to another (i.e., frontline versus rearguard) in a conventional civil war.

order that they deemed unfair" (Casanova et al. 2001: 221). Also regarding Nationalist violence in Aragon, Cenarro (2002b) argues that "among the first to die we find the members of the military loyal to the Republic, labor leaders who opposed the coup energetically, and the Republican and Socialist politicians who occupied important positions in the local institutions" (Cenarro 2002b). Casanova explains that "Mayors, provincial government presidents, city council representatives and hundreds of political officials were killed in this way, dumped in meadows, outside towns or against cemetery walls" (Casanova 2010: 183).[2]

In this book, I contend that political identities in the prewar period are critical cues in targeting and victimizing the enemy. In territories under the complete control of armed groups and with few exit options for dissident civilians, prewar political behavior is more informative than wartime behavior, as open non-collaborative behavior is not strategic. We can therefore expect this type of behavior to be uncommon.[3] In these contexts, people have strategic incentives to falsify their preferences (Kuran 1994). For example, in the most affluent districts of Barcelona during the early stages of the civil war – when Barcelona was undergoing a revolutionary process – Kaminski argues that, although there was "relative calm," this "uncovered a fear and distrust of the 'Revolution'" (Kaminski 1937/2002: 37). Regarding the bourgeois living in these areas of the city, he says, "They will shut up while everything goes well, but if things changed, they would immediately become active. It is very easy to guess that a whole social class hates [the revolution] in these districts" (Kaminski 1937/2002: 37). He also explains how women had stopped wearing hats, as this was a distinctive sign of being part of the bourgeoisie, the "enemy class" (i.e., this would endanger them) (35). Regarding the Francoist period, Ventura explains that in the town of Valls "it seemed like a miracle to see *Falangists* who days earlier had been affiliated with leftist political parties such as PSUC, ERC, UGT, CNT, FAI" (1993: 33). In his memoirs, Pablo Uriel recounts that "in the Francoist zone, everybody makes sure to come across as a supporter of the rebels" (2005: 377).

The importance of civilian agency in the perpetration of selective killings is acknowledged in numerous primary and secondary sources, some of which were reviewed in the previous chapter. For example, Ester Casanova (2007)

---

[2] There is obviously much "gray area" in the selection of targets. In Spain, many testimonies report the assassination of individuals who were not involved in politics. Also, the identification of political enemies was sometimes based on very weak evidence (if any): Chaves (1995), for example, reports the case of a couple of men who were killed simply because they were seen greeting with a Marxist sign. In his memoirs, the priest of Zaragoza Gumersindo de Estella uncovers many cases of individuals who were executed after false accusations.

[3] There are some exceptions. For example, in Solivella, in Catalonia, the right-wingers of the *Requeté* would hold clandestine meetings in order to counteract the actions of the leftist local committee (Causa General, Legajo 1446, Exp. 24); many of them were executed by leftist militiamen.

provides detailed evidence pertaining to several cases of individuals in Aragon who risked their lives in order to warn neighbors that their names were included in the "black list"; such actions sometimes helped people escape and avoid being killed. She also provides evidence on the agency of local political committees: "The committee of Azaila managed to help some neighbors return who had been resettled to Caspe; its intervention saved many lives. In some villages such as Vinaceite, the neighbors reached an agreement according to which, no matter which group entered the locality, nobody would be killed" (Casanova 2007: 41).

An oral testimony collected in Sànchez (1999) explains that the intervention on the part of the local committee prevented violence from taking place in their village:

[In September 1936] some FAI murderers from Caspe came to the village of [Móra d'Ebre] with a list of more than 40 people who were to be assassinated. Members of the local committee stopped them and offered them a big lunch while the father [the priest] left by car to Barcelona to see Rouret, who sent the Mossos d'Esquadra [the Catalan police]. The FAI left without killing anyone. (Sànchez 1999)

This same oral testimony recalls acts of resistance by the mayor of another village in the province of Tarragona (Benifallet): "Armed militiamen came from Pinell de Brai with a list that included the name of my father, but the representative of the local committee, Armengol, and other men from the Republican Center, urged those on that list to escape. And they left, so nobody was killed" (Sànchez 1999). In his published memoirs, Gil (2006) explains that – together with other theology students in Barbastro – he survived thanks to the intervention on the part of the members of the local committee, who encouraged them to leave in time. In Malaga, Gamel Woolsey (Gerald Brenan's wife) writes in her memoirs (1998) that they confronted the militia that came to their village, near Malaga city, to take one of the residents.

Several civil war survivors I interviewed (see Table A.4.12 in the appendix of the book) offered evidence along similar lines. For example, witness 38 a – who was 16 years old when the civil war began and was living in Alba de Tormes (in Castile), which had been controlled by the Nationalists since the beginning of the war – recounted that lists of suspects were given to the Falange militiamen, who were on patrol throughout the localities, and they killed the people identified from the lists. In his town, according to him, only three out eight people on a list were killed because the other five had received protection from neighbors. Witness 30 explained that the local authorities had released the priest from her village so that he could escape harm before the anarchist militias arrived. Witness 56 told me: "My father was the mayor of the town right before the civil war, and he was affiliated with the Lliga Catalana. No harm came to him during the war because he was protected by a socialist leader."

Chaves's historical research in the province of Cáceres furnishes additional examples of the key role played by civilian agency in the violence perpetrated on the Nationalist side. Sometimes the priest of the locality exercised his local influence to avoid killings, as in the case of Valverde del Fresno (Chaves 1995: 121).[4] In a similar vein, in the town of Quicena, in Huesca (Aragon), the *Falangist* militiamen wanted to take members of the local council away with them (presumably, to execute them). Yet the newly designated mayor, Ramón Pardo, opposed it. He allegedly told them: "I am as fascist as you are; nobody is going to leave Quicena" (Azpíroz 2007: 385). On other occasions, this veto was exerted by groups of organized individuals who would talk to the militiamen and convince them not to kill their targets. However, the veto of the local authorities was sometimes not sufficient to avoid killings. In Talaveruela, in the province of Cáceres, although the priest and local members of the Falange had agreed not to allow executions or *paseos*, two men were killed by militiamen from a neighboring locality. Allegedly, a sympathizer of the Falange led the militias to the spot where their victims were hiding (Junquera 2009).

In an interview with a former Nationalist combatant who fought under the command of the General Sagardía in the Catalan county of El Pallars, Armengou and Belis (2004) quote him as saying: "The population does not have very fond memories of Sagardía because they say that he was very violent. But the people who did the informing are to blame because Sagardía could not know who was on one side or the other" (156). Obviously, this combatant was trying to excuse the responsibilities of Sagardía, but there is some truth in the fact that local collaboration was necessary for soldiers such as Sagardía to identify targets and kill rather selectively. In the village of Arbúcies (Causa General, Legajo 1437, Exp. 18–22), several individuals were killed by militiamen who came from a different village, but who were informed by the local committee as to who the would-be targets were. In a report included in the *Causa General* archive, the widow of a right-wing man who was killed by three gunmen in their village (Seu d'Urgell) says: "The assassination was carried out by the militiamen, but the instigators were the leaders of the left-wing organizations in Seu d'Urgell for the militiamen did not know the village, and they were just mercenaries." She adds that her husband was killed because "he was an influential right-winger and a firm Catholic" (Causa General, Legajo 1465, Exp. 36, page 250).

In the Republican rearguard, there were numerous cases of people hiding priests, nuns and other clergy members. Witness 26 told me that not only was the priest of the town hidden in her family's house during the whole period of leftist control, but that he officiated clandestine masses. Gutiérrez Flores writes that in the rightist county of Campoo, in the province of Santander, people "protected the clergy ... In some localities they hid them, they helped

---

4 Though, on other occasions, the priest would be the main denouncer of suspected leftists, as in the case of Badajoz (Vila Izquierdo 1984).

them to flee or they refused to turn them [over to the armed group]" (2000: 78). In Ametlla del Vallès (Catalonia) the clergymen were also protected by members of the local council. One of them hid in the house of a relative of the mayor (Barbé 2006: 319). According to Juan Linz, Melchor Rodriguez Garcia, a CNT leader in charge of prisons, saved the lives of hundreds of right-wing men imprisoned in Alcalá de Henares by standing up to militiamen who wanted to execute the prisoners (Linz 1996: 396). He also writes that, on the nationalist side, there were priests who gave "guarantees" to people affiliated with communist parties in order to save their lives (Linz 1996: 397).

Local civilians played a role not only in lethal violence but also in other forms of victimization such as expropriations and destruction or desecration of religious buildings (in Republican-controlled areas). Two prominent examples are the cases of the Catalan villages of Bellver de Cerdanya (described in Pous and Solé i Sabaté 1988) and La Fatarella (described in Termes 2005). In these two locations, moderate leftists (i.e., Republicans) organized an armed resistance against radicals or revolutionaries (i.e., anarchists, communists) who intended to confiscate lands and provisions as well as to carry out assassinations against some right-wingers.

In the village of Creixell, the mayor ordered the burning of religious objects. By contrast, in the [neighboring] village of Tamarit, the mayor decided to have religious objects placed in different houses for their preservation (Piqué 1998: 129). In his study of the county of Vallès Oriental (Catalonia), Alcalá argues that the main churches of two villages (Ametlla del Vallès and Lliçà d'Amunt) were not destroyed because the mayors of these localities vehemently opposed it (Alcalá 2001: 236). In the village of San Vicente de Alcántara, in the province of Badajoz, there were no attacks against priests and the local church was not desecrated because the mayor of the Popular Front kept the keys in requisition" (Casanova 2004: 209).[5]

First-hand evidence of civilian collaboration being shaped by local political configurations is generally unavailable. However, there is some evidence on political motives being behind executions. For example, in his research on the civil war dynamics in Extremadura, Chaves argues that "The *Falangist* leaders and influential people who belonged to this organization determined who was to be executed, and they were guided not only by political criteria, but also by professional, economic and personal interests ... *With these criminal acts, the murderer assured that his power advanced in the area*" (Chaves 1995: 102; emphasis mine). The priest of Zaragoza reports the case of a Franco supporter who was executed by the Francoists because he had been denounced by a local political enemy: "Some time later, I learned that Martín Sancho was accused by a political adversary, who was appointed mayor when Franco's troops entered

---

[5] Casanova (2004) argues that common people had a profound respect for religious images and hence the population was often more strongly opposed to attacks against symbols than against the clergy.

the village; he was his bitter enemy" (de Estella 2003: 152). In Puigcerdà, a village with high levels of parity between Left and Right which I discussed in Chapter 1, a witness believes that her husband was executed because the local committee had decided to kill all the local influential right-wingers (Causa General, Legajo 1437, Exp. 4, Page 90).

The fact that the killing of affiliates of political parties was relatively more important in areas where the groups' supporters approached parity is also quite indicative of political strategy being behind such killings. Out of the 8,352 individuals executed by the Left in Catalonia, 1,521 have been identified as being affiliated with right-wing political parties (e.g., TYRE, LlR, CEDA, Acción Ciutadana, FE, RE, Unión Patriótica de la Dictadura) (Solé i Sabaté and Villarroya 1989).[6] Figure 4.1 shows the percentage of right-wing affiliates who were killed in the municipalities of Catalonia, by levels of support for the Left in the 1936 elections. We can observe that the killing of right-wingers peaked in the municipalities where the Left obtained between 40 and 50 percent of support in the elections, thus at the highest levels of parity. The

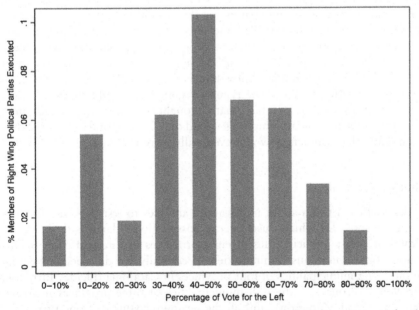

FIGURE 4.1 Percentage of Right-Wing Affiliates Executed, by Percent Support for the Left

[6] There were also 232 intra-leftist killings, which constitutes less than 3 percent of all recorded assassinations. Figure A.4.1 in the Appendix shows the distribution of deaths among members of leftist political parties, members of right-wing political parties, and non-members.

percentage of right-wingers assassinated decreases as the distribution of support for the Left moves away from the center – and therefore away from parity between the Left and the Right.

In my theoretical framework, the use of direct violence by local political elites is strategic, but did it actually achieve the goal of switching the balance of power at the local level? We cannot know this in the case of Spain because the Francoist Right imposed their political domination in all localities after the war ended.[7] In other words, the Right became dominant in all localities, regardless of the wartime events and regardless of prewar configurations. For example, in the locality of Olesa de Montserrat, as in most Catalan localities, the Falange did not have any presence before the war; after Franco's victory, this party was the one ruling the municipality, and its members were conservative individuals who had been members of other right-wing political parties before the civil war (Dueñas 2007). In many localities, and especially in those where wartime violence was greater, leftists were killed, they fled or were imprisoned, so the right-wingers had fewer obstacles in establishing themselves as the new elites. Interestingly, those who were appointed as mayors had often been persecuted by the leftists during the civil war (Gimeno 1989: 116), suggesting that the political cleansing logic was indeed at work during the civil war. Put another way: some right-wingers anticipated that they would be killed by their political enemies, and that is why they fled and only returned after the Francoist army controlled the localities. The fact that the goal of switching the local balance of power was not achieved in the case of Spain does not contradict the theory because the local elites did not know that Franco would win the civil war, and there was uncertainty about the type of regime that would follow if Franco were to win the civil war. In fact, many thought that, were Franco to win the war and establish a dictatorship, this would only be temporary – to reestablish order – and that democracy would eventually be restored.

## Multivariate Analyses

In this section, I run a set of multivariate analyses to test the main hypotheses in the book, for which I use several cross-sectional datasets that comprise a total of 2,103 municipalities of eight provinces in three different Spanish regions (or Autonomous Communities). Specifically, the datasets include data on the 1,062 municipalities of four provinces in Catalonia (Lleida, Tarragona, Barcelona, Girona); all the 948 municipalities of three provinces in Aragon (Huesca, Teruel, Zaragoza); and all the 93 municipalities of one province in Andalusia (Malaga).

---

[7] Casanova explains that, in the immediate postwar, most mayors were affiliated to the Falange (the mayor was also the local chief of Falange), and some were political leaders from the predemocratic (i.e., pre-1931) period. All of them operated under military (i.e., fascist) rule and served the interests of industrial and agricultural landlords (Casanova et al. 2001: 223).

The municipality, the lowest administrative level in Spain, is the unit of analysis. As I have already argued, a local-level approach is appropriate from both a theoretical and an empirical perspective. On the one hand, it is consistent with a micro-level explanation of the phenomenon of intentional violence against civilians. A smaller administrative unit permits a closer approximation to the geographic and social spaces that people occupy in their daily lives (Fujii 2009: 187), which are those that matter the most in accounting for dynamics of violence. On the other hand, the local-level approach allows measurement error to be minimized: using the municipality as the level of analysis permits us not only to collect fine-grained data but also better control for potential sources of unit heterogeneity that could otherwise bias the empirical results. Data on violence was coded at the municipal level by "group/period under which the municipality was under its control." In other words, all the executions perpetrated by one group in a locality are pooled together.

The critical independent variable in all the regression models in this chapter is the variable *Competition*, which captures the degree of parity between political factions (e.g., Left and Right) in a locality. As will be explained, I use a quadratic measure for competition (formula provided below), although I run a set of robustness tests with alternative measures. Following the theoretical framework, I expect wartime violence in a first stage of the civil war (on either side of the conflict) to be associated with prewar competition, and violence taking place in further stages (e.g., when an armed group conquers a locality previously controlled by another group) to be correlated with previous violence perpetrated by the rival group in the locality, as well as with competition. I will implement different tests with the aim of capturing the effects of each of these variables in the non-initial periods of the civil war.

The Spanish Civil War has a number of characteristics that make it very suitable for the study of the effect of local political configurations on wartime violence. The electoral results that are used to proxy local political configurations precede the civil war and its violence. Given that the 1936 elections took place five months before the onset of the civil war, it cannot be the case that violence, or the prospect of violence, had an impact on electoral results.[8] For all the provinces under scrutiny, the local-level electoral data that will be used in the main empirical analyses comes from the national elections that took place in Spain on 16 February 1936. Data on these elections is the most suitable for a number of reasons: firstly, while being early enough to guarantee exogeneity, these are the closest democratic elections to the outbreak of the civil war; this assures us that they are measuring political configurations that existed at the time of the civil war, and not older ones. Secondly, as explained in Chapter 3, these elections were extraordinary in terms of levels of political participation: specifically, 71 percent of the Spanish adult population went

---

[8] The latter is the case for elections that take place in wartime, where electoral results are not independent of war dynamics (e.g., those in Afghanistan, Iraq, and the US Civil War).

to the polls. The high turnout implies that the electoral results can give us a clear snapshot of local-level political configurations. Thirdly, we can expect that vote buying and patronage, which was common in rural areas of Spain since the period of *La Restauración* (1874–1923) (Brenan 1967; Tusell 1991), were less widespread in national than in local elections for the simple reason that local *caciques* would exert more pressure to assure their own power than to help national leaders keep theirs.[9] Finally, using national results at the local level has the advantage that level of competition is going to be less dependent on unobservables at the local level than if we were to look at local-level results. Thus, national elections data should be the most reflective of local social and political configurations as well as the most reliable for analytical purposes. Because I also have data from the 1933 national elections at the local level, I use these election results for robustness checks.[10]

As explained in Chapter 3, the electoral system of the Second Republic, the *panachage*, promoted the creation of pre-electoral coalitions (for example, the CEDA, created in 1933 – also called *Frente Nacional*[11] – or the *Frente Popular*,[12] created in 1936), despite citizens voting for individual candidates. In some of the historical sources, the results of the 1936 elections are gathered by electoral blocs instead of by political parties (e.g., Zubero 1982; Vilanova 2005); that is, the vote for the individual parties cannot be distinguished from the vote for these macro pre-electoral coalitions.[13] The analysis will therefore be based on the vote for the main blocs, whose division (i.e., Left and Right) corresponds to the macro-cleavage of the civil war.[14]

I estimate zero-inflated negative binomial (ZINB) regressions on total number of executions perpetrated by the Left or by the Right in each of the regions under scrutiny. The ZINB is a count regression model, which is the most suitable for the nature of the dependent variable. Linear regression models would lead to inefficient, inconsistent, and biased estimates (Long and Freese 2001: 223). In contrast with Poisson, the ZINB model allows us to

---

[9] Brenan explains that *caciquismo* was widespread in Spain (Brenan 2014/1943: 300). However, Vilanova (2005) argues that Catalonia had election monitoring mechanisms and less patronage than other areas of Spain, partly because it was less rural.

[10] The 1933 and 1936 results were significantly correlated, although the level of turnout was lower in 1933 due to the anarchosyndicalist campaign for absenteeism. Also, we still do not have all the information on the local elections of the time, but evidence from the city of Barcelona and the province of Girona indicates that there was a significant correlation between results in the national elections and those in the local elections (Vilanova 1979; 2005).

[11] In some places, this coalition was named Counterrevolutionary Candidature (*Candidatura Contrarevolucionaria*). In Catalonia, it was called Catalan Order Front (*Front Català d'Ordre*).

[12] In Catalonia, this received the name of Catalan Leftist Front (*Front Català d'Esquerres*).

[13] These were purely electoral coalitions. Once the the members of the parliament took possession of their seats, the political parties would behave autonomously in the Parliament (Linz and De Miguel 1977: 15).

[14] I will not use the results of the second electoral round in the empirical analyses because, as explained in Chapter 3, this was not generalized across the territory.

control for overdispersion, which leads to inefficient and downward-biased standard errors. It also allows us to control for the excess of zeros in the dependent variable. In all the analyses below, the ZINB shows itself to be more adequate than the NB model.[15] Later in the chapter, I use spatial econometric techniques in order to test for the spatial dependence in the data, which can bias ordinary regression estimates. Also, the study of the spatial dynamics in the data can provide us with useful insights into the dynamics of violent repression on the ground. Finally, I use matching estimators to test some of the hypotheses.

### Catalonia

Table 4.1 describes all the variables in the estimations ran with the 1,062 municipalities of Catalonia as well as their sources. *Executed by the Left* and *Executed by the Right* are the dependent variables in the analyses; they measure the total number of noncombatant victims of direct violence by leftist and rightist armed groups in a locality, respectively. *Support Left* indicates the percentage of support for the leftist coalition in the Spanish general elections of 1936; this variable will be included in a set of models to test for the alternative hypothesis that there is a monotonic effect of electoral alignments on violence. From the electoral results data, I compute a quadratic index to generate the variable *Competition*, which measures the extent to which there is parity in electoral support for the two blocs: $1-[(\%\text{VoteLeft}-\%\text{VoteRight}/100)]^2$. This index has value 0 when one of the groups received all votes in the elections (i.e., a 100 percent share), and it has value 1 when both groups received 50 percent of the votes. Following my theoretical framework, we expect this variable to exert a positive effect on the number of executions. An alternative Competition index, which will be used in robustness checks, is *Compabs*: $1-|(\%\text{VoteLeft}-\%\text{VoteRight}/100)|$. The index with absolute values has a greater variance than the quadratic measure of Competition and allows us to be sure that the results are not a product of the way this variable is constructed and of its low variance. In addition, to test for robustness, I run all the analyses with a simpler measure: the absolute difference between vote for the Left and Right.[16]

The control variables are either theoretically grounded in the civil war literature or connected to particular features of the Spanish Civil War: the dummy variable, *Catholic Center*, allows us to control for the presence of members of the clergy in a locality, which we can expect to have a positive effect on leftist violence. Members of the clergy were considered committed supporters of the Right and thus a target of violence. Density of clergymen can also have

---

[15] I have performed different analyses with Poisson, NB, and ZINB regressions and checked which of them adjusts better to the data: the ZINB models fit the data best. Also, the Vuong selection model statistic confirms the need for a ZINB model.

[16] Not all of the robustness checks are included in the chapter, but some are available in the Appendix and others are available upon request.

TABLE 4.1 *Description of Variables (Catalonia Dataset)*

| Name of the Variable | Characteristics | Data Sources |
|---|---|---|
| Executed by the Left | Total number of people executed by the Left in a locality | Solé i Sabaté and Villarroya (1989) |
| Executed by the Right | Total number of people executed by the Right in a locality | Solé i Sabaté (2000) |
| Support Left | Percentage Support for the Popular Front in the 1936 general elections | Vilanova (2005) |
| Competition | Index from 0 (minimum parity) to 1 (maximum parity) | Calculated from Vilanova (2005) |
| CNT Affiliation | Percentage inhabitants affiliated with the CNT in a locality | CNT (1936), Cucó i Giner (1970) |
| UGT Affiliation | Percentage inhabitants affiliated with the UGT in a locality | UGT (1931) |
| Population | Inhabitants of the municipality in 1936 | *Instituto Nacional de Estadística* |
| Catholic Center | Dummy variable: 1 if the municipality had an archbishop in 1936; 0 otherwise | *Conferencia Episcopal Española* |
| Frontline | Dummy variable: 1 if the municipality is in a county that shares the military frontline at any time during the war; 0 if not | Solé i Sabaté and Villarroya (2005) |
| Border | Dummy variable: 1 if the municipality is in a county that shares the French border; 0 if not | *Institut Cartogràfic de Catalunya* |
| Sea | Dummy variable: 1 if the municipality is in a county with a coastline; 0 if not | *Institut Cartogràfic de Catalunya* |
| Elevation | Elevation of the municipality, in meters | *Institut Cartogràfic de Catalunya* |
| Latitude | Degrees (UTM, fus 31, datum ED50) | *Institut Cartogràfic de Catalunya* |
| Longitude | Degrees (UTM, fus 31, datum ED50) | *Institut Cartogràfic de Catalunya* |
| Percent Literate | Percentage inhabitants in a locality who are able to read and write | *Instituto Nacional de Estadística* |

a positive effect on violence by the Right, as these individuals were likely to collaborate with the right-wing militias on the elimination of leftist supporters; indeed, there are several pieces of historical evidence that suggest that the priests of the localities were often involved in the prosecution of leftists in areas controlled by the Nationalists (e.g., Vila Izquierdo 1984). Unfortunately, more fine-grained data on the presence of religious people in a locality is not available from existing sources.

*CNT Affiliation* and *UGT Affiliation* capture the presence of syndicalists, who were strong supporters of the Left and who we can assume were more likely to denounce and help perpetrate violence against supporters of the rival bloc. In some cases, trade union organizations (and, quite particularly, the CNT) were armed, so they could perpetrate violence against neighbours without needing to acquire information or without facing major constraints on the perpetration of violence (e.g., they knew who the local leaders of the Right were and/or where they lived). In addition, in places with higher proportions of affiliates, there should be greater ratios of (identifiable) left-wing sympathizers and, therefore, more would-be targets of the Right. Thus, we can expect these variables to have a positive effect on both leftist and rightist violence.

The dummy variable *Frontline* should allow the capture of the lack of military persistence that is likely to characterize zones close to the war frontline(s), which we can expect to boost levels of violence. As I argued in Chapter 2, in areas where military control is more precarious, groups face greater incentives to target potential defectors and local civilians have greater incentives to collaborate with the armed group in order to single out defectors.[17] The dummy variables *Sea* and *Border* capture the effect of potential escape routes, which should reduce the number of assassinations.[18] *Elevation* is a measure for rough terrain; in mountainous locations, people can more easily hide to avoid being assassinated; thus, we can expect it to have a negative sign. Finally, I also include inhabitants of the village in 1936 (*Population*) in order to control for size of the locality, which is likely to have a positive effect on the number of executions. *Latitude* and *Longitude* are geographical measures that I will use in the spatial analyses, as well as in robustness checks. *Percentage Literate* is a proxy for the level of development of the municipality, which I also will also include in robustness checks.

Table 4.2 depicts the results of the ZINB model for *Executed by the Left* in Catalonia, with standard errors clustered at the level of the county (there were 38 counties in 1936 Catalonia). Note that the ZINB models have two set

---

[17] In Aragon, Ester Casanova explains that "in those villages located in the frontline, militiamen controlled peasants that could transfer information from one side to another" (2007: 49); and she mentions the example of a postman who was imprisoned by the leftist militias after being accused of transferring information to the Nationalists.

[18] Exile by sea was very important at the beginning of the Spanish Civil War. In Catalonia, it was even co-sponsored by the Catalan Republican government (Dòll-Petit 2004).

TABLE 4.2 *Executed by the Left in Catalonia (ZINB)*

|  | (1) | (2) |
| --- | --- | --- |
| **NB: Number of Executed** | | |
| Competition | 1.44** | |
|  | (0.39) | |
| Frontline | 0.32 | 0.33 |
|  | (0.31) | (0.33) |
| Population | 0.000059 | 0.000058 |
|  | (0.00011) | (0.00012) |
| CNT Affiliation | 0.12* | 0.13* |
|  | (0.057) | (0.056) |
| UGT Affiliation | 0.081 | 0.088 |
|  | (0.095) | (0.096) |
| Border | −0.37** | −0.47** |
|  | (0.14) | (0.17) |
| Sea | −0.12 | −0.16 |
|  | (0.25) | (0.27) |
| Elevation | −0.00071 | −0.00077 |
|  | (0.00065) | (0.00065) |
| Catholic Center | 2.16** | 2.25* |
|  | (0.84) | (0.88) |
| Support Left | | 0.004 |
|  | | (0.0072) |
| _cons | 0.33 | 1.45** |
|  | (0.63) | (0.50) |
| **Logit: Non-violence** | | |
| Population | −0.0071** | −0.0077** |
|  | (0.0017) | (0.0026) |
| Competition | 1.76 | |
|  | (2.00) | |
| Frontline | 0.86 | 0.84 |
|  | (1.09) | (1.53) |
| UGT Affiliation | 0.068 | 0.093 |
|  | (0.23) | (0.27) |
| Border | −0.38 | −0.64 |
|  | (0.48) | (0.55) |
| Sea | 1.58 | 1.71 |
|  | (1.77) | (2.17) |
| Elevation | 0.0014 | 0.0016 |
|  | (0.0019) | (0.0022) |
| Support Left | | 0.019 |
|  | | (0.015) |
| _cons | −1.66 | −1.09 |
|  | (1.44) | (1.76) |
| lnalpha | | |
| _cons | 0.33** | 0.36** |
|  | (0.10) | (0.096) |
| N | 870 | 870 |
| ll | −2110.5 | −2115.9 |

Clustered standard errors in parentheses
+*p* < 0.10, *p* < 0.05, **p* < 0.01

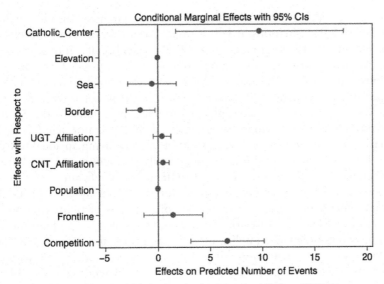

FIGURE 4.2 Executed by the Left in Catalonia: Marginal Effects (ZINB)

of estimates each: one for a logit regression estimating the non-occurrence of violence, and another for a negative binomial regression estimating numbers of executions in places with positive numbers of deaths. The first model in the table includes *Competition* as the main independent variable; the second model includes *Support Left* as the main independent variable in order to test the alternative hypothesis that political domination by the rival leads to higher levels of direct violence.[19]

*Competition* is substantively and statistically significant in explaining levels of direct violence (see Figure 4.2 for marginal effects). Only *Catholic Center* leads to a greater number of predicted executions, confirming that the presence of large numbers of clergymen led to increased levels of violence by leftist armed groups. *Competition* is not relevant in explaining the occurrence of violence, as shown in the logit part of the ZINB models. This implies that there are some factors that affect the occurrence of violence and are independent of the degree of competition in a locality. For example, one could think that clergymen victimization was somewhat independent of political dynamics for their assassinations had a symbolic value – killing the priest became a sort of a revolutionary obligation (Delgado 1992).

The variable *Support Left* is not significant in explaining violence (neither its occurrence nor its intensity); thus, the competing domination hypothesis can be ruled out in light of these results. *CNT Affiliation* takes a significant

---

[19] The inclusion of this variable also permits us to check for the possibility that the results obtained with the variable Competition are not driven by the imposition of a particular functional form (i.e., non-linearity).

positive sign, which indicates that the presence of anarchosyndicalists increases the number of assassinations by leftist armed groups. In fact, this variable cannot be included in the logit part of the ZINB model because it overdetermines the occurrence of violence: executions took place both in CNT and non-CNT locations, but all CNT locations experienced executions. UGT affiliation is also positive in explaining levels of violence, but it is not statistically significant. With regard to the geographical variables, proximity to the *Frontline* has a positive effect on violence, as expected, but it is not significant; *Border* has a negative effect because would-be targets living in localities close to the French border could escape more easily. *Elevation* and *Sea* have the hypothesized negative effect, even if not statistically significant.

Figure 4.3 shows the regression plots for the ZINB models (1) for three different dependent variables: the number of members of right-wing political parties (e.g., CEDA, Lliga Regionalista) who were killed by the Left; the number of members of left-wing political parties and trade unions (e.g., ERC, FAI, POUM, CNT, UGT) who were killed by the Left; and individuals who were not affiliated with any political party or trade union who were killed by the Left. This figure shows that political competition does not explain leftist violence against leftists, while it does explain violence against right-wingers and against those who were not affiliated to any political party.[20] This is consistent with the hypothesis that violence perpetrated by leftist armed groups was taking place in places where this served an instrumental purpose to leftist political elites.

Following my theory, we should expect strategic collaboration to be greater in localities where political cleavages are deeper and more stable. Violence could be seen as a more useful tool to change the state of affairs in such contexts. I develop a way to measure "deep cleavages" by using the differential in support for the Left between the 1936 and the 1933 elections in Catalonia and by identifying localities with deep cleavages as those in which the differences in levels of electoral support for the Left are smaller than 10 percent. Consistent with the strategic collaboration mechanism, the predicted number of executions is greater in localities with deeper cleavages than in localities with more electoral volatility and thus shallower cleavages (Figure 4.4). This also shows that the results are not driven by recent partisanship and that violence is more intense where political cleavages were more grounded.

### Aragon

In Aragon, a total of 366 municipalities were under Francoist control for the duration of the conflict; I call them "Nationalist Aragon." The rest of the municipalities in the region (a total of 582) were under leftist control at some

---

[20] The graphs also show that the most important variable in explaining violence against leftists in Catalonia is proximity to the frontline. This suggests that deserters were probably the targets of such violence.

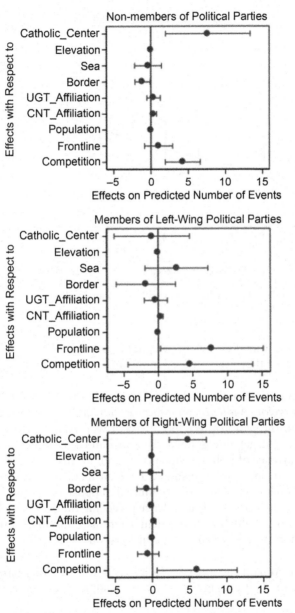

FIGURE 4.3 Executed by the Left in Catalonia: Marginal Effects (ZINB), by Political Party Membership (Conditional Marginal Effects at Means, with 95% CI)

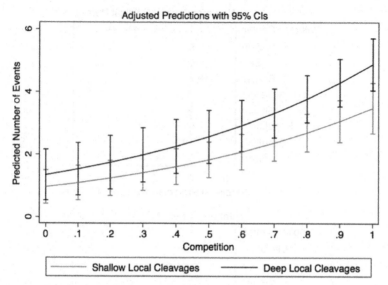

FIGURE 4.4 Depth of Local Cleavages and Executions by the Left

point during the war; I call them "Republican Aragon."[21] Table 4.3 presents
the description of the variables used in the analyses with municipalities of this
region.

In addition to the usual correlates, in the analyses for Aragon I also include
the variable *Previous Violence*, an indicator that allows me to control for political conflict in the period preceding the civil war. Aragon is the only region
for which I could get fine-grained data to build this indicator, which captures the occurrence of political violence in each locality between January and
July 1936.[22] Previous violence should have an incidence on victimization in
$t_1$, as priors on the existence of committed supporters should be greater in
places with incidents of political violence preceding the civil war. Also, dynamics of retaliation could be driving denunciations and enhance local civilian
collaboration with the armed groups in locations with a history of political
violence.

Republican Aragon encompasses locations that were either partially or fully
controlled by the Left during the civil war; in some cases, these municipalities

[21] Table 3.2 in Chapter 3 shows the distribution of municipalities by control zones (and provinces)
of this region.
[22] The data is obtained from Casanova (1985: 52). I built a dummy variable for each locality,
which has value 1 if any event of political violence occurred during this period, and 0 otherwise. The events that are included are: strikes; illegal occupation of private or communal rural
properties; disturbances or confrontations between groups; violent aggression toward peasants; governmental intervention in conflicts. They do not include crimes of passion or normal
delinquency.

TABLE 4.3 *Description of Variables (Aragon Dataset)*

| Name of the Variable | Characteristics | Data Sources |
| --- | --- | --- |
| **Executed by the Right** | Total number of people executed by the Right in a locality | Casanova et al. (2001) |
| **Competition** | Index from 0 (minimum parity) to 1 (maximum parity) | Calculated from Germán (1982) |
| **Support Left** | Percentage support for the Popular Front in the 1936 general elections | Calculated from Germán (1982) |
| **CNT Affiliation** | Percentage inhabitants affiliated with the CNT in a locality | CNT (1936), Cucó i Giner (1970) |
| **UGT Affiliation** | Percentage inhabitants affiliated with the UGT in a locality | UGT (1931) |
| **Population** | Inhabitants of the municipality in 1936 | *Instituto Nacional de Estadística* |
| **Catholic Center** | Dummy variable: 1 if the municipality had an archbishop in 1936; 0 otherwise | *Conferencia Episcopal Española* |
| **Latitude** | Latitude degrees | Global Gazetteer 2.1 |
| **Longitude** | Longitude degrees | Global Gazetteer 2.1 |
| **Elevation** | Elevation of the municipality, in feet | Global Gazetteer 2.1 |
| **Previous Violence** | 1 if violent events occurred in the prewar period; 0 if not | Casanova (1985) |

were conquered several times by different groups or militias. The patterns of direct violence against civilians that took place in these locations cannot be fully explained by my theoretical framework because the military contest between the armed groups was very intensive in this area and civilian victimization was usually a byproduct of this military struggle. Indeed, none of the groups had full control of the territory during a sufficient period of time for it to be considered a rearguard territory. In this battlefield zone, I predict violence to follow patterns similar to those observed for irregular civil wars; in other words, violence should be explained as the result of tactical maneuvers and relative control of the territory by each of the armed groups. As explained in Chapter 2, in areas with little military persistence, where military control is not complete, local collaboration relies more on military than on political considerations. I find that political competition does not have a significant impact on violence perpetrated by either rightist or leftist armed groups in this region (see A.4.6 in the Appendix), which suggests that the determinants of violence in battlefield areas are indeed different from those in rearguard territories. I will come back to this point further below.

I focus here on the subset of localities of Aragon that I have coded as Nationalist, focusing on violence perpetrated by the Francoist army and rightist militias. The vector of control variables is almost the same as that in the analyses of Catalonia, and it includes *Population, CNT Affiliation, UGT Affiliation, Elevation, Catholic Center, Frontline,* and *Border,* in addition to *Previous Violence.* In these regressions I use the longitude of the municipality to capture proximity to the frontline (since the frontline was to the east of all these territories, the greater the longitude the greater the proximity to the frontline). For a more refined measure of proximity to the French border, I use the latitude of the municipality (France is to the north of Aragon). The standard errors are clustered by counties (in Aragon called *partidos judiciales*).[23]

The results indicate that *Competition* at the local level is very relevant in explaining direct violence by the Right in Aragon, which is consistent with what we observed in Catalonia and supports the first theoretical hypothesis in the book. The marginal effects of the estimates are shown in Figure 4.5 (the table with the ZINB models are included in the Appendix).[24] As in Catalonia, *Catholic Center* and *Competition* are the two variables with the greatest explanatory power, and their effects are slightly larger than in Catalonia. *Catholic Center* were not locations where clergymen were assassinated, unlike

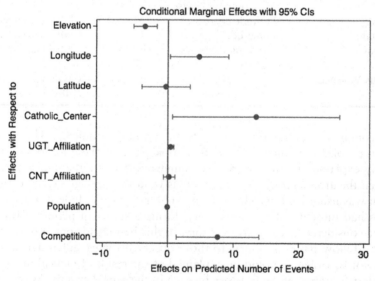

FIGURE 4.5 Executed by the Right in Aragon: Marginal Effects (ZINB)

[23] The variables *Previous Violence* and *Catholic Center* cannot be introduced into the second part of the ZINB model due to over-determination issues.

[24] Elevation significantly decreases the number of executions, and it decreases the likelihood of violence. Proximity to the frontline, proxied with *Longitude,* increases levels of violence. In Model 4 of Table A.4.3, *Support Left* is significant and positive; this result however does not hold when we include the quadratic term of *Support Left* (in Model 5), which takes a negative sign and indicates that the effect of the variable is nonlinear, as captured by the variable *Competition.*

Catalonia; in Aragon this variable is increasing levels of violence most probably because places with archbishops were relatively big localities and also locations in which the Nationalists had significant collaboration from local clergymen.

In Aragon, prewar political violence has a positive effect on levels of wartime violence, and it also explains the occurrence of violence: violence was more likely to occur and was more intense in places where there had been political confrontations in the immediate prewar. This variable does not rule out the relevance of political competition. In order to disentangle the effect of previous violence and competition, and to better identify causality, I match all the municipalities of Nationalist Aragon on levels of competition and look at the effect of previous violence on civil war violence perpetrated by the Right. Consistent with the multivariate results, previous violence has a strong impact on rightist violence: specifically, with propensity score (and a five nearest neighbors algorithm) matching, the average treatment effect of the treated is 34 (and significant at the 95 percent level). In other words, in those localities where there was political violence before the civil war, the Right executed 34 more people, on average, than in localities without prewar violent events.[25]

Overall, the results from the Nationalist area of Aragon are also supportive of the theoretical model and they show that levels of direct violence increase with levels of prewar competition between the two blocs. Importantly, these results show that the same mechanisms explaining variation in levels of violence perpetrated by the Left account for variation in levels of violence perpetrated by the Right, which implies that the logic of violence perpetrated by these two antithetical groups was similar: I argue that this is the case because local political dynamics were behind direct violence, regardless of the group carrying out the violence. Figure 4.6 illustrates this: it shows predictions drawn from the ZINB models for Catalonia (Executed by the Left) and Aragon (Executed by the Right). The graphs show that there is a similar impact of prewar electoral competition on the number of executions perpetrated by these two armed organizations.

## Malaga

The province of Malaga was controlled by the leftist militias – in particular, by the anarchists – from July 1937 to February 1937. The province was then conquered by the Nationalist army, which committed an outright slaughter (Rodrigo 2008). As explained in the previous chapter, fine-grained data on rightist killings is unfortunately still not available from primary or secondary sources, so I have to focus on the violence perpetrated by the leftist militias during the time they controlled the area. This province's patterns of

---

[25] The results are similar when using other algorithms; for example, with propensity score matching and one nearest neighbor, the ATET is 31.6, significant at the 90 percent level.

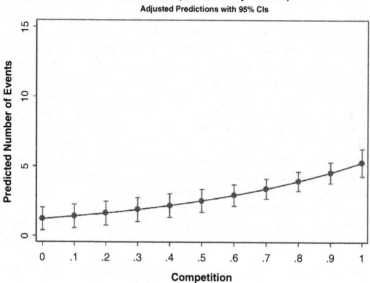

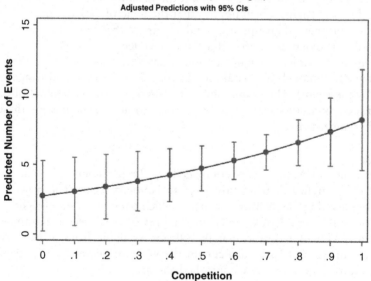

FIGURE 4.6 Predicted Executions, by Level of Prewar Competition

TABLE 4.4 *Description of Variables (Malaga Dataset)*

| Name of the Variable | Characteristics | Data Sources |
|---|---|---|
| Executed by the Left | Total number of people executed by the Left in a locality | Nadal (1984) |
| Support Left | Percentage Support for the Popular Front in the 1936 general elections | Velasco Gómez (2008) |
| Competition | Index from 0 (minimum parity) to 1 (maximum parity) | Calculated from Velasco Gómez (2008) |
| CNT Affiliation | Percentage Inhabitants affiliated with the CNT in a locality | CNT (1936), Cucó i Giner (1970) |
| UGT Affiliation | Percentage Inhabitants affiliated with the UGT in a locality | UGT (1931) |
| Population | Inhabitants of the municipality in 1936 | *Instituto Nacional de Estadística* |
| Elevation | Elevation of the municipality, in meters | *Infraestructura de Datos Espaciales de España* |
| Latitude | Latitude degrees | Global Ganzeeter Version 2.1 |
| Longitude | Longitude degrees | Global Ganzeeter Version 2.1 |
| Strikes | Number of workers' strikes in the locality during the Second Republic (1931–1936) | Velasco Gómez (2008) |

social and economic inequality diverge considerably from those in the other Spanish provinces analyzed in this book. In addition, since the attributes of chaos and anarchy have been quite definitional of the type of control held by the anarchist militias in this province (Seidman 2002), if *Competition* shows as significant to explain direct violence, we will have further evidence confirming the relevance of local-level political factors vis-à-vis organizational factors in explaining violence against civilians during civil war.

Table 4.4 describes the variables used to analyze leftist violence in the 93 municipalities in the province of Malaga. I do not include *Catholic Center* because there is only one location that had an archbishop – the capital city (Malaga) – and this variable correlates very strongly with other variables in the model, leading to a collinearity problem. I include a new variable that was available for this province: the number of workers' strikes during the

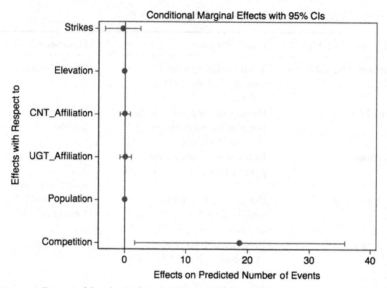

FIGURE 4.7 Executed by the Left in Malaga: Marginal Effects (ZINB)

Second Republic in each locality. The workers' movement was particularly strong in Malaga,[26] and it led a significant strike movement throughout the 1930s (Nadal 1981). I expect this variable to have a positive impact on levels of violence given that social conflict would lead to deeper cleavages, and to a greater degree of identification of strong supporters of the enemy. Indeed, at the descriptive level, there is a positive correlation between the number of strikes in a locality (coded from Velasco Gómez 2008) and leftist violence during the civil war (Figure A.4.2 of the Appendix).

Figure 4.7 shows the marginal effects of the estimates for Malaga, which are also supportive of the rivalry hypothesis (the coefficients are included in Table A.4.4 of the Appendix): *Competition* is the variable with the strongest significant and substantive effect on executions by leftist militias in this province. Workers' strikes in a locality are not statistically significant in the main models, but if we take out the outlier of the city of Malaga, where 899 people were executed by the leftists, this variable leads to significant greater levels of violence. This is consistent with what we observed in Aragon regarding prewar political violence.[27]

Overall, these results confirm the relevance of local-level political dynamics in explaining violence during wartime, even when violence is perpetrated by loose, decentralized, and what have been labeled as "chaotic" armed groups

---

[26] Among the three regions studied, Malaga was the one furthest to the left, as can be observed in the histograms of support for the leftist bloc in the 1936 elections included in the Appendix.

[27] Neither in Aragon nor in Malaga, previous violence explains levels of political competition at the local level.

such as the anarcho-syndicalist militias that controlled this province during the early stages of the Spanish Civil War. The results for this province provide external validity to those obtained with the regions of the Northeast of Spain, which were characterized by different socioeconomic and political dynamics. The South was more rural, poorer, and more unequal; social conflict between landowners and peasants was more salient than in the North. And yet, local parity between the Left and the Right also seems to underlie the local dynamics of violence in the rearguard territories of this region.

### All Regions

I pool all the municipalities from Catalonia, Malaga, and Aragon in the same database to run the same multivariate analyses above. When analyzing all the regions altogether, the dependent variable is the total number of noncombatants killed in a locality (by either side) in the first period of the war ($t_1$).[28] A dummy variable, Republican Zone, indicates if the municipality was located in a Republican/Nationalist zone. The remaining controls are the same as those included in the regressions above, with the exception of those variables for which information was available only for particular regions. Standard errors are clustered by province (there are eight of them).[29] The results of these analyses are depicted in Table 4.5, which includes two columns: one with the results for all the municipalities in these provinces – including the areas of Aragon that were in the battlefield – and one with the results excluding battlefield areas.

The results of the ZINB models (Table 4.5) show that *Competition* is a significant variable in explaining levels of violence by both armed groups in non-battlefield areas and is accounting for the occurrence of violence in all areas, increasing the probability of violence. Importantly, we observe that being in a Republican rearguard zone is associated to lower levels of violence: this is consistent with the fact that the Republicans were more restrained than the Nationalists in their use of violence against civilians. On July 19th, General Mola stated: "We must exterminate those who do not think as we do," implying that the Francoists should follow an extermination plan; nothing of this sort was ever stated by Republican political authorities (Preston 2013). However, in the logit part of the ZINB models, *Republican Zone* takes a negative value indicating that the likelihood of the occurrence of killings was greater in Republican zones. This suggests that, while overall levels of violence were greater in Nationalist zones, violence was more spread in Republican territories, with more localities suffering at least one killing (very often, the priest). In my data, 74 percent of localities in Republican zones suffered from at least

---

[28] I run robustness checks with the total number of killings, including $t_1$ and $t_2$, in Catalonia, and the results do not change.

[29] As for geographical measures, I include here only dummies for *Border* and *Sea*. I do not include a *Frontline* variable because this would have contradictory effects for the areas East and West of the Aragon frontline. Similar interpretation issues would arise if geo-referencing variables were included.

TABLE 4.5 *Determinants of Executions by the Two Groups (Combined Datasets) (ZINB)*

| | (1)<br>With Battlefield | (2)<br>Without Battlefield |
|---|---|---|
| **NB: Number of Executed** | | |
| Competition | 0.13 | 1.35** |
| | (0.24) | (0.24) |
| Catholic Center | 2.22** | 2.10** |
| | (0.50) | (0.46) |
| Republican Zone | −0.18 | −0.74** |
| | (0.20) | (0.11) |
| Population | 0.00011 | 0.000084* |
| | (0.000073) | (0.000037) |
| CNT Affiliation | 0.085** | 0.10** |
| | (0.020) | (0.026) |
| UGT Affiliation | 0.052 | 0.054* |
| | (0.038) | (0.025) |
| Border | −0.88** | −0.71** |
| | (0.18) | (0.17) |
| Elevation (range) | 0.000061 | 0.00021 |
| | (0.000075) | (0.00017) |
| _cons | 1.74** | 0.80** |
| | (0.21) | (0.17) |
| **Logit: Non-violence** | | |
| Competition | −2.96** | −2.61** |
| | (0.96) | (0.47) |
| Republican Zone | −24.6** | −25.9** |
| | (9.29) | (8.34) |
| Population | −0.0062* | −0.0062** |
| | (0.0025) | (0.0013) |
| Border | 21.1* | 22.7** |
| | (9.40) | (7.53) |
| Elevation (range) | 0.0028** | 0.0030* |
| | (0.0010) | (0.0012) |
| _cons | 3.08** | 2.67** |
| | (0.70) | (0.52) |
| lnalpha | | |
| _cons | 0.73** | 0.73** |
| | (0.094) | (0.091) |
| N | 1228 | 905 |
| ll | −3501.5 | −2332.7 |

Clustered standard errors in parentheses
$^+p < 0.10$, $^*p < 0.05$, $^{**}p < 0.01$

one execution, while this was the case for 65 percent of localities under Francoist control. Hence, violence by the Nationalists was more intense but also more territorially concentrated.[30] I ran propensity score matching estimators in order to compare balanced municipalities (I match them on their levels of political competition, population, CNT affiliation, UGT affiliation, elevation, proximity to the border, and presence of members of the clergy) and to evaluate the effect of being in a Republican zone vis-à-vis a Nationalist zone. The average treatment effect for the treated (ATET) – being in a Republican zone as the treatment – is negative (−12), but it is not statistically significant.[31]

Figure 4.8 shows very clearly that, in non-battlefield areas, direct violence (by both armed groups) increases as the distribution of support for the Left and the Right in the 1936 elections approaches parity. Yet, there are different violence dynamics in battlefield zones vis-à-vis non-battlefield zones: local political competition is less relevant in explaining violence in battlefield areas than in rearguard territories. This is consistent with the theory: in rearguard territories, where territory is not contested, local civilians weight political configurations in their decision to collaborate with the group. In the battlefield, military considerations are likely to weight more than political considerations. The difference with battlefield zones is striking when we compare killings by the Right in battlefield areas with non-battlefield areas (Figure 4.9): whereas

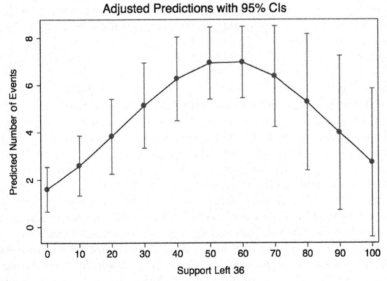

FIGURE 4.8 Total Executed in Non-Battlefield Areas, by Levels of Support for the Left in the 1936 Elections

---

[30] This contradicts Preston's hypothesis that the Republicans were killing in urban locations, while the Francoists tended to kill in rural locations (2013).

[31] These estimates are obtained with a five nearest neighbors algorithm.

political competition (i.e., parity between Left and Right) has a clear impact on killings in rearguard zones, it does not have any effect on killings in battlefield areas, where control is contested and military variables are likely driving the dynamics of violence.

## Focused Comparisons of Localities

Evidence from focused comparisons of local communities supports the mechanism of strategic collaboration by local political elites, namely that they made an instrumental use of violence to try to change the local balance of power. For example, if we look at different localities in the county of Ribera d'Ebre (Catalonia), which was a quite violent region due to its proximity to Aragon and the Ebro frontline, we observe the following patterns: in Torre de l'Espanyol (a village with 835 inhabitants), leftists were in the majority before the war (the Popular Front obtained 66.6 percent of the vote in the 1936 elections). The leftist militias killed three individuals in the locality: given the fact that their political bloc dominated the locality, violence was unlikely to change the state of affairs, and this is probably why local leftists did not push for further executions. In contrast, violence was, in relative terms, much greater in the village of Palma d'Ebre (with 608 inhabitants): the leftists killed 15 people. In Palma d'Ebre, the Left had won the elections in 1936, although only by small margins (it obtained 53.8 percent of the vote). Because of the close competition between Left and Right, the assassination of right-wingers could contribute to a change in the state of affairs in this locality. In the village of Rasquera, where the Left saw a comfortable victory (64 percent of the vote), there were only two deaths, while in the similarly sized village of Riba-Roja d'Ebre, where the Left had won with only 53 percent of the vote, the death toll was 15. Similarly, in Tivissa, where the Left also had won with a small margin (51.8 percent of the vote), the total number of deaths was 13. In this area, violence arose when militias passed through town on their way to fight on the Aragon frontline. Hence, militiamen were not from the area and required information from locals in order to identify and execute right-wing figures. These villages were all part of the same county, they had similar economic structures, their proximity to the frontline was roughly equal, and they saw the same level of military presence. The main differences between them concerned the local political cleavages, which determined the degree and kind of collaboration in the perpetration of violence when the leftist militias and the Republican soldiers passed by.

The county of Berguedà, also in Catalonia, was industrial and thus had a significant working class movement, which led to confrontations during the Second Republic and to significant violence during the civil war. Yet, violence was not similarly distributed across all the localities in this area: in the village of Puig-Reig, where the Left had won the elections with 61 percent of the vote, local historians argue that "there was not the degree of political party enmity that existed in other localities" (Montañà and Rafart 1991: 52), and

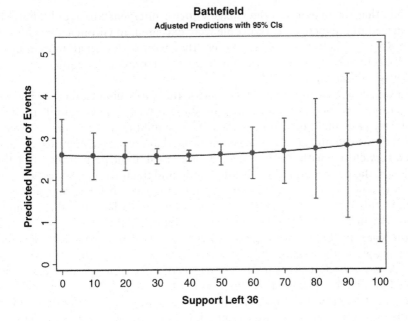

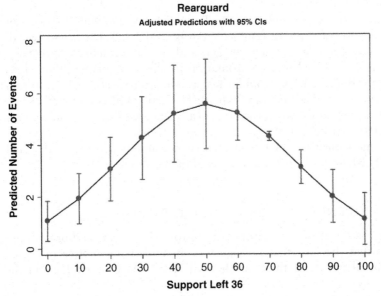

FIGURE 4.9 Executed by the Right in Battlefield and Rearguard Areas, by Levels of Support for the Left in the 1936 Elections

explain that the mayor and the village's doctor intervened to avoid killings by the armed militiamen; still, 13 people were executed. In Gironella, neighbor to Puig-Reig, the Left was less hegemonic (they won with a small margin in the 1936 elections) and violence was much greater: a total of 34 people were killed by leftist militiamen and soldiers.

In Canet de Mar, a Catalan locality with 4,984 inhabitants, the Left had lost the national elections with 49.3 percent of the vote: a close margin. During the civil war, 41 civilians died at the hands of leftist militias. In the *Causa General*'s archive, one can find ample evidence showing that the local committee collaborated very closely with the FAI's armed militiamen in the perpetration of lethal violence, the destruction of the local church, and the torture of some prisoners (Causa General Legajo 1587, Exp. 6, page 27). The CNT had a strong presence in this town, with 425 affiliates, so some locals had joined the militia. Similarly, in Arbúcies, the Left lost the national elections with 47.1 percent of the vote. In this town of 4,192 inhabitants the leftist armed forces killed eight people in the first period of the war (the Francoists killed ten people in the second period of the war). In the national archives, we find evidence that armed militiamen collaborated closely with the local political committee: "the men of action were local militiamen who were financially supported and led by the local Committee" (Causa General, Legajo 1437, exp. 18–22). Thus, the killings perpetrated by these militiamen were targeted and very much driven by the preferences expressed by local political elites. In Vilalba dels Arcs, a town with around 1,500 inhabitants, the Popular Front had won the elections with 47.3 percent of the vote. The village was so divided that it had two distinct cultural centers: one for right-wingers and another for leftists. Seventeen right-wingers were killed in a confrontation in which militiamen (both local and from neighboring villages) ambushed a right-wing meeting at a cultural center (Causa General, Legajo 1447, Exp. 8). The leftists killed a total of 40 people in Vilalba; afterwards, when the Francoists came in, at least 14 individuals were executed after being denounced by local residents.

We now turn to what happened in non-initial periods of the civil war, namely when the Francoists conquered the localities.

## 4.2 VIOLENCE IN NON-INITIAL PERIODS

There is a lot of evidence, from both historical accounts and oral testimonies, supporting the idea that revenge was an underlying motive of violence in non-initial phases of the Spanish Civil War.[32] As Ruiz explains in the case

---

[32] Some local and regional studies that provide clear evidence on revenge and retaliation dynamics are: Martín Rubio (1987); Garriga (1986, 2004); Gimeno (1989); Gabarda (1993); Ventura i Solé (1993); Ors (1995); Gavaldà (1997); Solé i Sabaté (2000); Gutiérrez Flores (2000); Espinosa (2005); Crosas (2004); Casanova (2007); Dueñas (2007); Ledesma (2009b); Langarita (2014); Moreno (2014).

of Madrid, "Death sentences issued after March 1939 indicate the importance of memories of the so-called 'red terror' and the desire to get revenge
for the Republican 'violent crimes'" (Ruiz 2005: 182). A historian from Granollers writes: "By the end of 1939, Granollers was, like all the localities in
Catalonia, ready for a settling of scores because revolutionary violence had
affected some families too directly" (Garriga 2003: 405). Azpíroz (2007),
for his part, explains the following with regard to the province of Huesca
(Aragon):

> When the Nationalists occupied the province of Huesca, many peasants were
> denounced by their landlords. Hundreds of people who were incarcerated in 1938 and
> 1939 were subjected to unilateral military trials ... In the trials, horrifying testimony
> was provided by mayors (many of them middle owners), priests, national guards officers
> and right-wing neighbors, but most testimony was not proved or sufficiently verified.
> Accusations were directed against those who had led the local committees and the col-
> lectivities, or against those who had sympathized with or supported the revolutionary
> processes (380).

Various accounts indicate that the nuclear family was the main agent of
retaliation (Linz 1996; Casanova 2007), following patterns that have been
observed in other settings, i.e., in conflicts that are not civil wars (see, for example, Gould 1999; 2000). Relatives of people who had been victimized in the
previous period played the most active roles in the denunciation processes. For
example, referring to the Francoist period in Aragon, Azpíroz (2007) argues
that official documents from the War Courts include declarations and testimonies from relatives of people who had been executed. These relatives "asked
for blood and more blood" (450). In his memoirs, Gumersindo de Estella documents many cases of people who were arrested and executed because they were
considered either perpetrators of violence against right-wingers or informants,
and who were singled out by relatives of victims. Somebody told the wife of
one right-winger who had been killed by the leftists: "Mrs. Pilar, congratula-
tions! The other day the girl who denounced your husband was executed" (de
Estella 2003: 88) – as if it were a cause for celebration. Langarita (2014) also
explains that local collaboration was indispensable to the Francoist regime in
the early postwar period. She notes that those responsible for denunciations
were mostly men (between 35 and 50 years old), but women also provided
accusatory information in retaliation, when their family members had been
victimized (they were "widows of those who died for God and for Spain").
This historian also explains that the Francoist regime, far from containing
revenge dynamics at the end of the conflict, welcomed denunciations; and she
also emphasizes the importance of what she calls "bottom-up" processes of
violence.

Another dimension of retaliatory dynamics is that relatives of those
allegedly responsible for crimes became targets when the perpetrators could
not be found in the locality. Such was the case for many women who were

victimized by *Falangists* or by Nationalist soldiers when their leftist husbands, who had fled, could not be found. The Francoists subjected these women to brutal humiliation, including shaving their hair, forcing them to ingest laxatives and subsequently parading them around the village. In addition, these women were often physically tortured and dispossessed of their property. Ruiz explains that the Francoists killed the brother of Atadell, a socialist who had led a militia that arrested and allegedly executed many right-wingers in Madrid: "Although there is no evidence that he worked in the brigade, Manuel was sentenced to die by garrotte in Madrid on April 17, 1939, barely a fortnight after the fall of the capital" (2007: 114). Although perpetrators of violence in the first period of the war had often fled the localities when the rival army came, this did not prevent revenge dynamics from taking place. The official "lists of suspects" drafted by the Nationalists were broad enough to include anybody with a link to events occurred during the previous war period. Residents of the locality – and especially rightist political elites – could get people arrested by merely saying that they were members of leftist political parties or trade unions, by saying that they were "collaborators," or simply by implying that they sympathized with the Left.[33] Reflecting on the innocence of many prisoners who were executed by the Francoists in Zaragoza, Gumersindo de Estella argues: "The true criminals left when the Francoists troops were approaching their villages. The right-wingers who remained and who had lost relatives at the hands of the reds sought revenge by punishing citizens who had a leftist ideology or who had identified as Republicans. And they would accuse them in front of the Francoist authorities" (2003: 177).

Dynamics of revenge and retaliation were especially severe in battlefield areas such as zones of Aragon that switched hands several times. The desire for revenge very often shaped the decisions made by local leaders and influenced the consequent levels of repression that were carried out (Casanova 2007: 43). Retaliatory dynamics, which caused deaths in every occupation, led to a high number of casualties over the course of the conflict. For example, in the town of Calanda, in the province of Teruel, a total of 75 people (18.5 per thousand of the population) were killed by the anarchist militias who conquered the locality (initially under Nationalist control) on their way to Zaragoza. When the Nationalist army reestablished their occupation of the locality in March 1938, revenge triggered further violence, now against leftists: a total of 23 people (5.67 per thousand) were then executed by the Right (Cenarro 2002a). The death toll in this town was therefore significant. In Extremadura, Espinosa

---

[33] A local historian from Valls (Catalonia) explains that, during the Francoist period, "The Information Office received denunciations for a wide variety of reasons, which included political activism and trade union support, being a member of a significant leftist family or having a powerful position in a public or private institution. Denunciations often involved exaggerated criminal accusations, such as robbery and illegal confiscation" (Ventura i Solé 1993: 41).

argues that the people victimized by the Right in the Western zone (e.g., Almendralejo, Fuente de Maestre, Mérida, and Badajoz) were those who carried out repressive actions in the Eastern part: the refugees who went to the Republican zones of Extremadura (fleeing from the Nationalists) "wanted to kill rightist detainees" (Espinosa 2005: 253).

According to my theory, both competition and revenge should be relevant factors in the violence that takes place in the non-initial periods of the civil war, and they should have an independent effect. Qualitative evidence supports the hypothesis that violence was indeed the result of a combination of strategic (i.e., political) and emotional (i.e., revenge) motivations. For example, according to the historian Jordi Font, who studied postwar attitudes in the province of Girona, "The denunciations made by many citizens (once the Francoist regime was in place) were not only made against those who were allegedly responsible for previous acts of violence; they were also driven by personal animosity that usually corresponded to political and ideological rivalries" (Font 2001: 118). According to the historian of El Pallars, Manuel Gimeno, people who were forcibly displaced by the Francoists in the early stages of the occupation of this territory were denounced by "old enemies and potential economic and professional competitors" (1989: 88). Linz argues that places occupied by different armed groups/blocs over the course of the civil war saw the most severe slaughter because every arrival of a new group at a locality was accompanied by "cleansing," following denunciations made by local inhabitants against certain people for their *political ideology* or for their *actions* during the previous period of the war (Linz 1996, emphasis is mine). According to Langarita (2014), those who reported others to authorities right after the Francoist victory expected to receive benefits that would be greater than the social costs of the violence.[34]

Revenge was driven by emotions such as anger, awakened by events that occurred in previous periods of the war. Anger was the consequence not only of previous lethal violence, but also of other forms of victimization (e.g., imprisonment, torture, conscription, confiscation of goods, etc.). Collectivization campaigns were a widespread phenomenon in the Republican areas of control during the war; according to Casanova (1985), there were more than 200 collectivization campaigns in the Republican zone of Aragon.[35] Landowners who produced lists of suspects that were to be used by the *Falangist* militiamen

---

34 Interestingly, Langarita (2014) also explains that the Francoist authorities did not give credence to all denunciations, and especially those made by people who were not known to be Francoists. In other words, right-wing local political elites had more agency than ordinary citizens.

35 On collectivization campaigns, much has been written by authors such as Casanova (1985), Bosch (1983), Casanova et al. (1988), or, for specific locations, by Termes (2005) for La Fatarella, and Blanchon (1987) for the county of La Cerdanya (1987). In his memoirs, Kaminski (1937/2002) describes the revolutionary process in Catalonia first hand, including the collectivization campaigns.

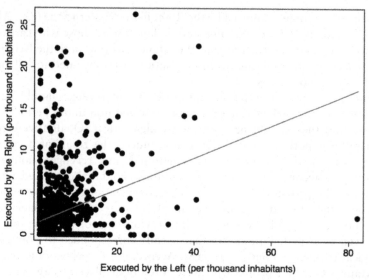

FIGURE 4.10 Executed by the Left ($t_1$) and Executed by the Right ($t_2$) in Catalonia

(Garriga 2004) were often denouncing leftists who had been involved in the confiscation of their properties.[36]

We can empirically test the revenge hypothesis by analyzing direct violence perpetrated by the Right in Catalonia after the Nationalist army conquered the territory, in $t_2$. The dependent variable is the total number of executions perpetrated by the Nationalist army and the right-wing militias during and after its occupation of the territory. Figure 4.10 shows the correlation of leftist and rightist violence (in per thousand inhabitants) for all the municipalities of Catalonia. We can observe a quite linear correspondence between these values, with only a few outliers.[37]

Table 4.6 shows the results of the multivariate analyses on *Executed by the Right* in Catalonia. The significance of the coefficient for *Executed by the Left* suggests that the revenge mechanism is explaining levels of violence: indeed, the greater the levels of leftist violence in a locality in one period, the greater the levels of rightist violence during the subsequent period. Importantly, the results indicate that the revenge mechanism also explains the occurrence of violence; thus, revenge is underlying both *occurrence* and *levels*

[36] In fact, in additional research I have conducted on the provinces of Valencia and Alicante, I find that levels of Nationalist violence were greater in localities where, during the Republican period, collectivities had been established and thus land or property had been expropriated.

[37] Those counties of Catalonia where the Left victimized much more than the Right correspond with counties close to the war frontline (e.g., Terra Alta).

TABLE 4.6 *Executed by the Right in Catalonia (ZINB)*

| | (1) | (2) | (3) |
|---|---|---|---|
| **NB: Number of Executed** | | | |
| Competition | 1.26** | 0.85* | 0.98** |
| | (0.41) | (0.37) | (0.37) |
| Frontline | 0.031 | −0.16 | −0.12 |
| | (0.22) | (0.20) | (0.20) |
| Population | 0.000025 | −0.000059** | 0.000083** |
| | (0.000086) | (0.000016) | (0.000033) |
| CNT Affiliation | 0.084 | 0.092* | 0.024$^+$ |
| | (0.071) | (0.033) | (0.013) |
| UGT Affiliation | 0.067 | 0.0063 | −0.0093 |
| | (0.10) | (0.04) | (0.032) |
| Border | −0.47$^+$ | −0.44$^+$ | −0.35* |
| | (0.25) | (0.23) | (0.17) |
| Sea | −0.088 | −0.024 | −0.11 |
| | (0.18) | (0.17) | (0.15) |
| Elevation | −0.0006 | −0.0007* | −0.00029 |
| | (0.0004) | (0.00030) | (0.00026) |
| Executed_left | | 0.019** | 0.015* |
| | | (0.0044) | (0.007) |
| Executed_left*Population | | | −0.000000056** |
| | | | (0.00000001) |
| _cons | 0.29 | 0.64 | 0.26 |
| | (0.51) | (0.39) | (0.38) |
| **Logit: Non-violence** | | | |
| Competition | −0.32 | −0.35 | −0.17 |
| | (0.84) | (0.80) | (0.80) |
| Frontline | 0.34 | 0.13 | 0.14 |
| | (0.40) | (0.43) | (0.46) |
| Population | −0.0056** | −0.0038** | −0.0034** |
| | (0.00096) | (0.00094) | (0.00084) |
| CNT Affiliation | 0.14* | 0.25** | 0.21** |
| | (0.063) | (0.074) | (0.076) |
| UGT Affiliation | 0.24 | 0.23$^+$ | 0.20 |
| | (0.15) | (0.14) | (0.14) |
| Border | −0.20 | −0.32 | −0.23 |
| | (0.51) | (0.44) | (0.39) |
| Sea | −0.61 | −0.76* | −0.77* |
| | (0.42) | (0.34) | (0.32) |
| Elevation | −0.00063 | −0.00075 | −0.00041 |
| | (0.00062) | (0.00053) | (0.00053) |
| Executed_left | | −0.67** | −0.60** |
| | | (0.16) | (0.14) |
| Executed_left*Population | | | 0.0000024** |
| | | | (0.00000044) |
| _cons | 2.79** | 3.14** | 2.70** |
| | (0.71) | (0.75) | (0.75) |
| **lnalpha** | | | |
| _cons | −0.029 | −0.26** | −0.54** |
| | (0.100) | (0.097) | (0.12) |
| N | 870 | 870 | 870 |
| ll | −1614.9 | −1557.9 | −1518.7 |

Clustered standard errors in parentheses
$^+ p < 0.10$, $^* p < 0.05$, $^{**} p < 0.01$

of violence.[38] In substantive terms, the effect of previous killings is greater than the effect of competition, suggesting that factors endogenous to the war (i.e., revenge) are more relevant than factors that are exogenous to it (i.e., political competition).[39]

In Model 3, we can see that there is an interactive effect between previous killings and size of the locality: as predicted, revenge mechanisms are stronger in smaller locations, where there is greater public knowledge about "who did what."[40]

It could be argued that the effects of *Competition* and *Executed by the Left* are endogenous and that including both of them in the same regression does not solve this problem (Achen 2005). I obtain matching estimators in which the "treatment" is having been victimized by the Left in $t_1$, balancing the sample for all the main covariates in the regressions above, including *Competition*. I find that the effect of having at least one individual killed by the Left (in $t_1$) in a locality is, on average, two individuals executed by the Right in $t_2$.[41] Thus, executions by the Left in $t_1$ have a significant impact on executions by the Right $t_2$, and this impact is independent of political competition.

To further explore the causal effect of previous executions, I identify a subset of localities that are highly similar in terms of prewar levels of political competition (i.e., they had high levels of competition), and I partition them into two groups: one that experienced *high* levels of leftist violence during the first period of the war and one that experienced *low* levels of leftist violence during the same period. I then compare the average levels of rightist executions during the second period of the war for each of these two sub-samples. Table 4.7 shows the results of this test: Sample 1 includes localities that had high levels of political competition in the prewar period[42] and experienced no violence or very low levels

---

[38] Proximity to the sea increases the likelihood of violence, which may reflect the limited possibilities of fleeing by sea during the period of Francoist control. In maritime locations, violence targets could have found themselves in a *cul-de-sac*. Proximity to the French border did permit people to flee, and that is why this variable has a negative effect on levels of violence.

[39] In Model 2, one standard deviation increase in Executed Left increases the expected count of Executed Right by 81 percent whereas a standard deviation increase in Competition increases the expected count by 0.15 percent.

[40] I test for the interactive effect of Executed by the Left and Competition, and it is not significant. Thus, it is not the case that the effect of competition increases with killings, and vice versa; these are independent factors.

[41] I use inverse probability weights, which provide a good balance; the average treatment effects among the treated is 2 (significant at the 99 percent level). I have run a similar set of analyses with Coarsened Exact Matching (Blackwell et al. 2009), and propensity score matching (with one and five nearest neighbours algorithms) the results are extremely consistent (ATET is 2.2 in both cases, significant at the 99 percent level).

[42] It includes those that have a *Competition* index equal or greater than 0.987, which is the value of the third quartile of this variable.

TABLE 4.7 *Comparison of Means Test for Sub-Samples of Competitive Municipalities with Different Levels of Leftist Violence*

|  | Sample 1 Low Leftist Violence | Sample 2 High Leftist Violence | Combined | Sample 2 – Sample 1 |
|---|---|---|---|---|
| Mean of Executed by the Right | 0.55 (0.09) | 6.58 (0.68) | 2.77 (0.32) | 6.03** (0.53) |
| Observations | 141 | 82 | 223 | |

Standard errors in parentheses
Sig Level: +.1 *.05 ** .01

of leftist executions,[43] while Sample 2 includes localities that also had high levels of competition in the prewar period, but that experienced high levels of leftist executions.[44] I calculate the difference in the mean number of executions by the Right (during period $t_2$) for each of these sub-samples, and I check to see if the difference in means is statistically significant.

The results of this test indicate that violence by the Left in $t_1$ is a key factor in explaining violence by the Right in $t_2$: indeed, localities that were highly competitive and experienced high levels of violence in $t_1$ display a much greater average number of rightist executions in $t_2$ – as compared to places that were also highly competitive but that experienced very low levels of leftist violence or no violence at all in $t_1$. The difference in the means of the two sub-samples is statistically significant at the 99 percent level. The results are very similar if we analyze non-competitive localities,[45] as shown in Table 4.8. Again, this confirms that the effect of previous killings (i.e., revenge) is independent of competition. Also, it shows that the effect of revenge is substantially stronger than the effect of political competition. In other words, in $t_2$, what explains violence in a given locality is whether there have been killings beforehand – more than political competition at the local level.[46]

[43] It includes those with no deaths or with one death.
[44] I code such localities as having had four or more deaths by the Left, which is the third quartile of the distribution of this variable.
[45] I code non-competitive those localities in which the *Competition* index was smaller than 0.9.
[46] The analyses in this subsection are all made with the electoral results of the prewar period. However, if I recalculate *Competition* and *Support for the Left* and *the Right* taking into consideration the killings of leftist supporters in the initial period of the civil war, the results are extremely consistent.

TABLE 4.8 *Comparison of Means Test for Sub-Samples of Non-Competitive Municipalities with Different Levels of Leftist Violence*

| | Sample 1 Low Leftist Violence | Sample 2 High Leftist Violence | Combined | Sample 2 – Sample 1 |
|---|---|---|---|---|
| Mean of Executed by the Right | 0.44 (0.07) | 7.56 (1.41) | 2.14 (0.38) | 7.12** (0.79) |
| Observations | 229 | 72 | 301 | |

Standard errors in parentheses
Sig Level: +.1 *.05 ** .01

## 4.3 LOCALITIES THAT FIT THE THEORY AND OUTLIERS

A closer look at some localities whose patterns of violence match the theory as well as at some outliers – namely, cases that do not fit the theory – provides additional evidence as to how local political competition between leftists and rightists gave rise to violence during the early periods of the civil war, as well as to how revenge had a strong impact on violence in later periods.

The village of Castelladral (now called Navàs), in Catalonia, is a case that fits the theory quite well. In this village, the Left lost the 1936 elections by a small margin, obtaining 47.2 percent of the vote. Conflict between workers and owners in the textile industry was intense during the Second Republic, and local historians describe a high degree of social and political polarization, which in fact affected many neighboring localities (the Bages was a markedly industrial county). The level of social conflict was such that the conservative mayor requested increased police presence in the village (Algué et al. 2015: 97–100). During the October Insurrection, in 1934, there were violent confrontations and the priest was killed. Over 45 people were detained and many leftist leaders left the village, not to return until July 1936. Some of the CNT members were imprisoned for 15 months (Algué et al. 2015: 111). After the 1936 national elections, some "normality" was restored to the political situation, but there was still much tension between leftist and rightist local elites. Shortly after the military coup, a new local council was formed, including members of leftist parties only. In the meantime, the CNT members became men of action (i.e., specialists of violence): they carried weapons and patrolled the area. Because the CNT members were local, they did not require much collaboration from the local committee in order to identify the right-wingers who were to be eliminated. However, the decision to kill some of these people was taken in town meetings (Algué et al. 2015: 139). A total of 17 people were executed by the leftist militia. When the Francoist forces conquered this village in January 1939, the former mayor, who had fled during the leftist period, was named chief of the local council (aka *junta gestora*). In the postwar period, political repression was fierce. Some people "disappeared," at least 88 men were taken to Francoist concentration camps (Algué et al. 2015: 197), and many people went into exile (including all those who had been in the militias and the local committee). Some men died in prison and five were executed as the result of accusations from residents; among them, four were CNT affiliates and one was a UGT affiliate; four were responsible for violence during the revolutionary period, but one was executed on dubious charges (local historians argue that he was probably executed because his son had been one of the CNT militiamen). A list of 15 leftist political leaders was drawn up, some of whom were sentenced to prison for 20–30 years; around 65 people were brought to military court. There were economic reprisals against leftists, and the right-wingers ruled the locality thereafter, until the end of the Francoist dictatorship in 1977.

Among all the municipalities under study, there are some outliers in the general "rivalry and revenge" patterns depicted in this chapter. One outlier is Olesa de Montserrat, a town with around 7,000 inhabitants in 1936. This was an industrial town with two large textile factories, as well as several family owned factories. Its local economy also had an important agricultural component. Tensions between the workers and the landlords were significant in Olesa during the period of the Second Republic. For example, there were strikes, which led to confrontations with the police in May 1933. New violent events occurred in December 1933, which ended up with the death of one trade unionist and were followed by detentions and by the banning of the CNT trade union in the locality. Tensions reached a peak in 1934, during the October Insurrection. Although there were very severe political confrontations (Dueñas 2007: 23), parity between Left and Right was not very significant in this locality: the Left obtained 70 percent of the votes in the 1933 national elections and 62 percent of the vote in the 1936 national elections. Following my theory, this would lead us to predict low levels of violence during the civil war. When the military coup occurred, workers (i.e., members of unions) in Olesa got weapons and they took control of the local council. As in the rest of Catalonia, a Revolutionary Committee was created, which in Olesa was led by the CNT-FAI leaders in town. Denunciations and executions started right away; the anarchist militias established systems of surveillance to impede people from escaping. Because the CNT-FAI militiamen were from the locality, they had great inside knowledge and did not need as much civilian collaboration. They managed to kill 36 people during the first months of the war: most of the victims were affiliates of right-wing parties or right-wing associations. Even though several members of the local committee tried to avoid violence (Dueñas 2007: 123), they did not manage to impede it because the most radical members of the militias managed to carry out the violence. In other words, Olesa is a case in which civilian local agency could have constrained violence, but it did not because militiamen were from the locality and they could overrule the desires of the (non-anarchist) local political elites, who did not have much interest in killing people. Thus, the presence of the CNT-FAI in the locality is behind the high levels of violence in Olesa, which the theory would under-predict. However, Olesa does fit the theory in that, when the locality changed hands and the Francoists achieved control of it (on January 25, 1939), revenge took place. Those who had lost their relatives at the hands of the militiamen denounced other individuals in the locality, including people who had not been involved in violence during the previous period. They also promoted the repression of the wives of some of these militiamen, who were shaved, forced to drink laxative oils, and paraded around the village (Dueñas 2007: 23). The desire for revenge among inhabitants of Olesa was such that 12 detainees were executed on their way to Barcelona, where they were supposed to be judged by a Military Court. According to Dueñas (2007: 335), the officer (Mariano Pérez) was pressured to execute them in the cemetery of a nearby locality and some of the neighbours even participated in the executions. A total of 24 people from Olesa were executed by the Nationalists (Solé i Sabaté 2000).

Another interesting outlier is the county of El Pallars (located in the Pyrenees, bordering Aragon and France), where the Right was very violent even though the leftists had not killed many civilians in this area. This case does not completely fit the theory because violence in $t_2$ was highly disproportional to violence in $t_1$. As stated in Chapter 2, because of escalation, violence might increase in each round of violence. Yet, in the case of Catalonia, we find a lot of proportionality throughout the region, except in El Pallars. The leftists had killed a total of nine people in this county; and while registered Francoist violence amounted to a total of ten deaths, non-registered Francoist violence was much greater. Gimeno (1989) estimates that 75 people were killed by the Francoists in this county, most of them in extra-legal killings. The Francoist general who conquered the area ordered indiscriminate assassinations, including pregnant women and elders. Also, at least one young woman was raped (Gimeno 1989; Barbal 1996; Witnesses 53, 54, 55, 56, 57). Local historians still wonder about the reasons behind this violence, but the presence of leftist guerrillas (i.e., *maquis*) in this mountainous area probably accounts for it. As explained in Chapter 3, guerrilla tactics were rare in the Spanish Civil War, and they concentrated in some mountainous areas such as El Pallars.[47] But the Francoist military leaders attempted to eradicate the guerrillas using "scorched earth" counterinsurgency tactics, which led to the terrorization of local civilians with indiscriminate violence, torture, and even sexual violence. The idea was not only to catch the *maquis*,

---

[47] Similarly, during the American Civil War (also a conventional civil war), high civilian victimization in Missouri was linked to the guerrilla warfare that took place there and in Eastern Kansas (Edwards 1877; McPherson 1988; Fellman 1989). The Union army was brutal in Missouri (Fellman 1989; Maben 2008), although 80 percent of white males voted for the Union in the 1861 elections (i.e., only 20 percent of voters had secessionist preferences).

but also to pre-empt local collaboration with them. In some cases, violence against civilians was a direct response to guerrilla attacks of *maquis* against Francoist military posts (Gimeno 1989). In a nutshell, El Pallars is an outlier to the logic of revenge because of the nature of the terrain and the guerrilla warfare that took place in this area (with ambushes and terrorist attacks), and the brutal attempts of Francoist armed forces to defeat the *maquis*.

## 4.4 ADDITIONAL EMPIRICAL CHECKS

Because I am using observational data, causal identification issues could be raised: for example, an omitted variable could be explaining both prewar distribution of power and violence. Absent a valid instrumental variable for *Competition*, I deal with this issue by checking if the results are robust when introducing county dummies in the regressions. This is quite an adequate way to control for a potential omitted variable bias (Clarke 2005). In Spain, counties are an economically significant administrative unit; therefore, all localities in a county tend to share economic characteristics that could potentially be having an impact on their levels of prewar competition as well as on violence in $t_1$. By including county dummies in the regressions, I look into the determinants of violence within these economic units and therefore control for the effect of these potential omitted variables.[48] With the county fixed effects, *Competition* remains statistically significant in all the regions under study (see Table A.4.1 of the Appendix).[49] I have also checked the determinants of *Competition* (Table A.4.5 of the Appendix) and none of the variables in the models significantly explains variation in levels of competition across localities.

---

[48] This type of strategy has been used by other scholars dealing with similar issues (e.g., Chacón et al. 2011).

[49] In addition, in order to make sure that the results above are not driven by the specification of the explanatory models, I run some alternative models. First, I run NB regressions with the same specifications above, and they provide consistent results. Second, I run a set of ZINB and NB regressions without including the variable *CNT Affiliation*. As we have seen, this variable correlates with the dependent variable *Executed by the Left* (it is a sufficient but not a necessary condition for this violence). The results do not change with this specification of the model(s), and, in fact, the estimate of the variable *Competition* has greater substantive and statistical significance when CNT is not included in the vector of covariates. Finally, I run OLS models with a normalized dependent variable (percent executed in a locality), instead of the count models. The results are broadly robust and they confirm the relevance of the variable *Competition* in explaining direct violence. The results are also consistent when we do not include *Elevation* in the main analyses: in this way, we have fewer missing cases in the regressions (n = 1,052). Finally, I have also done an assessment of fit of the ZINB models to the actual executions in Catalonia. The models fit the data well except in urban locations, where they over-predict killings. The latter indicates that, as expected, the theoretical model works better in smaller locations – where interpersonal relations are tighter and civilian collaboration may be more crucial for the perpetration of violence.

Table A.4.2 of the Appendix of this chapter shows the results of the ZINB models of leftist violence in Catalonia with the variables *Longitude* and *Latitude* (instead of the dummies *Border, Sea, Frontline*), with the index of *Competition* calculated in absolute (instead of quadratic) values, and with *Percentage Literacy* as a control variable. It also includes models with two additional independent variables: *Competition33* (that is, competition measured with electoral data from the 1933 elections instead of 1936), and Reynal-Querol's (2002) index of polarization *(Polarization33)*, also calculated with electoral data of 1933.[50] I find that *Competition33* is not statistically significant to explain number of executions by the Left in Catalonia, and neither is *Polarization33*.

Spatial autocorrelation can bias any type of regression analysis with geographical data (Anselin et al. 2004), and there are different techniques that permit us to control for it. I conduct different analyses with polygon and point spatial data in order to ensure that the results above are not biased due to any type of spatial dependence between municipalities. Also, the spatial analyses allow me to explore the possibility that there is some sort of contagion or neighboring effect between units, e.g., that violence in one locality has an impact on the probability of violence in nearby municipalities. A summary of the spatial analyses are included in the Appendix. The results provide robustness to the results in this chapter. In addition, an interesting pattern arises from the spatial analyses is the following: while spatial dependence is not the norm in the violence data, there is some spatial dependence in battlefield zones, which is consistent with the idea that violence in this region was determined by the military conquest. Violence in the battlefield areas of Aragon was predominantly determined by the paths that were followed by the different militia and units of the army that conquered the territory; being located in one place or another was highly decisive for a municipality's fate, and this is reflected in the spatial dependency of the data.

## 4.5  CONCLUDING REMARKS

Using extensive qualitative and quantitative evidence from the Spanish Civil War, this chapter has shown that in civil wars where the two sides have been mobilized before the war's outbreak, armed groups perpetrate violence against

[50] Reynal-Querol's polarization index seeks to capture how far the distribution of the groups is from the (1/2, 0, 0, ...0, 1/2) distribution, which represents the highest level of polarization (Montalvo and Reynal-Querol 2005: 798). I calculate this index with data from the 1933 elections because many parties were competing individually in those elections: that is, not under the umbrella of pre-electoral coalitions (vis-à-vis the 1936 elections, where all parties competed with a coalition). The polarization index captures the same as *Competition* in the context of two-party systems such as the 1936 elections.

supporters and sympathizers of the enemy group.[51] However, they manage to assassinate these individuals when they are able to count on collaboration from local supporters and meet with acquiescence on the part of the local population. In areas of military contestation, local supporters of armed groups collaborate with them regardless of local political configurations: they try to maximize the probability of their group establishing military control of the area. Yet, when an armed group has already full military control of an area, local political elites collaborate following other considerations. Specifically, they follow their political interests, maximizing their probability of political control in the postwar period. This futurity consideration leads violence to be greater in places where rival political groups are at parity, for these are places where violence against political enemies will provide greater returns to local political elites.

At the same time, there are dynamics of revenge that are very significant in explaining violence in non-initial war periods. Victimization in an early period promotes local collaboration and acquiescence toward a rival group's actions in a later period. This makes violence in subsequent periods to be highly related to violence in earlier periods of the civil war, as is the case of violence by the Francoists in Catalonia, which is significantly correlated to levels of violence perpetrated by leftist armed forces before the Francoists entered the region.

The "rivalry and revenge" framework better explains violence in smaller locations than in big cities: on the one hand, if we look at the fit of the statistical models, they perform better in villages than in large cities; on the other hand, the effect of revenge is more intense in smaller locations. This finding offers an interesting lesson, which is that violence is not necessarily lower in places where civilians have greater capacity for intervention (potentially, in smaller places), but the other way around; there is a somewhat "dark side" of civilian agency, which is that people can be malicious toward their neighbors (e.g., Sender Barayón 1986; Seidman 2002; Su 2011).

Then next chapter addresses the determinants of indirect violence, and it explores data from bombardments (i.e., aerial and naval strikes) perpetrated by fascist armed forces in Catalonia during the Spanish Civil War.

---

[51] Direct violence against civilians peaks soon after the beginning of the war or soon after the conquest of a new piece of territory. In Spain, leftist violence peaked during the summer of 1936, across all the Republican rearguard territories; it decreased in the fall of 1936. In a similar vein, the rightists would be very violent every time they conquered a new piece of the Spanish territory: violence would concentrate in the early months and years of conquest (see Figure 3.2 for Catalonia). This suggests that once committed supporters were eliminated, violence became less crucial for armed groups.

# 5

# Bombardments During the Spanish Civil War

"I heard an old man saying that the fighter planes had very meticulously bombed the most central points of the city, as if they had calculated it millimeter by millimeter."

Montserrat Roig, *Ramona, Adéu*

## 5.1 INTRODUCTION

In Chapter 2, I developed a theory on the determinants of direct violence in civil wars, with a focus on conventional civil wars. In this chapter, I extend my theoretical framework to indirect violence, and I generate a set of hypotheses that are tested with data on bombardments perpetrated by fascist armed forces (under Franco's leadership) in the region of Catalonia during the Spanish Civil War.

Following the taxonomy presented in Chapter 2, indirect violence is perpetrated with heavy weaponry (e.g., bomber aircraft, field artillery, naval gunfire) and does not require face-to-face interaction with victims; indirect violence can consist of aerial, artillery, or maritime bombardments.

As explained in Chapter 2, there are two main dimensions over which indirect violence differs from direct violence, and that make their respective theoretical explanation necessarily distinct: on the one hand, direct violence is perpetrated by an armed group in the territories they control, whereas indirect violence is mostly perpetrated in territories under the rival's control. On the other hand, direct violence implies an interaction between armed groups and civilians: this is not the case for indirect violence, which therefore leaves less room for civilian agency.

The use of air power became widespread during World War II, thanks to the technological development during World War I (Overy, 1980). The Spanish Civil War was the first conflict of the twentieth century in which air forces played an essential role (Payne, 2010: 471). Many bombs were dropped on cities full of noncombatants (Balcells 1987: 34; Leitz 1999). Since then, bombings against civilian targets have been frequent in any war where armed groups have access to air power. Artillery is much older than air power, but the underlying trend in artillery has been an increase in range, precision, and payloads, which has enabled it to reach "strategic" targets – deep inside enemy lines – rather than targets on the front or its immediate rear and so it can work much as a substitute for air power.

In the existing scholarly literature, bombings against civilians have often been interpreted as a bargaining and coercive tool (Pape 1996; Valentino 2004; Downes 2008) or as a tactic to win new territories (Downes 2008; Cochran and Downes 2012). They have been regarded as instrumental both from the perspective of eliminating the enemy's resources and destroying morale (Arreguín-Toft 2001; Pape 2006; Friedrich 2006). Arreguín-Toft argues that in asymmetric conflict, by means of barbarism (i.e., attacking civilians) the strong actor seeks to coerce its weaker opponent into changing its behavior. The goal is to destroy an adversary's will and capacity to fight (2001: 102). Downes (2008), for his part, argues that belligerents resort to targeting enemy civilians with coercive purposes when defeating military forces proves very difficult; killing civilians is a way to impose costs that cannot be imposed in the battlefield. In international security studies, aerial bombardments have not generally been interpreted as a tactic to annihilate particular groups of individuals, nor as a way to punish specific localities and communities. In the context of an international war, all civilians on the enemy's side are likely to be considered supporters of the enemy (Friedrich 2006), so they are often considered equally susceptible to being targeted. A few authors have, however, considered the targeting of specific collectivities in "eliminationist campaigns," which tend to occur in wars of territorial annexation, and are aimed at removing members of a target group from a certain piece of territory (Downes 2008; Cochran and Downes 2012).

In the study of civil wars, few authors have highlighted ideological factors as relevant in explaining bombings and other forms of indirect violence. For example, in their study of bombings in Vietnam, Kocher et al. (2011) show that they tended to occur in political strongholds of one side or the other. The counterinsurgency literature has, however, mostly focused on the consequences of violence for war outcomes, either with a focus on combat and strategic effectiveness (Arreguín-Toft 2001; Allen 2007; Downes 2007; Lyall 2009; Kocher et al. 2011; Condra and Shapiro 2012; Toft and Zhukov 2015), or with a more specific focus on attitudes toward or support for armed groups (Kalyvas 2006; Berman et al. 2011).

## 5.2   IS INDIRECT VIOLENCE NECESSARILY INDISCRIMINATE?

What I call indirect violence is often more indiscriminate than direct violence, but bombardments and other forms of indirect violence often display some degree of selectivity. As I explained in Chapter 2, we can think of the repertoire of indirect attacks in a continuum: from less to more selective. Attacks with precision-guided munition or drones can be very selective (i.e., targeting individuals), but airstrikes can be quite selective too because they can attack certain groups. As Pape explains, "bombing can focus on specific categories of targets, attacking either political, economic, population, or military targets in isolation or combination" (Pape 1996: 45). Since the Spanish Civil War and WWII, technological developments in warfare has increasingly allowed for indirect violence to be more precise, and therefore, potentially more selective.

In previous theoretical approaches, such as Kalyvas (2006), violence is considered indiscriminate insofar as the selection process does not take place at the individual level. Also, indiscriminate violence is normally understood as a consequence of information scarcity (and individual vulnerability) in zones under enemy control (Kalyvas 2006; Lyall 2009; Kocher et al. 2011). However, there often exists some information in zones under enemy control (for example, through fifth-columnists) and political allegiances can be used as cues for targeting at a collective level (Downes 2008; Steele 2009; Balcells and Steele 2016). I argue that if violence is intentionally targeting groups of individuals, we should recognize that it is not truly indiscriminate.

Kalyvas (2006) has explained that, while indiscriminate violence is counterproductive, selective violence can induce compliance toward the armed group perpetrating it. From a theoretical viewpoint, the effects of selective indirect violence can resemble those of selective direct violence in that they can both compel the targeted individuals to comply with the perpetrating group: when individuals are targeted because of their political loyalties, they can "learn" that their loyalties are "wrong-headed" and they can attempt to change them. Alternatively, they may choose to flee and seek protection elsewhere (Steele 2009).[1] Yet, shifts in loyalty and displacements can occur more easily in irregular wars than in conventional ones, in which civilians are "trapped" behind the frontlines, where rival armed groups cannot offer them protection. In contrast with irregular wars, in civil wars, with stable frontlines and large areas under full military control, the main objective of bombings cannot possibly be to provoke defections toward the perpetrating group because individuals cannot easily switch sides. Also, if the levels of prewar mobilization are high, shifts in loyalty are generally unlikely and non-credible, regardless of the type of civil war.

## 5.3   ACCOUNTING FOR INDIRECT VIOLENCE AGAINST CIVILIANS

In a country undergoing civil war, it is perhaps banal to say that armed groups are interested in using airstrikes and shellings against some territories more than others based on purely military motives. As Hegre et al. (2007: 5) explain,

---

[1] Displacement is not an obvious safe choice for civilians. During the Spanish Civil War, for example, the Francoists attacked refugee convoys using aerial bombardments: on the road from Malaga to Almeria, thousands of refugees were bombed by the Italian airforce and the Francoist navy (Prieto and Barranquero 2007).

in any war "both parties to a conflict will target strategic locations such as crossroads, bridges, ports and airports held by the opponent and invest resources to protect them". I do not dispute this view, but I argue that local political factors also weigh heavily in the targeting decisions of armed groups. Bombing raids can deliberately target collectivities or groups of people, and armed groups can use indirect violence to achieve the goal of eliminating enemies behind the frontlines.

Let us imagine the same country, civil war, and territory discussed in Chapter 2. Armed groups $A$ and $B$ fight a conventional war with heavy weaponry and relatively stable frontlines. $B$ is a well-equipped armed group with weaponry that allows shelling from land (in places close to the frontline), from sea (in places near the shore), and from the air (presumably anywhere). In addition to using this technological capacity to attack $A$ on the frontlines and/or in militarily strategic enclaves (e.g., harbors, nodal train stations, or roads), $B$ can choose to deploy some of its resources to attack civilian locations in $A$'s territory behind the frontlines. This can potentially diminish $A$'s morale and push them to surrender.[2] Yet, not all localities behind the enemy's lines will be bombed. Selecting localities to target will be necessary for armed groups due to limited resources; furthermore, genocide is not always in the strategic interest of military leaders (Valentino et al. 2004; Straus 2015). Hence, these indirect attacks, however barbaric, are likely to be perpetrated on a selective basis, with the groups deciding to target localities with certain profiles. In a context of political mobilization, $B$ is ultimately interested in eliminating highly mobilized $A$ supporters, who are potentially offering logistical, material, and informational support to $A$, or who will pose a potential threat at a future time, if and when the group comes to rule this territory. Given the nature of attacks with heavy weaponry such as bombs (not as precise as direct attacks), armed groups can be relatively confident that they are targeting enemy supporters only when attacking locations with relatively large proportions of such supporters. Thus, $B$ is likely to attack places with greater proportions of $A$'s sympathizers.

*Hypothesis 5.1:* Ceteris paribus, the greater the proportion of supporters of a given group in a locality, the greater the likelihood that a locality will be the target of lethal indirect violence by the rival armed group.

The relationship between level of support for the rival group and indirect violence is likely to be positive, but it might not be linear, as this violence might increase at the highest levels of support for the rival group, where the odds of targeting rival supporters are much greater.

Although frontlines are typically quite stable in conventional wars, information on violent events, the brutality of attacks, and other points of concern tend

---

[2] We can assume that $B$ will not use indirect violence in their own rearguard territory as this could damage their infrastructures and harm their resources, as well as their supporters.

to travel fast. Refugees and messengers have usually served as a source of information regarding events occurring on the other side of the frontline; in current
times, mass communications (e.g., radio, TV, internet) also serve this purpose.
Armed groups can use this information to retaliate for previous killings of
their supporters, for example, in places where their supporters are known to
have been repressed and victimized; they might be willing to punish these areas
collectively and send a signal that such actions will not be tolerated. In addition, armed groups' leaders might be driven by a desire to avenge the killing
of their supporters (Petersen 2011), or to respond to the vengeful emotions of
their "domestic audiences" (Fearon 1994). Stein (2015) has shown that leaders often respond to vengeful desires of citizens by using violence against their
international enemies; something similar could occur in the context of domestic conflict.[3] Following this assumption, we can conjecture that there will be a
greater incidence of indirect violence in places where armed groups have been
more violent against supporters of the group dropping the bombs:

*Hypothesis 5.2:* *The greater the number of killings perpetrated by one group
in a locality, ceteris paribus, the greater the likelihood that this locality will be
the target of lethal indirect violence by the rival armed group.*

Retaliatory attacks can be expected to come into play after the civil war has
been underway for some time and after executions or massacres (by the rival
group) have taken place.

Below, I use evidence from the Spanish Civil War in order to test these two
hypotheses. As explained in Chapter 3, the Nationalists perpetrated indirect
violence by means of aerial bombings and they did so more extensively than
the Republicans. The intervention of the German Condor Legion and Mussolini's air forces (*Regia Aeronautica*) contributed to the overwhelming use
of indirect violence by the Francoist side in contrast to the more limited use
of indirect violence by the Republicans (Payne 2004).[4] Furthermore, fascist
armed forces showed less restraint than the Spanish Republicans in the use of
airstrikes against civilian populated areas, as illustrated in the well-known and

---

[3] Armed groups can punish locations where violence on the part of their rivals has been reported,
whether such reports are based in fact or merely rumor. For example, Raymond Carr argues
that, during the Spanish Civil War, the Right invented atrocity stories, such as the rape of nuns
and the murder of priests, in order to produce an atmosphere in which extreme acts of vengeance
could be carried out (Carr, in Brenan 2014/1943: X).

[4] Again, external support on the part of fascist powers was a major determinant of the insurgents' victory in the Spanish Civil War. The Germans and the Italians used these airstrikes to
experiment and test bomber planes such as the *Junker 87 Stuka*, which would then be used in
WWII.

horrific case of *Guernica* and the airstrikes over the city of Barcelona in March 1938 (Marimon 2013).[5]

When it came to indirect attacks, the main commanders of each army were the ones who had the most agency. Indeed, despite the alliance with Italy and Germany, Franco exercised tight control over the actions of these foreign armed forces. Solé i Sabaté and Villarroya explain that General Franco had the power to decide whether or not to bomb rearguard cities (full of civilians): "During the years 1937 and 1938, Franco gave the order not to bomb any urban center without his explicit consent" (2003: 78).[6] While no agency is attributed to civilians in these attacks, sometimes local "fifth columnists" played a significant role by providing information to military commanders (see below). However, the role of civilian agency was much more limited in the perpetration of bombings than in the perpetration of executions and massacres.

## 5.4   BOMBARDMENTS IN CATALONIA DURING THE SPANISH CIVIL WAR

Historians of the Spanish Civil War usually understand bombings in rearguard territories either in terms of military targets or as distributed across localities somewhat randomly, with the sole aim of terrorizing the population. For example, Leitz (1999) argues: "Bombing raids on Spanish cities such as Madrid and Barcelona were often undertaken without any military targets in mind, but simply to frighten the Republican population into submission" (Leitz 1999: 130). Solé i Sabaté and Villarroya also suggest that bombs were dropped in rearguard territories quite indiscriminately, without clear military objectives (1986: 235).

I posit that the variation of bombings in the rearguard territory cannot be fully explained in terms of military factors, and that it can be explained with a "rivalry and revenge" theoretical framework. Following this framework, in early phases of the war, groups are expected to target areas dominated by supporters of the rival group; in later phases of the war, groups are also expected to undertake retaliatory attacks and to drop bombs in localities with a concentration of rivals who have victimized their own supporters.

In the empirical analyses included in this chapter, I use data on all 1,062 municipalities of Catalonia. The Francoists, aided by Italian and German air forces, continuously bombed this region until February 1939, when they finally secured full occupation of Catalonia. While the Republican army also bombed localities within the territory of Catalonia, they did so almost exclusively in locations on the frontline and in places affected by battles at the end of the

---

[5] For a detailed account of the Guernica attack by the Condor Legion, see, among others, Solé i Sabaté and Villarroya (2003: 82–92), Vidal (1997), or Casanova (2013: 59–60).

[6] Solé i Sabaté and Villarroya (1986: 133) argue that Franco's brother, Ramon, was in charge of giving orders to the Italians.

military conflict.[7] These Republican bombings, which caused an estimated total of 18 deaths in Catalonia (Solé i Sabaté and Villarroya 1986: 237), will thus not be taken into account in this chapter.

I use data from Catalonia because it is the only Spanish territory for which I have been able to collect fine-grained (i.e., municipal-level) data on bombardments during the civil war. Solé i Sabaté and Villarroya (1986) have collected disaggregated local level data on the number of bombings as well as on the number of lethal casualties directly linked to these attacks. These authors have relied on different primary sources including the civil registries in Catalonia, documentation from Catalonia's Defense Council (*Junta de Defensa Pasiva de Cataluña*) – located in the National Archive of the Spanish Civil War in Salamanca – and local archives and newspapers published at the time. The triangulation method pursued by these historians offers us a great deal of reliability. To the best of my knowledge, there is not similar fine-grained data on bombardments for any other Spanish regions.

Table 5.1 shows the distribution of bombings by the Nationalists across Catalan municipalities (the geographical distribution of bombings in Catalonia is mapped in Figure 3.5, in Chapter 3). Following the data collection in Solé i Sabaté and Villarroya (1986), bombings are coded such that each event captures a whole military operation, which may imply more than one strike. We can observe that 87 percent of Catalan municipalities were not bombed during the Spanish Civil War; others were targeted by a significant number of bombings. The estimations are of 700 bombing raids killing approximately 4,752 people. Many bombings targeted military outposts (many of those that took place in coastal regions were attempts to reconquer Catalonia from the sea), so deadly bombings were highly concentrated: 144 localities were targeted by bombings causing at least one death, 79 localities were affected by bombings causing at least five deaths, and 48 with bombings leading to 10 deaths or more.[8] The city of Barcelona, which suffered a total of 212 bombings (30 percent of them), is an outlier in the distribution.[9]

Although Catalonia is the empirical focus of this chapter, we can assume that the patterns observed in this region are generalizable to other areas of Spain. Existing qualitative evidence suggests that patterns of bombings in other Republican rearguard territories were similar. Regarding Nationalist bombings in Madrid (autumn–winter 1936), Solé i Sabaté and Villarroya (2003) write: "the neighborhood least affected by the bombs in Madrid was that of Salamanca, which was the one inhabited by many of the supporters of the

---

[7] Specifically, the locations affected were *Gandesa, Horta de Sant Joan, Móra d'Ebre, Valls, Serós, and Sort* (Solé i Sabaté and Villarroya 1987).

[8] Note that those who were wounded in these strikes are not counted in these figures.

[9] Albertí and Albertí (2013), who do not group the different strikes under the same attack, report 385 aerial and naval attacks in Barcelona, with 2,750 deaths, over 7,000 wounded, and 1,800 buildings destroyed.

TABLE 5.1 *Distribution of Bombings in Catalonia*

| Total Bombings | Frequency | Percentage |
|---|---|---|
| 0 | 920 | 86.83 |
| 1 | 78 | 7.34 |
| 2 | 23 | 2.17 |
| 3 | 9 | 0.85 |
| 4 | 12 | 1.13 |
| 5 | 2 | 0.19 |
| 7 | 5 | 0.47 |
| 9 | 3 | 0.28 |
| 11 | 1 | 0.09 |
| 12 | 1 | 0.09 |
| 13 | 2 | 0.19 |
| 14 | 1 | 0.09 |
| 15 | 1 | 0.09 |
| 21 | 1 | 0.09 |
| 39 | 1 | 0.09 |
| 89 | 1 | 0.09 |
| 212 | 1 | 0.09 |
| Total | 1,062 | 100 |

rebellion. Franco gave instructions not to bomb it" (56). Something similar happened in the city of Barcelona, where the wealthiest neighborhoods were the least affected by the bombardments. Conversely, one of the most affected neighborhoods in Barcelona was the Barceloneta (Marimon 2013), next to the harbor. In this neighborhood, the leftist coalition had overwhelmingly won the 1936 elections (Vilanova 2005).

I have argued that, in conventional civil wars, indirect violence in rearguard territories is likely to be determined by a combination of military, political, and revenge-related factors. For the sake of operationalization, and given the absence of more suitable indicators, I use geo-referencing and geographic variables (i.e., elevation, proximity to sea, to the French border and to the frontline – and, alternatively, latitude and longitude) to measure the "military value" of the localities. These are suitable indicators insofar as the military significance of a given locality has to do with its geographical location and terrain. I also include the size – proxied by population – of the locality in order to account for the presence of industrial resources and the coercive effect of bombing cities: densely populated locations are more likely to be targeted if the armed group intends to diminish the morale of the enemy (Friedrich 2006) and coerce them.

Political allegiances (manifested, for example, in electoral contests) can be very informative with regard to determining where an armed group's supporters reside: I incorporate different indicators of the political characteristics of the municipalities, including political competition, trade union affiliation, and percentage of support for the political blocs in the February 1936 national elections. Following my theory, indicators of political dominance, in contrast to indicators of political competition, should be significant in explaining indirect violence; this differs from the case of direct violence, which is explained by political competition (and not dominance).

I rely on data on executions committed by the rival group (i.e., leftist militias and the Republican army) in the previous period of the war in order to proxy revenge motives by the Nationalists, who were the ones dropping the bombs in Catalonia. The factors behind executions by the Left in a locality are different from those accounting for bombings by the Right, so there should be no endogeneity issues. Also, most executions in Catalonia took place in 1936, whereas most bombings took place after 1936, so executions cannot be endogenous to bombardments.[10]

The results in this chapter are displayed in two parts: first I present a set of multivariate analyses including military and political variables as the main correlates of bombings, and then I present a set of analyses building on the first model and incorporating the proxy for revenge. In the main set of analyses, I use different dummy variables to capture the occurrence of bombardments: *Bombdum* is a dummy with value 1 if the locality suffered a strike and 0 otherwise; *Bombdum1* is a dummy with value 1 if the locality suffered a strike that resulted in at least one civilian death and 0 otherwise; *Bombdum5* is a dummy with value 1 if the locality suffered a strike that resulted in at least five civilian deaths and 0 otherwise. Finally, *Bombdum10*, captures bombings involving at least 10 civilian deaths. By taking out bombings that involved few civilian deaths, I can better capture those attacks that did not target infrastructure, roads, and harbors. This is a rough way to clean the dependent variable, but it is the best option for identifying attacks that intentionally target civilians. I run robustness checks with different versions of the dependent variable: *Total Bombings*, which captures the total number of bombings in a locality, and *Killed Bombings*, which measures the total number of people in a locality killed in bombings. I run logit models for the dummy dependent variables, and negative binomial models for the count variables.

## Political Variables

The main independent variable in the analyses is a measure of the percentage of support for the left-wing bloc in the 1936 national elections (*Support Left*), which is expected to have a positive effect on bombings perpetrated by right-wing forces. In the main analyses, I include measures for proximity to the *Border*, to the *Sea* and to the civil war's *Frontline* to capture the geostrategic value of the locality; in alternative models, I use *Longitude* and

---

[10] Below I discuss a number of retaliatory mass killings that took place after bombardments, but these represent a narrow set of cases.

*Latitude.* In the case of Catalonia, proximity to the coastline should increase bombings, as many were perpetrated by Italian forces based in Mallorca, and naval attacks against harbors also were frequent. Proximity to the front-line and the French border are also likely to increase bombings, for these are more likely strategic locations. I include *Elevation* as a control variable because I expect higher and therefore more mountainous locations to be less important from a militaristic perspective, and therefore less prone to being targeted; more mountainous locations are more isolated and less likely to be crucial communication nodes or industrial centers.[11] The variable *Population* (in thousands of inhabitants) allows us to control for the size or level of urbanization of a given locality, which – as explained above – should have a positive effect on bombings. *CNT Affiliation* and *UGT Affiliation* are included as additional proxies for the local presence of strong supporters of the Left: I expect them to have a positive impact on bombings in a given locality.[12]

The results depicted in Table 5.2, are supportive of the main hypothesis in this chapter: percentage support for leftist parties in the 1936 elections has a significant and positive effect on the likelihood of bombings in a local-ity. The effect is stronger for more lethal bombings, which is consistent with the intuition that bombings behind the frontlines had an underlying "political cleansing" motivation. These results are consistent when estimating negative binomial models on total number of bombings in a locality, as well as on total number of people killed by bombs in a locality (Table A.5.1 of the Appendix). The results do not vary when Barcelona city is excluded from the analyses and, notably, *Support Left* remains significant when we run the analyses with county fixed effects, which allow to eliminate potential omitted variables bias.

Figure 5.1 depicts the predicted likelihood of bombings by levels of support for the Left (with all other variables set at their sample mean levels), for all bombings as well as for bombings that killed at least 10 people. The relation-ship between political support for the rival and indirect violence is positive, and it is not completely monotonic, as bombings decrease at the highest levels of support for the Left (this is, however, mostly due to the fact that there are not many localities in the dataset with more than 80 percent of support for the leftist bloc).

---

[11] In the regressions, the inclusion of the variable capturing elevation leads to the loss of 18 percent of the observations. Yet, if we run the same regressions without this variable the results do not vary and are even more supportive of my hypotheses.

[12] In robustness checks, I test for the alternative hypothesis that parity between groups – and not political dominance on the part of the enemy group – explains the likelihood of a locality being targeted in bombardments, with the independent variable *Competition* (details on this variable are included in chapter 4). This variable is not significant, which allows me to reject the hypothesis that the factors accounting for indirect violence are the same as those accounting for direct violence.

TABLE 5.2 *Logit on Lethal Bombings in Catalonia*

| | Bombing | Bombing 1 | Bombing 5 | Bombing 10 |
|---|---|---|---|---|
| Support Left | 0.014[+] | 0.015[*] | 0.022[*] | 0.032[**] |
| | (0.0071) | (0.0066) | (0.009) | (0.011) |
| Population (*1000) | 0.56[*] | 0.38 | 0.34 | 0.35 |
| | (0.23) | (0.30) | (0.28) | (0.32) |
| CNT Affiliation | 0.036 | 0.049 | 0.083[*] | 0.081[*] |
| | (0.034) | (0.036) | (0.035) | (0.035) |
| UGT Affiliation | 0.15[+] | 0.15[*] | 0.22[*] | 0.28[**] |
| | (0.090) | (0.07) | (0.09) | (0.10) |
| Border | −0.25 | 0.027 | −0.10 | −0.15 |
| | (0.40) | (0.34) | (0.42) | (0.51) |
| Sea | −0.20 | −0.061 | 0.26 | 0.17 |
| | (0.38) | (0.40) | (0.40) | (0.51) |
| Frontline | −0.016 | 0.32 | −0.052 | −0.028 |
| | (0.30) | (0.31) | (0.38) | (0.45) |
| Elevation | −0.0016[*] | −0.00087[+] | −0.0010[+] | −0.0009 |
| | (0.0006) | (0.00047) | (0.0006) | (0.0007) |
| _cons | −2.73[**] | −2.90[**] | −4.11[**] | −5.41[**] |
| | (0.43) | (0.50) | (0.66) | (0.97) |
| N | 870 | 870 | 870 | 870 |
| ll | −285.2 | −312.3 | −191.8 | −122.8 |

Clustered standard errors in parentheses
$^{+}p < 0.10, {}^{*}p < 0.05, {}^{**}p < 0.01$

In addition, the results in Table 5.2 indicate that lethal bombardments are more likely in localities with larger proportions of trade union affiliates. Overall, these results support the hypothesis that armed groups use bombings to target political enemies. Only by bombing enemy enclaves can groups maximize the odds of harming the enemy's supporters while minimizing the risk of harming their own supporters.

In order to better identify the causal relationship between *Support for the Left* in a locality and *Bombings* by the fascists in Catalonia, I obtain matching estimators of causal effects. I code all localities in which the Left obtained 50 percent or more of the vote in the 1936 elections as "leftist" localities, and I consider this as the treatment. By matching localities in all the other covariates (*Population, CNT* and *UGT Affiliation, Longitude, Latitude,* and *Elevation*) using different algorithms, I estimate the effect of being a leftist locality on number of bombings, on the one hand, and on total number of people killed in bombings, on the other. There is a significant (although not very large) effect of being a leftist locality on total number of bombings as well as on total number of killed in bombings. For example, using propensity score matching with one nearest neighbor, the average treatment effect on the treated is 0.47 (significant at the 95 percent level) for total number of bombings, and 2.5 (significant

**Bombings**

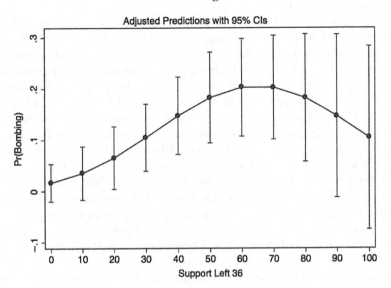

**Bombings with at least 10 deaths**

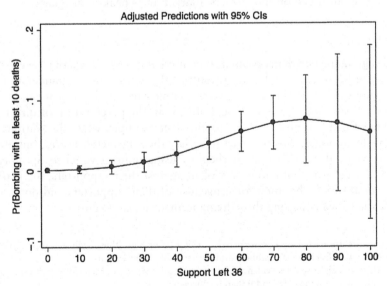

FIGURE 5.1 Fascist Bombings by Levels of Support for the Left

at the 99 percent level) for total number of people killed in bombings. Thus, leftist localities had, on average, between two and three more people killed in bombings than non-leftist localities.[13]

As we have seen in Chapter 4, many primary and secondary historical sources on the Spanish Civil War suggest that individuals were targeted largely because of their political loyalties. However, I have not found official military files with explicit resolutions on bombing locations based on the political identities of their citizens. This is partly due to the fact that access to many military documents is still blocked. Recent evidence provided by Guixé (2012) shows that there was an important network of fifth-columnists in Catalonia who provided relevant information to the Francoist commanders in Salamanca, who then relayed it to the German and Italian air bases in Mallorca, with information on where to bomb. This network of spies received the name of *Servicio de Información de la Frontera Nordeste de España* (*SIFNE*), and the information it provided to the fascists included more than 300 maps and more than 220 targets in Barcelona city.[14] In one of the several maps retrieved by Solé i Sabaté and Villarroya (1986) from Francoist intelligence services it is possible to see that the headquarters of political organizations and political parties were indicated as potential targets of bombings.

Perhaps surprisingly, given the military technology in the 1930s, aerial attacks during the Spanish Civil War seem to have been quite precise;[15] in *Vandellós*, for example, the bombing affected a camp with Republican soldiers in the outskirts of the town (Solé i Sabaté and Villarroya 1986). In Granollers, the bombs were dropped on the farmers' market at its peak hour (Garriga 2003).

### Revenge

Bombings against civilians could also be used as a way of exacting revenge. As we saw in Chapters 3 and 4, as a result of the actions of militiamen and soldiers against their friends and relatives, people came to develop anger, hatred, and other vengeful emotions. Collaboration in the perpetration of direct violence in subsequent phases of the conflict (for example, when the Nationalists occupied Catalonia) was one way to satisfy these vengeful desires, but armed groups could also seek to satisfy them by using indirect violence. Specifically, by punishing areas that had been violent against their supporters, the Nationalists could satisfy the thirst for vengeance of their supporters and potentially win further loyalty among those living in their areas of control.

---

[13] The results are extremely consistent when using other algorithms such as propensity score matching with five nearest neighbors and inverse probability weights.

[14] Guixé (2012) also provides evidence of the fact that the SIFNE worked closely with the French extreme Right and the Nazi and Italian intelligence services.

[15] Some of the bomber planes were quite precise, though. The Luftwaffe's Condor Legion used, among others, the Junkers 87 Stuka – precision ground-attack aircraft. The Italians provided the rebels with planes such as the Savoia-Marchetti S.M.79 – also used in WWII – or Savoia-Marchetti S.M.81.

TABLE 5.3 *Previous Violence by the Left and Lethal Bombings by the Right in Catalonia (Logit Models)*

|  | Bombing | Bombing 1 | Bombing 5 | Bombing 10 |
|---|---|---|---|---|
| Support Left | 0.014** | 0.017** | 0.026** | 0.038** |
|  | (0.006) | (0.007) | (0.009) | (0.01) |
| Population (* 1000) | 0.61** | 0.31 | 0.22 | 0.21 |
|  | (0.21) | (0.34) | (0.32) | (0.33) |
| UGT Affiliation | 0.16 | 0.16* | 0.22** | 0.28** |
|  | (0.09) | (0.06) | (0.083) | (0.09) |
| Border | −0.25 | −0.005 | −0.19 | −0.25 |
|  | (0.40) | (0.34) | (0.43) | (0.53) |
| Sea | −0.24 | −0.045 | 0.28 | 0.22 |
|  | (0.35) | (0.40) | (0.42) | (0.58) |
| Frontline | −0.055 | 0.27 | −0.16 | −0.15 |
|  | (0.30) | (0.30) | (0.38) | (0.47) |
| Executed by the Left | −0.0026 | 0.018 | 0.029+ | 0.032+ |
|  | (0.021) | (0.012) | (0.015) | (0.017) |
| Elevation | −0.0016* | −0.00089+ | −0.0011+ | −0.0011 |
|  | (0.0006) | (0.0005) | (0.0007) | (0.0007) |
| _cons | −2.73** | −2.98** | −4.25** | −5.66** |
|  | (0.42) | (0.49) | (0.65) | (0.95) |
| N | 869 | 869 | 869 | 869 |
| ll | −285.9 | −312.5 | −192.8 | −122.8 |

Clustered standard errors in parentheses
$^{+}p < 0.10$, $^{*}p < 0.05$, $^{**}p < 0.01$

Table 5.3 displays the results of the four logit models in Table 5.1 with an additional explanatory variable: *Executed Left*, a proxy for revenge motives.[16]

The results of the different models in Table 5.3 show that previous violence by leftist militias had a positive impact on the occurrence and incidence of lethal bombings leading to at least five deaths (model 3) and to ten deaths (model 4). The effect of previous killings is, however, not very large, substantively.[17] Matching estimators of causal effects (calculated with propensity-score matching and one nearest neighbour) indicate that, on average, localities in which the Left perpetrated executions had two more individuals killed in fascist bombardments.

Qualitative evidence regarding the hypothesis on the role of revenge is rather scarce, in large part due to the aforementioned absence of official reports explicitly stating the motives underlying the decision behind bombings. In any

[16] CNT Affiliation is not included in these models because they very strongly correlated to Executed Left and can produce collinearity. I exclude the city of Barcelona because it is an outlier in both number of leftist killings and bombings.

[17] If I run these regressions without the variable Elevation (hence, with 1,052 observations), Executed by the Left is very significant to explain Francoist bombings in all four models.

case, this is the kind of evidence that, if available, would make us much more confident about the theory but whose absence does not really undermine it because the Nationalists had powerful interests in avoiding making it visible, i.e., recording this kind of information.[18] There is some anecdotal evidence along these lines; for example, in the county of *La Cerdanya*, the locality of *Puigcerdà*, where the anarchist militias had brutally attacked rightist citizens, suffered bombardments that turned out to be very deadly. In contrast, the nearby town of *Bellver*, where local leaders constrained the actions of militiamen, was barely affected by indirect violence.[19]

Regarding executions and bombings, it could be argued that the relationship was in fact the reverse; that is, that the direct killings were a consequence and not a cause of indirect violence. In fact, several historical accounts (Sáiz Viadero 1979: 101–109; Preston 1986; Solé i Sabaté and Villarroya 1989; 2003) document the fact that aerial bombardments behind the frontlines sometimes made the groups perpetrate direct violence against civilians. Cases of retaliation very often involved the execution of groups of prisoners (in the so-called *sacas*) (Payne 2010: 476). This is what happened, for example, on the ship *Aragon*, where prisoners were being held by the Republican army on the island of Menorca (in the Balearic islands): "As a result of a bombardment by the Nationalist air force over Mahón, all the prisoners in the ship, even the doctors, were executed in retaliation" (Moreno de Alborán and Moreno de Alborán, 1998: 239).[20] Herreros and Criado (2009) have analyzed the effect of bombings on leftist violence in Catalonia, and they have argued that bombings had a significant impact on executions. However, the number of massacres carried out as reprisals for aerial and naval bombardments in Catalonia, as reported by historians, is quite limited and concentrated on very specific dates, which are the following: October 30, 1936, after an incursion into the harbor of *Roses* made by a naval boat, which led to a wave of killings across the territory; November 16, 1936 in *Palamós*; February 13, 1937 in Barcelona (Solé i Sabaté and Villarroya, 2003). Moreover, as I have explained, a large majority of bombardments in Catalonia were carried out after 1936 – that is, after

---

[18] "In May 1938, the German Condor Legion dropped bombs against four small villages of the region of Castelló in order to test bomber planes" (Suica Films 2015; Grau 2015). In these villages, the leftist militias had killed right-wingers: for example, in Albocasser – a population of 3,060 – the leftists had killed 23 people. There is no primary evidence that these were retaliatory strikes, though.

[19] According to a local historian (personal communication, February 2007), in Bellver "the bombs were falling into the river. Maybe they [the Nationalists] did not have much interest in killing people."

[20] Sometimes it seems that these retaliations were misguided; for example, a report made by the Toledo Police explains that there was a *saca* for a bombing that leftists had accidentally directed at their own forces: "around 80 people were taken out from the provincial prison during the night of August 23, 1936 and were killed as a reprisal for the bombardment by the Red air force, which accidentally targeted the Red barricades" (Informe 4741, Causa General, Pieza 4, Checas, 1049/1).

the largest share of leftist violence had already taken place; given this time-
line, executions in this region cannot really be regarded as a consequence of
bombings.

**Spatial Analyses**

As I did in Chapter 4 with regard to direct violence, I undertake a set of
analyses in order to check if there are patterns of spatial dependence in the indirect violence data, which could be biasing the results obtained with ordinary
regression techniques. Because I use point-based data, I calculate Euclidean distances to generate weights (distance band between 0 and 4, row standardized).
I estimate Moran's I for the dependent variables I have used in the analyses above, in order to check for autocorrelation. The results indicate that we
should not be concerned by patterns of autocorrelation when looking at total
number of bombs thrown in a locality, but that there is spatial autocorrelation in some of the dummy variables measuring occurrence of bombings: for
example, the Moran's I for Bombing with at least 1 death is 0.01, significant
at the 99 percent, and the Moran's I for Bombing with at least 10 deaths
is 0.005, also significant at the 99 percent. For these two dummy dependent
variables, I rerun the analyses above with spatial lag regression to make sure
the main results are not affected by this spatial autocorrelation. The results
(shown in Table 5.4) indicate that *Support Left* remains a significant variable in
explaining the occurrence of deadly bombings. I also run spatial error models
(included in the Appendix), which show that these results are not vulnerable
to contagion effects coming from the independent variables. The results on
revenge are, however, not robust to the spatial specifications.[21]

## 5.5   CONCLUSIONS

This chapter has explored the determinants of indirect violence in civil wars,
which consists of intentional violence perpetrated with what is often considered indiscriminate weaponry, but can nevertheless be used to quite precisely
target certain groups of people and localities. The results support the hypothesis that armed groups with access to weaponry such as bomber aircraft or
naval gunfire are likely to attack localities where the rival group is politically
dominant because it allows them to maximize the odds of eliminating enemy
supporters. This eliminationist approach to indirect violence complements the
coercive approach already adopted by other scholars (Pape 1996; Arreguín-
Toft 2001; Downes 2008). I consider these strategies not to be incompatible
with each other, though: by targeting enclaves of the rival, an armed group
can undermine the ability of the rival group to continue fighting while also

---

[21] I exclude Barcelona city from the spatial regressions, because it is an outlier both in number of
bombings and number of executions. The results are consistent, and slightly more supportive
of hypothesis 5.1, if Barcelona city is included.

TABLE 5.4 *Spatial Lag Regression for Bombings in Catalonia*

| | Bombing1 | Bombing1 | Bombing10 | Bombing10 |
|---|---|---|---|---|
| Support Left | 0.0017** | 0.0017** | 0.00076** | 0.00080** |
| | (0.00058) | (0.00059) | (0.00033) | (0.00035) |
| CNT Affiliation | 0.01+ | | 0.0067 | |
| | (0.0044) | | (0.0048) | |
| UGT Affiliation | 0.030** | 0.031** | 0.04** | 0.04** |
| | (0.0097) | (0.01) | (0.009) | (0.009) |
| Population(*1000) | 0.035** | 0.039** | 0.035** | 0.036** |
| | (0.010) | (0.012) | (0.0088) | (0.010) |
| Elevation | −0.069* | −0.069* | −0.022 | −0.021 |
| | (0.032) | (0.033) | (0.017) | (0.017) |
| Catholic Center | 0.30+ | 0.23 | 0.25+ | 0.18 |
| | (0.18) | (0.27) | (0.14) | (0.20) |
| Executed by the Left | | 0.00032 | | 0.00042 |
| | | (0.0017) | | (0.0014) |
| Constant | −0.070 | −0.069 | −0.022 | −0.027 |
| | (0.048) | (0.050) | (0.033) | (0.032) |
| rho | | | | |
| Constant | 0.71** | 0.69** | −0.13 | −0.071 |
| | (0.23) | (0.24) | (0.49) | (0.48) |
| sigma | | | | |
| Constant | 0.33** | 0.33** | 0.19** | 0.19** |
| | (0.012) | (0.012) | (0.014) | (0.014) |
| Observations | 869 | 869 | 869 | 869 |

Standard errors in parentheses
$+p < 0.10, *p < 0.05, **p < 0.01$

eliminating their supporters. The willingness to coerce might explain why bombings take place, but the willingness to eliminate can better explain why some localities are targeted while others are not.

It must be emphasized that the empirical evidence in this chapter comes from a civil war that took place in the 1930s and that aerial attacks against civilian locations were mostly inflicted by fascist armed forces. There is growing international and domestic legislation (for example, in the United States) that prohibits direct attacks on civilians (Thomas 2006), which should allow us to expect this kind of targeting to be less prevalent in today's world. Yet, recent evidence from the civil wars in Lybia (2011) and Syria (ongoing since 2011) is still quite consistent with this logic: in the Syrian city of Homs, a rebel enclave, the government carried out shellings with the intention not only to compel the rebels to surrender, but also to cleanse the area of enemies. As quoted in the *New York Times*, a pro-government fighter said, "This time we will clean

Homs completely and will not leave any germs behind us. Homs should be cleaned forever from all traitors" (Barnard 2013). Furthermore, within Homs, the mainly Sunni neighborhood of Baba Amr was highly damaged by the shelling. In the autumn of 2016, the city of Aleppo was targeted following a similar eliminationist logic (Wintour 2016; Rubin and Saad 2016). In Libya, the city that suffered the most indirect violence from the NATO international coalition forces, which supported the rebels, was Sirte, the enclave where the head of the government, Mouammar Al-Gadafi, resided (Stephen 2011).

In conflict studies, bombardments are not typically studied in conjunction with executions or massacres; in this book, however, I put them in the same explanatory framework and argue that they can be used for the same purpose, namely, cleansing the territories of political supporters of the rival group. The results in this chapter are important because they demonstrate that political variables are crucial when it comes to accounting for violence against groups of individuals, and not only against selected individuals – killed face-to-face. The results also suggest, albeit less strongly, that bombings are also partly influenced by war dynamics – for example, by direct killings perpetrated by the opposing group at the local level. This is consistent with the "rivalry and revenge" framework in this book, which highlights the role not only of political rivalry but also of vengeful emotions in civil war dynamics. The inclusion of revenge makes my theoretical framework slightly broader than those in the existing literature, which has largely focused on military factors, bargaining considerations and/or military balance of power between groups, or on a combination of military and political factors. As Roger Petersen has pointed out (2011), the rationalist literature has overlooked the experiences of people living through the war, the emotional effects of these experiences, and, in turn, the effects of these emotions on war-related decisions.

Weinstein (2007) argues that we can expect ideologically motivated rebels to inflict less indiscriminate violence than non-ideological ones; however, this book provides evidence of highly ideological (i.e., fascist) organizations perpetrating mass killings against civilians, and intentionally bombarding municipalities full of noncombatants. Thus, barbarism is not necessarily the byproduct of a lack of organization or discipline within armed groups. Nevertheless, this does not imply that ideology should be disregarded as a relevant factor accounting for violence. Genocidal ideologies like fascism are more prone to lead to eliminationist forms of indirect violence (Valentino 2004; 2014; Straus 2006), while groups with non-genocidal ideologies might be more prone to use indirect violence in a more strategic way, as a form of coercion without the intention to completely exterminate enemy supporters. Although we do not yet have sufficient fine-grained data on bombings in Nationalist rearguard territories, there is plenty of historical evidence showing that Republicans in Spain used bombings in a more selective way, mainly against military targets and not intending to kill civilians en masse behind the enemy's frontlines (Preston 2011).

The theoretical framework in this book has avoided grand strategy considerations among the determinants of indirect violence; instead I have focused on the question of why there is variation in targeting across large and clearly delineated rearguard territories. This focus is useful, theoretically as much as empirically, because grand strategies are usually very hard to determine with certainty. As Neely explains, in the case of the American Civil War, "we simply do not know what the grand strategies of the Civil War were. We must infer them from events and from passing remarks left us here and there in the military and political record, official and unofficial.... it is important to maintain a humble attitude and realize that the policies are not clear and never will be" (2007: 202–3). In the case of Spain, Solé i Sabaté and Villarroya (2003: 303) explain that, according to Francoist press releases, only military objectives, harbors, and railroad stations were attacked – yet, this was not the case; many rearguard territories full of civilians were targeted. Something similar is illustrated by the discrepancy between what the Italian air force claimed that they had destroyed in their aerial attacks on the city of Barcelona (i.e., the harbor), and what they had in fact destroyed (i.e., much more than the harbor). Hence, it is plausibly more reliable to look at objective damage (e.g., bombs thrown, number of people killed) than at stated strategies.

Previous research has shown that displacement is instrumental for armed groups in contested areas: by targeting groups of individuals, armed groups can provoke the displacement of peoples and the cleansing of territories, thereby facilitating their attempts at conquest (Downes 2008; Balcells and Steele 2016). Here I argue that indirect violence can also serve the purposes of cleansing in rearguard territories; as groups can use indirect violence as a substitute for direct violence in areas they do not control militarily.[22]

On the whole, the evidence from the Spanish Civil War adduced in Chapters 3, 4, and 5 supports the theory elaborated in this book. It consists of evidence from a single case, which explores subnational variation and maximizes leverage by combining quantitative and qualitative data. Yet, the theory would lack generalizability if only applied to the Spanish case. In the following chapter, I provide evidence from a very different civil war, which took place in Côte d'Ivoire between 2002 and 2011, in an attempt to provide external validity to the theory. In addition, Chapter 7 includes both systematic and anecdotal evidence from a number of additional cases (e.g., Northern Ireland, Colombia). The following two chapters should hopefully convince the reader that the theory in this book can be generalized beyond the Spanish case.

---

[22] Interestingly, patterns of indirect violence resemble those of collective violence leading to displacement, which also affect localities with an electoral profile indicating political dominance on the part the rival group (Steele 2010; Balcells and Steele 2016). I would argue that this similarity is linked to the unilateral character of both these types of victimization, which do not require much local collaboration.

# PART III

# 6

# The Conflict in Côte d'Ivoire (2002–2011)

## 6.1 INTRODUCTION

So far the empirical evidence adduced in favor of my theory of wartime violence has been drawn from a single case, namely, the Spanish Civil War. For the purposes of lending external validity to the results taken from the Spanish case, in this chapter and the following I will compare it to other cases, showing that they are broadly consistent. In this chapter, I present a study of the Ivorian Civil War(s) (2002–2007; 2010–2011), with a focus on the subnational dynamics of violence in this African conflict. My interest in Côte d'Ivoire stems from the fact that this civil war was fought along clear frontlines and characterized by uncontested control over large territories on the part of each of the armed groups. As with other cases of conventional civil wars, current theoretical approaches cannot fully explain violence against civilians in the Ivorian case. Thus, despite the fact that Côte d'Ivoire and Spain differ extremely in many respects, their civil wars exhibit commonalities that are relevant for the purposes of this book.

The main "master cleavage" during the Ivorian Civil War concerned ethnic identities: the underlying cause of the war was the political disempowerment of those considered "non-Ivorians," and recruitment into armed groups took place along ethnic lines.[1] Thus, following standard classifications (e.g., Sambanis 2001), this case can be considered an ethnic civil war, which is not the case with the Spanish Civil War.[2] As explained in Chapter 3, while ethnic

---

[1] According to the EPR-ETH dataset, cited by Vogt (2013), the politically relevant ethnic groups and their respective shares of the country's population are as follows: Northerners (Mandé and Voltaic) (34 percent), Southern Mandé (12 percent), Kru (11 percent), Baoulé (Akan) (20 percent), Other Akans (22 percent). The conflict took place along the northerners (commonly known as "Dioula") vs. southerners ethnic divide (Vogt 2013).

[2] For more on how dynamics of ethno-political exclusion can lead to civil war, see Horowitz (1985), Cederman et al. (2011), and Wimmer (2012). For more on the specific

issues did in fact surface during the Spanish conflict, and quite significantly during the postwar period – national minorities such as Catalans, Basques, or Galicians suffered particularly severe repression at the hands of Franco's regime – the Spanish Civil War was fought along a Left–Right cleavage.

Chapter 7 reports other results in the conflict studies literature that are consistent with the theory in this book. I draw from existing works that have dealt with dynamics of violence during internal conflict, not necessarily civil war. I also refer to results from research I have conducted on low-intensity sectarian violence in Northern Ireland that are consistent with the theoretical framework in this book. Furthermore, I explore some macro-level implications of the theory, and I empirically test one of them with a large-n dataset on civil wars.

In this chapter, I analyze dynamics of direct violence in Côte d'Ivoire. Indirect violence was quite marginal in this civil war, and mostly perpetrated by foreign armed forces. I test the hypothesis that direct violence peaks in areas where the distribution of political support for rival groups approaches parity. I also look into variation in levels of political mobilization over time, within Côte d'Ivoire, to evaluate the theoretical assumption that mobilization is a precondition for violence against civilians in conventional civil wars. Before going into these analyses, however, I will provide some historical background on Côte d'Ivoire and the civil war that began in 2002.

## 6.2  THE CIVIL WAR IN CÔTE D'IVOIRE

### Origins of the Conflict

Côte d'Ivoire is a West African country that shares borders with Mali, Guinea, Ghana, Liberia, and Burkina Faso. After gaining its independence from France on August 7, 1960, Côte d'Ivoire adopted its own constitution, which formally instituted a presidential system, recognized party plurality, and established separation of powers. However, *de facto*, the Ivorian political stage was dominated from 1960 to 1993 by President Félix Houphouët-Boigny, who exercised authoritarian rule and favored a form of neo-patrimonialism (Diarra 1997: 23).

Côte d'Ivoire was recognized as the "African Miracle" for the prosperity and political stability it attained during the 1960s and 1970s (Akindès 2007). As the global leader in cocoa exports, Côte d'Ivoire enjoyed a long period of political stability and economic development following its independence. With an average real GDP growth rate of 4.4 percent per year during 1965–1990, this country became an economic powerhouse in West Africa and it

case of Côte d'Ivoire, see Banégas (2006), McGovern (2011), Marshall-Fratani (2006), and Langer (2006).

attracted foreign investment and migrant workers from neighboring countries (Minoui et al. 2012: 3). The Ivorian economy depended heavily on cocoa exports and the cocoa business influenced many of the political developments in the post-colonial period (McGovern 2011). The cocoa revenues also allowed Houphouët-Boigny to maintain a system of patronage (Côté and Mitchell 2015). However, the 1980s were marked by a decline in public funding and the so-called *cocoa crisis*, which culminated in a series of mass protests and the formation of underground political organizations such as the Ivorian Popular Front (FPI) and the Rally of the Republicans (RDR) (Koné 2012).

Political tensions sharpened in Côte d'Ivoire after the death of Houphouët-Boigny in 1993 when his right-hand man Henri Konan Bédié (former president of the National Assembly) took power. In 1990, multi-party elections were introduced and some political parties started to mobilize along ethnic lines (Côté and Mitchell 2015). Under Houphouët-Boigny there was a complex system of ethnic balance, with the Baoulé ethnic group playing a "primum inter pares" role (Akindès 2007; Piccolino 2014). This balance was disturbed when Bédié introduced discriminatory laws that favored those considered nationals and initiated a wave of exaltation of the so-called *Ivoirité* (that is, the notion of "pure" Ivorian identity). This exclusionary ethnic mobilization was largely a reaction to the economic crisis and land-tenure issues that had arisen between natives and immigrants, which were particularly prominent in the Western region of the country – where Cocoa production is concentrated (Allouche and Zadi Zadi 2011; Klaus and Mitchell 2015).[3] Immigrants typically came from rural agricultural areas in the northern regions of the country and from neighboring countries, especially Burkina Faso.[4] The politics of *ivoirité* emboldened autochthons to reclaim their original lands (Côté and Mitchell 2015: 661).[5] At the same time, mobilization in the name of *ivoirité* also served to directly exclude those who could be politically threatening: Muslims, in general, and Alassane Ouattara, in particular.

---

[3] Land-tenure issues have led some to characterize the conflict as a "sons of the soil" civil war, in which members of regional ethnic groups considered to be indigenous revolt against colonizers or newly arrived economic immigrants, often from within the same country (Allouche and Zadi Zadi 2011; Côté and Mitchell 2015).

[4] Scott Straus (2015) writes: "Ivoirité initially was part of a tactic to insure the political dominance of the largest ethnic group in the country (the Akan) ... But Ivoirité crystallized anti-foreigner, anti-Northerner, and anti-Muslim sentiment in southern and western parts of the country. The doctrine of Ivoirité also dovetailed with nativist claims to land, in particular in the fertile Western and Southwestern areas of the country where large numbers of Muslim migrants and immigrants had settled" (2).

[5] A 1998 land reform made national citizenship a prerequisite for land ownership (Klaus and Mitchell 2015). As a consequence, disputes over land claims between autochthons and migrant populations arose.

## Conflict Outbreak

In 1999, General Robert Guéï led a military coup that brought an end to 39 years of domination by the PDCI-RDA (Houphouët-Boigny and Konan Bédié's party). Guéï created a government of national unity that was joined by Laurent Gbagbo's FPI and Alassane Ouattara's RDR. Nonetheless, he promoted the adoption of a controversial article in the 2000 Constitution (Article 35), which banned anyone whose parents were born outside the country from running in the presidential elections (presidential candidates had to be Ivorian, born to Ivorian parents, and at no time a possessor of foreign nationality). This law prohibited Ouattara from running for president.[6]

Guéï declared himself the winner in the 2000 elections, but was forced into exile after massive demonstrations decrying his part in electoral fraud and Gbagbo, who had in fact received a majority of the vote, was sworn in. The new government subsequently purged certain sectors of the army that were regarded as close to Guéï (i.e., military elites from the western regions of the country) or disloyal to the regime (i.e., soldiers from the north). None of this was able to prevent the rebellion that would occur two years later. Gbagbo refused to hold new elections open to both Bedié and Ouattara, and he continued playing on widespread xenophobic sentiments to marginalize "Northerners" (McGovern 2010: 69).

## Warfare in Côte d'Ivoire (2002–2003)

The 2002 rebellion started as a failed coup led on the night of 18–19 September by an armed organization trained in Burkina Faso: the Patriotic Movement of Côte d'Ivoire (MPCI).[7] After the assassination of Robert Guéï (along with his family) on September 19, 2002 (allegedly by Laurent Gbagbo's supporters, in reprisal for the uprising), there was a resurgence of two armed groups in the west closely allied to Guéï: the *Mouvement pour la justice et la paix* (MJP) and the *Mouvement populaire ivoirien du Grand Ouest* (MPIGO). These insurgent groups became important proxies to the main insurgent group, the MPCI, and in December 2002 they combined to form the *Forces Nouvelles* (FN). Although they did not achieve their goal of overthrowing the government, the FN managed to control the north of the country. The rebels – who called for the dismissal of Gbagbo, the modification of the Constitution, and more inclusive elections – retreated to Bouaké once they realized that they could not conquer Abidjan (the capital), and made Bouaké the capital of the north. Daloa and San Pedro, two strategically important western cities, remained in government hands. The French intervention facilitated the *de facto* partition

---

[6] For more details on the manipulation of the Constitution and the law in Côte d'Ivoire during that period, see Piccolino (2014).

[7] The MPCI soldiers were former Ivorian in exile, and they had a political faction led by Guillaume Soro.

(McGovern 2010: 69) of the country through their peacekeeping mission: the *L'opération Licorne*.

There is an extensive scholarly debate over the true causes of the coup and the outbreak of violence in Côte d'Ivoire. For example, Woods (2003) and Klaus and Mitchell (2015) argue that it was the consequence of disputes over land tenure and property rights. Nordas (2008), for her part, points to religious polarization. McGovern (2011) and Allouche and Zadi Zadi (2011) point to the cocoa business, which created incentives to seize control of lands and carry out redistribution campaigns. Langer (2006) highlights the combination of between-group political (at the elite level) and economic (at the non-elite level) inequality. Chelpi-den Hamer, for his part, argues that the causes of the coup and ensuing conflict was the discontent among soldiers who faced a process of demobilization under an army reform program introduced by the new government (2012: 25).

During the conflict, armed groups recruited from different sectors of society, mostly marginalized youth, unemployed students, and young soldiers (Koné 2011; 2012), and they waged what can be considered a conventional civil war. Both sides used a combination of heavy and light forms of weaponry and waged battle along a stable frontline, with clearly delimitated areas of control for each of the sides. In Côte d'Ivoire, groups did not seem to face much of a challenge to their territorial control, where they even levied taxes (Polgreen 2005; Akindès 2007), but they nevertheless organized commandos to patrol the localities and consolidate their presence (Chelpi-den Hamer 2012). Certain forms of governance were established in the rebel-controlled areas (Mampilly 2011). Following a common pattern in conventional conflicts, Ivorian fighters (many of them young militarized civilians) were divided into those engaged on the frontline and those performing rearguard functions "ranging from maintaining military positions when places were captured from the enemy, to securing particular locations through the set-up of checkpoints" (Chelpi-den Hamer 2012: 21). There were, however, few armed confrontations (Straus 2015); there was much less battlefield violence in the Ivorian than in the Spanish Civil War.

Despite the partition of the country, members of different ethnic and religious groups lived in communities on both sides of the north–south divide (Basset 2003; Polgreen 2005).[8] The lack of fluidity or mobility in this civil war, which was imposed by the nature of the war frontlines, led to some tensions at the local level. Yet, this was not always conducive to violence; for example, Polgreen (2005) writes that in Fengolo, villagers said they were determined to reconcile, because they had little choice short of wiping one another out. There was widespread displacement that affected mostly areas of the country

---

[8] While the majority of recruits to the *Forces Nouvelles* were indeed of northern origin, rebel forces have consistently denied any specific regional or ethnic affiliation (Langer 2006; Chelpi-den Hamer 2012).

that were bordering other countries (e.g., Burkina Faso, Liberia): that is, where more exit options existed.

## The "No War, No Peace" Situation (2003–2007)

After French mediation, in January 2003 a peace agreement (the Linas-Marcoussis agreement) was signed, and the war was officially over in August 2003. Yet, *de facto*, the conflict continued. In Abidjan, pro-Gbagbo groups (e.g., the Young Patriots) reacted violently to the peace agreement and they rebelled by destroying various symbols of French presence (McGovern 2011). Low levels of civil-war violence persisted until at least 2007. Thus, the initial, more violent phase of the war was followed by a tense period marked by iso-lated bouts of violence (Minoui et al. 2012: 5), what McGovern (2011) has called a "no war, no peace" situation.

After an arduous conflict-resolution process (involving UN and French peacekeeping interventions), Laurent Gbagbo and Guillaume Soro (leader of the Forces Nouvelles) signed a second peace agreement in Ouagadougou (Burkina Faso) on March 4, 2007. Among other things, both sides agreed on eliminating the peace line, which was controlled by the United Nations Opera-tion in Côte d'Ivoire (ONUCI) and the French peacekeeping forces. The agree-ment stipulated that the peace line was to be reduced gradually and replaced by domestic security forces (Caramés 2011). In spite of the peace agreement, there was a massive process of rearmament between September 2002 and April 2011. Reno (2011) argues that "actors prepared for a violent confrontation rather than focusing on peaceful interventions or resolutions" (186).

## The 2010 Elections and their Aftermath

In 2010, three and a half years after the signing of the Ouagadougou Peace Agreement, Côte d'Ivoire held presidential elections in two rounds. These elec-tions were thought to represent the closure of the peace process; tragically, they triggered a relapse into war. Indeed, these elections led to a political crisis, which eventually broke out into a full-scale military conflict between forces loyal to Laurent Gbagbo and supporters of the president-elect Alas-sane Ouattara, who was internationally recognized as such (Allouche and Zadi Zadi 2013: 72).

The climate before the elections was tense, with the presence of interna-tional observation missions, and an overall fear of electoral malfeasance and potential violent confrontations (Carter Center 2011). In the first round of the elections, held on October 31, 2010, Gbagbo and Ouattara received 38 and 32 percent of the votes, respectively (Bedié, the third most voted candi-date, obtained 25 percent of the votes). Gbagbo's support came mostly from the southeast, center-west and southwest (Bassett 2011: 471) of the coun-try; Ouattara received 80–95 percent of the vote in the northwestern and north-central regions. In the second round of the elections, Bedié endorsed Ouattara and this endorsement was key to Ouattara's victory (Bassett 2011: 477). Indeed, in the second round, Ouattara obtained a majority of electoral support in the northern and western areas of the country, while Gbagbo received more support in the southern provinces, particularly in the southwest, where the land-tenure conflict was most prevalent. Ouattara also performed well in the southern departments of Soubré, Sassandra, and in Abidjan, due to the presence of northerners in all three locations and because he managed to capture the vote of the Baoulé region, which was Bedié's enclave.[9]

Following the second round of elections, held on November 28, 2010, Ouattara was declared the winner with 54 percent of the vote by the Independent Electoral Commission with the certification of the international community (United Nations and the African Union).[10] Yet, the Constitutional Council dismissed the polling results in three northern regions (Bouaké, Dabakala, Katiola) – a total of seven districts – citing violent incidents, and declared Gbagbo as the winner. Despite the fact that violence and intimidation occurred at some polling stations, according to election observers these incidents did not warrant calling into question the general election results. Election observers from the EU and UN reported that violence and intimidation were in fact more widespread in the western and west-central regions where Gbagbo received a majority of the vote (Bassett 2011: 477–478). McGovern (2011) writes: "The Economic Community of West African States (ECOWAS), the African Union (AU), the European Union (EU) and the American Carter Center all had international electoral observation missions, and they unanimously said that the election was globally free and fair, that irregularities had been committed were done predominantly by Gbagbo supporters. They pronounced the Constitutional Court's ruling an act of blatant fraud" (211).

The Constitutional Court ruling led to a situation of dual authority, with two presidents:[11] one of them, Gbagbo, who was declared legitimate by the Constitutional body and had control of the main bodies of administration and the state; the other, Ouattara, who was recognized by the international community but who was sheltered in the Golf Hotel, in central Abidjan, protected by UN peacekeepers.

---

[9] Thus, while ethnicity was a clear determinant in the first round of the elections, as each candidate was dominant in their respective ethnic homelands (Lewis 2011), it was somewhat less relevant in the second round, as electoral results did not always follow ethnic lines. This regional divide in the vote was completely absent in the October 2015 presidential elections, in which Gbagbo did not compete (he was facing trial before the International Criminal Court in The Hague). In 2015, Ouattara received a majority of the vote in all but two of the country's thirty-plus regions (Koter 2015).

[10] As Basset (2011) points out, the UN certification of the elections as "fair and credible" was remarkable as it was the first ever such certification in an African country.

[11] On December 4, 2010, Gbagbo and Ouattara both took oaths of office (Mitchell 2015: 183).

The outcome of the election and the "Constitutional Coup" quickly triggered an armed confrontation, the so-called Second Ivorian Civil War (following McGovern 2011: 209, I take this to be part of one overarching conflict starting in 2002). The country became again split into North and South, with two competing armed forces: on the one hand, the Defense and Security Forces (FDS), with an estimated 55,000 soldiers, which remained under the command of Gbagbo; on the other hand, the former rebels of the Forces Nouvelles (FN) army, with an estimated 9,000 soldiers. At the beginning of the post-electoral crisis, most senior officers in the FDS pledged allegiance to the outgoing president, whereas the former FN lined up behind Ouattara. As the crisis unfolded, however, a share of the FDS defected to Ouattara.[12] Some remained loyal to Gbagbo while others deserted.

After several months of clashes between the Forces Nouvelles and the army units and militias loyal to Gbagbo, Ouattara (who was still under protection at Abidjan's Golf Hotel) announced the creation of the *Forces Républicaines de Côte d'Ivoire* (FRCI) on March 17, 2011. The latter were composed of FDS defectors and the former FN. The FRCI launched a countrywide military offensive on March 28, 2011 and gradually conquered the territory, starting from the west (specifically, from Blolequin, Toulepleu, and Duekoué), and ending up in Abidjan. They received indirect assistance from UN forces and were strongly backed by French troops (Mitchell 2015: 184). Figure 6.1 illustrates the 2010–2011 country divisions, as well as the FRCI offensives toward the capital.[13]

At the beginning of the 2010–2011 crisis, violence was more widespread in rural areas, particularly, in the country's "Far West" (Klaus and Mitchell 2015: 631). Many non-indigenous people in the region were violently threatened and attacked. By February 2011, much of the fighting was concentrated in Abidjan (*BBC News*, February 28, 2011), where violence escalated between Ouattara and Gbagbo supporters. Pro-Gbagbo state and non-state forces targeted people on a selective basis: their primary targets were Muslim Ivorians of northern provenance and West African nationals, who were cued as Ouattara supporters. In the same vein, pro-Ouattara forces were responsible for selective targeting leading to human rights violations. In northern areas, there were attacks against political party activists and the homes of pro-Gbagbo officials (Straus 2011: 487). In addition, the FRCI committed serious atrocities on their way to Abidjan: the International Crisis Group (2014: 13) documents a massacre of at least 300 people in Duékoué's Carrefour district, home of the Wê Patriotic Alliance (APWÊ) headquarters, allegedly perpetrated by the FRCI and Dozo and Burkinabe militias; and several assassinations and rapes

---

[12] Allouche and Zadi Zadi (2011: 82) argue that around 63 percent of the security forces of Côte d'Ivoire (including the police and gendarmerie) had voted in favor of Ouattara.

[13] The map on Figure 6.1 has been elaborated on the basis of information provided by Political Geography Now.

FIGURE 6.1 Côte d'Ivoire: Military Control Areas in the 2010–2011 Conflict

are reported by Human Rights Watch (HRW) (2011). Supporters from both sides were often singled out on the basis of their political identities. Also, Straus (2011: 487) argues that there was a "tit for tat spiral of retaliation and reprisals, whereby attacks against people associated with one community are followed by attacks against people associated with the other community." Thus, the dynamics of violence in this conflict seem to have followed a pattern consistent with the "rivalry and revenge" framework presented in this book.

The FRCI's arrival at the country's capital unleashed the bloodiest confrontations between the armed groups. The French Force Licorne and the ONUCI intervened in favor of Ouattara under the aegis of the UN Resolution

1975, which authorized the attack on Gbagbo's heavy weapons arsenals, in addition to imposing international sanctions on Côte d'Ivoire. Heavy and light weaponry were used by both sides: Gbagbo's military used heavy-caliber sniper fire as well as mortars and rocket-propelled grenades; the UN forces supporting Ouattara's troops used attack helicopters and armored vehicles. Gbagbo was finally captured on April 11, 2011, marking the end of the civil war. After that, the Constitutional Council overturned its initial decision and confirmed Ouattara's electoral victory. According to the ONUCI and HRW, more than 3,000 were killed (and more than 150 women raped) during the 2010–2011 armed confrontations. Estimates are of 1,497 killed in Abidjan, out of a national total of 3,248 (Klaus and Mitchell 2015: 631). Most of the killings have been described as extra-judicial and were committed by supporters of both parties (Lamin et al. 2011). According to the ONUCI, more than a million people sought asylum in neighboring countries.

There are important continuities in the patterns of political violence between the first period of conflict (2002–2007) and the second (2010–2011); one of them is the role of youth militias in the perpetration of violence (Straus 2011: 488). Yet, there are also significant differences. The rates of intentional violence against civilians were much higher in the second period: in less than a year there were almost as many killings as there were between 2002 and 2007. During the first period, although there were instances of violence perpetrated by pro-government militias in collaboration with local civilians (International Crisis Group 2014: 11), violence against civilians occurred mostly in areas close to the frontline; on many occasions, noncombatants were the victims of collateral damage (Nordas 2008). There were a few remarkable instances of violence in this first period of the war, such as the massacre of hundreds of anti-Gbagbo demonstrators in March 2004, in which Northerners and non-Ivorians were targeted (Straus 2015), but intentional violence in this period was overall quite limited – to the point that some have argued that the war in Côte d'Ivoire never fully took off (McGovern 2011: 208).

McGovern (2010) explains the restraint in violence during the first Ivorian Civil War as a result of considerations of normative standing and international reputation.[14] Yet, this cannot explain why violence reached much higher levels in 2010–2011: the effect of norms should also apply to this period. In a similar vein, Piccolino (2014) argues that one of the reasons why we did not observe high levels of violence against civilians in Côte d'Ivoire was the political game taking place in the background between the belligerent forces, France, and the UN. Both belligerent forces knew that openly targeting civilians would meet with international outcry and could invite serious military consequences.

[14] McGovern (2010) writes: "the threat of being disqualified or rendered illegitimate, whether this meant imprisonment or simply (local or international) censure, does appear to have played a role in Côte d'Ivoire in making some of the combatants 'think twice' about committing atrocities or allowing atrocities to be committed under their command" (81).

Yet, the deterrent effect of international intervention should have applied in the 2010–2011 period as well. Straus (2015), by contrast, argues that international factors are insufficient to explain why there was no genocide in Côte d'Ivoire, and he points to domestic factors such as national narratives, military institutions, and the country's economic structure, among others. However, these factors would also lead us to predict non-violence in 2010–2011. What explains the differences between these two periods?

### Mobilization and Violence in Côte d'Ivoire

Despite the fact that ethnic mobilization was remarkable during the 2000s, it could be argued that it did not reach all levels of society and did not convert average individuals into intense supporters of the groups. Ethnic mobilization was important since the country democratized, but, in order to constitute a precondition for political violence, mobilization has to turn significant shares of the population into potential activists, who armed groups will perceive as threatening and therefore worth persecuting. In addition, as I argued in Chapter 2, in order to be a precondition for violence, mobilization has to be distributed geographically such that groups will perceive potential threats behind their frontlines. In Côte d'Ivoire, I would argue that this was not the case in the 2000s, but it was the case in 2010, after accumulated years of conflict in which both sides invested increased resources in political mobilization, and in which mobilization in favor of northerners was much more widespread across the country (and not only in the north). Political mobilization was particularly salient around the 2010 elections, which implied a lot of expectations from both sides. These elections were a landmark of the peace process and the first elections in which Alassane Ouatara could compete after having been barred due to discriminatory citizenship rules. In the aftermath of the 2010 elections, the Ouattara camp perceived them as fraught with fraud and hence as having illegitimate results.[15] In short: when the failed coup occurred in 2002, Ivorian society was not mobilized to the extent that armed groups would perceive threats coming from citizens behind the frontlines. In 2010, in contrast, groups perceived the presence of substantial shares of mobilized supporters of the rival in their areas of control (e.g., Abidjan for Gbagbo), and they invested increased resources in eliminating these threats, or they simply gave leeway to the militias to do the job.

Political mobilization can be captured by a variety of indicators (e.g., attendance to rallies, number of political protests, strikes, etc.), as mobilization can take place beyond the conventional forms of participation (Chenoweth 2015), but I use turnout as a proxy. When democracy is functioning, electoral participation has the advantage of being a clean indicator of political mobilization.

---

[15] While the 2000 elections left many pro-Ouattara supporters bitter, they had not been not the proximate cause of the 2002 outbreak of violence.

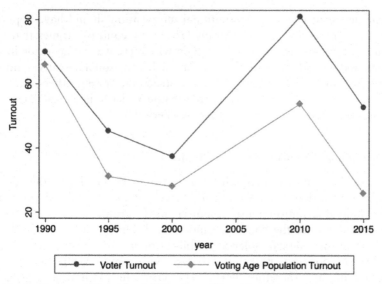

FIGURE 6.2 Turnout in Presidential Elections, Côte d'Ivoire

For example, it can be argued that mass political mobilization has been achieved when (non-compulsory) turnout is over 70 percent. Turnout data is also easier to obtain country-wide than other indicators, which can have an urban bias, for example.[16]

Figure 6.2 shows variation in turnout in presidential elections in Côte d'Ivoire from 1990 to 2015 (Presidential elections took place every five years, except for 2005).[17] Levels of electoral participation indicate that political mobilization reached its highest point in 2010, with over 81 percent turnout. Electoral mobilization was much lower in the 2000 and the 2015 elections, with levels of turnout below 70 percent.

I would argue that the peak in violence against civilians that we observe in 2010–2011 is related to the mobilization peak depicted in Figure 6.2. The fact that Ivorian society was much more politically mobilized than in previous periods contributed to greater victimization of political enemies. Yet, again,

[16] In Côte d'Ivoire, this indicator is not ideal because some candidates were barred from running in the 1995 and 2000 elections (Vogt 2013). The RDR and the PDCI-RCA boycotted the 2000 election in response to the exclusion of Alassane Ouattara and Emile Constant Bombet by the Supreme Court. Thus, we need to take the turnout figures with a grain of salt, as they do not perfectly reflect levels of political mobilization. However, we lack better objective and countrywide indicators. Also, the fact that voter registration was not significantly lower in 2000 than in 2010 speaks in favor of using turnout as an indicator.

[17] The turnout data comes from International IDEA's Voter Turnout Database (www.idea.int/ data-tools/data/voter-turnout). The voting age population turnout is over the estimated number of citizens above the legal voting age, while the voter turnout rate is over the actual number of people on the voters' roll.

violence did not target everyone in society. Like in Spain, violence behind the frontlines mostly involved targeting members of rival political groups. As reported by Human Rights Watch, direct violence in Côte d'Ivoire was highly selective and targeted at specific members of the rival groups. According to Banégas, violence was carried out by political militias "taking control of whole neighborhoods, developing into a form of ethno-political cleansing" (2011: 464). Straus (2011) highlights the political targeting behind lethal violence carried out by both pro-Gbagbo (e.g., Young Patriots; Liberian mercenaries) and pro-Ouattara groups. On the one hand, this followed ethnic lines: pro-Gbagbo forces targeted Muslim Ivorians of northern provenance and West African nationals (Straus 2011: 481). On the other hand, violence was clearly linked to mobilized political identities as "there were attacks against political party activists and the homes of pro-Gbagbo officials. Civilians who voted for Gbagbo in northern areas were also detained and beaten" (Straus 2011: 487). Violence was intended to be selective: house-to-house searches were undertaken by militias and checkpoints were installed in different parts of the country and within neighborhoods of Abidjan.

The following two paragraphs of a report issued by HRW on the post-electoral violence clearly illustrate a pattern of violence that both Gbagbo's and Ouattara's respective supporters directed at their perceived political enemies:[18]

"Elite security force units closely linked to Gbagbo dragged neighborhood political leaders from Ouattara's coalition away from restaurants or out of their homes into waiting vehicles; family members later found the victims' bodies in morgues, riddled with bullets. Women who were active in mobilizing voters – or who merely wore pro-Ouattara T-shirts – were targeted and often gang raped by armed forces and militia groups under Gbagbo's control, after which the attackers told the women to "go tell Alassane" their problems. Pro-Gbagbo militiamen stopped hundreds of real and perceived supporters of Ouattara at checkpoints or attacked them in their neighborhoods and then beat them to death with bricks, executed them by gunshot at point-blank range, or burned them alive" (HRW 2011: 4).

"In Duékoué, the Republican Forces and allied militias massacred hundreds of people, pulling men they alleged to be pro-Gbagbo militiamen out of their homes and executing them unarmed. Later, during the military campaign to take over and consolidate control of Abidjan, the Republican Forces again executed scores of men from ethnic groups aligned to Gbagbo – at times in detention sites – and tortured others" (HRW 2011: 4).

In the West, HRW also reported a wave of killings by pro-Gbagbo militias and pro-Gbagbo Liberian mercenaries against ethnic groups believed to support Ouattara (Mitchell 2014: 210). Political targeting did not necessarily follow ethnic divisions: it was based on political allegiances. The International Crisis Group reports that "in the village of Tinhou, several Guéré PDCI leaders

---

[18]  Human Rights Watch reported that "armed forces on both sides committed war crimes and likely crimes against humanity" (HRW 2011: 5).

were attacked by their Guéré neighbours, who were fervent FPI supporters"
(2014: 12). Amnesty International and Human Rights Watch reported attacks
on RHDP members who had been involved in ballot monitoring during the
election.

In short, the logic underlying civilian victimization in post-2010 Côte
d'Ivoire seems to be that of political targeting. Armed groups sought to
eliminate strong political supporters of the rival bloc, who earlier had been
politically mobilized and who now posed threats behind the war frontlines. The violence was not the byproduct of chaos and anarchy: it was
systematically perpetrated. As Human Rights Watch reported, "The scale
and organization of crimes committed by both sides, including murder,
rape, and persecution of individuals and groups on political, ethnic, and
national grounds, strongly suggest that they were widespread and systematic"
(HRW 2011: 7).

## 6.3 DIRECT VIOLENCE IN 2010–2011

According to the theory propounded in Chapter 2, political mobilization at
the national level is a precondition for violence to occur, and violence is likely
to vary across the territory depending on local political alignments. We should
observe higher levels of direct violence in areas with higher levels of political
competition, where the armed groups would enjoy a greater degree of collaboration with local civilians and therefore more opportunities to identify and
assassinate political supporters of their rival. To test this hypothesis in the Ivorian case, I use a provincial level dataset with electoral results in the second
round of the presidential elections, which serve as a proxy for the distribution
of supporters of the two blocs that opposed each other in the war. As in the
case of Spain, one of the advantages of the Ivorian case is that the two fighting blocs roughly correspond to the two blocs in the elections (particularly, in
the second round, which was contested between Gbagbo and Ouattara) and
that elections (especially with such high turnout) provide a strong indication of
the distribution of political support at the local level. In other words, electoral
results provide a way to measure the distribution of support for each of the
groups in the conflict.

I collected data for a total of 95 provinces or *départements* in Côte d'Ivoire,
relying on the United Nations Office for the Coordination of Humanitarian
Affairs (OCHA) administrative division. Unfortunately, I could not build a
dataset with lower units of analysis in this country. Generally, there is little to no data at the municipal level, especially when it comes to electoral
and violence indicators. For the presidential elections, I rely on the Independent Electoral Commission (CEI), which has provided the most exhaustive
data. The data from the Constitutional Court is more limited because several
regions were excluded due to alleged electoral malfeasance and violence at
polling places; again, Gbagbo made these allegations in hopes of discarding

the results from these northern departments, which helped Ouattara achieve victory.[19]

While the collection of data in Côte d'Ivoire was not straightforward, in general terms, the most complicated to obtain has been information on the crucial variable: direct violence against civilians. I built a dataset relying on the reports by Human Rights Watch, the International Crisis Group, ONUCI, and the ACLED dataset (Hegre and Raleigh 2005).[20] I estimated a total of 1,117 victims of acts of direct violence against civilians: 482 (43 percent) of them were perpetrated by armed forces and militias associated with Gbagbo, while 635 (57 percent) were perpetrated by pro-Ouattara forces (mostly, the FRCI). These figures are smaller than the total number of estimated victims in the conflict (over 3,000): yet, again, I have limited my data to direct violence perpetrated by clearly identified actors. Geographically, most killings concentrated in the region of Moyen-Cavally, in the west. The two provinces with the highest levels of violence were Duékué and Abidjan, both of which had high levels of parity between Ouattara and Gbagbo supporters. Indeed, in the second round of the Presidential elections, neither of the two candidates had obtained an overwhelming majority (in Abidjan, Gbagbo had obtained 51.9 percent of the votes; in Duékué, it had won with 52.9 percent of the vote). I also collected demographic data, such as data on the ethnic composition of the departments, and economic data, such as cocoa production in the province, as well as data on violence during the 2002–2007 period (all the data sources are listed in Table 6.1).

I will not study the perpetration of indirect violence in Côte d'Ivoire because this type of violence was extremely rare in this conflict, even though both groups had weaponry that would have made it possible. Indirect forms of violence were mostly used by international forces against Gbagbo's weapons arsenals or in the frontal clashes in Abidjan between armed forces of the two sides. I do not analyze the few events in which indirect violence targeted civilians (for example, according to Human Rights Watch, the Abobo suburb of Abidjan was targeted by heavy weapons on March 17, 2011; at least 12 people were killed when a market was shelled).

---

[19] The CEI provides information on electoral results for 75 provinces, so 20 of the OCHA departmental units go missing in the empirical analysis. I have tried to obtain the electoral data for these additional provinces and the "sous-prefectures" but it has proven impossible to acquire. Fortunately enough, there were no killings in any of these missing cases during the war, so we are not missing relevant cases when we analyze variation among provinces with nonzero levels of violence.

[20] I built the dataset after reading all the reports and taking notes on the figures reported on the violence perpetrated by each of the armed group and their associated militias. I do not include the data when the perpetrators are not identified. I also exclude cases of communal violence when these can be identified. I tried to be as precise as possible, but the data has clear measurement issues, and it could be that the figures change as new research is conducted to uncover the crimes committed during the 2010–2011 period.

TABLE 6.1 *List of Sources in the Côte d'Ivoire Côte d'Ivoire's Dataset*

| Variable | Source |
| --- | --- |
| Total Killings (2010–2011) | Estimated from Human Rights Watch (HRW); International Crisis Group; Regroupement des Acteurs Ivoiriens des Droits de l'Homme (RAIDH); Armed Conflict Location Event Data Project (ACLED) |
| Killed by Ouattara (2010–2011) | Estimated from HRW; International Crisis Group; RAIDH; ACLED |
| Killed by Gbagbo (2010–2011) | Estimated from HRW; International Crisis Group; RAIDH; ACLED |
| Competition (2010) | Elaboration with data from Independent Electoral Commission (CEI) |
| Surface in cocoa prod | Food and Agriculture Organization (FA) of the United Nations (Agro-Maps) |
| Population 2010 | OCHA (2011) |
| Killed by Pro-Gbagbo (2002–2007) | Uppsala Conflict Data Program (UCDP) |
| Killed by FN (2002–2007) | UCDP |
| Elevation | Global Gazetteer (Version 2.3) |
| Ethnic Polarization Index (2002) | Dabalen et al. (2012) |
| Gini Coefficient of Land Ownership (2002) | Dabalen et al. (2012) |
| Horizontal Income Inequality | Dabalen et al. (2012) |

Table 6.2 shows an initial set of models with the results of a negative binomial (NB) regression on victims of violence in Côte d'Ivoire.[21] As in the case of Spain, I use the electoral results in the second round of the elections to build a quadratic measure of *Competition* between Ouattara's and Gbagbo's supporters at the province level. Given the distribution of the dependent variable, with many zeros and very few cases with positive levels of violence, I do not include many controls in the models: I include basic variables such as the total surface of the province devoted to cocoa production (in thousand meters) and population figures for the province (in thousands). I also incorporate three measures provided by Dabalen et al. (2012), which seem important from a theoretical point of view: *Land Gini Coefficient* (inequality of land ownership in the province; ownership is measured by the area of land owned in hectares by each household), *Horizontal Income Inequality* (capturing inequality between the richest and the poorest ethnic group in the province), and *Ethnic Polarization* (measuring, in each province, how far the distribution of the ethnic group

---

[21] Following Long and Freese (2001), I test for the suitability of count models, and I find that NB and ZINB are equally valid for these estimations.

TABLE 6.2 *Negative Binomial on Killings in Côte d'Ivoire, 2010–2011*

|  | (1)<br>Total Killed | (2)<br>Killed by Out. | (3)<br>Killed by Gb. |
|---|---|---|---|
| Competition | 10.6** | 9.31** | 17.5** |
|  | (2.37) | (3.02) | (4.56) |
| Surface in cocoa prod, in | −0.0058 | −0.0055 | −0.0046 |
| thousand mt | (0.0043) | (0.0051) | (0.0032) |
| Population (*1000) | 0.00096* | 0.00093$^+$ | 0.0011** |
|  | (0.00039) | (0.00054) | (0.00036) |
| Gini Coefficient (Land) | 2.48 | 0.48 | 5.47$^+$ |
|  | (1.94) | (2.19) | (2.97) |
| Horizontal Inc. Ineq | −0.11 | 0.078 | −0.89 |
|  | (2.03) | (3.74) | (2.58) |
| Ethnic Pol. | 25.9** | 21.6** | 41.1** |
|  | (6.02) | (6.96) | (11.6) |
| Constant | −27.8** | −22.8** | −48.0** |
|  | (4.81) | (5.35) | (12.5) |
| lnalpha |  |  |  |
| Constant | 2.98** | 3.36** | 3.07** |
|  | (0.51) | (0.53) | (0.65) |
| Observations | 50 | 50 | 50 |
| Pseudo $R^2$ | 0.091 | 0.081 | 0.104 |

Clustered standard errors in parentheses
$^+ p < 0.10$, $^* p < 0.05$, $^{**} p < 0.01$

is from the bipolar distribution).[22] Standard errors are clustered by region (there are 19 regions in Côte d'Ivoire). A first column shows the results for all killings – namely, all the people executed by both Ouattara's and Gbagbo's armed forces in a given province –, a second column shows the results only for the total number executed by Ouattara's armed forces (against Gbagbo's supporters), and the third column shows the number executed by Gbagbo's armed forces (against Ouattara's supporters).

In Table 6.2, we can observe that *Competition* is significant in explaining variation in levels of violence across Ivorian provinces. Also consistent with my theory and with the evidence from Spain, *Competition* is relevant in explaining levels of violence perpetrated by all groups (i.e., Ouattara's supporters and Gbagbo's supporters), both when taken separately and when they are pooled together. Population of the province has a positive sign, indicating that violence was more intense in more populated areas. Even though previous accounts (i.e., McGovern 2011) suggest that cocoa-producing regions experienced massive influxes of internal immigrants (not only Northerners but also Baoulé) and

---

[22] These variables are not available for all provinces, so a number of cases are dropped.

intense land-tenure disputes, and that violence should be concentrated in areas producing cocoa, the results of this variable are not totally supportive of this hypothesis: land Gini Coefficient only has an impact on violence perpetrated by pro-Gbagbo armed forces and militias. Ethnic polarization has a strong impact on violence perpetrated by all groups, suggesting that the ethnic polarization mechanism leading to violence is independent of political competition.[23]

I run a number of additional tests in which I incorporate two new variables in the models: violence (against civilians) perpetrated by pro-Gbagbo armed groups, on the one hand, and violence (against civilians) perpetrated by FN in the 2002–2007 period. The idea is to test for the revenge hypotheses, although the data at the provincial level does not allow for the kind of fine-grained test that I have undertaken in Spain. The effect of revenge on violence is supported by qualitative evidence on the events that took place in Côte d'Ivoire. For example, the International Crisis Group writes: "Vengeance became the third major reason for communities to fight each other, in addition to land conflicts and political divisions." (2014: 11), and they add that, in the context of the massacre of Carrefour (Duékoué) mentioned above, "town residents, victims of APWÊ atrocities, took part, in a spirit of vengeance, directly or indirectly by pointing out the homes of militia families or those alleged to be such" (International Crisis Group 2014: 13). The quantitative results (not included here) are, however, not fully supportive of the revenge hypothesis; only previous FN killings have an impact on violence perpetrated by pro-Ouattara forces. Also, in contrast with the case of Spain, previous killings have no effect when we obtain matching estimators. In fact, at the provincial level, the correlation between levels of violence from 2002 to 2007 and levels of violence from 2010 to 2011 is quite small.[24]

Abidjan, the capital of Côte d'Ivoire, was the site of intensely violent conflict between Ouattara's supporters and Gbagbo's supporters. The post-election conflict became a real urban war (Banégas 2011: 464). There are ten communes in Abidjan.[25] Table 6.3 summarizes the relevant indicators for these communes: the electoral results, a quadratic measure of competition (which

---

[23] Ethnic polarization is not underlying levels of political competition in Côte d'Ivoire; in fact, these variables are not significantly correlated.

[24] In additional robustness checks, I use geographical indicators such as kilometers of foreign borders (with Burkina Faso, Liberia, Ghana, Mali, and Guinea) in a given province; as well as latitude, longitude, and altitude of the centroid in each department. I also run the models clustering the standard errors by departments instead of regions. Finally, I use different measures of parity at the province level, such as absolute vote difference between Ouattara and Gbagbo, or a measure of *Competition* with absolute (instead of quadratic) values. All these analyses are available upon request.

[25] I coded levels of lethal violence in Abidjan relying on the 2011 Human Rights Watch report, which was the result of six research missions conducted between December 2010 and July 2011, the ACLED, and information gathered from other NGO sources reporting on violent events, such as the RAIDH.

TABLE 6.3 *Elections and Killings in Abidjan Communes, 2010–2011*

| Commune | %Gbagbo %(2nd round) | %Ouattara %(2nd round) | Competition (2nd round) | Killings by Ouattara Supp | Killings by Gbagbo Supp |
|---|---|---|---|---|---|
| Adjame | 32.5% | 67.51% | 0.87 | 1 | 19 |
| Plateau | 65.08% | 34.92% | 0.91 | 0 | 0 |
| Port-Bouet | 61.43% | 38.57% | 0.94 | 0 | 0 |
| Treichville | 39.52% | 60.48% | 0.95 | 0 | 2 |
| Cocody | 59.42% | 40.58% | 0.96 | 4 | 40 |
| Abobo | 41.23% | 58.77% | 0.97 | 24 | 130 |
| Yopougon | 58.48% | 41.52% | 0.97 | 70 | 0 |
| Attecoube | 52.66% | 47.34% | 0.99 | 0 | 9 |
| Koumassi | 47.69% | 52.31% | 0.99 | 0 | 40 |
| Marcory | 52.22% | 47.78% | 0.99 | 0 | 0 |

goes from 0 to 1), and the total number of killings committed by supporters of both political leaders.

In Abidjan, violence was particularly intense in the commune of Abobo (with 24 people killed by Ouattara's supporters and 130 people killed by Gbagbo's supporters). In this commune, there were reports of electoral malfeasance in the second round of elections. It was a quite contested commune (although not the most competitive one), which Ouattara ended up winning with 58.7 percent of the vote. In the commune of Koumassi there were 40 deaths at the hands of Gbagbo supporters; Ouattara had won this commune by a slim margin, with 52.3 percent of the vote. In Yopougon, Gbagbo won the second round of the presidential elections with 58 percent of the vote and Ouattara supporters killed 70 people. We do not see evidence of any violence in Plateau or Port-Bouet, where Gbagbo had won by a greater margin; and two people were killed in Treichville, where Ouattara had obtained over 60 percent of support. The only outlier in this subset of cases is Adjame, a commune where Ouattara had won by a larger margin (67 percent of the vote) and Gbagbo supporters killed 19 people. I cannot run reliable regressions with only ten cases, yet the micro-level descriptive evidence from Abidjan is overall quite consistent with what we observed in the country as a whole: killings are positively related to levels of parity between the two blocs in conflict. The rationale is, again, that violence brings greater returns in areas where there is such parity, as violence can help tip the local balance of power in favor of the group perpetrating the violence. Because of this, groups find greater collaboration toward the perpetration of direct violence in parity areas.

## 6.4 CONCLUDING REMARKS

This book represents an attempt to advance knowledge about the determinants of violence against civilians in civil war. In this chapter, I have explored the case of Côte d'Ivoire, and I have tested my main hypothesis on the determinants of direct violence with data from this civil war. This case poses some data limitations, so the statistical results have to be taken with a grain of salt. With the existing data sources, it was not possible to build a dataset with more fine-grained information on violence, as well as data on the main correlates of violence at units of analysis that are smaller than the province. Nonetheless, it is relevant that the Côte d'Ivoire's case provides us with evidence that is very much consistent with the evidence on violence during the Spanish Civil War presented in previous chapters. In Côte d'Ivoire, provincial-level parity between Ouattara's and Gbagbo's respective supporters has a significant impact on levels of direct violence against civilians. In addition, the case of Côte d'Ivoire illustrates the importance of political mobilization in explaining violence in conventional wars: in the first period of the war, mobilization (proxied with turnout) was less massive and victimization of civilians was lower than in the second period of the civil war, when levels of mobilization were higher and targeting of civilians was likely perceived as more paramount by the armed organizations.

There are very important differences between the Spanish and the Ivorian civil wars. Comparing these very different civil wars that nevertheless share an important common feature (i.e., both were conventional civil wars) is a useful exercise, despite the challenges, and it leads to more robust and generalizable results. The Ivorian case is particularly relevant because it is a "new" civil war (as opposed to Spain, which is an "old" civil war – in Kaldor's (1999) terminology), and because it is a civil war that was fought along politicized ethnic lines – as opposed to the Spanish case, where the fighting took place along ideological lines. Overall, the results in this chapter suggest that the theory in this book is applicable across different civil wars. In the following chapter, I present further evidence contributing to the external validity of the book.

# 7

# Additional Evidence and Macro-Level Implications

## 7.1 INTRODUCTION

In the previous chapter, we saw that the main theoretical predictions in the book fit not only the patterns of violence during the Spanish Civil War but also violence during the civil war in Côte d'Ivoire. This chapter introduces additional evidence complementing the main analyses in the book. Firstly, I present evidence from research on low-intensity inter-group violence in post-civil war Northern Ireland, which provides results consistent with the prediction that violence increases with parity between groups in conflict (in this case, Catholics and Protestants), even in non-civil war contexts. I also refer to research conducted by other scholars that provides evidence broadly supportive of my theory. Secondly, using a cross-national dataset covering all civil wars with more than one hundred battle deaths in the second half of the twentieth century, I explore macro-level variation in intentional violence against civilians and I explain it through the lens of my theoretical framework.

## 7.2 EVIDENCE FROM OTHER CASES

In research with Lesley Ann-Daniels and Abel Escribà-Folch, we explore geographical and temporal variation in inter-group violence (i.e., between Protestants and Catholics) in Northern Ireland. We use an original dataset of incidents of sectarian violence in this region from 2005 to 2012, with the ward-year as the unit of analysis.[1] Low-intensity sectarian violence has been prevalent in Northern Ireland since 1998, when a peace agreement put an end to the civil war that had plagued this region since 1969 (the so-called "the

---

[1] There is a total of 582 wards in Northern Ireland, and the time period for which data on sectarian violence is available is 2005–2012, so our dataset consists of 4,656 ward-year observations.

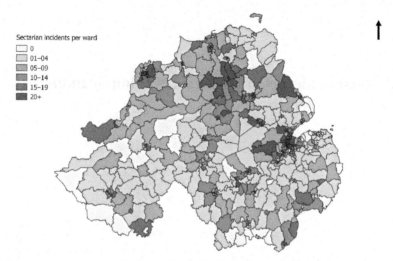

FIGURE 7.1 Low-Intensity Violence Between Catholics and Protestants in Northern Ireland (2005–2012)
*Source*: Balcells, Daniels, and Escribà-Folch (2016)

Troubles"). Incidents of sectarian violence are not necessarily lethal, and they include violence against individuals, symbols, and buildings, verbal threats, and even riots (all of these constitute what we call low-intensity inter-group violence). Thus, the type of violence explored is different from the type of violence that I have analyzed in this book, which has focused on wartime lethal violence.[2]

Figure 7.1 reveals the geographical variation in low-intensity violence across Northern Ireland's wards during the period under study (in some wards, violence could reach as many as 78 incidents in a year, while 7 percent of wards witnessed no incidents during this time period). When performing multivariate analyses, the determinants of variation in low-intensity violence in Northern Ireland appear to be strikingly similar to what I have observed in Spain and in Côte d'Ivoire regarding lethal wartime violence. Indeed, we find systematic evidence that inter-group *parity* at the ward level explains sectarian violent events. As shown in Figure 7.2, the predicted number of violent incidents in a given ward increases as the distribution of Catholics and Protestants approaches a parity distribution. Violence peaks in wards with 50 percent of Catholics, and where Protestants and Catholics are thus at parity. As shown in Balcells

---

[2] Although they tend to be studied separately, there are important connections between different forms of political violence: for example, popular protests very often precede coups; coups sometimes precede civil wars (Fearon 2004; Balcells and Kalyvas 2014); acts of terror are very often a part of civil war fighting (Fortna 2016); and low-intensity violence often takes place in post-war settings (Reno 2011). Bringing different forms of political violence under the same explanatory umbrella is challenging and not always possible, though.

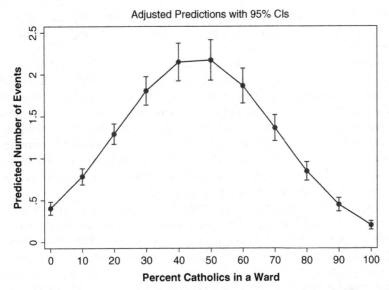

FIGURE 7.2 Predicted Low-Intensity Inter-Group Violence Events in Northern Ireland (2005–2012)

et al. (2016), results are consistent if we use a quadratic index of competition or parity between groups.

The findings from Northern Ireland are relevant because they show that the logic of violence outlined in Chapter 2, which aims to explain violence against civilians during civil wars, broadly travels to different settings. In the case of Northern Ireland, violence is not perpetrated by armed groups but by individuals, who act collectively on the basis of politicized ethnic identities. Yet, these individuals also behave strategically, using violence to shape demographic and political control of territories in a manner that resembles dynamics of violence in armed conflict. Individuals use harassment, intimidation, and violence in areas with ethnic parity in order to make the other group leave an area and secure control of it; indeed, where groups are demographically hegemonic, violence is less instrumental and thus violence is generally less prevalent. In the case of Northern Ireland, within-ward ethnic parity is crucial to understand sectarian violence, but the ethnic composition of neighboring wards is also very relevant in explaining confrontations between Protestants and Catholics. Violence takes place not only in internally divided wards (with parity), but also in the interface areas of highly segregated wards: for example, in the area where a predominantly Protestant ward meets a predominantly Catholic ward.[3] However, these neighboring effects do not rule out the effect of local-level demographic parity between groups; they are basically capturing

---

[3] For further details on the neighboring effects, see Balcells et al. 2016.

the effect of parity at higher levels of aggregation. In other words, competition between segregated groups does not take place at the ward level but at the district level.

The main finding in this book, which is that local political parity (or competition) is very relevant in explaining direct violence against civilians during civil war, connects with existing research on other civil wars. In the case of Colombia's "La Violencia" (1948–1958), Chacón et al. (2011) also observe that violence was greater in municipalities where prewar electoral support for the two competing blocs was more evenly balanced.[4] A shared feature of "La Violencia" and the Spanish Civil War, in addition to the historical time period in which they both took place (i.e., they are both "old" civil wars), is the high levels of political mobilization characterizing the periods preceding them, which led to severe violence against civilians in these two conflicts.[5] In contrast with my approach, Chacón et al. (2011) do not conceptualize direct violence as "jointly produced" between armed groups and civilians, but rather as unilaterally produced by the armed group. However, other authors have pointed out that local political elites were crucial actors in the perpetration of direct violence during *La Violencia*. For example, citing Roldán (2002), Auyero argues: "Political elites did not simply tolerate or instigate the violence; they were its perpetrators. While party members organized attacks on places and peoples, police acted as partisan shock troops" (Ayuero 2007: 35).

In the civil war in Bosnia (1992–1995), one of the most lethal conventional civil wars of the post-Cold War period (in the battlefield and outside of it), several authors (e.g., Weidmann 2011; Klasnja and Novta 2016; Costalli and Moro 2012) find that violence is to a great extent explained by intermixed demographic patterns.[6] Kalyvas and Sambanis (2005) argue that, in Bosnia, spatial variation in violence was explained by the strategic and economic importance of the area, and they also write that, at the local level, "polarization seems more significant than either fractionalization or dominance" (221). Gagnon (2004), for his part, argues that heterogeneous communities in the most ethnically plural parts of Croatia were those more intensively targeted by the elites of Belgrade and Zagreb.[7]

The results in this book are also in line with some results from the study of insurgency and counterinsurgency (i.e., irregular wars): for example, regarding

---

[4] "La Violencia" took place mostly in the form of raids or incursions into the enemy's territory. In Kalyvas and Balcells (2010), it is classified as a symmetric non-conventional (SNC) civil war.

[5] The total estimates are circa 200,000 deaths in "La Violencia," including both combatants and civilians (Karl 2016).

[6] In contrast with my theory, most of these authors refer to the "ethnic dilemma" (Posen 1993), which is less applicable to ideological wars than to ethnic ones. The ethnic dilemma assumes an inherent misperception of threat between groups belonging to different ethnic groups.

[7] It must be noted that violence in the former Yugoslavia was very much connected to nationally and internationally motivated ethnic cleansing dynamics (Mylonas 2012; Bulutgil 2015), which are not the norm in all civil wars.

the recent civil war in Iraq (2003–2011), Condra and Shapiro (2012) find that violence was more intense in mixed areas than in places dominated by either Shia or Sunnis. As I argued in Chapter 2, the structure of incentives considered in my theory should exist in areas of full military control in the context of any type of civil war, not only those fought conventionally. Anecdotal evidence from international wars of annexation and in wars where populations claiming different "nationhoods" share the same territory is also broadly consistent with my theory. For example, in the August 2008 war in South Ossetia between Russia and Georgia, local-level political dynamics seem to have played an important role in the violence taking place on the ground: "In a swath of villages in central Georgia, some killings were carried out for revenge, since feuds in this lush farmland go back generations. Some acts were outright cases of theft. And in still other cases, the message seemed to be that the *power balance was shifting, away from ethnic Georgians to the Ossetian separatists and their Russian backers*" (Tavernise 2008: A1, emphasis mine). During the Irish war of independence, Augusteijn claims that the level of violence directed at the Crown Forces and civilians depended on local-level collaboration in a given area (Augusteijn 1996: 334).

## 7.3   LARGE-N ANALYSES

So far I have theorized about individuals and armed groups interacting in a local context, and I have empirically tested the observable implications of the theory at the meso level, namely at the level of the locality (in Spain) and the province (in Côte d'Ivoire). Yet, dynamics taking place at a micro and meso level aggregate and generate macro-level dynamics and patterns. Micro-level approaches should allow us to better understand some of these macro-level dynamics and patterns (Balcells and Justino 2014). In what follows, I draw two macro-level implications of the results in this book, and I test one of them with large-n data on civil wars in the world between 1956 and 2004.

A first macro-level implication of the theory in this book is that civil wars – and, more specifically, conventional civil wars – should be more deadly when levels of prewar political mobilization are greater. When prewar political mobilization is high, armed groups have greater incentives to persecute civilians in territories that they control militarily. Ideally, I would use a cross-national proxy for prewar political mobilization to test this hypothesis, but there is no such proxy. Prewar mobilization could be captured by levels of turnout in prewar elections, but not all countries have elections before a civil war outbreak; and cross-national data on political party membership or trade union affiliation, which could also be a proxy for political mobilization, is generally unavailable for countries outside the Organisation for Economic Cooperation and Development (OECD). However, we can empirically establish a very general division between two different time periods in the second half of the twentieth century: the Cold War, in which levels of political and social mobilization were overall high because of the powerful ideological grip of Marxism and anti-Marxism (Kalyvas and Balcells 2010), and the post-Cold War period, in which the ideological cleavage lost relevance and political and social mobilization were overall less salient; Brubaker and Laitin talk about the "eclipse of the left–right ideological axis" (1998: 424). The external intervention of the superpowers contributed to the greater degree of social and political mobilization along the ideological cleavage during the Cold War: political movements seeking external sponsorship by either the United States or the Soviet Union took a stance in the cleavage.[8] Yet, as Adam Przeworski (1991) explains, the end of the Cold War destroyed the belief in radical political change (100); this lead to the demise of revolutionary activism and to political demobilization. Hence, contrary to the "new wars" approach (Kaldor 1999), I would argue that civil wars taking place during the Cold War were to be more violent than those in the post-Cold War period, precisely because of the overall lower degree of political mobilization in the post-1990 period.

I build a dataset that is based on Balcells and Kalyvas's (2014) PRIO100 dataset, to which I have added an indicator of violence against civilians from Melander et al. (2009). Balcells and Kalyvas's PRIO100 dataset includes those cases in the original UCDP/PRIO dataset (Gleditsch et al. 2002) that have more than 100 battle deaths per year.[9] Melander et al. (2009) compiled an indicator of intentional civilian victimization (that is, excluding battle deaths or collateral damage) in civil conflicts between 1956 and 2004. The indicator is called genocide/politicide, defined and coded by the State Failure project, and it includes: "massacres, unrestrained bombing and shelling of civilian-inhabited areas, declaration of free-fire zones, starvation by prolonged interdiction of food supplies, forced expulsion ('ethnic cleansing') accompanied by extreme privation and killings" (Marshall et al. 2006: 15, cited in Melander et al. 2009: 516). Thus, this measure, which ranges from 0 to 5, captures both direct and indirect forms of intentional violence against civilians.

Figure 7.3 shows the mean of the civilian victimization index across the two time periods considered: the Cold War, and the Post-Cold War (I date the end of the Cold War as 1991, coinciding with the dissolution of the Soviet Union). The differences between periods are stark, with the civil wars in the 1956–1990 period displaying significantly greater levels of civilian victimization than civil wars taking place from 1991 onwards. To test this implication on more solid ground, I use a multivariate regression analysis including a number of control variables, which are common in the cross-national analyses of conflict

---

[8] This mobilization did not exclude ethnically based movements, which on several occasions were organized as Marxist national liberation movements, e.g., FLN, Polisario (Balcells and Kalyvas 2016).

[9] To build this dataset, we used version 2009-4 of the UCDP/PRIO Armed Conflict dataset, which includes conflicts between 1946 and 2008. We took out interstate armed conflicts, but we did not exclude anti-colonial wars. The dataset has a total of 903 conflict-years that correspond to 212 conflicts.

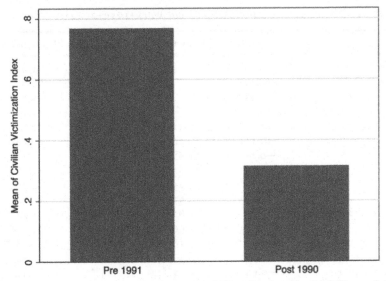

FIGURE 7.3 Civilian Victimization Across Civil Wars During the Cold War and After

(the descriptive statistics of all the variables are listed in the appendix of the book): GDP per capita (in thousands of 1990 international $) – from Maddison (2008); Rough Terrain, Democracy, Population, Ethnic Fractionalization, Oil Export – from Fearon and Laitin (2003); regional dummies;[10] a Cold War dummy, Post-1990 (with value 1 if the war takes place after 1990, and 0 otherwise), as well as dummies for the Technologies of Rebellion (Irregular, Conventional, SNC; Irregular is the base category). I transform the victimization variable (i.e., the dependent variable) into an ordinal variable with three categories (0 for no violence, 1 for low violence, 2 for high violence).[11] I use an ordinal logit to estimate the effect of the time period and the type of civil war on civilian victimization.

Table 7.1 presents the results, which show that the end of the Cold War led to a decrease of civilian victimization across all types of civil wars and that this decrease was quite significant if we only look at the subset of conventional civil wars (model 2). The results also show that irregular civil wars are more deadly against civilians – which is consistent with the idea that violence in guerrilla wars is very much related to military competition and to the strategy often followed by strong actors of trying to strike insurgents via the population

---

[10] The regional dummies are coded following Fearon and Laitin (2003), who distinguish between Western Democracies and Japan, Eastern Europe, Asia (without Japan), MENA, Sub-Saharan Africa and Latin America. MENA is the base category in the regressions.

[11] I transform the variable because there is little variation between some of the categories in the 0–5 scale. The results with the original variable are consistent.

TABLE 7.1 *Civilian Victimization Across Civil Wars (1956–2004)*

| | All | Only Conv. | Cold War | Post-Cold War |
|---|---|---|---|---|
| Conventional | −0.93** | | −0.36 | −1.97* |
| | (0.34) | | (0.36) | (0.88) |
| SNC | −1.43 | | −1.03 | −1.82 |
| | (0.91) | | (1.05) | (1.29) |
| Population (Log) | −0.23* | 0.31 | −0.35* | −0.100 |
| | (0.11) | (0.26) | (0.13) | (0.28) |
| Democracy | −0.21 | 21.6** | 0.071 | 0.21 |
| | (0.38) | (1.82) | (0.39) | (1.78) |
| Oil | 1.57** | 2.25** | 1.58** | 2.23** |
| | (0.29) | (0.57) | (0.31) | (0.70) |
| Ethnic Fractionalization | 0.28 | 3.82 | 0.26 | 4.24* |
| | (0.52) | (2.96) | (0.61) | (2.04) |
| Rough Terrain | 0.21+ | −0.18 | 0.36** | 0.68** |
| | (0.11) | (0.30) | (0.14) | (0.24) |
| Gdp per capita | −0.64** | −1.44** | −0.64** | −0.42 |
| | (0.15) | (0.46) | (0.18) | (0.34) |
| Post 1990 | −1.60** | −3.09+ | | |
| | (0.34) | (1.87) | | |
| West. Europe | 4.13** | 0 | 4.47** | 0 |
| | (0.78) | (.) | (0.87) | (.) |
| East. Europe | 3.14** | 16.8** | 4.88** | 2.49** |
| | (0.57) | (1.77) | (0.88) | (0.91) |
| Asia | 0.94+ | 14.0** | 1.64* | −17.2** |
| | (0.56) | (1.53) | (0.64) | (1.87) |
| Sub-Sah. Africa | 0.58 | 10.8** | 0.60 | 1.42 |
| | (0.58) | (2.25) | (0.66) | (1.22) |
| Latin America | 1.12* | 15.7** | 1.34* | −15.7** |
| | (0.51) | (1.72) | (0.56) | (0.65) |
| cut1 | | | | |
| Constant | −1.28 | 16.2*** | −1.61 | 5.28+ |
| | (1.18) | (2.53) | (1.35) | (3.00) |
| cut2 | | | | |
| Constant | −0.53 | 17.1*** | −0.73 | 5.56+ |
| | (1.19) | (2.62) | (1.37) | (2.97) |
| Observations | 624 | 86 | 444 | 180 |
| Pseudo $R^2$ | 0.200 | 0.270 | 0.177 | 0.415 |

Standard errors in parentheses
$^+p < 0.10$, $^*p < 0.05$, $^{**}p < 0.01$

(Downes 2008) – whereas it is less connected to military dynamics in conventional wars. However, if we disaggregate the sample between 1956–1990 (Cold War) (model 3) and 1991–2004 (post-Cold War) (model 4) civil wars, we observe that conventional civil wars were not significantly less deadly than irregular civil wars in the first period. I would argue that this is due to the high levels of political mobilization during the Cold War, which made conventional civil wars particularly deadly. In other words, in conditions of high political mobilization, conventional civil wars are as deadly as irregular civil wars. Again, that is the case, according to my theory, because armed groups perceive threats behind the front lines as coming from mobilized noncombatants and they invest resources in targeting them. Armed groups perceive less of a need to persecute civilians behind the front lines if prewar mobilization is insignificant.[12]

Another macro-level implication of the theory is that the spatial distribution of supporters of the different armed groups will correlate with violence against civilians during civil wars. Among civil wars with similar levels of prewar mobilization and fought between similarly equipped armed groups, we can expect direct violence to be relatively more prevalent, and indirect violence to be relatively less so, in countries with mixed settlements, and we can expect direct violence to be less prevalent, and indirect violence to be more so, in countries with segregated settlements. In other words: while segregation reduces direct violence, it increases the likelihood of indirect violence against civilians. Testing this implication is not straightforward because disaggregated data on direct and indirect violence against civilians are not available from large-n datasets: information on casualties from executions, massacres, and bombings are often pooled together. In addition, large-n country-level data are not available on the spatial distribution of supporters, especially for non-ethnic civil wars. In a recent paper, Wimmer and Miner (2016) use data from geographical cells, from which they calculate levels of ethnic parity in these geographical units. They find that, in ethnic civil wars, violence against civilians is higher in areas with greater parity between ethnic groups. Hultman et al. (2013), for their part, find evidence in favor of the idea that collective targeting (often perpetrated with indirect violence) against civilians is higher in areas dominated by rival groups. Their findings are thus generally consistent with my marco-level prediction, although they do not suffice to validate them because they are focused on ethnic conflicts and they do not precisely distinguish direct and indirect violence. Ideally, data should be collected for all types of wars (i.e., ethnic and non-ethnic) and should distinguish between victims of executions/massacres and victims of bombardments/shellings with further precision.

---

[12] Regarding battlefield deaths, which I have not addressed in this book, conventional wars are those most severe in relative terms (i.e., controlling for duration) and irregular wars are the most severe in absolute terms – as they are significantly longer (Balcells and Kalyvas 2014).

## 7.4 CONCLUSIONS

Chapters 6 and 7 have provided additional external evidence in support of the theory in the book and have explored some of its implications. Chapter 6 showed that the patterns of direct violence against civilians in the recent conflict in Côte d'Ivoire are broadly consistent with the patterns predicted by my theory, and that they are coherent with what we have observed in the case of Spain. Chapter 7 has discussed evidence from additional cases, as well as two macro-level observable implications of the theory, one of which I have been able to test with cross national data on civilian victimization. At the macro level – compared to irregular ones – conventional civil wars are overall less deadly toward civilians. Irregular civil wars are the "dirtiest" type (Valentino 2004; Balcells and Kalyvas 2014). Nonetheless, I find that conventional civil wars can be very deadly when prewar social and political mobilization is salient, as was the case during the Cold War. During the Cold War, most civil wars took place in countries with mobilized constituencies, due to the ideological grip and the mobilizational capacity of Marxism and anti-Marxism. Marxism constituted a powerful ideology, but also a transnational movement that established a military doctrine (Kalyvas and Balcells 2010); revolutionary socialism (and the reactions to it) contributed to mass political mobilization, which was often bolstered by the activity of trade unions and mass political parties. Because societies were overall less politically mobilized after the end of the Cold War, civilian victimization decreased significantly after 1990 across all types of civil wars.[13]

The next chapter discusses the main lessons of the book and considers competing explanations for the phenomena under scrutiny. It also addresses some caveats and discusses further avenues of research.

---

[13] From a normative perspective we tend to think of political mobilization in positive terms. However, the results in this book suggest there might be a "dark side" to it, which is that it can lead to greater levels of noncombatant victimization in the event of a civil war.

# 8

## Conclusions

"Tristes guerras,
si no es amor la empresa.
Tristes, tristes."

Miguel Hernández, *Cancionero y Romancero de Ausencias*

"The world is so lovely, yet we turn our backs on it to manufacture private sordid little hells."

Joan Sales, *Incerta Glòria*

### 8.1 MAIN LESSONS

This book makes several theoretical and empirical contributions. Firstly, it shows that theories of victimization in civil war should take into consideration differences between types of civil wars, and that we should be careful when applying theories that are largely inspired by one particular context to other civil war settings. Civil war should not be confounded with irregular warfare, and this holds true especially in the post-Cold War period. Yet, most research on civilian victimization still focuses on irregular warfare, both theoretically and empirically. In this book, I have extended the analytical focus to conventional warfare, which is a quite overlooked type of war that poses relevant theoretical puzzles. However, the theory extends beyond conventional conflicts and explains violence wherever the structure of incentives characterizing conventional civil wars exists, or whenever this structure of incentives is sharpened by specific warfare conditions. That is the case, for example, in areas of irregular civil wars that are fully controlled by one armed group – where there is no military contestation[1] – or of international civil wars where armed groups have military control of areas inhabited by people loyal to a

---

[1] For example, in Peru, a civil war fought irregularly: "Senderista groups apparently visited communities in the wake of the Peruvian military and executed those they considered to be state

rival nation (i.e., in wars of annexation, Downes 2008), including non-core national groups linked to external actors (Mylonas 2012).[2]

Secondly, this book has brought together types of violence that are often studied separately, namely executions/massacres and bombings, which I have called direct and indirect violence, respectively. While most studies focus exclusively on one type or the other, I posit that these two different forms of lethal violence can be explained within a common "rivalry and revenge" framework. Armed groups use direct and indirect violence to target political enemies as well as to satisfy vengeful desires, once wartime violence has taken place.

Thirdly, I put politics at the center of an explanation of wartime violence. As Eckstein put it, the political realm is crucial for the understanding of civil wars: "Internal wars belong to the realm not only of social force but also to political competition, since their object is to obtain political outputs advantageous to the groups that urge them favorable policies, offices, or general control of the political structure of society" (Eckstein 1964: 12). Clausewitz, for his part, argued that "war is a mere continuation of politics by other means" (1832/1968: 23) and that "under all circumstances War is to be regarded not as an independent thing, but as a political instrument" (25). I posit that insights of both the first and second generations of scholars of violence – that is, those defending a political approach to violence on the one hand and those arguing for a strategic approach on the other – should be incorporated into a single theoretical framework. In this framework, political variables do not exhibit an immediate connection with violence; in other words, while wartime violence is connected to prewar politics, the former does not constitute a mere continuation of politics by other means. The main reason behind the complex relationship between politics and direct violence is civilian agency – namely, the joint production of direct violence on the part of armed groups and civilians – and the strategic use of violence by local civilians.[3] Indeed, in this book I oppose approaches that conceive all civil war violence as unilaterally inflicted by armed groups that do not require public cooperation (Mueller 2004, cited in Valentino 2014: 98); direct forms of violence leave significant room for civilian agency, and without civilian cooperation, groups have limited maneuvering capacity.

Relatedly, while previous research has conceived behavior during civil war as disconnected from attitudes, preferences, and political allegiances

---

collaborators" (Metelits 2008: 10). In Colombia, Vargas (2009) finds that the distribution of political loyalties explains selective violence in the city of Barrancabermeja.

[2] In a world of nation-states, national identity is often taken as a strong signal of personal loyalty. This is why thousands of people of Japanese ancestry living in the USA were forcedly relocated and incarcerated during World War II.

[3] The relationship between the master cleavage of the civil war and violence is more straightforward in the case of indirect violence because this type of violence does not provide much agency to local civilians.

(Kalyvas 2006), I argue that political mobilization makes individual wartime behavior to be very much related to political attitudes, preferences, and allegiances. Mobilized individuals are committed to a cause, and they are likely to behave in coherence with this commitment. Consequently, armed groups target mobilized individuals (e.g., activists, members of political parties, syndicalists) because they know that mobilized individuals are likely to behave in coherence with their ideology, even if they mask their preferences to maximize their odds of survival.[4] This explains why we observe violence in areas where military considerations would not lead us to expect it.

At the same time, in this book I incorporate emotional factors – endogenous to wartime events – in an explanation of violence. Emotions such as anger and shame – spawned by wartime victimization – are behind revenge, which is an important factor in accounting for violence in non-initial phases of a civil war. Because of these emotions related to violent experiences, what Petersen (2011) has called "residuals of experiences," civil wars have endogenous dynamics, which make political factors lose some of their relevance over time.[5] Empirically, I find that there is a clear endogenous trend whereby, at the local level, subsequent levels of direct violence perpetrated by one group are highly correlated with initial levels of direct violence perpetrated by the rival group. Thus, the book sheds some light on the relationship between levels of violence on the part of rival actors in war, which to date has remained quite unclear (Eck and Hultman 2007: 241), and it shows that understanding the determinants of violence requires a theory that combines the effects of political cleavages and wartime dynamics.

In addition, this book shows that civilian targeting is not a mere consequence of guerrilla warfare and counterinsurgency operations. Although irregular wars tend to be more violent against noncombatants, civilians are also widely targeted in conventional wars. This holds regardless of whether the conflict is based on ethnic identities or not. Indeed, the literature on ethnic, conflict as well as the social psychology literature, has often emphasized the dangers of ethnic mobilization, ethnic outbidding, ingroup–outgroup differentiation, and subsequent violence (Horowitz 1985; Hechter 2001; Fearon and Laitin 2003; Fujii 2009; Littman and Paluck 2015). This book posits that these processes of political and social mobilization leading to the outbreak of conflict and collective violence are not necessarily reduced to ethnic conflict: they can also take place along ideological lines. Furthermore, the book challenges

---

4 In territory under *A*'s full control, *B* supporters will behave in public "as if" they support *A*. In a way, they will falsify their preferences (Kuran 1994). But they might undertake clandestine actions to support *B*, which is why *A* is concerned about them.

5 Emotions obviously also have a role in accounting for violence that takes place in initial phases of the civil war (for instance, one group can be resentful toward another, or some individuals can hate others for a variety of reasons). Yet, I have focused on revengeful emotions, which become particularly relevant as the civil war develops and violence is perpetrated, and which we can expect to be systematically connected to this violence.

the literature that argues that there are fundamental differences between ethnic and non-ethnic wars (Kaufmann 1996; Denny and Walter 2014). For example, Chaim Kaufmann argues that ideological civil wars tend to feature dynamics of guerrilla warfare whereas ethnic civil wars tend to feature conventional warfare, and that this divergence is due to the difference between ethnic and ideological loyalties. According to him, while in ethnic wars loyalties remain rigid and visible, in ideological wars "loyalties are changeable and difficult to assess, and the same population serves as the shared mobilization base for both sides" (Kaufmann 1996: 139). The evidence in this book challenges his approach. Firstly, ideological identities were quite rigid in the Spanish Civil War: those who had been mobilized by leftist political forces before the war were not easily turned into right-wingers afterwards, and vice versa.[6] Members of the working class and members of the bourgeoisie were not a shared mobilization base for both blocs: they were clearly aligned with one of them. Secondly, the Spanish Civil War was an ideological civil war fought conventionally (this is also the case with the civil wars in Russia, China, the U.S., and in several former Soviet Republics).[7] Finally, the evidence from the conflict in Côte d'Ivoire, a war that has been labeled as ethnic, is quite consistent with my theory and with the evidence from the Spanish Civil War, which was fought along non-ethnic, ideological lines. This indicates that dynamics of targeted killing in ideological conflicts are similar to those in ethnic civil wars. While ascriptive characteristics may make supporters of the enemy somewhat easier to identify (i.e., ascriptive characteristics they can serve as a relevant informational cue), armed groups always have difficulty in distinguishing between strong and weak supporters of the rival, and thus they always require some civilian collaboration in the perpetration of direct violence.

## 8.2 LESSONS ABOUT CASE STUDIES

This book is grounded on comparative micro-level evidence from two case studies. In addition to generate inferences from these cases, I hope I have made a contribution to the understanding of what happened in Spain and in Côte d'Ivoire during their respective civil wars. The research I have undertaken on the civil war in Côte d'Ivoire supports McGovern's conjecture (2011) that this conflict does not come down to a simple division between ethnic or

---

[6] Mobilized identities are sticky, but they are not immutable. This applies to both ideological and ethnic identities, as ethnic identities can be mobilized (or not), and people can renounce ethnic identities or they can behave in ways that are theoretically inconsistent with their identities (Kalyvas 2008; Lyall 2009).

[7] In fact, the characteristics and dynamics of warfare in the Spanish Civil War run nearly parallel to those that describe "ethnic civil wars" in Kaufmann's theory: the decisiveness of territory and of military operations, collective violence against particular communities, the inherent risk in mixed communities (Kaufmann 1996: 146–148).

religious groups. There is more complexity in the processes underlying civilian victimization than the simple notion of a fight between Muslims and Christians, or northerners against southerners. Political identities mobilized during the first phase of the conflict and before the 2010 elections were behind civilian victimization by pro-Gbagbo and pro-Ouattara armed groups in 2010–2011. Also, as in Spain, the fact that local-level competition is explaining levels of direct violence indicates that there was a strategic use of violence by local political actors.

With regard to the Spanish Civil War, which I have analyzed in greater depth, my goal is not to provide a new historiographic account of this civil war. My intent is to present an overarching explanation of dynamics of violence against non-combatants, which should help explain what happened during this civil war, among many other cases. In general terms, I have shown that violence behind the war frontlines, which has been labeled as "terror" in many historical accounts, was less indiscriminate than is usually thought. Violence was targeted toward political enemies and emanated from dynamics of political rivalry at the local level. I have also shown that violence was the consequence of vengeful emotions which led individuals who suffered the loss of relatives, friends, and even properties, to push for violence in non-initial stages of the civil war.

Several historians have argued that the logic of violence during the Spanish Civil War was different on both sides. The two blocs were indeed fundamentally different, ideologically and organizationally, but the evidence in this book shows that the local dynamics of direct violence were strikingly similar across control zones. I would argue that this is the case because civilians living on both sides behaved in similar ways toward the armed groups and their repressive actions: on both sides, local political actors were instrumental in the use of this violence against their enemies. The differences between blocs are more clear-cut with regards to indirect violence, for which local civilian agency was mainly absent: while the Nationalists clearly intended to perpetrate mass killings through the bombing and shelling of cities full of noncombatants, the Republicans were much more restrained.[8]

Arguing that the local dynamics of direct violence followed a similar logic should not be taken to mean that the two sides were equivalent; still less should this be interpreted as a normative statement regarding the legitimacy of these two groups. The Nationalists were insurgents who plotted and organized a *putsch* against a legitimate democratic government. In addition, they received extensive support from the fascist regimes, they perpetrated at least twice more direct violence against civilians than the Loyalists, and they killed thousands

---

[8] The conduct of the two armies in battlefield areas was also different, with the Nationalist army being more brutal as they were conquering new areas, perpetrating mass killings and inducing mass displacement (Preston 2011; Balcells and Steele 2016).

in bombardments. On the Republican side, the army was more restrained and the government tried to avoid executions on many occasions.[9] However, the above cannot lead us to establish that leftist violence was not strategic and that it did not involve the targeting political enemies, who were seen as particularly dangerous during the war as they posed a threat to the democratic order (as the coup itself had demonstrated), and to the revolution (the ultimate goal of anarcho-syndicalists and communists).[10] If that was the case, we would not find any systematic effect of local political factors on leftist violence. The historian José Luis Ledesma puts it as follows: "Massacres in the Republican zone did not come from the higher levels of power and were not ordered by Government authorities, as was the case in the Francoist rearguard. However, they were also not the result of obscure uncontrolled squads or groups acting outside any authority or organization. It would be wrong to conclude that local powers, political parties, trade unions, or even certain sectors of the Republican state had nothing to do with them. Whether by action or omission, the authorities and anti-fascist organizations adopted an ambiguous stance toward such violent practices, and sometimes took direct responsibility for them" (Ledesma 2003: 8). For her part, Clara Campoamor, who was a Republican politician and first-hand witness of the violence in the Republican rearguard, wrote: "One cannot avoid thinking that these crimes would not have happened if the men in power had felt their horror. It seemed that they were indifferent to them and even that they closed their eyes, convinced that this purging could be useful and necessary for internal security reasons" (Campoamor 2005: 115).

Finally, although it is overall very rich, some of the historical research on violence during the Spanish Civil War exhibits flaws that I hope to have addressed in this book. First, some historical accounts of violence are affected by a selection bias on the dependent variable – for example, they focus on the analysis "of executions in municipalities where these were most relevant" (Chaves 1995: 104), which leads them to draw biased inferences. Secondly, the unit of analysis of historians has very often been the whole country or the region (Linz 1996; Casanova 1985), and this overaggregation has sometimes led to omitted variable bias.[11] Relatedly, these researchers do not

---

[9] Julián Casanova explains that "there was a large number of people, including the CNT leader Joan Peiró, senior politicians in the *Generalitat* and ordinary political activists, as well as Pere Bosch-Gimpera, the rector of the university, who tried to prevent bloodshed, something that can hardly be said of the rebel officers and authorities on the other side"(Casanova 2010: 196). Nearly 5,000 right-wing individuals left Barcelona after the military coup failed in this city (Benet 1989: XII–XIII), and many received help from Republican political authorities (Dòll-Petit 2003).

[10] Eduardo de Guzmán, an anarchist, put it in the following way: "The execution of fascists is the revolution" (2004: 92).

[11] For example, when analyzing provincial-level patterns, Juan Linz (1996) contends that violence was at higher levels in provinces with a higher proportion of *latifundios* and heightened social

usually conduct systematic econometric analyses and thus they draw inferences that lack internal validity. Finally, until very recently (see Casanova 2014; Moreno 2014; Langarita 2014), historians had not undertaken systematic analyses of civilian agency. While the role of political committees and local civilians on the perpetration of violence has been acknowledged in many local and regional histories, their implications for lethal violence had not been theorized in depth.

## 8.3   COMPETING EXPLANATIONS

Conclusions should not be drawn in a scientific work without giving serious attention to alternative explanations (Green and Shapiro 1996). In what follows, I address competing explanations for the main takeaway from in the book, which is that direct violence increases with parity between groups at the local level, and I discuss how we can evaluate and discard these alternative explanations with the empirical evidence at hand.

One potential rival hypothesis is the *security dilemma* (Posen 1993). According to the security dilemma, civil war violence takes place in ethnically mixed settlements because, in a situation of anarchy (i.e., absence of state authority), members of different ethnic groups compete for security up to a point at which they generate threats to the other groups; eventually one of them attacks the other, trying to make use of a first mover's advantage, and leading to conflict and civilian victimization. Violence does not occur in segregated territories, because no security dilemma emerges when groups are not in contact with each other (Kaufmann 1996). The security dilemma could thus lead us to predict violence in areas of parity between groups, but it cannot really account for the dynamics of violence explored in this book for a number of reasons: first, in most civil war contexts, including those analyzed here, there is neither pure anarchy nor absence of authority. In civil wars, competing armed groups are in control of the territory, which they govern. Second, even though civilians play an important role in the perpetration of violence, the agents of violence are the armed groups and not the communities themselves (with some exceptions) – contrary to the security dilemma scenario. Third, at the empirical level, the fact that we observe the same dynamic in ethnic (e.g., Ivory Coast) and in non-ethnic (e.g., Spain) civil wars challenges an explanation of violence based on the security dilemma, because the latter would apply only to ethnic conflicts and not to ideological ones. Indeed, according to the security dilemma theoretical framework, mutual threat perception does not occur between individuals from the same ethnic group who are divided along ideological lines. Finally, if violence were the mere outcome of a security

agrarian conflict (e.g., Malaga, Ciudad Real, Córdoba). Yet, Linz did not conduct statistical analyses to test this conjecture and he did not control for patterns of military presence and other variables that most likely had an impact on levels of violence.

dilemma, we would not find prewar political dynamics to matter; wartime behavior of individuals would instead be more crucial in explaining violent outcomes.

Killing civilians could be just a way to show strength to the opposing side; a *coercive* tool to push the rival to surrender (Pape 1996; Valentino 2004; Hultman 2007; Downes 2008; Wood 2010). In the Spanish case, for example, Ors (1995: 297) argues that violence on the Republican side increased in correlation with acts of violence on the Nationalist side; according to him, this was a way to show strength. This alternative hypothesis can be ruled out in light of the finding that local political factors are underlying levels of direct violence. If violence were a mere coercive tool, it would be randomly distributed geographically and would not be systematically related to local factors.

Trying to reverse *domination* could be behind direct violence. At the operational level, this competing hypothesis implies that there is a linear relationship between political support for a group and levels of violence perpetrated by the rival group. In the case of Spain, a number of authors have made this conjecture (e.g., Linz 1996; Casanova et al. 2001; 2010; Herreros and Criado 2009).[12] The political domination hypothesis can, however, be discarded in light of the multivariate results in this book, which show a robust nonlinear effect of support for one group on levels of direct violence perpetrated by the rival group.

Violence could be driven by *military control*, reaching higher levels in areas of military competition or where military control is contested (Kalyvas 2006; Metelits 2009). Yet, as I have argued previously in the book, military control cannot adequately account for violence occurring in uncontested areas such as the rearguard territories of a conventional civil war. One could challenge the idea that there is full control in the rearguard areas of a conventional civil war like the Spanish one; it may be the case, for example, that armed groups are incapable of exerting full authority in more inaccessible areas (e.g., mountainous areas). However, even in these areas, the other group is militarily absent: in other words, there is no military contestation. Also, in my analyses, elevation – a potential proxy for state absence (Fearon and Laitin 2003; McLauchlin 2014) – does not have a systematic effect on violence. A related alternative hypothesis is that of *economic competition*. Metelits (2009) argues that groups treat civilians coercively when they face competition or "active rivalry" from other groups that can draw from the same pool of resources. However, this hypothesis can be discarded for the same reasons as the military control hypothesis.

---

[12] For example, historian Julián Casanova argues that violence against left-wing loyalists was greater in places where the *Frente Popular* had gained more votes in the February 1936 elections (Casanova 2010: 188). And, he writes that "In those places where landlord property was more equally distributed and the Popular Front had a smaller share of the electoral results, the terror was less severe" (Casanova et al. 2001: 222).

Some theories relate wartime violence to the *degree of urbanization* or to the proximity of urban centers (Mkandawire 2002). Both in Côte d'Ivoire and in Spain, violence was greater in urban and hence more populated settings, but this is driven by the fact that larger locations have a higher population density and hence more would-be targets. This alternative hypothesis can be discarded because the relevance of political competition in explaining violence is robust to the inclusion of an indicator of urbanization in the vector of independent variables, and the results do not change if I use a normalized measure of the dependent variable (i.e., killings per capita).

Finally, it could be argued that direct violence was driven by the characteristics of armed groups, and in particular by their level of *internal discipline*. Weinstein (2007) predicts that well-disciplined organizations will be more selective and inflict lower levels of violence than organizations that lack mechanisms of internal control, which as a result will be more violent and inflict more indiscriminate violence against civilians. Yet, in this book we have observed that local-level competition explains direct violence across armed groups. Behind the frontlines, both tightly organized (e.g., the rebels) and loosely organized (e.g., the Loyalists) groups perpetrated direct violence following similar patterns. Furthermore, in Spain, violence by Nationalists was more intense and indiscriminate (for example, with many more bombing raids and shellings) than violence by leftist armed forces, which contradicts the prediction that loose and decentralized organizations are more violent than disciplined ones.[13]

## 8.4 BROADER IMPLICATIONS AND NEXT STEPS

The results in this book have several implications for phenomena that go beyond civil war violence. In the comparative politics literature, political competition is usually perceived as a positive characteristic for democratic politics. In some rationalist approaches, elections are deemed to function peacefully only when the electoral chances of competing parties are similar. According to Przeworski (1991), "democracy is an equilibrium" when there is parity between competitors; in other words, democracy becomes stable when the two competing blocs have a high chance of winning the election. The results here indicate that electoral competition has the potential of leading to

---

[13] Another way to test the principal-agent hypothesis in Spain could be by measuring the presence of anarchist militias. In areas controlled by the anarchists, the Republican government's orders would not necessarily be followed and militiamen would be more likely to kill "opportunistically." In Catalonia we have observed that CNT affiliates at the local level did have a significant impact on left-wing violence: there were no localities with CNT affiliates that were not victimized by the Left. However, CNT militias were in charge of patrolling large territories and they moved from one municipality to another. As pointed out in Chapter 1, there were entire counties with a strong presence of anarchist militias and still there was variation across the municipalities in these counties. Furthermore, my results are consistent when using county fixed effects.

disastrous consequences in wartime environments. In this regard, the findings here are coherent with previous literature that has found that political competition can have negative effects at the economic (Bardhan and Yang 2004), and social (Wilkinson 2004; Chacón et al. 2011) levels. In a similar vein, the evidence in the book suggests that mass political mobilization can lead to terrible consequences in the event of a civil war. When individuals are politicized, they are more likely to be perceived as threatening by armed groups, which might then devote resources to their persecution. Thus, the book might be uncovering a "dark side" of both political mobilization and political competition.[14]

In a similar vein, the results have certain implications for the theoretical discussion in international relations, which considers "power parity" to have a deterrent effect and therefore to be conducive to interstate peace (see, among others, Organski and Kugler 1980; Kugler and Lemke 1996). If we were to measure power with the number of supporters each group has, at the micro level, the results in this book suggest that power parity between two antagonistic parties does not entail deterrence, but rather leads to violence.[15] Nevertheless, the decision to engage in violence – in the context of an ongoing conflict – is somehow different than the decision to start a conflict.

There are various synergies between my theory and the study of other forms of political violence such as genocide or riots. As I argued in Chapter 2, some of the assumptions in my theoretical model do not hold when groups have genocidal goals: the marginal benefits of violence are always increasing for a group if their ultimate objective is to completely eliminate another group. So, I do not expect the model to apply perfectly to cases of genocide. However, there are some interesting points in common with recent research on genocide conducted by Gross (2001), Fujii (2009), Finkel (2015), and Straus (2015), who have highlighted the role of civilian agency in the perpetration of genocidal violence. In addition, one of the implications of my findings on revenge is that violence is likely to haunt the perpetrators if they lose control of a given territory. This parallels experiences of mass violence that were triggered by reprisals for previous killings (e.g., Rwanda), and it also parallels experiences of ethnic cleansing in which supporters of one group are forced to abandon territories in punishment for previous victimization inflicted by their group (e.g., Krajina, in Croatia/Serbia).

My approach also has connections to Wilkinson's (2004) and Auyero's (2007) research on riots in that it unpacks violence that many have considered chaotic (and therefore unexplainable) and provides an explanation that

---

[14] Still I would stress caution when considering the evidence in this book as speaking in favor or against theories of democracy. Even though wartime violence is used to shape electoral politics, wartime and peacetime politics do not admit direct comparability.

[15] Regarding interpersonal relations, Gould (2003) finds that the more evenly balanced they are with regard to power, the greater the odds of violent conflict.

puts political actors (and their strategic interests) at the heart of the story. In his seminal book, Steven Wilkinson (2004) finds riots in India to be positively associated with levels of competitiveness in state elections. The crucial actors are national-level politicians, who are in charge of the security forces and who use these riots in the run-up period to the elections to win popular support. Javier Ayuero, for his part, shows that the 2001 lootings in Argentina were selective and followed a political logic. Even though it was perpetrated by others (e.g., specialists of violence), political brokers, political authorities and policemen created the opportunities for looting. He writes: "The genesis of many episodes of collective violence should be located in the area where the actions of political entrepreneurs and those specialists in violence meet and mesh" (Auyero 2007: 33). In a similar vein, I also find that there is a gray area in which local political elites and specialists of violence (i.e., militias, armed groups) collaborate in the perpetration of violence against civilians during civil war.

This book also speaks tangentially to the social capital literature. We have observed that wartime events lead to emotions such as anger, which – in turn – lead to vengeful actions. These emotions and associated behavior are likely to have an impact on social trust and community cohesion: as a consequence of violence, we can expect members of a community to be less willing to cooperate and more likely to betray one another (Putnam et al. 1993; Varshney 2002). Although exploring the consequences of violence on social capital is out of the scope of this book, the results here suggest that, as civil wars go by, we might be observing increasingly less cooperative societies, and that postwar societies are likely to have lower levels of social capital as compared to societies not having experienced a civil war.

Political cleavages are very relevant in my explanation of wartime violence. I have assumed that civil wars are fought around one "macro-cleavage." Political spaces do not need to be unidimensional, but they are likely to become so during war. In the case of Spain, we have observed that a multidimensional political space became somewhat one-dimensional during the war – the ideological cleavage prevailed over the religious or territorial cleavages. With the explosion of the civil war, some of the other cleavages collapsed in the civil war cleavage to the point that people sometimes fell on one side or the other without having taken a deliberate decision about it. Interviewee 9 explained, for example, "Religious people were not necessarily supporters of the right. But they automatically became right-wingers when the coup took place." This has implications for the configuration of cleavages and political party systems in the postwar, which can be transformed because of the war (Mayhew 2005), as well as for the perception of cleavages. For example, in contemporary Basque Country and Catalonia, voters often confound the ideological and territorial cleavages (Dinas 2012): that is probably because the territorial cleavage somehow collapsed in the Left–Right cleavage during the civil war and the Francoist dictatorship. In short, cleavage dynamics during armed conflict have interesting implications for the study of the dimensionality of political spaces, and they can have implications on political dynamics in the postwar periods.

In this book, I have argued that prewar mobilization leads to higher levels of violence, but I have set aside the causes of political mobilization. A question for further research is exploring why some civil wars are preceded by high levels of political mobilization while others are not. The international system could have a strong impact on the nature and levels of mobilization. As I argued in the previous chapter, during the Cold War, Marxism and revolutionary Socialism had a strong influence on political and social mobilization. During the interwar period in Europe, ideologies such as Communism, Anarchism, and Nazism also had a very powerful impact on political mobilization preceding popular revolutions and civil wars. Yet, domestic factors such as the nature of domestic electoral institutions undoubtedly also affect levels of political mobilization. Further research might explore the international and domestic sources of prewar political mobilization and how they are intertwined.

## 8.5 CONCLUDING REMARKS

Understanding why unarmed civilians are killed in the context of civil wars is a major question in social science. In this book, I have provided an explanation that puts a lot of emphasis on political mobilization and political identities. While this cannot explain all the violence taking place across the whole spectrum of civil wars, I would argue that it can account for an important share of the violence that takes place within them. Civil wars are, after all, political conflicts, and those who are involved in these civil wars are inevitably plagued by the political rivalries that lead to the outbreak of violence in the first place. Recent approaches to violence and conflict have tended to overlook the importance of politics, either because they have considered armed actors as highly rational and narrowly driven by greedy factors, or because they have considered them totally irrational and prompted by wanton barbarism. Neither of these extremes considers that actors in conflict are often rational, but that their goals do not boil down to economic profit. Political goals are relevant too, and that is especially the case when individuals are politically mobilized and therefore politically committed to a cause.

At the same time, in this book I have highlighted the relevance of emotions in explaining violence. Emotions are not necessarily at odds with rationality, but they often trigger behavior that otherwise would not unfold. In the civil wars explored in this book, many of those who denounced or killed others would not have done so if they did not have vengeful emotions in the first place. Although vengeful emotions can be driven by a myriad of factors, they are often a response to violence. Revenge is the mechanism behind spirals of violence that we often observe in civil wars and that make these conflicts lose some of their political content over time.

Studying atrocities from an analytical perspective is not painless. Yet, only by being analytical can we obtain insights from which we can hopefully derive useful policy implications aimed at reducing conflict and human rights violations. The lessons of this book suggest that policymakers should pay more attention to political dynamics at the local level in order to understand and prevent atrocities in ongoing civil wars. The nature of local political alignments is relevant if we want to understand why some individuals and localities are being targeted while others are not. Local politics can thus inform us on where to put efforts if we wish to avoid casualties. In non-initial periods of the civil war, we also have to pay attention to revenge dynamics, and thus focus on areas with greater victimization in early periods, where violence spirals are likely to emerge. Furthermore, because patterns of direct and indirect violence are different, the efforts should vary depending on the technology available to armed groups and the ways in which they use it to target civilians. As we have seen in previous chapters, mixed locations with high levels of parity are vulnerable to executions and massacres, but segregated locations with clear majorities are vulnerable to bombings and shellings, if armed groups have heavy weaponry at their disposal. Furthermore, the determinants of violence in militarily contested areas are different from those in uncontested areas, and thus patterns of civilian victimization in civil wars with porous frontlines and large areas of military contestation (i.e., irregular wars) are likely to be broadly different from those in civil wars with clear frontlines and relatively stable zones of uncontested military control (i.e., conventional). Overall, the results in this book tell us that we need to pay more attention to the type of warfare (i.e., how the war is being fought), local politics, and revenge dynamics, if we want to better understand why noncombatants are being killed during civil wars, as well as if we want to do something about it.

# Appendix

TABLE A.4.1 *Executed by the Left in Catalonia & Executed by the Right in Aragon (ZINB with County Fixed Effects)*

|  | Executed_left | Executed_right |
|---|---|---|
| Competition | 1.60** | 1.23** |
|  | (0.38) | (0.45) |
| inflate |  |  |
| Competition | 2.94+ | −1.37 |
|  | (1.75) | (0.98) |
| lnalpha |  |  |
| _cons | 0.31** | 0.088 |
|  | (0.070) | (0.15) |
| N | 870 | 250 |
| ll | −2092.1 | −597.6 |

Control variables in specification not shown. Standard errors in parentheses
$^+p < 0.10, ^*p < 0.05, ^{**}p < 0.01$

TABLE A.4.2 *Executed by the Left in Catalonia (Alternative ZINB Models)*

|  | (1) | (2) | (3) | (4) | (5) |
|---|---|---|---|---|---|
| **NB: Number of Executed** | | | | | |
| Competition (Abs.) | 0.92** | | | | |
|  | (0.32) | | | | |
| Frontline | 0.34 | 0.34 | 0.36 | 0.50 | |
|  | (0.32) | (0.33) | (0.30) | (0.33) | |
| Population | 0.000062 | 0.000058 | 0.000064 | 0.000049 | 0.000052 |
|  | (0.00011) | (0.00012) | (0.00012) | (0.00011) | (0.00011) |
| CNT Affiliation | 0.13* | 0.13* | 0.13* | 0.12+ | 0.13* |
|  | (0.060) | (0.055) | (0.057) | (0.06) | (0.06) |
| UGT Affiliation | 0.082 | 0.085 | 0.086 | 0.097 | 0.071 |
|  | (0.097) | (0.094) | (0.092) | (0.11) | (0.078) |
| Border | −0.36* | −0.41** | −0.42** | −0.39* | |
|  | (0.15) | (0.13) | (0.14) | (0.16) | |
| Sea | −0.11 | −0.12 | −0.11 | −0.083 | |
|  | (0.27) | (0.28) | (0.24) | (0.27) | |
| Elevation | −0.00072 | −0.00076 | −0.00076 | −0.00064 | −0.00055 |
|  | (0.00067) | (0.00069) | (0.00062) | (0.00064) | (0.00037) |
| Catholic Center | 2.17* | 2.18** | 2.19** | 1.94** | 2.23** |
|  | (0.85) | (0.72) | (0.84) | (0.53) | (0.80) |
| Competition33 | | 0.68 | | | |
|  | | (0.46) | | | |
| Polarization33 | | | 0.19 | | |
|  | | | (0.36) | | |
| Competition | | | | 0.75* | 1.44** |
|  | | | | (0.38) | (0.40) |
| Percentage Literate | | | | 0.023** | |
|  | | | | (0.0075) | |
| Longitude (*1000) | | | | | −0.0020 |
|  | | | | | (0.0015) |
| Latitude (*1000) | | | | | −0.0040 |
|  | | | | | (0.0026) |
| _cons | 0.92 | 1.04* | 1.44** | −0.62 | 19.6+ |
|  | (0.63) | (0.42) | (0.53) | (0.81) | (11.7) |

*(continued)*

TABLE A.4.2 *(continued)*

| | (1) | (2) | (3) | (4) | (5) |
|---|---|---|---|---|---|
| **Logit: Non-violence** | | | | | |
| Competition (Abs.) | 0.81 | | | | |
| | (1.45) | | | | |
| Frontline | 1.08 | 1.32 | 1.68 | 1.11 | |
| | (1.41) | (1.92) | (1.69) | (1.15) | |
| Population | −0.0075** | −0.0076* | −0.0085** | −0.0063** | −0.0070** |
| | (0.0024) | (0.0036) | (0.0033) | (0.0014) | (0.0013) |
| UGT Affiliation | 0.10 | 0.15 | 0.23 | 0.068 | 0.0022 |
| | (0.30) | (0.41) | (0.39) | (0.26) | (0.18) |
| Border | −0.37 | −0.46 | −0.54 | −0.67 | |
| | (0.51) | (0.58) | (0.54) | (0.49) | |
| Sea | 1.92 | 2.35 | 2.99 | 2.09 | |
| | (2.46) | (3.68) | (3.38) | (2.05) | |
| Elevation | 0.0017 | 0.0021 | 0.0027 | 0.0022 | −0.000085 |
| | (0.0026) | (0.0039) | (0.0034) | (0.0022) | (0.00094) |
| Competition33 | | 0.58 | | | |
| | | (1.54) | | | |
| Polarization33 | | | −0.37 | | |
| | | | (1.31) | | |
| Competition | | | | 0.024 | 2.27 |
| | | | | (1.69) | (1.65) |
| Percentage Literate | | | | 0.067* | |
| | | | | (0.032) | |
| Longitude (*1000) | | | | | −0.0030 |
| | | | | | (0.0060) |
| Latitude (*1000) | | | | | 0.0015 |
| | | | | | (0.0088) |
| _cons | −0.98 | −1.33 | −1.06 | −5.23* | −6.46 |
| | (1.86) | (2.32) | (2.50) | (2.54) | (39.0) |
| *lnAlpha* | | | | | |
| _cons | 0.35** | 0.37** | 0.40** | 0.28** | 0.28** |
| | (0.11) | (0.13) | (0.11) | (0.11) | (0.085) |
| N | 870 | 865 | 867 | 832 | 870 |
| ll | −2112.0 | −2101.2 | −2113.1 | −1990.5 | −2106.7 |

Clustered standard errors in parentheses
$^{+}p < 0.10$, $^{*}p < 0.05$, $^{**}p < 0.01$

TABLE A.4.3 *Executed by the Right in Nationalist Aragon (ZINB)*

| | M1 | M2 | M4 | M5 |
|---|---|---|---|---|
| | NB: Number of Executed | NB: Number of Executed | NB: Number of Executed | NB: Number of Executed |
| Competition | 1.29* | 1.11[+] | | |
| | (0.63) | (0.66) | | |
| Population(*1000) | 0.041 | 0.027 | 0.033 | 0.051 |
| | (0.17) | (0.022) | (0.025) | (0.18) |
| CNT Affiliation | 0.038 | −0.036 | −0.066 | 0.017 |
| | (0.072) | (0.054) | (0.054) | (0.087) |
| UGT Affiliation | 0.085* | 0.072* | 0.052[+] | 0.067* |
| | (0.035) | (0.031) | (0.030) | (0.032) |
| Catholic Center | 2.04** | 1.67** | 1.61** | 2.01* |
| | (0.79) | (0.51) | (0.47) | (0.80) |
| Latitude | −0.018 | −0.15 | −0.082 | 0.046 |
| | (0.34) | (0.35) | (0.34) | (0.36) |
| Longitude | 0.86* | 0.73[+] | 0.72[+] | 0.82[+] |
| | (0.41) | (0.40) | (0.42) | (0.42) |
| Elevation | −0.57** | −0.58** | −0.58** | −0.56** |
| | (0.12) | (0.068) | (0.072) | (0.12) |
| Previous Violence | | 1.06** | 1.10** | |
| | | (0.17) | (0.15) | |
| Support Left | | | 0.021* | 0.029 |
| | | | (0.010) | (0.021) |
| SuppLeft2 | | | | −0.00011 |
| | | | | (0.00026) |
| Constant | 3.93 | 9.21 | 6.75 | 1.43 |
| | (13.8) | (14.5) | (14.1) | (14.7) |
| **INFLATE** | **Logit:** | **Logit:** | **Logit:** | **Logit:** |

*(continued)*

TABLE A.4.3 *(continued)*

|  | M1 | M2 | M3 | M4 |
|---|---|---|---|---|
|  | Logit Non-violence | Logit Non-violence | Logit Non-violence | Logit Non-violence |
| Competition | −1.36 | −1.46 |  |  |
|  | (1.10) | (1.06) |  |  |
| Population | −0.0019** | −0.0019** | −0.0021** | −0.0021** |
|  | (0.00070) | (0.00064) | (0.00063) | (0.00065) |
| CNT Affiliation | −0.091* | −0.072+ | −0.11 | −0.073 |
|  | (0.045) | (0.042) | (0.065) | (0.059) |
| Latitude | 1.29+ | 1.14 | 0.91 | 1.56+ |
|  | (0.70) | (0.70) | (0.61) | (0.89) |
| Longitude | 1.00 | 0.92 | 1.03 | 0.53 |
|  | (1.53) | (1.41) | (1.27) | (1.54) |
| Elevation | 1.28** | 1.15** | 1.17** | 1.35** |
|  | (0.43) | (0.39) | (0.38) | (0.45) |
| Previous Violence |  | −20.1** | −20.3** |  |
|  |  | (0.70) | (0.65) |  |
| Support Left |  |  | −0.0048 | −0.12+ |
|  |  |  | (0.015) | (0.066) |
| SuppLeft2 |  |  |  | 0.0017+ |
|  |  |  |  | (0.00086) |
| Constant | −54.1+ | −47.8 | −38.8 | −65.6+ |
|  | (30.1) | (29.7) | (26.1) | (37.7) |
| *lnAlpha* | 0.23 | 0.10 | 0.089 | 0.22 |
|  | *(0.15)* | *(0.15)* | *(0.15)* | *(0.15)* |
| Observations | 250 | 250 | 250 | 250 |
| ll | −603.1 | −596.4 | −597.2 | −600.5 |

Clustered standard errors in parentheses
Sig Level: +.1 *.05 **.01

TABLE A.4.4 *Executed by the Left in Malaga (ZINB)*

| | All | All | Without Malaga City |
|---|---|---|---|
| **NB: Number of Executed** | | | |
| Competition | 1.35* | 1.36* | 0.83[+] |
| | (0.61) | (0.61) | (0.46) |
| Population | 0.000040** | 0.000030 | 0.000064** |
| | (0.000010) | (0.000020) | (0.000020) |
| UGT Affiliation | 0.021 | 0.019 | 0.023 |
| | (0.034) | (0.034) | (0.025) |
| CNT Affiliation | 0.0073 | 0.0029 | −0.0069 |
| | (0.029) | (0.031) | (0.024) |
| Elevation | −0.00091[+] | −0.00090[+] | −0.00070[+] |
| | (0.00048) | (0.00048) | (0.00039) |
| Strikes$_{1931\_1936}$ | | 0.052 | 0.20* |
| | | (0.096) | (0.092) |
| _cons | 1.94** | 1.92** | 1.80** |
| | (0.52) | (0.52) | (0.43) |
| **Logit: Non-violence** | | | |
| Competition | 0.29 | 0.14 | 0.040 |
| | (1.00) | (1.03) | (0.97) |
| Population | −0.00032* | −0.00047** | −0.00046** |
| | (0.00013) | (0.00017) | (0.00016) |
| UGT Affiliation | 0.059 | 0.061 | 0.060 |
| | (0.056) | (0.057) | (0.055) |
| Elevation | −0.0014 | −0.0012 | −0.0012 |
| | (0.0011) | (0.0012) | (0.0011) |
| Strikes$_{31\_36}$ | | 0.50[+] | 0.49[+] |
| | | (0.29) | (0.28) |
| _cons | 0.99 | 0.98 | 1.10 |
| | (1.15) | (1.17) | (1.12) |
| **lnalpha** | | | |
| _cons | −0.46* | −0.46* | −1.09** |
| | (0.23) | (0.22) | (0.24) |
| N | 90 | 90 | 89 |
| ll | −269.1 | −267.4 | −245.8 |

Clustered standard errors in parentheses
[+] $p < 0.10$, * $p < 0.05$, ** $p < 0.01$

TABLE A.4.5 *Competition as a Dependent Variable*

| Variable | Catalonia | Aragon |
|---|---|---|
| Population | 0.000 | −0.000 |
|  | (0.00) | (0.00) |
| CNT Affiliation | 0.004* | 0.006 |
|  | (0.00) | (0.01) |
| UGT Affiliation | 0.002 | 0.013 |
|  | (0.00) | (0.01) |
| Latitude | 0.000 | 0.082 |
|  | (0.00) | (0.12) |
| Longitude | 0.001$^+$ | 0.186 |
|  | (0.00) | (0.13) |
| Elevation | −0.000 | −0.000 |
|  | (0.00) | (0.00) |
| Catholic Center | 0.104$^+$ | 0.062 |
|  | (0.06) | (0.19) |
| Previous Violence |  | 0.106 |
|  |  | (0.07) |
| **County FE** | Yes | Yes |

Standard errors in parentheses
Sig Level: +.1 *.05 **.01

TABLE A.4.6 *Executed by the Right in Battlefield Areas of Aragon (ZINB)*

|  | (1) | (2) | (3) | (4) | (5) |
|---|---|---|---|---|---|
| **NB: Number of Executed** | | | | | |
| Competition | 0.039 | 0.0053 | | | |
|  | (0.31) | (0.32) | | | |
| Population | 0.00070** | 0.00069** | 0.00068** | 0.00067** | 0.00069** |
|  | (0.00015) | (0.00014) | (0.00014) | (0.00014) | (0.00014) |
| CNT Affiliation | 0.014 | 0.012 | 0.015 | 0.024 | 0.016 |
|  | (0.033) | (0.033) | (0.034) | (0.042) | (0.033) |
| UGT Affiliation | 0.095* | 0.091* | 0.095$^+$ | 0.11$^+$ | 0.096$^+$ |
|  | (0.045) | (0.041) | (0.049) | (0.062) | (0.052) |
| Catholic Center | −0.41 | −0.38 | −0.39 | −0.41 | −0.41 |
|  | (1.05) | (1.03) | (1.00) | (1.03) | (1.03) |
| Latitude | 0.45 | 0.49 | 0.52$^+$ | 0.51$^+$ | 0.49 |
|  | (0.37) | (0.32) | (0.28) | (0.28) | (0.32) |
| Longitude | −0.94* | −0.91* | −0.90* | −0.91* | −0.92* |
|  | (0.43) | (0.39) | (0.37) | (0.37) | (0.41) |

|  | (1) | (2) | (3) | (4) | (5) |
|---|---|---|---|---|---|
| Elevation | −0.077 | −0.059 | −0.047 | −0.040 | −0.061 |
|  | (0.23) | (0.20) | (0.19) | (0.18) | (0.21) |
| Previous Conflict |  | −0.0016 | −0.011 |  |  |
|  |  | (0.41) | (0.39) |  |  |
| Support Left1936 |  |  | −0.0019 | 0.0062 | −0.0013 |
|  |  |  | (0.0055) | (0.015) | (0.0058) |
| Support Left Squared |  |  |  | −0.00012 |  |
|  |  |  |  | (0.00022) |  |
| _cons | −18.8 | −20.5 | −21.7[+] | −21.2[+] | −20.4 |
|  | (15.2) | (13.2) | (11.7) | (11.6) | (13.1) |
| **Logit: Non-violence** |  |  |  |  |  |
| Competition | −0.75 | −0.85 |  |  |  |
|  | (1.37) | (1.35) |  |  |  |
| Population | −0.0092 | −0.0074[+] | −0.0068* | −0.0071* | −0.0079 |
|  | (0.0068) | (0.0041) | (0.0029) | (0.0028) | (0.0052) |
| CNT Affiliation | −0.71** | −0.68** | −0.69** | −0.74** | −0.70** |
|  | (0.13) | (0.16) | (0.16) | (0.12) | (0.14) |
| Latitude | 1.65[+] | 1.61* | 1.59* | 1.44* | 1.60* |
|  | (0.88) | (0.68) | (0.67) | (0.65) | (0.75) |
| Longitude | 4.02** | 3.45** | 3.28** | 3.17** | 3.65** |
|  | (1.45) | (1.15) | (1.08) | (1.14) | (1.21) |
| Elevation | 0.35 | 0.35 | 0.39 | 0.35 | 0.39 |
|  | (0.53) | (0.39) | (0.35) | (0.33) | (0.40) |
| Previous Conflict |  | −21.5** | −21.7** |  |  |
|  |  | (0.65) | (0.62) |  |  |
| Support Left1936 |  |  | −0.026 | 0.097 | −0.025 |
|  |  |  | (0.016) | (0.091) | (0.017) |
| Support Left Squared |  |  |  | −0.0022 |  |
|  |  |  |  | (0.0016) |  |
| _cons | −63.2[+] | −62.2* | −61.6* | −56.3* | −61.4* |
|  | (35.1) | (28.3) | (27.7) | (26.9) | (30.7) |
| lnalpha |  |  |  |  |  |
| _cons | 0.88** | 0.85** | 0.83** | 0.83** | 0.86** |
|  | (0.17) | (0.17) | (0.17) | (0.16) | (0.17) |
| N | 395 | 395 | 395 | 395 | 395 |
| ll | −665.2 | −664.2 | −663.8 | −664.2 | −664.9 |

Clustered standard errors in parentheses
[+] $p < 0.10$, * $p < 0.05$, ** $p < 0.01$

TABLE A.4.7 *Descriptive Statistics (Catalonia Dataset)*

| Variable | Obs. | Mean | Std. Dev. | Min | Max |
|---|---|---|---|---|---|
| Population | 1,058 | 1,647.56 | 19,726.11 | 50 | 637,841 |
| Executed Left | 1,062 | 7.5414 | 73.65 | 0 | 2,328 |
| Executed Right | 1,062 | 2.79 | 14.29 | 0 | 431 |
| Support Left 1936 | 1,058 | 52.27 | 16.94 | 2.2 | 100 |
| Support Left 1933 | 1,052 | 54.51 | 19.08 | 0 | 100 |
| Competition | 1,058 | 0.88 | 0.16 | 0 | 1 |
| Competition (Abs.) | 1,058 | 0.725 | 0.2 | 0 | 1 |
| CNT Affiliation | 1,062 | 0.56 | 2.72 | 0 | 29.79 |
| UGT Affiliation | 1,058 | 0.088 | 1.02 | 0 | 20.36 |
| Frontline | 1,060 | 0.20 | 0.40 | 0 | 1 |
| Border | 1,060 | 0.22 | 0.41 | 0 | 1 |
| Sea | 1,060 | 0.28 | 0.45 | 0 | 1 |
| Elevation (in mt.) | 875 | 368.22 | 317.3 | 0 | 1,539 |
| Catholic Center | 1,062 | 0.0075 | 0.0865 | 0 | 1 |
| Competition 1933 | 1,057 | 0.831 | 0.158 | 0 | 1 |
| Longitude | 875 | 396,935.3 | 66,009.08 | 269,050 | 522,850 |
| Latitude | 875 | 4,621,514 | 4,6029.15 | 4,491,400 | 4,745,550 |

TABLE A.4.8 *Descriptive Statistics (Aragon Dataset)*

| Variable | Obs. | Mean | Std. Dev. | Min | Max |
|---|---|---|---|---|---|
| Population | 940 | 1,118.3 | 5,414.86 | 71 | 162,12 |
| Executed Left | 948 | 4.09 | 11.88 | 0 | 188 |
| Executed Right | 948 | 8.89 | 117.64 | 0 | 3,543 |
| CNT Affiliation | 938 | 0.633 | 3.545 | 0 | 77.22 |
| UGT Affiliation | 938 | 0.124 | 1.07 | 0 | 13.23 |
| Catholic Center | 948 | 0.0063 | 0.0793 | 0 | 1 |
| Latitude | 914 | 41.54 | 0.709 | 39.91 | 42.76 |
| Longitude | 914 | −0.736 | 0.652 | −2.15 | 0.716 |
| Elevation (in ft.) | 914 | 2,481.62 | 1,187.65 | 0 | 6,676 |
| Support Left 1936 | 659 | 27.39 | 16.75 | 0.2503 | 85.068 |
| Competition | 659 | 0.683 | 0.264 | 0.009 | 0.99 |
| Previous Violence | 948 | 0.036 | 0.186 | 0 | 1 |
| Competition (Abs.) | 659 | 0.499 | 0.25 | .005 | 0.99 |

TABLE A.4.9 *Descriptive Statistics (Malaga Dataset)*

| Variable | Obs. | Mean | Std. Dev. | Min | Max |
|---|---|---|---|---|---|
| Executed Left | 91 | 23.24 | 95.71 | 0 | 899 |
| Population | 93 | 6,315.4 | 19,073.38 | 360 | 180,105 |
| UGT Affiliation | 93 | 1.09 | 4.02 | 0 | 21.92 |
| CNT Affiliation | 93 | 1.46 | 3.85 | 0 | 19.005 |
| Competition | 93 | 0.77 | 0.25 | 0 | 0.99 |
| Elevation (in mt.) | 92 | 517.75 | 234.67 | 39.9 | 1061.2 |
| Strikes | 93 | 1.55 | 4.2 | 0 | 39 |

TABLE A.4.10 *Description of Variables (Combined Dataset)*

| Name of the Variable | Characteristics | Data Sources |
|---|---|---|
| Competition | Index from 0 (minimum parity) to 1 (maximum parity) | Sources listed in Chapter 4 |
| Killed_t1 | Total number of people executed in a locality in the first period of the war | Sources listed in Chapter 4 |
| Killed | Total number of people executed in a locality | Sources listed in Chapter 4 |
| Support Left | Percentage support for the Popular Front in the 1936 general elections | Sources listed in Chapter 4 |
| ZoneRep | 1 if Republican control zone; 0 if Nationalist control zone | Solé i Sabaté and Villarroya (2005), Casanova (2001), Ledesma (2009) |
| CNT Affiliation | Percentage inhabitants affiliated with the CNT in a locality | CNT (1936), Cucó i Giner (1970) |
| UGT Affiliation | Percentage inhabitants affiliated with the UGT in a locality | UGT (1931) |
| Population | Inhabitants of the municipality in 1936 | *Instituto Nacional de Estadística* |
| Catholic center | Dummy variable: 1 if the municipality had an archbishop in 1936; 0 otherwise | *Conferencia Episcopal Española* |
| Border | Dummy variable: 1 if the municipality is in a county that shares the French border; 0 if not | Sources listed in Chapter 4 |
| Battlefield | Dummy variable: 1 if the municipality is in a county in a battlefield area; 0 if not | Sources listed above |
| Elevation | Elevation range of the locality | Sources listed above |

TABLE A.4.11 *Descriptive Statistics (Combined Dataset)*

| Variable | Obs. | Mean | Std. Dev. | Min | Max |
|---|---|---|---|---|---|
| Competition | 1,229 | .78 | .24 | 0 | 1 |
| Population | 1,229 | 2180.8 | 19569.42 | 59 | 637,841 |
| Killed_t1 | 1,229 | 15.5 | 127.04 | 0 | 3543 |
| Killed | 1,229 | 15.17 | 134.56 | 0 | 3567 |
| ZoneRep | 1,229 | .82 | .38 | 0 | 1 |
| CNT Affilation | 1,229 | 0.76 | 3.05 | 0 | 34.07 |
| UGT Affiliation | 1,229 | .21 | 1.54 | 0 | 21.91 |
| Support Left 1936 | 1,229 | 40.88 | 21.19 | 0 | 100 |
| Border | 1,229 | .08 | .28 | 0 | 1 |
| Catholic Center | 1,229 | .01 | .1 | 0 | 1 |
| Elevation | 1,228 | 395.8 | 363.88 | 0 | 2108 |
| Battlefield | 1,229 | .26 | .44 | 0 | 1 |

TABLE A.4.12 *Summary of Interviewed Civil War Survivors*

| Id | Year Birth | Gender | Province during war | Side during War | Combatant | Victimization |
|---|---|---|---|---|---|---|
| 1 | 1908 | Female | Barcelona | Republican | No | No |
| 2 | 1929 | Female | Tarragona | Republican | No | Yes. Uncle disappeared |
| 3 | 1926 | Male | Tarragona | Republican | No | No |
| 4 | 1917 | Male | Barcelona | Republican | Yes | No |
| 5 | 1930 | Female | Barcelona | Republican | No | Yes. Sister killed bombing (Nat) |
| 6 | 1930 | Male | Barcelona | Republican | No | No |
| 7 | 1930 | Female | Girona | Republican | No | Yes. Father killed in combat (by Nat) |
| 8 | 1930 | Male | Barcelona | Republican | No | Yes. Father killed in Mathausen |
| 9 | 1917 | Male | Various locations | Nationalist | Yes | No |
| 10 | 1928 | Female | Barcelona | Republican | No | Yes. Two uncles killed by Left |
| 11 | 1921 | Male | Barcelona | Republican | No | No |
| 12 | 1928 | Male | Barcelona | Republican | No | No |
| 13 | 1924 | Male | Madrid | Republican | No | No |
| 14 | 1929 | Female | Madrid | Republican | No | No |
| 15 | 1914 | Male | Moroco, Sevilla, others | Nationalist | Yes | No |

| Id | Year Birth | Gender | Province during war | Side during War | Combatant | Victimization |
|----|-----------|--------|---------------------|-----------------|-----------|---------------|
| 16 | 1920 | Female | Madrid | Republican | No | No |
| 17 | 1929 | Female | Barcelona | Republican | No | No |
| 18 | 1919 | Male | Guipuzcoa, others | Republican, Nationalist | Yes | Yes |
| 19 | 1923 | Female | Girona | Republican | No | No |
| 20 | 1920 | Female | Aragon | Republican | Yes | Yes. Mutilated |
| 21 | 1924 | Female | Girona | Republican | No | No |
| 22 | 1914 | Female | Barcelona | Republican | No | Yes. Brother wounded in combat |
| 23 | 1926 | Female | Tarragona | Republican | No | Yes. Brother-in-law killed by Left |
| 24 | 1924 | Male | Tarragona | Republican | No | No |
| 25 | 1920 | Male | Tarragona | Republican | Yes | No |
| 26 | 1920 | Female | Tarragona | Republican | No | No |
| 27 | 1923 | Male | Tarragona/France | Republican | No | Yes (exiled in France 10 years) |
| 30 | 1926 | Female | Tarragona, Barcelona | Republican | No | No |
| 31 | 1928 | Male | Tarragona | Republican | No | No |
| 32 | 1922 | Male | Barcelona | Republican | No | Yes. Brother killed in combat |
| 36 | 1917 | Male | Lleida | Republican, Nationalist | Yes | No |
| 37 | 1926 | Female | Lleida | Republican, Nationalist | No | Yes. Brothers had to hide |
| 38 | 1923 | Male | Castile-Leon | Nationalist | No | No |
| 39 | 1920 | Male | Salamanca | Nationalist | Yes | No |
| 40 | 1929 | Female | Salamanca | Nationalist | No | No |
| 41 | 1919 | Female | Zamora | Nationalist | No | No |
| 42 | 1919 | Female | Bilbao | Republican, Nationalist | No | No |
| 43 | 1922 | Male | Madrid | Republican | No | No |
| 44 | 1923 | Female | Madrid | Republican | No | Yes. Brother wounded in combat |
| 45 | 1918 | Male | Madrid | Republican | Yes | Yes (concentration camp) |
| 46 | 1911 | Female | Madrid | Republican | No | No |
| 47 | 1919 | Male | Various locations | Republican, Nationalist | Yes | No |
| 48 | 1923 | Female | Barcelona | Republican | No | No |
| 49 | 1926 | Male | Barcelona | Republican | No | No |

*(continued)*

TABLE A.4.12 *(continued)*

| Id | Year Birth | Gender | Province during war | Side during War | Combatant | Victimization |
|----|-----------|--------|---------------------|-----------------|-----------|---------------|
| 50 | 1930 | Female | Barcelona | Republican | No | Yes. Father killed (by Left) |
| 51 | 1926 | Male | Valencia | Republican | No | No |
| 52 | 1923 | Female | Barcelona | Republican | No | No |
| 53 | 1922 | Male | Lleida | Rep, Nat (switched sides) | No | No |
| 54 | 1923 | Male | Lleida | Republican, Nationalist | No | No |
| 55 | 1923 | Male | Lleida | Republican, Nationalist | No | Father exiled in France |
| 56 | 1923 | Male | Lleida | Republican, Nationalist | No | No |
| 57 | 1918 | Male | Lleida | Republican, Nationalist | No | Yes. Brother mutilated in combat |
| 58 | 1925 | Male | Tarragona | Republican | No | Yes, uncle and aunt killed (bombings by Nat.) |
| 59 | 1928 | Female | Tarragona | Republican | No | No |
| 60 | 1925 | Male | Lleida | Republican, Nationalist | No | Father imprisoned (by Nat) |

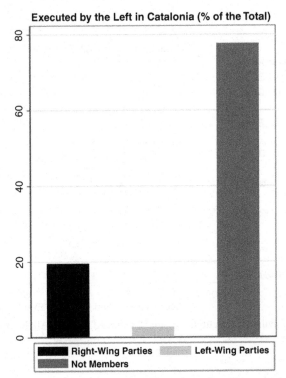

FIGURE A.4.1 Executed by the Left in Catalonia, by Political Party Membership

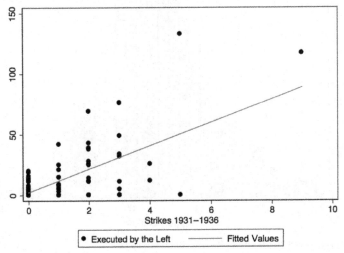

FIGURE A.4.2 Workers's Strikes in a Locality (1931–1936) and Leftist Executions in Malaga

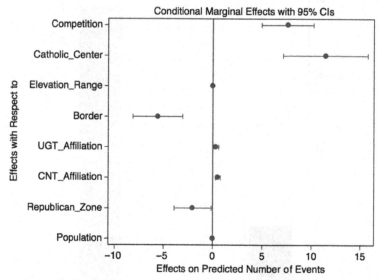

FIGURE A.4.3 Civilians Executed outside Battlefield Zones (All Regions); Marginal Effects (ZINB)

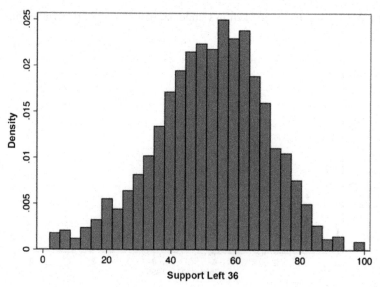

FIGURE A.4.4 Support for the Left in Catalonia (1936)

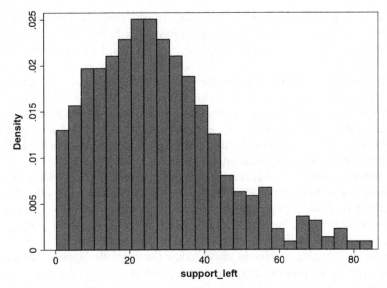

FIGURE A.4.5 Support for the Left in Aragon (1936)

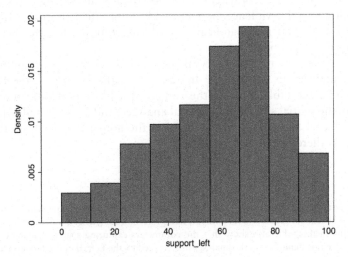

FIGURE A.4.6 Support for the Left in Malaga (1936)

## APPENDIX CHAPTER 4 (II). SPATIAL ANALYSES

I first run diagnostic tests to see if the data in the different datasets present relevant spatial dependence or autocorrelation patterns that could be biasing the results; I then run spatial regression analyses. I begin by checking for spatial autocorrelation in the violence data from Catalonia. I first test for the existence of spatial autocorrelation by employing a Euclidean specification of the neighborhood between municipalities.[1] With this, I calculate the statistic *Moran's I*, which indicates the level of association between the values of this variable and the lagged version of the variable (the weighted averages of the values for neighboring localities).[2] The value of the *Moran's I* statistic is very small (close to 0), which means that the relationship between the spatially lagged variable (i.e., *w_killed_left*) and the variable (i.e., *killed_left*) is almost nonexistent, but it is statistically significant for both *Executed by the Left* and *Executed by the Right* in Catalonia.

In order to make sure that there is not any distortion in the ordinary regression results due to spatial autocorrelation in the dependent variables, I run a spatial lag regression model, which includes a spatially lagged version of the dependent variable in the matrix of independent variables. I also run a spatial error model, which allows us to test for the existence of spatial error dependence in the weights matrix (it checks that the spatially lagged independent variables are not having an effect on the dependent variable; for example, that political competition of a locality does not have an impact on the level of violence perpetrated in a neighboring locality). The results for Catalonia (in Table A.4.13) show that the main results remain unaltered when controlling for spatial dependence: consistent with the "rivalry and revenge" framework, competition explains violence, perpetrated by either the Left or the Right, and violence by the Left is a significant variable accounting for violence by the Right in subsequent periods.[3]

TableA.4.14 depicts a summary of spatial analyses for the remaining zones of Spain analyzed in Chapter 4.[4] In addition to the *Moran's I*, the Rho and the Lambda, the table includes the results of a likelihood ratio test, which compares the spatial and the non-spatial analyses, and tests the null hypotheses that the spatial analyses are different from the non-spatial analyses (in other words, that there is spatial dependence).[5]

---

[1] I have created a weight matrix using a distance band between 0 and 4, row-standardized.

[2] *Moran's I* checks for global spatial autocorrelation in the data (Anselin 2003).

[3] The results in this table also show that the parameters capturing spatial dynamics (Rho and Lambda) are not significant in the analyses of Executed by the Left; they are however significant in the analyses of violence perpetrated by the Right in Catalonia.

[4] The analyzes for *Aragon Nat* are for the Nationalist zone of Aragon, while the analyses for *Aragon Rep* are for the Republican zone of Aragon.

[5] For each of the regional datasets, I have used point data, and I have built the weights matrix with Euclidean distances, with the three nearest neighbors. For the combined dataset, I have used polygon data, with which I have been able to compute contiguity based spatial weights; specifically, I have built the weights matrix with Rook contiguity weights, which are defined according to common boundaries between localities (Anselin 2003). I have used first-order contiguity neighborhood indicators.

TABLE A.4.13 *Spatial Lag and Spatial Error Regressions; Violence by the Left* $(t_1)$ *and Violence by the Right* $(t_2)$ *in Catalonia*

| | Spatial Lag Executed_left | Spatial Error Executed_left | Spatial Lag Executed_right | Spatial Error Executed_right |
|---|---|---|---|---|
| Competition | 2.51[+] | 2.72[*] | 1.44[**] | 1.38[**] |
| | (1.28) | (1.32) | (0.50) | (0.52) |
| Frontline | 2.16 | 2.34 | 0.024 | −0.22 |
| | (1.51) | (1.63) | (0.33) | (0.35) |
| Population(*1000) | 3.5[**] | 3.5[**] | 3.8[**] | 3.9[**] |
| | (0.070) | (0.070) | (0.13) | (0.13) |
| CNT Affiliation | 0.60[**] | 0.54[*] | 0.36[*] | 0.39[*] |
| | (0.25) | (0.26) | (0.16) | (0.17) |
| UGT Affiliation | 1.05 | 1.04 | 0.013 | 0.015 |
| | (0.88) | (0.89) | (0.19) | (0.18) |
| Border | −0.99 | −0.48 | −0.20 | −0.44 |
| | (0.72) | (0.68) | (0.27) | (0.30) |
| Sea | −2.14[**] | −2.16[**] | 0.11 | 0.19 |
| | (0.70) | (0.70) | (0.39) | (0.44) |
| Elevation | −0.0026[*] | −0.0023[*] | −0.00074[+] | −0.0011[*] |
| | (0.0011) | (0.0011) | (0.00039) | (0.00043) |
| Catholic Center | 97.9[*] | 98.5[*] | −0.81 | −0.87 |
| | (44.5) | (44.5) | (3.99) | (3.93) |
| Executed_left | | | 0.080[*] | 0.078[*] |
| | | | (0.037) | (0.037) |
| _cons | 2.01 | −0.32 | −1.38 | 0.74 |
| | (1.53) | (1.16) | (1.00) | (0.59) |
| rho | | | | |
| _cons | −0.22 | | 0.59[*] | |
| | (0.14) | | (0.27) | |
| sigma | | | | |
| _cons | 10.9[**] | 10.9[**] | 3.95[**] | 3.97[**] |
| | (2.23) | (2.23) | (0.71) | (0.74) |
| lambda | | | | |
| _cons | | −0.050 | | 0.65[*] |
| | | (0.52) | | (0.30) |
| N | 832 | 832 | 832 | 832 |
| ll | −3165.4 | −3167.0 | −2325.1 | −2329.4 |

Standard errors in parentheses
[+] $p < 0.10$, [*] $p < 0.05$, [**] $p < 0.01$

TABLE A.4.14 *Summary of Spatial Analyses*

| DV (Dataset) | Moran's I | Spatial Autocorrelation | Spatial Lag Regression | Spatial Error Regression |
|---|---|---|---|---|
| Executed by the Right (Aragon Nat) | −0.0047 | No | Lagged DV is not sig. | Lambda non-sig. LR test for spatial dependence not sig. |
| Executed by the Right (Aragon Rep) | −0.0014 | No | Lagged DV is not sig. | Lambda has value 0.16 and is statistically significant at the 95% level. LR test for spatial dependence is significant |
| Executed by the Left (Aragon Rep) | 0.09 | Maybe | Lagged DV is not sig. | Lambda non-sig. LR test for spatial dependence not sig. |
| Executed by the Left $t_1$ (Malaga) | 0.067 | No | Lagged DV is not sig. | Lambda non-sig. LR test for spatial dependence not sig. |
| Executed by the Left $t_1$ (All) | 0.0066 | No | Lagged DV is not sig. | Lambda non-sig. LR test is sig at the 95% level |
| Executed by the Right $t_1$ and $t_2$ (All) | 0.0116 | No | Lagged DV is not sig. | Lambda non-sig. LR test for spatial dependence not sig. |
| Executed Total $t_1$ and $t_2$ (All) | 0.0034 | No | Lagged DV is not sig. | Lambda non-sig. LR test for spatial dependence not sig. |

## APPENDIX CHAPTER 4 (III). NOTES ON SOURCES AND CODING

### Electoral Results

The availability of electoral data at the local level during the Second Republic is extremely fragmented, and it varies a lot with the region. For the purposes of this book, my task has consisted of digitalizing previously collected data. Electoral data for the regions of Catalonia and Malaga has been compiled in rich secondary sources, mainly Vilanova (1989; 2005) – for Catalonia – and Velasco Gómez (2008) – for Malaga. Vilanova provides remarkable fine-grained data on electoral results for the whole period of the Second Republic (1931–1936) for all municipalities of Catalonia. For Aragon, I have obtained data from Zubero (1982); the collection of the data from primary historical sources had been done by the author, but the information was poorly organized and the original manuscript poorly preserved; this implies that some data went missing in the digitalization process. It is important to note that the unreadable figures in Zubero's manuscript were from randomly distributed localities; in other words, there are no systematic factors that can explain the missing cases on this variable.

### Violence Data

Data on *direct violence* has been obtained from very rich and reliable secondary sources: Solé i Sabaté and Villarroya (1989) (for executions by the Left in Catalonia), Solé i Sabaté (2000) (for executions by the Right in Catalonia), Casanova et al. (2001) and Ledesma (2009b) (for executions by the Right and the Left in Aragon), and Nadal (1984) (for executions by the Left in Malaga).

In the places where I visited local archives during fieldwork, I could double-check the data with primary sources (local and county archives). I did likewise with many cases that I did not visit, but for which I read local histories. When there were discrepancies between sources, which was rarely the case, I coded the case with the source that had been more refined in the use of methods (i.e., triangulation of different sources) and which was therefore more reliable.

For Catalonia, I have obtained data on direct violence from the books by Solé i Sabaté and Villarroya (1989) and Solé i Sabaté (2000). These authors have put together data on the number of executions at the municipal level (classifying victims by place of residence). They use a triangulation of sources method. This method was applied for the first time by Josep Maria Solé i Sabaté in order to obtain actual figures of right-wing repression in Catalonia (given that he could not access military archives as a consequence of censorship under the Francoist regime), and it became a model for local historians working on violence during the Spanish Civil War. Following this methodology, oral testimonies and similar sources would be considered reliable only when corroborated by local cemetery and death registers (Solé i Sabaté 2000; Ruiz 2009). The triangulation method implies that these authors collected the data from local civil registries (death certificates), which they double-checked with data in different historical archives (e.g., national, regional, local), and which they also checked with available oral sources (e.g., neighbors of the locality who were still alive). For leftist violence, they have also relied on *La Causa General*, a section of the Spanish National Historical Archive where the Francoist authorities meticulously documented the wartime crimes presumably carried out by leftist forces during the Spanish Civil War. The data in this archive is upwardly biased, making leftists responsible for more crimes than those they actually committed, so these historians have – very wisely – not relied on it blindly.

The same methodology and types of sources have been used by the authors whose data I used to build the Aragon dataset (Casanova et al. 2001; Ledesma 2009b). With regard to Nationalist violence in Aragon, the collection of the data has been complicated by the lack of a general register such as the *Causa General*. Casanova et al. (2001) argue that they base their figures on the death certificates in the civil registers of the localities; they do not count non-registered killings because they cannot make sure that they were really assassinated (228–229). Thus, it is possible that the figures are downwardly biased and some of the irregular violence perpetrated by Nationalist forces in Aragon has been left uncounted.

For Malaga, the main source of data on leftist violence is the book by Nadal (1984), who uses similar procedures to the authors above: he complemented the data of the *Causa General* with oral sources and data in local archives and civil registers. As explained in chapter 3, data on Nationalist violence in Malaga is unfortunately still unavailable.

## Population Data

The data on population that was not available from secondary sources (e.g., Vilanova 1989) has been acquired from the official 1930 census (*Instituto Nacional de Estadística*). Gabarda (1993), among many others, emphasizes the convenience of using this census as a proxy for the population of Spanish localities at the beginning of the civil war, especially given the fact that the Municipal Census of 1936 (*el Padrón*) has been in most cases been destroyed. However, when available, I have used the 1936 Municipal Census data in robustness checks.

## APPENDIX CHAPTER 5

TABLE A.5.1 *Negative Binomial; Bombings and Killed in Bombings in Catalonia*

|  | Total Bombings | Killed in Bombings |
|---|---|---|
| Support_left | 0.025** | 0.026** |
|  | (0.0082) | (0.0094) |
| Population (*1000) | 0.37** | 0.89** |
|  | (0.11) | (0.19) |
| CNT Affiliation | 0.033 | 0.065+ |
|  | (0.027) | (0.038) |
| UGT Affiliation | 0.11 | 0.19+ |
|  | (0.088) | (0.10) |
| Longitude (*1000) | −0.0018 | −0.0068* |
|  | (0.0026) | (0.0033) |
| Latitude (*1000) | 0.0048 | 0.0077 |
|  | (0.0033) | (0.0053) |
| Elevation | −0.0025** | −0.0015* |
|  | (0.0006) | (0.00064) |
| _cons | −24.1+ | −35.3 |
|  | (14.3) | (23.4) |
| lnalpha |  |  |
| _cons | 1.37** | 2.48** |
|  | (0.23) | (0.13) |
| N | 869 | 869 |
| ll | −508.7 | −752.1 |

Clustered errors in parentheses
$^+ p < 0.10, ^* p < 0.05, ^{**} p < 0.01$

TABLE A.5.2 *Spatial Error Regression for Bombings in Catalonia*

| | Bombing1 | Bombing1 | Bombing10 | Bombing10 |
|---|---|---|---|---|
| Support_left | 0.0017** | 0.0017** | 0.00076* | 0.0008** |
| | (0.00058) | (0.00058) | (0.0003) | (0.0003) |
| CNT Affiliation | 0.012$^+$ | | 0.0068 | |
| | (0.0068) | | (0.0048) | |
| UGT Affiliation | 0.030** | 0.031** | 0.040** | 0.040** |
| | (0.0097) | (0.010) | (0.0090) | (0.0092) |
| Population(*1000) | 0.035** | 0.040** | 0.035** | 0.036** |
| | (0.011) | (0.013) | (0.0088) | (0.010) |
| Altitude(*1000) | −0.097* | −0.099* | −0.020 | −0.020 |
| | (0.039) | (0.039) | (0.018) | (0.018) |
| Catholic Center | 0.29$^+$ | 0.23 | 0.25$^+$ | 0.18 |
| | (0.18) | (0.27) | (0.14) | (0.20) |
| Executed by the Left | | 0.000024 | | 0.00044 |
| | | (0.0018) | | (0.0014) |
| Constant | 0.053 | 0.050 | −0.029$^+$ | −0.031* |
| | (0.063) | (0.058) | (0.015) | (0.015) |
| lambda | | | | |
| Constant | 0.80** | 0.78** | 0.27 | 0.24 |
| | (0.17) | (0.19) | (0.40) | (0.41) |
| sigma | | | | |
| Constant | 0.33** | 0.33** | 0.19** | 0.19** |
| | (0.012) | (0.012) | (0.014) | (0.014) |
| Observations | 869 | 869 | 869 | 869 |

Standard errors in parentheses
$^+p < 0.10$, $^*p < 0.05$, $^{**}p < 0.01$

# APPENDIX CHAPTER 6

TABLE A.6.1 *Descriptive Statistics; Côte d'Ivoire's Dataset*

| Variable | Obs | Mean | Std. Dev. | Min | Max |
|---|---|---|---|---|---|
| Total Killings (2010–2011) | 69 | 16.18 | 67.21 | 0 | 389 |
| Executed by Ouattara (2010–2011) | 69 | 9.2 | 41.37 | 0 | 300 |
| Executed by Gbagbo (2010–2011) | 69 | 6.98 | 31.9 | 0 | 241 |
| Competition (2010) | 69 | .68 | .29 | .06 | 0.99 |
| Surface in cocoa prod, in mt | 69 | 30,901.59 | 108,941.2 | 0 | 877,779 |
| Population 2010 | 69 | 286,088.5 | 537,327.9 | 41,944.53 | 4,483,122 |
| Civilians killed by Gbagbo (2002–2007) | 69 | 6.39 | 25.24 | 0 | 151 |
| Civilians killed by FN (2002–2007) | 69 | 2.43 | 13.29 | 0 | 102 |
| Elevation | 69 | 759.76 | 422.29 | 0 | 1971 |
| Ethnic Polarization Index (2002) | 50 | .63 | .21 | 0 | .91 |
| Gini Coefficient of Income (2002) | 50 | .35 | .06 | .25 | .52 |
| Gini Coefficient of Land Ownership (2002) | 50 | .62 | .15 | .27 | .97 |
| Horizontal Income Inequality | 50 | .6 | .19 | 0 | .88 |

APPENDIX CHAPTER 7

TABLE A.7.1 *Descriptive Statistics Large-n Dataset*

| Variable | Obs | Mean | Std. Dev. | Min | Max |
| --- | --- | --- | --- | --- | --- |
| Civilian Victimization (original variable) | 710 | .58 | 1.24 | 0 | 5 |
| Civilian Victimization (recoded variable) | 710 | .33 | .67 | 0 | 2 |
| Battledeaths | 913 | 7,237.09 | 26,853.9 | 100 | 350,000 |
| Rough Terrain | 913 | 2.62 | 1.11 | 0 | 4.42 |
| Oil | 913 | .14 | .34 | 0 | 1 |
| GDP per capita | 901 | 2.69 | 2.99 | .20 | 17.93 |
| Conventional | 979 | .12 | .33 | 0 | 1 |
| SNC | 979 | .02 | .15 | 0 | 1 |
| Post 1990 | 913 | .42 | .49 | 0 | 1 |
| Population (Log) | 644 | 9.94 | 1.71 | 6.11 | 13.79 |
| Democracy | 652 | .34 | .47 | 0 | 1 |
| Ethnic Fractionalization | 913 | .55 | .28 | .03 | .90 |
| West Europe | 913 | .018 | .13 | 0 | 1 |
| East Europe | 913 | .05 | .22 | 0 | 1 |
| Asia | 913 | .35 | .48 | 0 | 1 |
| MENA | 913 | .16 | .36 | 0 | 1 |
| Sub-Saharan Africa | 913 | .28 | .45 | 0 | 1 |
| Latin America | 913 | .13 | .34 | 0 | 1 |

# Bibliography

1 SPAIN AND THE SPANISH CIVIL WAR

## Archival Sources

Archivo de la Guerra Civil de Salamanca. Generalitat de Catalunya. Departament de
Defensa. Informes Reservats (Leg. 335).
Archivo General de la Administración del Estado. Fondo Gobernación (Sig 44/266).
Archivo Histórico Nacional, Fondo Causa General:

- Pieza 1.
- Pieza 3. Cárceles o sacas.
- Pieza 4. Checas.

Arxiu Comarcal del Priorat. Expedientes de Depuración. Falange Española Tradicional-
ista y de las J.O.N.S.

## Statistical and Mapping Sources

Ministerio de Trabajo, Sanidad y Previsión, Subdirección Nacional de Estadística.
1936. *Pequeño anuario estadístico de España*. Año I – 1936. Madrid: Talleres
Tipográficos Plutarco.
Generalitat de Catalunya, Departament de la Presidència. Servei General d'Estadística.
*Butlletí mensual d'Estadística de Catalunya*:

- Gener del 1936. Any III. Núm. 1.
- Març del 1936. Any III. Núm. 3.
- Abril del 1936. Any III. Núm. 4.
- Maig del 1936. Any III. Núm. 5.

Consorci d'Informació i Documentació de Catalunya (CIDC). 1981. *Població dels
municipis i comarques de Catalunya 1975–1981*. Barcelona: CIDC.

Conferencia Episcopal Española: www.conferenciaepiscopal.es

Global Ganzeeter Version 2.1: www.fallingrain.com/world

Infraestructura de Datos Espaciales de España and Ministerio de Fomento, Infraestructura de Datos Espaciales de España: www.idee.es

Institut Cartogràfic de Catalunya. Coordenades de Caps de Municipi de Catalunya: www.icc.cat

Instituto Nacional de Estadística. *Censo de Poblacion 1930, Provincia de Huesca.*

Instituto Nacional de Estadística. *Censo de Poblacion 1930, Provincia de Teruel.*

Instituto Nacional de Estadística. *Censo de Poblacion 1930, Provincia de Zaragoza.*

Instituto Nacional de Estadística. *Censo de Poblacion 1930, Provincia de Malaga.*

Servei General d'Estadistica (SGE). Població de Catalunya. 1936. Generalitat de Catalunya.

## Periodicals

*Acció Sindical.* Portantveu de la CNT de la Comarcal de Valls-Montblanch.

*Butlletí d'Esquerra Republicana de Catalunya, Federació de Barcelona-Ciutat.* 1937–1938.

CNT. *Solidaridad Obrera.* "Memoria del Congreso Extraordinario celebrado en Madrid los dias 11 al 16 de junio de 1931."

CNT. *Solidaridad Obrera.* "El Congreso Confederal de Zaragoza, Mayo 1936."

*El Sembrador,* CNT Puigcerdà.

*Humanismo,* Ripoll.

*Llibre d'Actes del Congrés de la FAI,* Arxiu Comarcal de la Cerdanya.

*Solidaridad Obrera,* CNT La Cerdanya.

*Triomf,* Ripoll.

*La Planenca. Revista d'informació, opinió i debat.* Fira de Tardor 2006. Especial núm. 3. Associacionisme planenc a principis del segle XX. Vivències i records del poble.

UGT. *Boletin de la Unión General de Trabajadores de España.* Noviembre 1931. Año III. No. 35.

UGT. *Boletin de la Unión General de Trabajadores de España.* Diciembre 1931. Año III. No. 36.

## Newspaper and Magazine Articles

Balcells, Albert. "Los horrores de la guerra en Cataluña." *La Vanguardia,* July 16, 1987: 34.

"Moments," *Diari de Barcelona,* May 25, 1937.

"Catalans Sota Franco." *L'Avenç. Revista d'Historia i Cultura.* Num. 266, February 2002.

Del Rey, Fernando. "La Memoria Democrática de todos." Opinión. Tribuna Libre. *El Mundo,* September 28, 2007.

"Els morts del Baix Camp al front 1936–1939." *Reus Diari,* 1987.

"Ellos no Olvidan." Domingo, *El Pais,* July 23, 2006.

"Falset bajo el signo de los rojos," La Comisión Pro-Mártires Falset, Septiembre de 1940.

Garriga, Joan. "Els silencis de la memòria." *El 9 Nou,* May 14, 2007: 25.

Garriga, Joan, Montserrat Salvador and Francesc Sànchez. "Els anys de la guerra civil. Fets i seqüeles (2). El cost humà." *El 9 Nou*, May 17, 2007: 3–20.

Grau, Josep. "Por qué Hitler bombardeó cuatro pacíficos pueblos de Castellón?" *El Pais*, December 26, 2015.

Junquera, Natalia. "En busca de un alcalde del Frente Popular y su ayudante, cantante de flamenco." *El País*, August 6, 2009.

Marimon, Sílvia. "Els morts oblidats." *Sàpiens 67*, May 2008: 20–27.

Raguer, Hilari. "La Patria ya está salvada." *El País*, May 27, 2007: 36.

Solé, Queralt. "El secret del Valle de los Caídos. Els noms dels milers de morts traslladats per Franco des de les fosses catalanes." *Sàpiens 67*, May 2008.

## Memoirs

Anonymous. *Vivències al Front d'Arago*. Unpublished manuscript.

Azaña, Manuel. 1986. *Causas de la guerra de España*. Madrid: Crítica.

Barbal, Joaquim. 1996. *Els fets de la guerra civil a Rialp*. Tremp: Garsineu Edicions.

Bueso, Adolfo. 1978. *Recuerdos de un cenetista. De la Segunda República al final de la guerra civil*. Barcelona: Ariel.

Campoamor, Clara. 2005. *La Revolución Española vista por una Republicana*. Sevilla: Espuela de Plata.

Castillo, Sofia. 1989. "Ripoll 1936–1939. Records Personals. Una entrevista amb en Daniel Maideu i Auguet." Pp. 17–28 in *Annals 1988–1989*. Ripoll: Centre d'Estudis Comarcals del Ripollès.

De Guzmán, Eduardo. 2004 (first edition 1938). *Madrid Rojo y Negro*. Madrid: Oberón.

Gil Imirizaldu, Plácido. 2006. *Un adolescente en la retaguardia. Memorias de la guerra civil (1936–1939)*. Madrid: Encuentro.

Kaminski, Hans Erich. 2002 (first edition 1937). *Los de Barcelona*. Translated by C. S. Barberá. Barcelona: Ediciones del Cotal. (Original title: *Ceux de Barcelone*).

Llaó Brull, Josep. 2006. "Ulls de xiquet. La Guerra Civil al Perelló." *Memòria del Perelló*. Butlletí num. 1. Abril: 5–11.

Uriel, Pablo. 2005. *No se fusila en domingo*. Aldaia, Valencia: Guada Impresores.

Woolsey, Gamel. 1998. *Malaga burning. An American Woman's Eyewitness Account of the Spanish Civil War*. Paris: Pythia Press.

## Student Research Papers

Gaitx Motlló, Jordi. 2003. *República i revolució en l'exili català de 1939*. MA Thesis, Universitat de Girona.

Sànchez Delgado, Irene. 2006. *Memoria Recuperada. El Pallars Sobirà*. High School Senior Project, IES Hug Roger III, Sort.

Travesa, Gerard. 2005. "Refugiats, desplaçats i exiliats durant la Guerra Civil Espanyola a Camprodon." Olot: IES-SEP La Garrotxa.

## Local Studies

Aragó, Narcís-Jordi. 2000. "1939, l'any zero a les comarques gironines." Pp. 135–156 in *Guerra Civil i Franquisme seixanta anys després*, eds. N. Figueras and A. Reyes. Santa Coloma de Farners: Centre d'Estudis Selvatans.

Arnabat, Ramon, and Anna Sabanés. 2006. *Víctimes de la Guerra Civil (1936–1939) al Penedès*. Vilafranca del Penedès: Andana.

Badia, Lluís. 1989. "Les víctimes de la persecució religiosa al Berguedà 1936–1939." *L'Erol* 28: 35–40.

Barbarà, Andreu, and Josep Maria Roig i Rosich. 1980. "La guerra civil a Alcover i la repressió de la postguerra." *Centre d'Estudis Alcoverencs* 11: 19–25.

Barbé i Pou, Elisenda. 2006. "De la creació del municipi a l'actualitat." In *Història General de l'Ametlla del Vallès*, ed. S. Cucurella. La Garriga: Fundació Martí l'Humà.

Blanch, Josepa. 1994. "Mort, on és la teva victòria? Aproximació al cost humà de la Guerra Civil a la Terra Alta." *Butlletí del Centre d'Estudis de la Terra Alta* 20 (segon semestre).

Blanchon, Jean-Louis. 1987. "Une expérience libertaire en Cerdagne: Puigcerdà sous le pouvoir des anarchistes (juillet 1936–juin 1937)." *Annales du Midi* 99(177): 87–124.

Bonjorn, Robert, Glòria Comas, and Jaume Torres. 1991. "Soldats de l'Urgell morts a la Guerra Civil (1936–1939) i civils morts per material de guerra abandonat." *Urtx* 3.

Bonjorn, Robert, Josep Pla, Joan Civit, and Delfí Solé. 1995. "Combatents de la Noguera morts al front i civils víctimes d'accidents derivats de la guerra." *Urtx* 7.

Borràs i Dòlera, Mercè. 2000. *Refugiats/des (1936–39)*, Quaderns de la Revista de Girona. Girona: Diputació de Girona.

Bosom i Isern, Sebastià. 1993. *Puigcerdà*. Quaderns de la Revista de Girona 23 (Monografies Locals). Girona: Diputació de Girona.

Bragulat Sirvent, Jaume. 1969. "Pròleg." In *Vint-i-cinc anys de vida puigcerdanesa 1901–1925*. Barcelona: Gráficas Casulleras.

Burgués, José P. 1999. *Tiempo de Violencia, Tiempo de Reconciliación. Dos años de la historia de Torrecilla de Alcañiz (1936–1938)*. Alcañiz: Boletín del Centro de Estudios Bajoaragoneses.

Castillo, Sofia. 1988. "Els primers dies de la guerra civil a Ripoll: un testimoni escrit." Pp. 43–49 in *Annals 1987–1988*. Ripoll: Centre d'Estudis Comarcals del Ripollès.

———. 1991. "El cost humà de la guerra civil: Ripollesos morts al front." Pp. 115–125 in *Annals 1989–1990*. Ripoll: Centre d'Estudis Comarcals del Ripollès.

Castillo, Sofia, and Olga Camps. 1994. *La Guerra Civil a Ripoll (1936–1939)*. Ripoll: Ajuntament de Ripoll.

Clara, Josep. 1991. "La repressió de postguerra al Ripollès: els empresonats del 1940." Pp. 127–139 in *Annals 1989–1990*. Ripoll: Centre d'Estudis Comarcals del Ripollès.

———. 1996. "Militars i la guerra civil: els carrabiners de Ripoll." Pp.161–166 in *Annals 1994–1995*. Ripoll: Centre d'Estudis Comarcals del Ripollès.

———. 2003. "El sometent franquista al Ripollès." In *Annals 2001–2002*, ed. F. Crivillé. Ripoll: Centre d'Estudis Comarcals del Ripollès.

Crosas Casadesús, Jaume. 2004. *Guerra i repressió al Collsacabra 1936–1943*. Santa Coloma de Gramenet: Grupo de Historia José Berruezo.

Delgado, Manuel. 1993. "Cultura de la violencia y violencia de la historia en Centelles, verano de 1936." *Historia y fuente oral* 9 (Junio): 103–117.

Dueñas Iturbe, Oriol. 2007. *La violència d'uns i altres. La repressió de la guerra i la postguerra 1936–1945. El cas d'Olesa de Montserrat*. Barcelona: Publicacions de l'Abadia de Montserrat.

Estrada i Planell, Gemma. 1995. *La Guerra Civil al Bruc*. Barcelona: Publicacions de l'Abadia de Montserrat.

Figueras, Narcís, and Antoni Reyes (Eds). 2000. *Guerra Civil i Franquisme seixanta anys després*. Santa Coloma de Farners: Centre d'Estudis Selvatans.

Gabarda, Vicent. 1994. "El Camp de Morverdre, 1936–1942. Las muertes violentas en la retaguardia bélica y la inmediata postguerra." *Braçal* 9: 31–52.

Gaitx Motlló, Jordi, and Esther Plaza. 2006. "Introducció. El context històric previ al franquisme." Pp. 23–30 in *Franquisme i Repressió a Sant Feliu de Guíxols durant la postguerra*, eds. J. Gaitx, *et al*. Sant Feliu de Guíxols: Diputació de Girona.

Gaitx Motlló, Jordi. 2007. *L'exili del Baix Empordà al 1939*. La Bisbal d'Empordà: Ajuntament de la Bisbal d'Empordà.

Gaitx Motlló, Jordi, Marc Auladell, Verònica Garcia, Àngel Jiménez, and Esther Plaza. 2006. *Franquisme i Repressió a Sant Feliu de Guíxols durant la postguerra*. Sant Feliu de Guíxols: Diputació de Girona.

Gallardo Moreno, Jacinta. 1994. *La Guerra Civil en La Serena*. Badajoz: Diputacion Provincial de Badajoz.

García, José María, and Carlos Polanco. 1995. *La II República y la Guerra Civil en la villa de Logrosán*. Mérida: Editora Regional de Extremadura.

Garriga i Andreu, Joan. 1986. *Revolta i guerra civil a la Garriga (Vallès Oriental) 1936–1939*. Argentona: L'Aixernador.

2003. *Granollers, caciquisme i fractura democratica (1848–1939)*. Barcelona: Publicacions de l'Abadia de Montserrat.

2004. *Franquisme i poder polític a Granollers (1939–1975)*. Barcelona: Publicacions de l'Abadia de Montserrat.

Gavaldà Torrents, Antoni. 1997. *Jo delato, tu inculpes, ell denúncia... Repressió Franquista a Valls i Comarca*. Valls: Institut d'Estudis Vallencs.

Gil, Fernando, and Albert Garcia. 2009. "La mortalidad en la infancia durante la Guerra Civil. Impacto territorial estimado a partir del Censo de 1940." *Revista Española de Investigaciones Sociológicas* (127): 55–91.

Gimeno, Manuel. 1989. *Revolució, guerra i repressió al Pallars (1936–1939)*. Barcelona: Publicacions de l'Abadia de Montserrat.

Gutiérrez Casalá, José Luis. 1998. *La Segunda República en Badajoz*. Badajoz: Universitas.

Gutiérrez Casalá, José Luis. 2006. *La Guerra Civil en la provincia de Badajoz*. Badajoz: Universitas.

Gutiérrez Flores, Jesús. 2000. *Guerra civil en una comarca de Cantabria: Campoo. Análisis de la represión republicana y de la represión franquista*. Comité Organizador del Festival Cabuerniga Música de los Pueblos del Norte.

Manent, Albert. 2002. "La guerra civil a tres pobles de les muntanyes de Prades: Arbolí, Mont-ral i Vilaplana." *Butlletí del Centre d'Estudis Alcoverencs* 97–100: 42–53.

2006. *La guerra civil i la repressió del 1939 a 62 pobles del Camp de Tarragona.* Valls: Cossetània Edicions.

Marina, Francesc. 2000. "Arbúcies 1939–1949: Les gestoras provisionales i la repressió de la posguerra." Pp. 245–264 in *Temps de Postguerra. Estudis sobre les comarques gironines (1939–1955)*, ed. S. Castillo. Girona: Cercle d'Estudis Històrics i Socials.

Martín Rubio, Ángel David. 2006. "Represión Republicana en Badajoz." Pp. 205–240 in *Badajoz Agosto de 1936. Historia y Memoria de la Guerra Civil en Extremadura*, ed. J. Chaves Palacios. Badajoz: Diputación de Badajoz.

Martorell Garau, Miquel. 2006. *Els refugiats de les zones de Guerra al Priorat. 1936–1939.* Torroja del Priorat: Arxiu Comarcal del Priorat.

Mateu, Xavier (Coord.). 1981. *La Cerdanya. Recursos Econòmics i Activitat Productiva.* Barcelona: Caixa de Catalunya.

Maymí Rich, Josep. 2001. *Entre la violència política i el conflicte social. Els comitès antifeixistes de Salt i d'Orriols en el context de la Guerra Civil 1936–1939.* Barcelona: Publicacions de l'Abadia de Montserrat.

Maymí Rich, Josep, Josep Ros Nicolau, and Turró Ventura. 2006. *Els refugiats de la Guerra Civil a les comarques del Gironès i el Pla de l'Estany (1936–1939).* Barcelona: Publicacions de l'Abadia de Montserrat.

Montañà, Daniel, and Josep Rafart 1991. "La Guerra Civil al Berguedà." Barcelona: Publicacions de l'Abadia de Montserrat.

Mota Muñoz, José Fernando. 2001. *La República, la guerra i el primer franquisme a Sant Cugat del Vallès (1931–1941).* Barcelona: Publicacions de l'Abadia de Montserrat i Ajuntament de Sant Cugat del Vallès.

Nadal, Antonio. 1981. *Andalucía ante el advenimiento de la República: coyuntura política y movimientos huelguísticos en la Malaga de 1930.* PhD Dissertation, Departamento de Historia Contemporánea, Universidad de Malaga, Malaga.

1984. *La guerra civil en Malaga.* Malaga: Argubal.

Noguera Canal, Josep. 1989. "El poder municipal durant la República, la Guerra Civil i l'inici del Franquisme a la ciutat de Berga." *L'Erol* 28: 18–21.

1989. "Els morts del Berguedà al front durant la guerra civil de 1936–1939." *L'Erol* 28: 24–39.

Oliva i Llorens, Jordi. 1992. "Els soldats de la Segarra morts a la Guerra Civil (1936–1939) i els civils víctimes d'accidents de la guerra." *Miscellània cerverina* 8.

1999. *El cost humà de la Guerra Civil a les comarques gironines: combatents morts i víctimes del material bèl·lic abandonat.* Girona: El Punt.

Pijiula, Jordi. 1993. *Els morts per la Guerra Civil a la Garrotxa (1936–1945).* Olot: Llibres de Batet.

2000. "L'exili olotí del 1939." Pp. 117–136 in *Temps de Postguerra. Estudis sobre les comarques gironines (1939–1955)*, ed. S. Castillo. Girona: Cercle d'Estudis Històrics i Socials.

Piqué i Padró, Jordi. 1998. *La crisi de la rereguarda. Revolució i guerra civil a Tarragona (1936–1939).* Tarragona: Diputació de Tarragona i Publicacions de l'Abadia de Montserrat.

Planes, Jordi. 1989. "Exili republicà i exili berguedà, cinquanta anys després." *L'Erol* 28: 59–63.

Pous, Joan, and Josep M. Solé i Sabaté. 1988. *Anarquia i República a la Cerdanya (1936–1939). El "cojo de Malaga" i els fets de Bellver.* Biblioteca Serra d'Or, 74. Barcelona: Publicacions de l'Abadia de Montserrat.

Prats i Armengol, Francesc. 1991. *La Ciutat de Tremp Durant la Segona República i la Guerra Civil (1931–1938).* Barcelona: Fundació Salvador Vives i Casajuana.

Radcliff, Pamela Beth. 1996. *From mobilization to civil war: the politics of polarization in the Spanish city of Gijón, 1900–1937.* New York: Cambridge University Press.

Sabaté i Alentorn, Jaume. 2002. *Víctimes d'una guerra al Priorat (1936–19...).* Collecció Camí Ral, núm. 21. Barcelona: Rafael Dalmau.

Sabín Rodríguez, Jose Manuel. *"La represión en Toledo: 1936–1950."* Unpublished manuscript.

Sabio, Alberto. 1997. *A las puertas de la memoria. La historia local en Samper de Calanda (1850–1970).* Samper de Calanda: Ayuntamiento de Samper de Calanda & Instituto de Estudios Turolenses.

Sánchez Cervelló, Josep. 1999. "Entre el perill feixista i les divergències republicanes: la guerra civil a les terres de l'Ebre." In *Guerra Civil a les Comarques Tarragonines (1936–1939)*, eds. J. Piqué Padró and J. Sánchez Cervelló. Tarragona: Cercle d'Estudis Històrics i Socials Guillem Oliver del Camp de Tarragona.

Santacana, Carles. 2004. *Guerra i repressió al Collsacabra.* Barcelona: Centre d'Història Contemporània de Catalunya.

Serra, Jaume. 1989. "Notes sobre el moviment obrer al Berguedà durant la segona república." *L'Erol* 21: 13–17.

Sitjar i Serra, Miquel. 1994. *Ribes de Freser.* Girona: Diputació de Girona.

Sitjar i Serra, Miquel. 2000. *Campelles.* Ripoll: Maideu.

Térmens, Miquel. 1991. *Revolució i guerra civil a Igualada (1936–1939).* Barcelona: Publicacions de l'Abadia de Montserrat.

Velasco Gómez, José. 2008. *La Segunda República en Malaga. 1931–1936.* Malaga: Ágora.

Ventura i Solé, Joan. 1993. *La postguerra a Valls. 1939–1940.* Valls: Consell Comarcal de l'Alt Camp.

## Documentaries and Audiovisual Material

BBC. 1983. "The Spanish Civil War." Eds. Neal Acherson and James Cameron. London: BBC.

CCRTV. 2006. "Entre el jou i l'espasa." Ed. M. D. Genovès. Barcelona: CCRTV

Montanyà, Xavier. 2010. "Espies de Franco." Sàpiens Publicacions, DL 2010.

Suica Films. "Stuke Experiment." Retrieved on January 30, 2016 from www.suicafilms.com/experiment-stuka/

## General Bibliography on Spain and the Spanish Civil War

Anonymous. 1939. *Bombardeos de la aviación nacional a la retaguardia republicana.* Barcelona: Seix y Barral.

Anonymous. 1938. *Bombardements et agressions en Espagne.* Paris: Comité Mondiale contre le Fascisme.

Amat, Francesc, Carles Boix, Jordi Muñoz, and Toni Rodon. 2016. "From Political Mobilization to Electoral Participation: Turnout in Barcelona in the 1930s." Paper presented at the First Annual LSE Historical Political Economy Conference. London, UK, January 25, 2016.

Abellà, Rafael. 1973. *La vida cotidiana durante la Guerra Civil. La España Nacional.* Barcelona: Planeta DeAgostini.

1975. *La vida cotidiana durante la guerra civil. La España Republicana.* Barcelona: Planeta DeAgostini.

Albertí, Santiago, and Elisenda Albertí. 2013. *Perill de Bombardeig! Barcelona sota les bombes (1936–1939).* Barcelona: Albertí.

Alcalá, César. 2001. *Persecución en la Retaguardia. Cataluña 1936–1939.* Madrid: Actas Editorial.

Alía Miranda, Francisco. 1994. *La Guerra Civil en Retaguardia, Ciudad Real (1936–1939).* Ciudad Real: Diputación de Ciudad Real.

Algué, Jordi, Miquel Arceda, Ester Llobet, Rossend Sellarés, and Arcadi Vilà. 2015. *Silencis. República, Guerra Civil i Repressió Franquista a Navàs (1931–1945).* Navàs: Ajuntament de Navàs.

Alós, Vicente. 1978. *Castellón y la Segunda República: aspectos electorales.* Zaragoza: Anubar Ediciones.

Anderson, Jon Lee. 2009. "Letter from Andalusia. Lorca's bones. Can Spain finally confront its civil-war past?" *The New Yorker*, June 22, 2009: 44–48.

Anderson, Peter, and Miguel Ángel del Arco Blanco. 2015. *Mass killings and violence in Spain, 1936–1952.* London: Routledge.

Arcarazo García, Luis. 2004. "El 'sector Huesca' del frente de Aragón. Los combates entre 1936 y 1938." Pp. 95–188 in *Guerra Civil Aragón*, vol 1, ed. F. Martínez de Baños. Zaragoza: Delsan.

Arcarazo, Luis Alfonso, Pedro Barrachina, and Fernando Martínez de Baños. 2007. *Guerra civil Aragón V: Huesca "el cerco."* Cuarte de Huerva: Delsan.

Armengou, Montse, and Ricard Belis. 2004. *Les fosses del silenci. Hi ha un Holocaust espanyol?* Barcelona: Televisió de Catalunya.

Arrué, Vicente. 1969. *Las elecciones de febrero de 1936 en el País Valenciano.* PhD Dissertation, Història Contemporània, Universitat de València: València.

1974. "L'ambient electoral durant les eleccions de febrer de 1936." *Arguments* 1: 157–172.

Artís Gener, Avellí. 1976. *La diàspora republicana.* Barcelona: Euros.

Ayala Vicente, Fernando. 2001. *Las elecciones en la provincia de Cáceres durante la II República.* Vol. 18. Mérida: Editora Regional de Extremadura.

2002. *La vida política en la provincia de Cáceres durante la II República.* Cáceres: Diputación Provincial de Cáceres.

Azpíroz Pascual, José María. 2007. *La Voz del Olvido.* Huesca: Diputación Provincial de Huesca.

Balcells, Albert. 1971. *Crisis económica y agitación social en Cataluña de 1930 a 1936.* Ariel: Barcelona.

1980. *El problema agrario en Cataluña: la cuestión rabassaire. 1890–1936.* Madrid: Ministerio de Agricultura, Pesca y Alimentación.

Balfour, Sebastian, and Paul Preston. 1999. "Introduction." Pp. 1–12 in *Spain and the Great Powers*, eds. S. Balfour and P. Preston. London: Routledge.

Ballarín, Josep Maria. 1989. "La lleva del biberó." *L'Erol* 28: 22–23.

Banqué i Martí, Jordi. 2004. *Comunistes i Catalans*. Reus: Associació d'Estudis Reusencs.

Barallat i Barés, Mercè. 1991. *La repressió a la postguerra civil a Lleida (1938–1945)*. Barcelona: Publicacions de l'Abadia de Montserrat.

Benet, Josep. 1989. "Pròleg." Pp. V–XVIII in *La Repressió a la Reraguarda de Catalunya (1936–1939)*, eds. J. M. Solé i Sabaté and J. Villarroya. Puigcerdà, Barcelona: Publicacions de l'Abadia de Montserrat.

Bermejo, Benito, and Sandra Checa. 2006. *Libro Memorial. Españoles deportados a los Campos Nazis (1940–1945)*. Madrid: Ministerio de Cultura.

Bernecker, Walter. 1982. *Colectividades y Revolución Social*. Trans. G. Muñoz. Barcelona: Grijalbo.

Beevor, Antony. 1982. *The Spanish Civil War*. London: Orbis Publishing.

2006. *The battle for Spain. The Spanish Civil War (1936–1939)*. New York: Penguin Books.

Bosch Sánchez, Aurora. 1983. *Ugetistas y Libertarios. Guerra Civil y Revolución en el País Valenciano 1936–1939*. Valencia: Institución Alfonso el Magnánimo. Diputación Provincial de Valencia.

Brenan, Gerald. 2014 (first edition 1943). *The Spanish labyrinth: an account of the social and political background of the Civil War*. New York: Cambridge University Press.

Calzado, Antonio. 2006. "La represión franquista durante la Guerra Civil." Pp. 9–27 in *Violencia y represión en la retaguardia*, eds. M. Ors and J. M. Santacreu. Valencia: Prensa Alicantina.

Calzado, Antonio, and Ricard Torres Fabra. 1999. "República i guerra civil al País Valencià. Un estat de la qüestió." *El Contemporani* 17 (gener-abril).

Canales Serrano, Antonio Francisco. 2002. *Derecha y poder local en el siglo XX: evolución ideológica y práctica política de la derecha en Vilanova i la Geltrú (Barcelona) y Barakaldo (Vizcaya) 1898–1979*. PhD Dissertation, Autonomous University of Barcelona, Barcelona.

Capel Martínez, Rosa María. 1992. *El Sufragio Femenino en la Segunda República Española*. Madrid: Dirección General de la Mujer.

Cardona, Gabriel (Director Científico). 2005. *La guerra civil española*. Madrid: Arlanza Ediciones.

Carrión, Pascual. 1932. *Los latifundios en España; su importancia, origen, consecuencias y solución*. Madrid: Gráficas reunidas.

Casanova, Ester. 2004. *Violencia Anticlerical y Memoria de los Mártires (1936–1945)*. PhD Dissertation, Departamento de Historia Moderna y Contemporánea, Universidad de Zaragoza, Zaragoza.

2007. *La violencia política en la retaguardia republicana de Teruel durante la guerra civil*. Teruel: Instituto de Estudios Turolenses.

Casanova, Julián. 1985. *Anarquismo y revolución en la sociedad rural Aragonesa. 1936–1938*. Madrid: Siglo Veintiuno de España Editores.

1988. *El sueño igualitario: campesinado y colectivizaciones en la España republicana 1936–1939*. Zaragoza: Institución Fernando el Católico.

2005. "Terror and violence: the dark face of Spanish anarchism." *International Labor and Working-Class History* 67 (Spring): 79–99.

2010. *The Spanish Republic and Civil War*. NY: Cambridge University Press.

2013. *A short history of the Spanish Civil War*. London: Tauris.

2014. "La Guerra Civil que nunca se aprendió en las escuelas." *El Pais*, 1 Abril 2014. Retrieved from: http://blogs.elpais.com/historias/2014/04/la-guerra-civil-que-nunca-se-aprendio-en-las-escuelas.html

Casanova, Julián, and Angela Cenarro. 2014. *Pagar las Culpas: la Represión Económica en Aragón (1936–1945)*. Barcelona: Crítica.

Casanova, Julián, Angela Cenarro Lagunas, Julita Cifuentes, Ma Pilar Maluenda, and Ma Pilar Salomón. 2001. *El Pasado Oculto. Fascismo y Violencia en Aragón (1936–1939)*, 3rd ed. Zaragoza: Mira Editores.

Cattini, Giovanni C. 2005a. "La violència revolucionària. Terror i repressió a la rereguarda." Pp. 142–152 in *Breu Història de la Guerra Civil a Catalunya*, eds. J. M. Solé i Sabaté and J. Villarroya. Barcelona: Edicions 62.

Cattini, Giovanni C. 2005b. "Els combatents morts a la Guerra Civil." Pp. 180–182 in *La Guerra Civil a Catalunya (1936–1939). Vol 4. Derrota, ocupació militar i exili*. Barcelona: Edicions 62.

Cenarro, Angela. 1998. "Muerte y subordinación en la España franquista: el imperio de la violencia como base del 'Nuevo Estado.' " *Historia Social* 30: 5–22.

2006. "Movilización femenina para la guerra total (1936–1939): un ejercicio comparativo." *Historia y política: ideas, procesos y movimientos sociales* 16: 159–182.

1994. *Los orígenes y la naturaleza del franquismo en Aragón (1936–1945)*. PhD Dissertation, Facultad de Filosofía y Letras, Universidad de Zaragoza, Zaragoza.

2002a. "La lógica de la guerra, la lógica de la venganza: violencia y fractura social en una comunidad bajoaragonesa, 1939–1940." Pp. 703–715 in *Segon Congrés Recerques. Enfrontaments civils: postguerres i reconstruccions*, Lleida.

2002b. "Matar, Vigilar y Delatar: La Quiebra de la Sociedad Civil Durante la Guerra y la Posguerra en España (1936–1948)." *Historia Social* 44: 65–86.

Cenarro, Angela, and Victor Pardo Lancina. 2006. *Guerra Civil en Aragón. 70 años después*. Zaragoza: Departamento de Educación, Cultura y Deporte.

Chamocho Cantudo, Miguel Ángel. 2004. *La Justicia del Pueblo. Los tribunales populares de Jaén durante la Guerra Civil*. Jaén: Instituto de Estudios Giennenses.

Chaves Palacios, Julián. 1995. *La represión en la provincia de Cáceres durante la guerra civil (1936–39)*. Cáceres: Universidad de Extremadura.

2000. *Violencia Política y Conflictividad Social en Extremadura. Cáceres en 1936*. Salamanca: Diputación Provincial de Badajoz.

2004. *La Guerra Civil en Extremadura. Operaciones Militares (1936–1939)*, 3rd ed. Mérida: Junta de Extremadura.

2006. "Represión Republicana en Badajoz." Pp. 205–240 in *Badajoz en agosto de 1936. Historia y Memoria de la Guerra Civil en Extremadura*, ed. J. Chaves Palacios. Badajoz: Diputación de Badajoz.

Cifuentes, Julita, and Maria Pilar Maluenda. 2006. "Alcaldes y concejales, objetivo prioritario del terror." In *La guerra civil en Aragón. Terror "azul" y violencia "roja,"* eds. M. P. Salomon and J. L. Ledesma Vera. Barcelona and Zaragoza: Ciro and Prensa Diaria Aragonesa.

Colomer, Josep Maria. 2004. "Spain: from civil war to proportional representation." Pp. 253–264 in *Handbook of electoral system choice*, ed. J. Colomer. London: Palgrave-Macmillan.

Cruz, Rafael. 2006. *En el nombre del pueblo. República, Rebelión y Guerra en la España de 1936.* Madrid: Siglo XXI.

Cucó i Giner, Antonio. 1970. "Contribución a un estudio cuantitativo de la C.N.T." *Saitabi* XX: 181–202.

De Estella, Gumersindo. 2003. *Fusilados en Zaragoza. 1936–1939. Tres años de asistencia espiritual a los reos.* Zaragoza: Mira Editores.

De la Cueva, Julio. 1998. "Religious persecution, anticlerical tradition and revolution: on atrocities against the clergy during the Spanish Civil War." *Journal of Contemporary History* 33(3): 355–369.

De Riquer, Borja. 1991. "El sistema de partidos políticos en Cataluña durante el primer bienio republicano (1931–1933)." *Historia Contemporánea* 6: 85–93.

Delgado, Manuel. 1992. *La ira sagrada. Anticlericalismo, iconoclastia y antirritualismo en la España contemporánea.* Barcelona: Humanidades.

——— 1997. "Anticlericalismo, espacio y poder. La destrucción de los rituales católicos, 1931–1939." *Ayer* 27: 149–180.

——— 2001. *Luces iconoclastas. Anticlericalismo, espacio y ritual en la España contemporánea.* Barcelona: Ariel.

Desfor Edles, Laura. 1998. *Symbol and Ritual in the New Spain.* New York: Cambridge University Press.

Díaz-Balart, Mirta, and Antonio Rojas Friend. 1997. *Consejo de guerra: Los fusilamientos en el Madrid de la posguerra (1939–1945).* Madrid: Compañía Literaria.

Díaz i Esculies, Daniel. 2003. "Aproximació bibliogràfica als exilis catalans de la Guerra Civil (1936–1939)." In *L'exili català del 1936–1939,* ed. E. Pujol. Girona: Cercle d'Estudis Històrics i Socials.

Díaz Nosty, Bernardo. 1975. *La Comuna Asturiana. Revolución de Octubre de 1934.* Bilbao: Zero S.A.

Díaz-Plaja, Fernando. 1994. *La vida cotidiana en la España de la guerra civil.* Madrid: Edaf.

Dòll-Petit, Rubèn. 2003. *Els "Catalans de Gènova" historia de l'èxode i l'adhesió d'una classe dirigent en temps de guerra.* Barcelona: Publicacions de l'Abadia de Montserrat.

——— 2004. "Repressió, Salvament i Fugida a la Reraguarda Catalana, 1936–1939." *Revista Internacional de la Guerra Civil Ebre* 38(2): 49–60.

Equip de Sociologia Electoral (U.A.B). 1978. *Sobre les eleccions legislatives del 1977.* Vol. 1, Estudis Electorals. Barcelona: Fundació Jaume Bofill.

Escribano Bernal, Francisco. 2004. "Una primavera de conspiraciones." Pp. 21–49 in *Guerra Civil Aragón,* vol. 1, ed. F. Martínez de Baños. Zaragoza: Delsan.

Espinosa, Francisco. 2005. *La columna de la muerte: el avance del ejército franquista de Sevilla a Badajoz.* Barcelona: Planeta-De Agostini.

Fillol, Vicente. 1971. *Los perdedores: memorias de un exiliado español.* Madrid: Ediciones Gaceta Ilustrada.

Flores, Miguel, Antonio Gascón, and Fernando Martínez de Baños. 2008. *Guerra civil Aragón VI: El Pirineo.* Cuarte de Huerva: Delsan.

Font i Agulló, Jordi. 2001. *Arriba el Campo! Primer franquisme i actituds polítiques en l'àmbit rural nord-català.* Girona: Diputació de Girona.

Fraser, Ronald. 2001. *Recuérdalo tú y recuérdalo a otros. Historia oral de la guerra civil española,* 3rd ed. Barcelona: Crítica.

Gabarda, Vicent. 1982. "La continuación de la guerra civil: la represión franquista." *Estudis d'Història Contemporània del Pais Valencia* 7: 229–248.

1993. *Els afusellaments al País Valencià.* València: Alfons el Magnànim.

1996. *La Represión en la Retaguardia Republicana. País Valenciano, 1936–1939.* València: Alfons el Magnànim.

Gaite, Jesús. 1994. "Fondos de Guerra Civil y Posguerra en la Sección Fondos Contemporáneos del Archivo Histórico Nacional." *Espacio, Tiempo y Forma, Historia Contemporánea* 7: 455–477.

Gaitx Motlló, Jordi. 2006. "Orígens socials i polítics de l'exili català de 1939." Pp. 21–39 in *L'exili català del 1936–39. Noves aportacions,* ed. E. Pujol. Girona: Cercle d'Estudis Històrics i Socials.

García de Cortázar, Fernando, and José Manuel González. 1994. *Breve Historia de España.* Madrid: Alianza.

García Miralles, Manuel. 1962. *Los Dominicos de la Provincia de Aragón en la Persecución Religiosa de 1936.* Valencia: Editorial F.E.D.A.

García Piñeiro, Ramón. 2002. "Marginación Política y Exclusión Social en la Asturias de la posguerra (1937–1952)." Pp. 137–147 in *L'exili republicà,* ed. F. Bonamusa. Barberà del Vallès: Ajuntament de Barberà del Vallès.

Germán Zubero, Luis Gonzalo. 1984. *Aragón en la II República. Estructura económica y comportamiento político.* Zaragoza: Institución Fernando el Católico.

Germán Zubero, Luis Gonzalo. 1982. *Elecciones y partidos políticos en Aragón durante la Segunda República: estructura económica y comportamiento político.* PhD Dissertation, Facultad de Filosofia y Letras, Departamento de Historia Moderna y Contemporánea, Universidad de Zaragoza, Zaragoza.

González Calleja, Eduardo. 2014. *En hombre de la autoridad. La defensa del orden público durante la Segunda República Española (1931–1936).* Granada: Comares Historia.

González Duro, Enrique. 2003. *El Miedo en la Posguerra. Franco y la España derrotada: la política del exterminio.* Madrid: Oberon.

Graham, Helen. 1999. "La movilización con vistas a la Guerra Total: la experiencia Republicana." Pp. 175–199 in *La Repubica asediada. Hostilidad internacional y conflictos internos durante la Guerra Civil.* ed. P. Preston. Barcelona: Ediciones Península.

Güell, Manel. 2002. "Servicio Nacional de Regiones Devastadas y Reparaciones de l'Arxiu Històric de la Diputació de Tarragona." Paper presented at Segon Congrés Recerques. Enfrontaments civils: postguerres i reconstruccions, Universitat de Lleida.

Guixé, Jordi. 2003. "Fons per a l'estudi de l'exili republicà." In *L'exili català de 1936–1939,* ed. E. Pujol. Girona: Cercle d'Estudis Històrics i Socials.

2012. *La República perseguida. Exilio y represión en la Francia de Franco, 1937–1951.* València: Universitat de València.

Gunther, Richard, Giacomo Sani, and Goldie Shabad. 1988. *Spain after Franco. The making of a competitive party system.* Los Angeles, Berkeley & London: University of California Press.

Gutiérrez Flores, Jesús. 2006. *Guerra civil en Cantabria y pueblos de Castilla.* Libros en Red. Available from www.librosenred.com

Hansen, Edward. 1977. *Rural Catalonia under the Franco regime.* Cambridge: Cambridge University Press.

Harding, Susan Friend. *Remaking Ibieca. Rural Life in Aragon under Franco.* Chapel Hill and London: The University of North Carolina Press.

Heredia, Iván. 2006. "Fusilamientos en el cementerio de Torrero." In *La guerra civil en Aragón. Terror "azul" y violencia "roja,"* eds. M. P. Salomon and J. L. Ledesma Vera. Barcelona and Zaragoza: Ciro and Prensa Diaria Aragonesa.

Hinojosa Durán, José. 2007. "La vida política en la Extremadura republicana durante la guerra civil. Estudio de los grupos dirigentes." Pp. 335–390 in *La depuración de funcionarios, maestros y otros colectivos "desafectos" en la provincia de Badajoz durante la Guerra Civil*, ed. J. García Pérez. Badajoz: Estudios Provinciales.

Jackson, Angela. 2008. *Els brigadistes entre nosaltres*. Barcelona: Cossetània.

Jackson, Gabriel. 1965. *The Spanish Republic and the Civil War 1931–1939*. Princeton: Princeton University Press.

Jackson, Gabriel (Ed.). 1985. *Octubre 1934: cincuenta años para la reflexión*. Madrid: Siglo XXI.

Juliá, Santos. 2004. *Víctimas de la guerra civil*, 2nd ed. Madrid: Temas de Hoy.

Langarita, Estefanía. 2014. "Si no hay castigo, la España Nueva no se hará nunca. La colaboración ciudadana con las autoridades franquistas." Pp. 145–174 in *Pagar las Culpas: la Represión Económica en Aragón (1936–1945)*, eds. J. Casanova and A. Cenarro. Barcelona: Crítica.

Lannon, Frances. 2002. *The Spanish Civil War, 1936–1939*. Oxford: Osprey.

Laparra, Alvaro. 2013. "An institutional study of the army during the Spanish Second Republic and Civil War (1931–1939)." Unpublished paper. University of Maryland.

Ledesma Vera, José Luis. 2001. "Espacios de poder, violencia y revolución: una perspectiva política de la represión en el Aragón republicano durante la guerra civil." Pp. 249–268 in *El difícil camino hacia la democracia*, ed. A. Morales Moya. Madrid: Sociedad Estatal España Nuevo Milenio.

Ledesma Vera, José Luis. 2003. *Los días de llamas de la revolución. Violencia y política en la retaguardia republicana de Zaragoza durante la Guerra Civil*. Zaragoza: Institución "Fernando el Católico" (C.S.I.C.).

Ledesma Vera, José Luis. 2006a. "Se rompió el tiempo. Fragores de ruina y muerte en el Aragón en guerra." Pp. 29–58 in *Paisajes para después de una guerra*, ed. J. Lambán, *et al.* Zaragoza: Diputación Provincial de Zaragoza.

Ledesma Vera, José Luis. 2006b. "La violencia en el Aragón republicano: negras sombras del alba roja." Pp. 87–100 in *Guerra Civil en Aragón. 70 años después*, eds. A. Cenarro Lagunas and V. Pardo Lancina. Zaragoza: Departamento de Educación, Cultura y Deporte.

Ledesma Vera, José Luis. 2006c. "Un baño de sangre: terror rebelde y violencia revolucionaria." Pp. 16–95 in *La guerra civil en Aragón. Terror "azul" y violencia "roja,"* eds. M. P. Salomón and J. L. Ledesma Vera. Barcelona and Zaragoza: Ciro and Prensa Diaria Aragonesa.

Ledesma Vera, José Luis. 2008. "Total war behind the frontlines? An inquiry into the violence on the Republican side in the Spanish Civil War." Pp. 154–168 in *If you tolerate this: the Spanish Civil War in the Age of Total War*, eds. M. Baumeister and S. Schüler-Springorum. Campus: Frankfurt-Nueva York.

Ledesma Vera, José Luis. 2009a. "Delenda est Ecclesia. De la violencia anticlerical y la Guerra Civil de 1936." Presentado en Seminario de Historia, Instituto Universitario Ortega y Gasset, Madrid, June 25, 2009.

Ledesma Vera, José Luis. 2009b. *Las justicias del pueblo: Violencia, justicia y revolución en la zona republicana durante la Guerra Civil española (1936-1939)*. PhD Dissertation, History, The European University Institute, Florence.

Ledesma, José Luis. 2011. "Las violencias contra el clero español (1936–1939): una interpretación histórica." *Razón y Fe* (1347): 45–60.

Leitz, Christian. 1999. "Nazi Germany and Francoist Spain, 1936–1945." Pp. 127–150 in *Spain and the Great Powers in the Twentieth Century*, eds. S. Balfour and P. Preston. London: Routledge.

Linz, Juan J. 1967. "The party system of Spain." Pp. 197–282 in *Party systems and voter alignments: cross-national perspectives*, eds. S. M. Lipset and S. Rokkan. New York: The Free Press.

Linz, Juan J. 1978. "From great hopes to Civil War: the breakdown of democracy in Spain." Pp. 142–215 in *The Breakdown of Democratic Regimes: Europe*, eds. J. Linz and A. Stepan. Baltimore: The Johns Hopkins University Press.

Linz, Juan J. 1996. La violencia en la guerra civil y en la posguerra. Unpublished manuscript, Yale University.

Linz, Juan J., and Jesus M. De Miguel. 1977. "Hacia un análisis regional de las elecciones de 1936 en España." *Revista Española de la Opinión Pública* 48: 27–68.

Linz, Juan J., and José Ramón Montero. 1999. The party systems of Spain: old cleavages and new challenges. Juan March Institute. Estudio Working Paper 1999/138.

Linz, Juan J., José Ramón Montero, and Antonia Ruiz. 2005. "Elecciones y Política." In *Estadísticas históricas de España: siglos XIX y XX*, eds. A. de Carreras and X. Tafunell. Madrid: Fundación BBVA.

Luengo, Félix. 1998. Algunas características de las violencias durante la Guerra Civil de 1936." *Vasconia* 26: 251–258.

Maldonado, José María. 2006a. "La guerra desde el aire. Los bombardeos y sus efectos." In *Guerra Civil en Aragón 70 años después*, eds. A. Cenarro and V. Pardo. Zaragoza: Departamento de Educación, Cultura y Deporte.

Maldonado, José María. 2006b. "Los bombardeos aéreos en Aragón." Pp. 143–158 in *Paisajes para después de una guerra*, eds. J. Lambán, *et al.* Zaragoza: Diputación Provincial de Zaragoza.

Maldonado, José María. 2007. *El frente de Aragón. La guerra civil en Aragón (1936–1938)*. Zaragoza: Mira Editores.

Malefakis, Edward. 1976. *Reforma Agraria y Revolución Campesina en la España del Siglo XX*, 3rd ed. Barcelona: Ariel.

Malefakis, Edward (Ed.) 1996. *La guerra de España (1936–1939)*. Madrid: Taurus.

Marín, Martí. 1995. "Franquisme i poder local. Construcció i consolidació dels ajuntaments feixistes a Catalunya, 1938–1949." *Recerques: història, economia, cultura* 31: 37–52.

Marimon, Sílvia. 2013. Els Bombardejos a Barcelona. *Sàpiens*. Retrieved on January 14, 2014 from: www.sapiens.cat/ca/notices/2013/03/els-bombardejos-a-barcelona-3275.php

Martín Jiménez, Ignacio. 2000. "La Guerra Civil en Menorca: entre la sublevación y las matanzas republicanas." In *Aportaciones a la historia de la guerra civil en Menorca*, ed. I. Martin Jiménez. Menorca: Nura.

Martín Rubio, Ángel David. 1987. *Paz, piedad, perdón... y verdad. La Represión en la guerra civil: una síntesis definitiva*. Madridejos: Fénix.

Martínez Cuadrado, Miguel. 1969. *Elecciones y partidos políticos de España: 1868–1931.* Madrid: Taurus.

Martínez Cuadrado, Miguel. 1980. *El sistema político español y el comportamiento electoral regional en el sur de Europa (1976–1980).* Madrid: Instituto de Cooperación Intercontinental.

Martínez de Baños, Fernando. 2004a. "Tras las líneas de frente." Pp. 367–410 in *Guerra Civil Aragón,* ed. F. Martínez de Baños. Zaragoza: Delsan.

Martínez de Baños, Fernando (Ed.). 2004b. *Guerra Civil Aragón.* Cuarte de Huerva: Delsan.

Martínez de Baños, Fernando (Ed.). 2006. *Guerra Civil IV.* Madrid. Cuarte de Huerva: Delsan.

Mateos Rodríguez, Miguel-Angel. 1991. "Fuentes y metodologia para el estudio electoral de la II República española." *Ayer* 3: 139–164.

Maymí Rich, Josep. 2000. "L'organització política i la dinàmica repressiva: la gestió dels comitès antifeixistes." Pp. 49–68 in *Guerra Civil i Franquisme seixanta anys després,* eds. N. Figueras and A. Reyes. Santa Coloma de Farners: Centre d'Estudis Selvatans.

Meléndez Badillo, Jorell A. 2009. "An interview with Noam Chomsky on the Spanish revolution." Libcom.org. Retrieved on 7 January 2016 from: https://libcom.org/

Miguélez, Faustino. 1984. "Sindicalismo y reconstrucción en Catalunya." *Papers* 21: 47–69.

Mintz, Jerome R. 1982. *The Anarchists of Casas Viejas.* Chicago: University of Chicago Press.

Mir Curcó, Conxita. 1999. "Violencia política, coacción legal y oposición interior." *Ayer* 33: 115–145.

Molas, Isidre (Ed). 2000. *Diccionari dels Partits Polítics de Catalunya: Segle XX.* Barcelona: Enciclopèdia Catalana.

Molas, Isidre. 1972. *Sistema de partidos politicos en Catalunya (1931–1936).* Barcelona Edicions 62.

Molas, Isidre. 1986. "Proleg." In *Atlas Electoral de Catalunya durant la Segona República,* ed. M. Vilanova. Barcelona: Edicions La Magrana.

Molinero, Carme. 2001. "Les actituds polítiques a Catalunya durant el primer Franquisme." *Butlletí de la Societat Catalana d'Estudis Històrics* 12: 97–106.

Montero Moreno, Antonio. 1961. *Historia de la persecución religiosa en España.* Madrid: Biblioteca de Autores Cristianos.

Moradiellos, Enrique. 1999. "The Allies and the Spanish Civil War." Pp. 96–126 in *Spain and the Great Powers in the Twentieth Century,* eds. S. Balfour and P. Preston. London: Routledge.

Moreno, Nacho. 2014. "'Por el bien de la Patria y de la Justicia.' Denuncias e informes de las autoridades aragonesas." Pp. 119–144 in *Pagar las Culpas: la Represión Económica en Aragón (1936–1945).* eds. J. Casanova and A. Cenarro. Barcelona: Crítica.

Moreno de Alborán, Fernando, and Salvador Moreno de Alborán. 1998. *La Guerra Silenciosa y Silenciada. Historia de la campaña naval durante la guerra de 1936–39.* Madrid: F. Moreno de Alborán y de Reyna.

Moreno Juliá, Xavier. 1999. "María y Miquel: Memorias de Guerra y Posguerra en España: 1936–1939." *Historia, Antropología y Fuentes Orales* 21: 67–81.

Nadal, Antonio. 1981. *Andalucía ante el advenimiento de la República: coyuntura política y movimientos huelguísticos en la Malaga de 1930.* PhD Dissertation, Departamento de Historia Contemporánea, Universidad de Malaga, Malaga.

Nadal, Antonio. 1984. *La guerra civil en Malaga.* Malaga: Argubal.

Oliva i Llorens, Jordi. 1994. "El cost humà de la Guerra Civil de 1936–1939." *Recerques: història, economia, cultura* 30: 87–102.

Oliver, Joan. 1983. *La II República en Baleares: elecciones y partidos políticos. Ensayo de sociologia electoral balear.* Palma de Mallorca: Institut d'Estudis Baleàrics.

Ors, Miguel. 1995. *La represión de guerra y posguerra en Alicante.* Alacant: Institut de Cultura "Juan Gil Albert."

Ortega, Carmen. 2005. "Participación y abstención electoral: la segunda república en perspectiva comparada." *Cuadernos Ciere* 2049: 1–15.

Orwell, George. 1938. *Homage to Catalonia.* London: Secker and Warburg.

Payne, Stanley. 1985. "Representative government in Spain: the historical background." Pp. 1–29 in *Spain at the polls, 1977, 1979, and 1982. A study of national elections,* eds. H. Penniman and E. Mujal-León. Durham: Duke University Press.

Payne, Stanley. 1990. "Political violence during the Spanish Second Republic." *Journal of Contemporary History* 25: 269–288.

Payne, Stanley. 2004. *The Spanish Civil War, the Soviet Union, and Communism.* New Haven and London: Yale University Press.

Payne, Stanley. 2010. *La Guerre d'Espagne. L'histoire face à la confusión mémorielle.* Paris: Les Éditions du Cerf.

Payne, Stanley. 2011. *Civil War in Europe, 1905–1949.* New York: Cambridge University Press.

Peirats, José. 2002. "Prólogo." In Kaminski, Hans Erich. *Los de Barcelona.* Trans. C. S. Barberá. Barcelona: Ediciones del Cotal.

Piñeiro, García. 2002. "Marginación Política y Exclusión Social en la Asturias de la posguerra (1937–1952)." In *L'exili republicà,* ed. F. Bonamusa. Barberà del Vallès: Ajuntament de Barberà del Vallès.

Pozo González, Josep Antoni. 2002. *El Poder Revolucionari a Catalunya durant els mesos de Juliol a Octubre de 1936. Crisi i Recomposició de l'Estat.* PhD Dissertation, Departament d'Història Moderna i Contemporània, Universitat Autònoma de Barcelona, Barcelona.

Preston, Paul. 1986. *Història de la Guerra Civil Espanyola.* Barcelona: Base.

Preston, Paul. 1994. *The Coming of the Spanish Civil War. Reform, reaction and revolution in the Second Republic.* London: Routledge.

Preston, Paul. 1999. "Italy and Spain in Civil War and World War, 1936–1943." Pp. 151–184 in *Spain and the Great Powers,* eds. S. Balfour and P. Preston. London: Routledge.

Preston, Paul. 2006. *Botxins i Repressors. Els crims de Franco i dels franquistes.* Barcelona: Base.

Preston, Paul. 2011. *El Holocausto Español. Odio y Exterminio en la Guerra Civil y Después.* Barcelona: Debate.

Preston, Paul. 2013. "Franco's Terror in an European Context: the Volksgemeinschaft That Got Away." *LSE Works.* Retrieved on January 26, 2016 from: www.lse.ac.uk/Events

Prieto, Lucía and Encarnación Barranquero. 2007. *Población y Guerra Civil en Malaga: Caída, Éxodo y Refugio*. Malaga: Diputación de la Provincia de Malaga.

Prieto, Lucía and Encarnación Barranquero. 2015. "Political Violence in the Republican Zone: Repression and Popular Justice in a City Behind the Lines: Malaga, July 1936–February 1937." In Anderson, Peter, and Miguel Ángel del Arco Blanco. 2015. *Mass Killings and Violence in Spain, 1936–1952*. London: Routledge.

Pujadas, Joan. 2000. "La recuperació de la memòria col.lectiva: reflexions metodològiques sobre guerra civil i franquisme." Pp. 33–48 in *Guerra Civil i Franquisme seixanta anys després*, eds. N. Figueras and A. Reyes. Santa Coloma de Farners: Centre d'Estudis Selvatans.

Pujol, Enric. 2003. *L'exili català del 1936–1939*. Vol. 19, Quaderns del Cercle. Girona: Cercle d'Estudis Històrics i Socials.

Radosh, Ronald, Mary Habeck, and Grigory Sevostianov. 2001. *Spain betrayed: the Soviet Union in the Spanish Civil War*. New Haven: Yale University Press.

Raguer, Hilari. 2001. *La pólvora y el incienso. La Iglesia y la Guerra Civil española (1936–1939)*. Barcelona: Península.

Recolons, Lluís. 1976. *La població de Catalunya. Distribució territorial i evolució demogràfica 1900–1970*. Barcelona: Laia.

Reig Tapia, Alberto. 1984. *Ideología e historia: sobre la represión franquista y la Guerra Civil*. Madrid: Akal.

Reverte, Jorge M. 2003. *La batalla del Ebro*. Madrid: Crítica.

Reverte, Jorge M. 2006. *La caída de Cataluña*. Barcelona: Crítica.

Riesco, Sergio. 2006. *La Reforma Agraria y los origenes de la Guerra Civil (1931–1940)*. Madrid: Biblioteca Nueva.

Rodrigo, Javier. 2008. *Hasta la raíz. Violencia durante la Guerra Civil y la dictadura Franquista*. Madrid: Alianza Editorial.

Roig, Montserrat. 1977. *Els catalans als camps nazis*. Barcelona: Edicions 62.

Roig, Montserrat. 2007 (first edition 1972). *Ramona, adéu*. Barcelona: Edicions 62.

Rubio, Javier. 1977. *La emigración de la guerra civil de 1936–1939: historia del éxodo que se produce con el fin de la II República*. Madrid: San Martín.

Ruiz, Cándido. 1993. *Política y Educación en la II República (Valencia 1931–1936)*. Valencia: Universidad de Valencia.

Ruiz Carnicer, Miguel A., and Angela Cenarro Lagunas. 1991. "La 'represión politica' y sus formas: fuentes y métodos de estudio." Pp. 245–290 in *Metodología de Investigación Científica sobre fuentes Aragonesas*. Zaragoza: Instituto de Ciencias de la Educación. Universidad de Zaragoza.

Ruiz, Julius. 2005. *Franco's Justice. Repression in Madrid after the Spanish Civil War*. Oxford: Oxford University Press.

Ruiz, Julius. 2007. "Defending the Republic: The García Atadell Brigade in Madrid, 1936." *Journal of Contemporary History* 42(1): 97–115.

Ruiz, Julius. 2009. "Seventy Years On: Historians and Repression during and after the Spanish Civil War." *Journal of Contemporary History* 44(3): 449–472.

Sagués San José, Joan. 2001. "La historia de la Guerra Civil española, un campo con puertas aún por abrir." Pp. 277–289 in *La Represión bajo el Franquismo*, ed. C. Mir Curcó. Madrid: Marcial Pons.

Sáiz Viadero, José Ramón. 1979. *Crónicas sobre la guerra civil en Santander*. Santander: Institución Cultural de Cantabria.

Salas Larrazábal, Ramón. 1977. *Pérdidas de la Guerra*. Barcelona: Planeta.

Sales, Joan. 2007 (first edition 1957). *Incerta Glòria*. Barcelona: Club Editor.

Salomón, Ma Pilar, and José Luis Ledesma (Eds.). 2006. *La guerra civil en Aragón. Terror "azul" y violencia "roja."* Zaragoza & Barcelona: Ciro Ediciones y Prensa Diaria Aragonesa.

Sànchez Agustí, Ferran. 1999. *Els maquis a Catalunya*. Lleida: Pagès Editors.

Sánchez Marroyo, Fernando. 1995. "Prólogo. Vida y muerte entre la arbitrariedad y el azar." Pp. 15–22 in *La represión en la provincia de Cáceres durante la guerra civil (1936–39)*, ed. J. Chaves Palacios. Cáceres: Universidad de Extremadura.

Sánchez Recio, Glicerio. 1991. *Justicia y Guerra en España. Los Tribunales Populares (1936–1939)*. Alicante: Diputación de Alicante.

Sanz Hoya, Julián. 2003. *El Primer Franquismo en Cantabria. Falange, Instituciones y Personal Político (1937–1951)*. PhD Dissertation, Departamento de Historia Moderna y Contemporánea, Universidad de Cantabria, Santander.

Segura, Antoni. 1999. "Pròleg." In *La Guerra Civil a les comarques Tarragonines*, eds. J. Piqué Padró and J. Sánchez Cervelló. Tarragona: Cercle d'Estudis Històrics i Socials Guillem Oliver del Camp de Tarragona.

Seidman, Michael. 2002. *Republic of Egos. A Social History of the Spanish Civil War*. Madison: University of Wisconsin Press.

Sender, Ramón. 1992 (first edition 1950). *Réquiem por un campesino español*. Barcelona: Destinolibro.

Sender Barayón, Ramón. 1986. *A Death in Zamora*. Albuquerque: University of New Mexico Press.

Serrallonga, Joan. 2004. *Refugiats i Desplaçats dins la Catalunya en guerra 1936–1939*. Barcelona: Ed. Base.

Silva, Emilio, and Santiago Macías. 2003. *Las fosas de Franco. Los republicanos que el dictador dejó en las cunetas*. Madrid: Temas de Hoy.

Sociedad Benéfica de Historiadores Aficionados y Creadores (S.B.H.A.C.). 2009. "Balance Aproximativo de la Represión durante la Guerra Civil." [Retrieved on 31 January 2009 from: www.sbhac.net/Republica/Victimas/Repre.htm.

Solano, Valentín. 2006. *Guerra Civil Aragón III: Teruel*. Cuarte de Huerva: Delsan.

Solano Sanmiguel, Valentín. 2004. "La Guerra Civil en Teruel." Pp. 297–330 in *Guerra Civil Aragón*, by F. Martínez de Baños. Zaragoza: Delsan.

Solé i Sabaté, Josep M. 2000. *La repressió franquista a Catalunya. 1938–1953*. Barcelona: Edicions 62.

Solé i Sabaté, Josep Maria, and Oriol Dueñas. 2007. *El Franquisme contra Esquerra*. Barcelona: Fundació Josep Irla.

Solé i Sabaté, Josep M., and Joan Villarroya. 1986. *Catalunya sota les bombes*. Barcelona: Publicacions de l'Abadia de Montserrat.

Solé i Sabaté, Josep M., and Joan Villarroya. 1987. *L'ocupació militar de Catalunya. Març 1938- Febrer 1939*. Barcelona: L'Avenç.

Solé i Sabaté, Josep M., and Joan Villarroya. 1989. *La Repressió a la Reraguarda de Catalunya (1936–1939)*. Vol. I. Barcelona: Publicacions de l'Abadia de Montserrat.

Solé i Sabaté, Josep M., and Joan Villarroya. 1996. "La Represión en la Zona Republicana." Pp. 113–127 in *La Guerra Civil Española*, ed. M. T. de Lara, V. 6. Madrid: Folio.

Solé i Sabaté, Josep M., and Joan Villarroya. 2003. *España en llamas*. Madrid: Temas de Hoy.

Solé i Sabaté, Josep M., and Joan Villarroya. 2005. *Breu Historia de la Guerra Civil a Catalunya*. Barcelona: Edicions 62.

Solla Gutiérrez, Miguel Ángel. 2005. *La sublevación frustrada: los inicios de la Guerra Civil en Cantabria*. Santander: Universidad de Cantabria.

Su, Yang. 2011. *Collective Killings in Rural China during the Cultural Revolution*. NY: Cambridge University Press.

Termes, Josep. 2003. "Pròleg." In *La repressió franquista a Catalunya. 1938–1953*, ed. J. M. Solé i Sabaté. Barcelona: Edicions 62.

Termes, Josep. 2005. "El pòsit de la Guerra Civil: al fons del sac, les engrunes. La desintegració de l'estat de dret en un conflicte fraticida." In *Breu Historia de la Guerra Civil a Catalunya*, eds. J. M. Solé i Sabaté and J. Villarroya i Font. Barcelona: Edicions 62.

Termes, Josep. 2005. *Misèria contra pobresa. Els fets de la Fatarella del gener de 1937: un exemple de resistència pagesa contra la col.lectivització agrària durant la Guerra Civil*. Barcelona: Afers.

Thomas, Hugh. 1986. *La Guerra Civil Española*. Madrid: Grijalbo.

Thompson, John Patrick. 2005. "The Civil War in Galiza, the Uncovering of the Common Graves, and Civil War Novels as Counter-Discourses of Imposed Oblivion." *Iberoamericana* 18: 75–82.

Torres, Rafael. 2002. *Desaparecidos de la guerra de España (1936–?)*. Madrid: La Esfera de los Libros.

Tusell, Javier. 1971. *Las elecciones del Frente Popular en España*. Vol. 1. Edicusa: Madrid.

Tusell, Javier. 1991. "El sufragio universal en España (1891–1936): un balance historiográfico." *Ayer* 3: 13–62.

Tusell, Javier. 1999. *Historia de España en el siglo XX (II) La crisis de los años treinta. República y Guerra Civil*. Madrid: Editorial Taurus.

Vallverdú i Martí, Robert. 2008. *El carlisme català durant la Segona República Espanyola (1931–1936). Anàlisi d'una política estructural*. Barcelona: Publicacions de l'Abadia de Montserrat.

Vidal, César. 1997. *La destrucción de Guernica: un balance sesenta años después*. Madrid: Espasa.

Vidal Tur, Gonzalo. 1991. *Persecución Religiosa. Provincia de Alicante (1936–1939)*. Alicante: Diputación de Alicante.

Vila Izquierdo, Justo. 1984. *Extremadura: la guerra civil*. Badajoz: Universitas.

Vilanova, Mercedes. 1979. "La stabilité de l'electorat catalan dans la circonscription de Gerone entre 1931–1936." *Tijdschrift Voor Geschiedenis* 473–491.

Vilanova, Mercedes. 1989. *Atlas electoral de Catalunya durant la Segona República. Orientació del vot, participació i abstenció*. Vol. 5, Estudis Electorals. Barcelona: Edicions de la Magrana.

Vilanova, Mercedes. 2005. *Atles Electoral de la Segona República a Catalunya*. Barcelona: Enciclopèdia Catalana.

Vilar, Margarita, and Elvira Lindoso. 2009. "El negocio de la guerra civil en Galicia, 1936–1939." *Revista de Historia Industrial* 39: 153–192.

Vilar, Pierre. 1986. *La Guerra Civil Española*. Barcelona: Crítica.

## 2 CÔTE D'IVOIRE

### Reports and Data Sources

Carter Center. 2009. *Côte d'Ivoire: Identification de la Population et Recensement Electoral: Appréciation Générale et Perspectives.* Atlanta: The Carter Center.

Human Rights Watch (HRW). 2011. *"They Killed Them Like it Was Nothing" The Need for Justice for Côte d'Ivoire Post-Election Crimes.* New York: Human Rights Watch.

Human Rights Watch (HRW). 2003. *Trapped between Two Wars: Violence against Civilians in Western Côte d'Ivoire.* New York: Human Rights Watch.

Human Rights Watch (HRW). 2001. *Le Nouveau Racisme: La Manipulation Politique de l'Ethnicité en Côte d'Ivoire.* New York: Human Rights Watch.

Global Witness. 2007. *Hot Chocolate: How Cocoa Fueled the Conflict in the Ivory Coast.* London: Global Witness.

International Crisis Group. 2008. *Côte d'Ivoire: Garantir un Processus Électoral Crédible, Africa Report.* Brussels: International Crisis Group.

International Crisis Group. 2009. *Côte d'Ivoire: Les Impératifs de Sortie de Crise, Africa Report.* Brussels: International Crisis Group.

International Crisis Group. 2014. *Côte d'Ivoire's Great West: Key to Reconciliation.* Brussels: International Crisis Group.

International Idea (IDEA). Voter Turnout Database. Retrieved in 2016 from: www.idea.int/data-tools/data/voter-turnout

Peace Reporter. 2007. "Per presidente Gbagbo la guerra e finite." April 17, 2007. Available at: www.peacereporter.net

UN Office for the Coordination of Human Affairs (OCHA). 2008. *La Communauté Humanitaire Exprime sa Préoccupation Suite à d'Inhabituels Mouvements de Retour et Repli des Populations Déplacées en Zone Ouest.* Abidjan: OCHA.

United Nations Operation in Côte d'Ivoire (ONUCI). 2007. *L'Organisation et le Fonctionnement du Système Judiciaire en Côte D'Ivoire.* Abidjan: ONUCI.

### General Bibliography on Côte d'Ivoire

Akindès, Francis. 2007. "Côte d'Ivoire: de la Stabilité Politique à la Crise. Vers une Politique de Réhabilitation Basée sur la Responsabilisation des Communautés à la Base." Abidjan: World Bank.

Allouche, Jeremy, and Patrick Anderson Zadi Zadi. 2013. "The Dynamics of Restraint in Cote d'Ivoire." *IDS Bulletin* 44(1): 72–86.

Banégas, Richard. 2006. "Côte d'Ivoire: Patriotism, Ethnonationalism and Other African Modes of Self-Writing." *African Affairs* 105(421): 535–552.

Banégas, Richard. 2011. "Post-Election Crisis in Côte d'Ivoire: The gbonhi War." *African Affairs* 110(440): 457–68.

Barbeito, Cecile, Albert Caramés, and Patricia García. 2008. "Côte d'Ivoire: Retos y Perspectivas un Año Después de Ouagadougou." In *Quaderns de Construcció de Pau.* Barcelona: School for a Culture of Peace.

Basset, Thomas. 2003. "Nord Musulman et Sud Chrétien: les moules mediatiques de la crise ivorienne." *Afrique Contemporaine* 206: 13–27.

Basset, Thomas. 2011. "Winning Coalition, Sore Loser: Côte d'Ivoire's 2010 Presidential Elections." *African Affairs* 110(440): 469–79.

Caramés, Albert. 2011. Elections in 2009? Progress and Obstacles in the Construction of Peace in the Ivory Coast. International Catalan Institute for Peace, Working Paper No. 2009/3.

Carter Center. 2011. *International Election Observation Mission to Côte d'Ivoire. Final Report. 2010 Presidential Elections and 2011 Legislative Elections.* Atlanta: The Carter Center.

Chelpi-den Hamer, Magali. 2012. "Militarized Youth in Western Côte d'Ivoire: Who are They? Why Did They Fight?" Pp. 21–45 in *Understanding Collective Political Violence*, ed. Yvan Guichaoua. New York: Palgrave Macmillan.

Cohen, Michael A., 1973. "The Myth of the Expanding Centre: Politics in the Ivory Coast." *The Journal of Modern African Studies* 11: 227–246.

Côté, Isabelle, and Matthew I. Mitchell. 2016. "Elections and 'Sons of the Soil' Conflict Dynamics in Africa and Asia." *Democratization* 23(4): 657–677.

Dabalen, Andrew L., Ephraim Kebede, and Paul Saumik. 2012. "Causes of Civil War: Micro Level Evidence from Côte d'Ivoire." In HiCN Working papers. Brighton: Institute of Development Studies, University of Sussex.

Diarra, Samba. 1997. *Les Faux Complots d'Houphouët-Boigny: Fracture dans le Destin d'une Nation.* Paris: Karthala.

Human Rights Watch (HRW). 2003. *Trapped between Two Wars: Violence against civilians in Western Côte d'Ivoire.* New York: Human Rights Watch.

International Crisis Group. 2008. "The Ivory Coast: Garantir un Processus Electoral Credible." Rapport Afrique n 139, available at: http://refworld.org

International Crisis Group. 2009. "The Ivory Coast: Les imperatifs de sortie de crise." Briefing Afrique 62, available at: http://www.refworld.org

International Crisis Group. 2011. "A Critical Period for Ensuring Stability in Côte d'Ivoire." Africa Report Num. 176. August 1, 2011.

Koné, Gnangadjomon. 2011. "Logiques des Pillages dans la Crise Postelectorale en Côte d'Ivoire." *Politique Africaine* 122: 145–159.

Koné, Gnangadjomon. 2012. "The Politics of Counter-Insurgency: How did the young patriots emerge in Côte d'Ivoire?" Pp. 222–245 in *Understanding Collective Political Violence*, ed. Yvan Guichaoua. New York: Palgrave Macmillan.

Klaus, Kathleen and Matthew Mitchell. 2015. "Land Grievances and the Mobilization of Electoral Violence: Evidence from Côte d'Ivoire and Kenya." *Journal of Peace Research* 52(5): 622–635.

Koter, Dominika. 2015. "Incumbent Alassane Ouattara's electoral sweep might be a good outcome for Côte d'Ivoire." *Africa is a Country*. Retrieved on November 5, 2015 from: www.africasacountry.com

Kouman H. Y. 1999. *Les conflicts fonciers. L'ivoirité, un concept incompris.* Abidjan: Fraternite Matin.

Langer, Arnim. 2006. "Horizontal Inequalities and Violent Group Mobilization in Côte d'Ivoire." *Oxford Development Studies* 33(1): 25–45.

Mitchell, Matthew. 2014. "Land Tenure Reform and Politics in Post-Conflict Côte d'Ivoire: A Precarious Peace in the Western Cocoa Regions." *Canadian Journal of African Studies* 48(2): 203–221.

Mitchell, Matthew. 2015. "Power-Sharing and Peace in Côte d'Ivoire: Past Examples and Future Prospects." *Conflict, Security & Development* 12(2): 171–191.

Lewis, Martin. 2011. "Ethnic Dimensions of the Conflict in Ivory Coast." Geocurrents. Retrieved on 28 February 2011 from www.geocurrents.info/geopolitics/ethnicdimensions-of-the-conflict-in-ivory-coast

Marshall-Fratani, Ruth. 2006. "The War of 'Who is Who': Autochthony, Nationalism, and Citizenship in the Ivoirian Crisis." *African Studies Review* 44(2): 9–43.

McGovern, Mike. 2010. "Proleptic Justice. The Threat of Investigation as a Deterrent to human rights abuses in Côte d'Ivoire." Pp. 67–86 in *Mirrors of Justice. Law and Power in the Post-Cold War Era*, eds. Kamari Maxine Clarke and Mark Goodale. New York: Cambridge University Press.

McGovern, Mike. 2011. *Making War in Côte d'Ivoire*. Chicago: The University of Chicago Press.

Muggah R. 2006. *Reflections on Disarmament, Demobilization and Reintegration in Sudan*. London: Humanitarian Practice Network.

Minoiu, Camelia and Olga N. Shemyakina. 2012. "Armed Conflict, Household Victimization, and Child Health in Côte d'Ivoire." HINC Working Paper 115.

United Nations Operation in Côte d'Ivoire (ONUCI). 2007. *Rapport sur l'organisation du système judiciaire en Côte d'Ivoire*. Abidjan: ONUCI.

Piccolino, Giulia. 2014. "Ultranationalism, Democracy and the Law: Insights from Côte d'Ivoire." *Journal of Modern African Studies* 52(1): 45–68.

Nordas, Ragnhild. 2008. "Côte d'Ivoire Conflict Information and Battle Events." ACLED Manuscript, Center for the Study of Civil War, PRIO, Oslo.

Polgreen, Lydia. "Ivory Coast's Ethnic Lines Harden, Hobbling Economy." *The New York Times*, October 31, 2005.

Straus, Scott. 2011. "'It's Sheer Horror Here': Patterns of Violence during the First Four Months of Côte d'Ivoire's Post-Electoral Crisis." *African Affairs* 110(440): 481–489.

## 3 GENERAL BIBLIOGRAPHY

Achen, Chris. 2005. "Let's Put Garbage Can Regressions and Garbage Can Probits Where They Belong." *Conflict Management and Peace Science* 22(4): 327–339.

Aldrich, John. 1995. *Why Parties?: The Origin and Transformation of Political Parties in America*. Chicago: University of Chicago Press.

Alesina, Alberto, and Ekaterina Zhuravskaya. 2011. "Segregation and the Quality of Government in a Cross Section of Countries." *American Economic Review* 101(5): 1872–1911.

Allen, Susan. 2007. "Time Bombs. Estimating the Duration of Coercive Bombing Campaigns." *Journal of Conflict Resolution* 51(1): 112–133.

Anonymous. 1985. *Handbook for Volunteers of the Irish Republican Army*. Boulder, CO: Paladin Press.

Anselin, Luc. 2003. *Geoda 9.5 User Guide Center for Spatially Integrated Social Science* Retrieved on 22 December 2007.

Anselin, Luc, Raymond Florax, and Sergio Rey. 2004. *Advances in Spatial Econometrics. Methodology, Tools and Applications*. Berlin: Springer-Verlag.

Anselin, Luc, Ibnu Syabri, and Youngihn Kho. 2006. "GeoDa: An Introduction to Spatial Data Analysis." *Geographical Analysis* 38(1): 5–22.

Arendt, Hannah. 1972. *Du mensonge au violence*. Trans. G. Durand. Paris: Calmann-Lévy.

Arjona, Ana. 2016. *Rebelocracy: Social Order in the Colombian Civil War*. NY: Cambridge University Press.

Arjona, Ana, and Stathis Kalyvas. 2008. "Rebelling against Rebellion: Comparing Insurgent and Counter-insurgent Recruitment." Unpublished manuscript, Yale University.

Arreguín-Toft, Ivan. 2001. "How the Weak Win War: A Theory of Asymmetric Conflict." *International Security* 26(1): 93–128.

Augusteijn, Joost. 1996. *From Public Defiance to Guerrilla Warfare: The Experience of Ordinary Volunteers in the Irish War of Independence*. Dublin: Irish Academic Press.

Auyero, Javier. 2007. *Routine Politics and Violence in Argentina. The Gray Zone of State Power*. NY: Cambdridge University Press.

Azam, Jean-Paul. 2001. "The Redistributive State and Conflicts in Africa." *Journal of Peace Research* 38(4): 429–444.

Azam, Jean-Paul. 2006. "On Thugs and Heroes." *Economics of Governance* 7(1): 53–73.

Azam, Jean-Paul, Paul Collier, and A. Cravinho. 1994. "Crop Sales, Shortages and Peasant Portfolio Behaviour: An Analysis of Angola." *Journal of Development Studies* 30(2): 361–379.

Azam, Jean-Paul, and Anke Hoeffler. 2002. "Violence against Civilians in Civil Wars: Looting or Terror?" *Journal of Peace Research* 39(4): 461–485.

Balcells, Laia. 2010. "Rivalry and Revenge. Violence against Civilians in Conventional Civil Wars." *International Studies Quarterly* 54(2): 291–313.

Balcells, Laia. 2011. "Continuation of Politics by Two Means: Direct and Indirect Violence in Civil War." *Journal of Conflict Resolution* 55(3): 327–339.

Balcells, Laia. 2013. "Mass Schooling and Catalan Nationalism." *Nationalism and Ethnic Politics* 19(4): 467–486.

Balcells, Laia, and Patricia Justino. 2014. "Bridging Micro and Macro Approaches on Civil Wars and Political Violence: Issues, Challenges, and the Way Forward." *Journal of Conflict Resolution* 58(8): 1343–1359.

Balcells, Laia, and Stathis Kalyvas. 2014. "Does Warfare Matter? Severity, Duration, and Outcomes of Civil Wars." *Journal of Conflict Resolution* 58(8): 1390–1418.

Balcells, Laia, and Stathis Kalyvas. 2016. "Revolutionary rebels and the Marxist paradox." Unpublished Manuscript, Duke University and Yale University.

Balcells, Laia, and Abbey Steele. 2016. "Warfare and Displacement in Spain and Colombia." *Political Geography* 51: 15–29.

Balcells, Laia, Lesley-Ann Daniels, and Abel Escribà-Folch. 2016. "The Determinants of Low-intensity Intergroup Violence. The Case of Northern Ireland." *Journal of Peace Research* 53: 33–48.

Ball, Patrick, Wendy Betts, Fritz Scheuren, and Jana Dudukovic. 2002. "Killings and Refugee Flow in Kosovo, March–June 1999: Analysis and Conclusions." In *Report to the International Criminal Tribunal for the Former Yugoslavia*. Washington: American Association for the Advancement of Science.

Barnard, Anne. 2013. "Ruins in a Center of Syria's Uprising." *New York Times*, July 16, 2013.

Bardhan, Pranab, and Tsung-Tao Yang. 2004. Political Competition in Economic Perspective. BREAD Working Paper 78.

Bashir, Omar S. 2012. "Who Watches the Drones? The Case For Independent Oversight." In *Foreign Affairs: Council on Foreign Relations*. Retrieved on September 24, 2012 from: www.foreignaffairs.com/articles/138141/omar-s-bashir/who-watches-the-drones.

Bates, Robert. 1999. "Ethnicity, Capital Formation, and Conflict." CID Working Paper No. 27.

Bearman, Peter S. 1991. "Desertion as Localism. Army Unit Solidarity and Group Norms in the U.S. Civil War." *Social Forces* 70(2): 321–342.

Beissinger, Mark R. 2002. *Nationalist Mobilization and the Collapse of the Soviet State.* New York: Cambridge University Press.

Berman, Eli, Jacob N. Shapiro, and Joseph H. Felter. 2011. "Can Hearts and Minds Be Bought? The Economics of Counterinsurgency in Iraq." *Journal of Political Economy* 119(4): 766–819.

Bernard, Cheryl. 1994. "Rape as Terror: The Case of Bosnia." *Terrorism and Political Violence* 6(1): 29–43.

Blackwell, Matthew, Stefano Iacus, Gary King, and Giuseppe Porro. 2009. "cem: Coarsened Exact Matching in Stata." *The Stata Journal* 9(4): 524–546.

Bowles, Samuel. 2004. *Microeconomics. Behavior, Institutions, and Evolution.* New Jersey: Princeton University Press.

Brubaker, Rogers and David D. Laitin. 1998. "Ethnic and nationalist violence." *Annual Review of Sociology* 24: 423–452.

Bulutgil, Zeynep. 2015. "Social cleavages, wartime experience, and ethnic cleansing in Europe." *Journal of Peace Research* 52(5): 577–590.

Bundorvoet, Tom. 2009. "Livestock, land and Political Power: the 1993 Killings in Burundi." *Journal of Peace Research* 46(3): 357–376.

Cederman, Lars-Erik, Nils B. Weidmann, and Kristian S. Gleditsch. 2011. "Horizontal Inequalities and Ethnonationalist Civil War: A Global Comparison." *American Political Science Review* 105(3): 478–495.

Chacón, Mario, James A. Robinson, and Ragnar Torvik. 2011. "When Is Democracy an Equilibrium? Theory and Evidence from Colombia's 'La Violencia.'" *Journal of Conflict Resolution* 55(3): 366–396.

Chandra, Kanchan. 2004. *Why Ethnic Parties Succeed: Patronage and Ethnic Headcounts in India.* New York: Cambridge University Press.

Chenoweth, Erica. 2015. "Political mobilization and institutions." In *Routledge Handbook of Comparative Political Institutions*, eds. Jennifer Gandhi and Ruben Ruiz. London: Routledge.

Chenoweth, Erica, and Maria J. Stephan. 2011. *Why Civil Resistance Works: The Strategic Logic of Nonviolent Conflict.* New York: Columbia University Press.

Christia, Fotini. 2008. "Following the Money. Muslim versus muslim in Bosnia's Civil War." *Comparative Politics* 40(4): 461–480.

Christia, Fotini. 2012. *Alliance Formation in Civil Wars.* NY: Cambridge University Press.

Clarke, Kevin A. 2005. "Phantom Menace: Omitted Variable Bias in Econometric Research." *Conflict Management and Peace Science* 22(4): 341–352.

Clausewitz, Carl Von. 1968 (first edition 1832). *On War*. Edited by Colonel F. N. Maude and translated by Colonel J. J. Graham. London: Routledge and Kegan Paul.

Cochran, Kathryn, and Alexander Downes. 2012. "Targeting Civilians to Win? Assessing the Military Effectiveness of Civilian Victimization in Interstate War." In *Rethinking Violence: States and Non-State Actors in Conflict*, eds. A. Lawrence and E. Chenoweth. Cambridge: MIT Press.

Cohen, Dara. 2013. "Explaining Rape during Civil War: Cross-National Evidence (1980–2009)." *American Political Science Review* 107(3): 461–477.

Condra, Luke N., and Jacob N. Shapiro. 2012. "Who Takes the Blame? The Strategic Effects of Collateral Damage." *American Journal of Political Science* 56(1): 167–87.

Costa, Dora L., and Matthew E. Kahn. 2008. *Heroes and Cowards. The Social Face of War*. Princeton and Oxford: Princeton University Press.

Costalli, Stefano, and Niccolò Moro. 2012. "Ethnicity and strategy in the Bosnian civil war: Explanations for the severity of violence in Bosnian municipalities." *Journal of Peace Research* 49(6): 801–815.

Darden, Keith. 2006. "Nationalism, Networks, and Armed Resistance to Occupation: Lessons from a Natural Experiment." Paper presented at the Seminar on Networks, Institutions, and Economic Transformation in Post-Socialism Harriman Institute, Columbia University, November 29, 2006.

De la Calle, Luis. 2007. "Fighting for Local Control: Street Violence in the Basque Country." *International Studies Quarterly* 51(2): 431–455.

Denny, Elaine and Barbara Walter. 2014. "Ethnicity and Civil War." *Journal of Peace Research* 51(2): 199–212.

Dinas, Elias. 2012. "Left and Right in the Basque Country and Catalonia: The Meaning of Ideology in a Nationalist Context." *South European Society and Politics* 17(3): 467–485.

Downes, Alexander. 2006. "Desperate Times, Desperate Measures: The Causes of Civilian Victimization in War." *International Security* 30(4): 152–195.

Downes, Alexander. 2007. "Restraint or Propellant? Democracy and Civilian Fatalities in Interstate Wars." *Journal of Conflict Resolution* 51(6): 872–904.

Downes, Alexander. 2008. *Targeting Civilians in War*. Ithaca: Cornell University Press.

Dube, Oeindrila, and Juan Vargas. 2013. "Commodity Price Shocks and Civil Conflict: Evidence from Colombia." *Review of Economic Studies* 80(4): 1384–1421.

Duyvesteyn, Isabelle. 2005. "Conventional War and Collapsed States." Pp. 65–87 in *Rethinking the Nature of War*, ed. D. I. a. J. Angstrom. London & New York: Franc Cass.

Eck, Kristine, and Lisa Hultman. 2007. "One-Sided Violence against Civilians in War: insights from New Fatality Data." *Journal of Peace Research* 44(2): 233–246.

Edwards, John N. 1877. *Noted Guerrillas or the Warfare of the Border*. St. Louis: Bryan, Brand & Company.

Elster, Jon. 1986. *Rational Choice*. Oxford: Blackwell Publisher.

Elster, Jon. 1990. "Norms of Revenge." *Ethics* 100(4): 862–885.

Elster, Jon. 2007. *Explaining Social Behavior: More Nuts and Bolts for the Social sciences*. New York: Cambridge University Press.

Esteban, Joan, and Debraj Ray. 1994. "On the Measurement of Polarization." *Econometrica* 62: 819–51.

Eckstein, Harry. 1964. "Introduction. Toward the Theoretical Study of Internal War." In *Internal War. Problems and Approaches*, ed. H. Eckstein. New York: The Free Press.

Fearon, James. 1994. "Domestic Audiences and the Escalation of International Disputes." *American Political Science Review* 88(3): 577–592.

Fearon, James D., and David D. Laitin. 2003. "Ethnicity, Insurgency and Civil War." *American Political Science Review* 97(1): 75–90.

Fellman, Michael. 1989. *Inside War. The guerrilla conflict in Missouri during the American Civil War*. New York & Oxford: Oxford University Press.

Finkel, Evgeny. 2015. "The Phoenix Effect of State Repression: Jewish Resistance during the Holocaust." *American Political Science Review* 109(2): 339–353.

Fortna, Virginia Page. 2016. "Is Terrorism Really a Weapon of the Weak?" Unpublished Manuscript, Columbia University.

Frank, Robert H. 1988. *Passions within Reason. The Strategic Role of the Emotions*. New York & London: W. W. Norton & Company.

Franzese, Robert, and Cindy D. Kam. 2007. *Modeling and Interpreting Interactive Hypotheses in Regression Analysis*. Ann Arbor: University of Michigan Press.

Fraser, Ronald. 2008. *Napoleon's Cursed War: Popular Resistance in the Spanish Peninsular War*. New York and London: Verso.

Frésard, Jean-Jacques. 2004. *The roots of behavior in war. A survey of the literature*. Geneva: International Committee of the Red Cross.

Fridja, Nico H. 1994. "The Lex Talionis: On Vengeance." Pp. 263–289 in *Emotions: Essays on Emotion Theory*, eds. S. H. M. Van Goozen, N. E. Van de Poll, and J. Sergeant. Hillsdale: Lawrence Erlbaum Associates.

Friedrich, Jorg. 2006. *Fire: The Bombing of Germany, 1940–1945*. New York: Columbia University Press.

Fujii, Lee Ann. 2009. *Killing Neighbors. Webs of violence in Rwanda*. Ithaca: Cornell University Press.

Gagnon, Philip. 2004. *The Myth of Ethnic War: Serbia and Croatia in the 1990s*. Ithaca: Cornell University Press.

Gates, Scott. 2002. "Recruitment and Allegiance. The Microfoundations of Rebellion." *Journal of Conflict Resolution* 46(1): 111–130.

Gleeson, D. T. 2008. "Why Confederates Fought: family and Nation in Civil War Virginia." *Journal of American History* 95(2): 547.

Gleditsch, Nils Petter, Peter Wallensteen, Mikael Eriksson, Margareta Sollenberg, and Håvard Strand. 2002. "Armed Conflict 1946–2001: A New Dataset." *Journal of Peace Research* 39(5): 615–637.

Goodwin, Jeff. 2006. "A Theory of Categorical Terrorism." *Social Forces* 84(4): 2027–2046.

Gould, Roger V. 1995. *Insurgent Identities. Class, Community, and Protest in Paris from 1848 to the Commune*. Chicago & London: University of Chicago Press.

Gould, Roger V. 1999. "Collective Violence and Group Solidarity: Evidence from a Feuding Society." *American Sociological Review* 64(3): 356–380.

Gould, Roger V. 2000. "Revenge and as Sanction and Solidarity Display: An Analysis of Vendettas in Nineteenth-Century Corsica." *American Sociological Review* 65(5): 685–705.

Gould, Roger V. 2003. *Collision of Wills. How Ambiguity about Social Rank Breeds Conflict*. Chicago & London: University of Chicago Press.

Green, Donald, and Ian Shapiro. 1996. *Pathologies of Rational Choice Theory. A Critique of Applications in Political Science*. New Haven: Yale University Press.

Gross, Jan T. 2001. *Neighbors. The Destruction of the Jewish Community in Jedwabne, Poland*. Princeton: Princeton University Press.

Guevara, Ernesto. 1967. *Episodes of the Revolutionary War*. Trans. E. Bernat. Havana: Book Institute.

Gurr, Ted Robert. 1970. *Why Men Rebel*. Princeton: Princeton University Press.

Gurr, Ted Robert. 2000. *Peoples versus States: Minorities at Risk in the New Century*. Washington: USIP.

Hacker, J. David. 2011. "A Census-Based Count of the Civil War Dead." *Civil War History* 57(4): 307–348.

Hart, Peter. 1998. *The I.R.A. & Its Enemies*. New York: Oxford University Press.

Hart, Peter. 2003. *The I.R.A. at War 1916–1923*. New York: Oxford University Press.

Hechter, Michael. 2001. *Containing Nationalism*. Oxford: Oxford University Press.

Hegghammer, Tomas. 2010. "The Rise of Muslim Foreign Fighters. Islam and the Globalization of Jihad." *International Security* 35(3): 53–94.

Hegre, Håvard, Ostby, Gudrun, and Clionadh Raleigh. 2007. "Economic Deprivation and Civil War Events: A Disaggregated Study of Liberia." Paper presented at Annual meeting of the American Political Science Association, Chicago, IL.

Hegre, Håvard, and Clionadh Raleigh. 2005. "Introducing ACLED: An Armed Conflict Location and Event Dataset." Paper presented at the Conference on Disaggregating the Study of Civil War and Transnational Violence, University of California Institute of Global Conflict and Cooperation, San Diego, CA, 7–8 March.

Herreros, Francisco, and Henar Criado. 2009. "Pre-Emptive or Arbitrary. Two Forms of Lethal Violence in a Civil War." *Journal of Conflict Resolution* 53(3): 419–445.

Hinton, Alexander Laban. 1998. "A Head for an Eye: Revenge in the Cambodian Genocide." *American Ethnologist* 25(3): 352–377.

Hoffman, Stanley. 1968. "Collaboration in France during WWII." *Journal of Modern History* 40(3): 375–395.

Hoover-Green, Amelia. 2006. "Beyond Body Count: Disaggregating 'Atrocity' During Armed Conflict." Unpublished manuscript, Yale University.

Horowitz, Donald L. 1985. *Ethnic Groups in Conflict*. Berkeley and Los Angeles: University of California Press.

Horowitz, Michael, and Dan Reiter. 2001. "When Does Aerial Bombing work?: Quantitative Empirical Tests, 1917–1999." *Journal of Conflict Resolution* 45(2): 147–173.

Hultman, Lisa. 2007. "Battle Losses and Rebel Violence: Raising the Costs of Fighting." *Terrorism and Political Violence* 19(2): 205–222.

Humphreys, Macartan, and Jeremy Weinstein. 2006. "Handling and Manhandling Civilians in Civil War." *American Political Science Review* 100(3): 429–447.

Humphreys, Macartan, and Jeremy Weinstein. 2008. "Who fights? The Determinants of Participation in Civil War." *American Journal of Political Science* 52(2): 436–455.

Hussein, Tam. 2014. "Jihad, then and now." *The Majalla*, February 8, 2014. Available from: www.majalla.com/eng/2014/02/article55248465

Jacoby, Susan. 1976. *Wild Justice: The Evolution of Revenge*. New York: Harper and Row.

Jentzsch, Corinna, Stathis Kalyvas, and Livia Schubiger. 2015. "Militias in Civil Wars." *Journal of Conflict Resolution* 59(5): 755–769.

Kaldor, Mary. 1999. *New and Old Wars: Organized Violence in a Global Era.* Cambridge: Polity Press.

Kalyvas, Stathis N. 2001. "'New' and 'Old' Civil Wars. A Valid Distinction?" *World Politics* 54(1): 99–118.

Kalyvas, Stathis N. 2005. "Warfare in Civil Wars." Pp. 88–108 in *Rethinking the Nature of War*, ed. J. Angstrom. Abingdon: Frank Cass.

Kalyvas, Stathis N. 2006. *The Logic of Violence in Civil War.* New York & London: Cambridge University Press.

Kalyvas, Stathis N. 2007. "Civil Wars." Pp. 416–434 in *The Oxford Handbook of Comparative Politics*, ed. C. Boix and S. Stokes. Oxford: Oxford University Press.

Kalyvas, Stathis N. 2008. "Ethnic Defection in Civil War." *Comparative Political Studies* 41(8): 1043–1068.

Kalyvas, Stathis N. 2009. "Conflict." Pp. 592–615 in *Oxford Handbook of Analytical Sociology*, ed. P. Hedstrom. Oxford: Oxford University Press.

Kalyvas, Stathis. 2012. "Micro-Level Studies of Violence in Civil War: Refining and Extending the Control-Collaboration Model." *Terrorism and Political Violence* 24(4): 658–668.

Kalyvas, Stathis, and Laia Balcells. 2010. "International System and Technologies of Rebellion: How the End of the Cold War Shaped Internal Conflict." *American Political Science Review* 104(3): 415–429.

Kalyvas, Stathis N., and Matthew A. Kocher. 2007a. "Ethnic Cleavages and Irregular War: Iraq and Vietnam." *Politics and Society* 35(2): 183–223.

Kalyvas, Stathis N., and Matthew A. Kocher. 2007b. "How 'Free' Is Free Riding in Civil Wars? Violence, Insurgency, and the Collective Action Problem." *World Politics* 59(2): 177–216.

Kalyvas, Stathis N., and Nicholas Sambanis. 2005. "Bosnia's Civil War: Origins and Violence Dynamics." Pp. 191–229 in *Understanding Civil War: Evidence and Analysis*, eds. P. Collier and N. Sambanis. Washington: The World Bank.

Kaplan, Oliver. 2013. "Nudging Armed Groups: How Civilians Transmit Norms of Protection." *Stability: International Journal of Security & Development* 2(3): 62, pp. 1–18,

Karl, Robert. 2016. "Here's the century-long history behind Colombia's peace agreement with the FARC." The Monkey Cage-Washington Post. October 1st 2016.

Kaufmann, Chaim. 1996. "Possible and Impossible Solutions to Ethnic Conflict." *International Security* 20(Spring): 136–175.

King, Gary, Robert Keohane, and Sidney Verba. 1994. *Designing Social Inquiry: Scientific Inference in Qualitative Research.* Princeton: Princeton University Press.

Klasnja, Marko, and Natalija Novta. 2016. "Segregation, Polarization, and Ethnic Conflict." *Journal of Conflict Resolution* 60(5): 927–955.

Kocher, Matthew, Thomas Pepinsky, and Stathis N. Kalyvas. 2011. "Bombing as an Instrument of Counterinsurgency in the Vietnam War." *American Journal of Political Science* 55(2): 201–218.

Kopstein, Jeffrey and Jason Wittenberg. 2010. "Deadly Communities: Local Political Milieux and the Persecution of Jews in Occupied Poland." *Comparative Political Studies* 44(3): 259–283.

Korge, Johannes. 2013. " Ms. Kalashnikov: The Women Rebels of Congo" *Das Spiegel Online* Retrieved on 2 October 2013 from:www.spiegel.de/international/world/francesca-tosarelli-photographs-women-rebel-fighters-in-congo-a-925283.html

Krause, Jana. 2011. "Resilient Communities: Non-Violence and Civilian Agency in Communal War." Presented at Harvard-MIT-Yale Graduate Student Conference on Political Violence, New Haven, CT, 23 April 2011.

Kudo, Timothy. 2015. "How We Learned to Kill." *New York Times*, February 27, 2015. Page SR1.

Kuran, Timur. 1995. *Private Truth, Public Lies.* Cambridge: Harvard University Press.

Kugler, Jacek, and Douglas Lemke (eds.) *Parity and War. Evaluations and Extensions of the War Ledger.* Ann Arbor: University of Michigan Press.

Liberman, Peter. 2013. "Retributive Support for International Punishment and Torture." *Journal of Conflict Resolution* 57(2): 285–306.

Littman, Rebecca, and Elizabeth Levy Paluck. 2015. "The Cycle of Violence: Understanding Individual Participation in Collective Violence." *Political Psychology* 36: 79–99.

Long, Scott J. 1997. *Regression Models for Categorical and Limited Dependent Variables.* Vol. 7, Advanced Quantitative Techniques in the Social Sciences: Sage Publications.

Long, Scott J., and Jeremy Freese. 2001. *Regression Models for Categorical Dependent Variables Using Stata.* College Station: Stata Press.

Luebbert, Gregory. 1987. "Social Foundations of Political Order in Interwar Europe." *World Politics* 39(4): 449–478.

Lyall, Jason. 2009. "Does Indiscriminate Violence Incite Insurgent Attacks? Evidence from Chechnya." *Journal of Conflict Resolution* 53(3): 331–362.

Maben, Michael. 2008. "Review of The Civil War's first blood: Missouri 1854–1861." *Journal of the West* 47(2): 82.

Maddison, Angus. 2008. Historical Statistics of the World Economy: 1-2008 AD. Available at: www.ggdc.net/maddison/.

Mampilly, Zachariah. 2011. Rebels with a Cause. The History of Rebel Governance, from the U.S. Civil War to Libya. *Foreign Affairs*, 13 April 2011.

Mao, Zedong. 1978. *On Guerrilla Warfare.* Trans. S. Griffith. Garden City: Anchor Press.

Maoz, Zeev. 1990. "Framing the National Interest: The Manipulation of Foreign Policy Decisions in Group Settings." *World Politics* 43(1): 77–110.

Mayhew, David R. 2005. "Wars and American Politics." *Perspectives on Politics* 3(3): 473–493.

McAdam, Doug, Sidney Tarrow, and Charles Tilly. 2001. *Dynamics of Contention.* NY: Cambridge University Press.

McLauchlin, Theodore. 2014. "Desertion, Terrain, and Control of the Home Front in Civil Wars." *Journal of Conflict Resolution* 58(8): 1419–1444.

McPherson, James. 1988. *Battle Cry of Freedom.* New York: Oxford University Press.

McPherson, James M. 2008. "Was It More Restrained than You Think?" *The New York Review of Books* 55(2).

Melander, Erik, Magnus Oberg, and Jonathan Hall. 2009. "Are 'New Wars' More Atrocious? Battle Intensity, Genocide and Forced Migration before and after the End of the Cold War." *European Journal of International Relations* 15(3):505–536.

Metelits, Claire. 2009. *Inside Insurgency. Violence, Civilians, and revolutionary group Behavior*. New York: New York University Press.

Mkandawire, Thandika. 2002. "The Terrible Toll of Post-Colonial 'Rebel Movements' in Africa: Towards an Explanation of the Violence against the Peasantry." *Journal of Modern African Studies* 40(2): 181–215.

Montalvo, Jose G., and Marta Reynal-Querol. 2005. "Ethnic Polarization, Potential Conflict, and Civil Wars." *American Economic Review* 95(3): 796–813.

Morales, Laura. 2004. *Institutions, Mobilisation, and Political Participation: Political Membership in Western Countries*. Madrid: Centro de Estudios Avanzados en Ciencias Sociales, Juan March Institute.

Moskalenko, Sophia, and Clark McCauley. 2009. "Measuring Political Mobilization: The Distinction between Activism and Radicalism." *Terrorism and Political Violence* 21(2): 239–260.

Mylonas, Harris. 2012. *The Politics of Nation-Building*. NY: Cambridge University Press.

Neely Jr., Mark E. 2004. "Was the Civil War a Total War?" *Civil War History* 50(4): 434–458.

Neely Jr., Mark E. 2007. *The Civil War and the Limits of Destruction*. Cambridge: Harvard University Press.

Organski, A. F. K. and Jacek Kugler. 1980. *The War Ledger*. Chicago: University of Chicago Press.

Overy, Richard J. 1980. *The Air War. 1939–1945*. New York: Stein and Day.

Pape, Robert A. 1996. *Bombing to Win. Air Power and Coercion in War*. Ithaca: Cornell University Press.

Petersen, Roger. 2001. *Resistance and Rebellion: Lessons from Eastern Europe*. New York: Cambridge University Press.

Petersen, Roger. 2002. *Understanding Ethnic Violence: Fear, Hatred, and Resentment in Twentieth-Century Eastern Europe*. New York: Cambridge University Press.

Petersen, Roger. 2011. *Western Intervention in the Balkans. The Strategic Use of Emotion in Conflict*. New York: Cambridge University Press.

Pinker, Steven. 2011. *The Better Angels of our Nature. Why Violence has Declined* Londong: Viking Penguin

Posen, Barry. 1993. "The security dilemma and ethnic conflict." Pp. 103–124 in *Ethnic Conflict and International Security*, ed. M. Brown. Princeton: Princeton University Press.

Posner, Daniel. 2004. "The Political Salience of Cultural Difference: Why Chewas and Tumbukas Are Allies in Zambia and Adversaries in Malawi." *American Political Science Review* 98(4): 529–545.

Przeworski, Adam. 1985. *Capitalism and Social Democracy*. New York: Cambridge University Press.

Przeworski, Adam. 1991. *Democracy and the Market. Political and Economic Reforms in Eastern Europe and Latin America*. NY: Cambridge University Press.

Przeworski, Adam. 2005. "Democracy as an Equilibrium." *Public Choice* 123(3–4): 253–273.

Przeworski, Adam. 2007. "Is the Science of Comparative Politics Possible?" Pp. 146–171 in *Oxford Handbook of Comparative Politics*, eds. C. Boix and S. Stokes. New York: Oxford University Press.

Przeworski, Adam, and John Sprague. 1989. *Paper Stones. A History of Electoral Socialism*. Chicago: University of Chicago Press.

Putnam, Robert, Robert Leonardi, and Raffaela Nanetti. 1993. *Making Democracy Work: Civil Traditions in Modern Italy*. Princeton: Princeton University Press.

Rangel, Alfredo. 2001. *Guerra Insurgente. Conflictos en Malasia, Perú, Filipinas, El Salvador y Colombia*. Bogotá: Intermedio Editores.

Reno, William. 2011. *Warfare in Independent Africa*. New York: Cambridge University Press.

Reynal-Querol, Marta. 2002. "Ethnicity, Political Systems, and Civil War." *Journal of Conflict Resolution* 46(1): 29–54.

Roberts, Adam. 1967. *The Strategy of Civilian Defence: Non-Violent Resistance to Aggression*. London: Faber and Faber Ltd.

Ross, Michael. 2004. "How do Natural Resources Influence Civil War? Evidence from Thirteen Cases." *International Organization* 58: 35–67.

Rowan, Steven (Ed). 1983. *Germans for a Free Missouri. Translations from the St. Louis Radical Press, 1857–1862*. Columbia: University of Missouri Press.

Roxborough, Ian. 2009. "The Rise of the Global State System and Waves of Irregular Warfare." Presented at the Comparative Research Worskhop, Yale University, March 23, 2009.

Rubin, Alissa J., and Hwaida Saad. 2016. "Aleppo Bombs Leave Quarter Million 'Living in Hell' and without Hospital Care." *New York Times*, November 20, 2016.

Sambanis, Nicholas. 2001. "Do Ethnic and Nonethnic Civil Wars Have the Same Causes? A Theoretical and Empirical Inquiry (Part 1)." *Journal of Conflict Resolution* 45(3): 259–282.

Schmitt, Carl. 1976. *The Concept of the Political*. New Brunswick: Rutgers University Press.

Sen, Amartya K. 1977. "Rational Fools: A Critique of the Behavioral Foundations of Economic Theory." *Philosophy and Public Affairs* 6(4): 317–344.

Silke, Andrew. 2003. "Becoming a Terrorist." In *Victims and Society. Psychological Perspectives on Terrorism and its Consequences*, ed. A. Silke. New Jersey: Wiley. Pp. 29–54.

Slim, Hugo. 2008. *Killing Civilians. Method, Madness, and Morality in War*. New York: Columbia University Press.

Speckhard, Anne, and Khapta Ahkmedova. 2006. "The Making of a Martyr: Chechen Suicide Terrorism." *Studies in Conflict and Terrorism* 29(5): 429–92.

Stanton, Jessica. 2015. "Regulating Militias: Governments, Militias, and Civilian Targeting in Civil Wars." *Journal of Conflict Resolution* 59(5): 899–923.

Starn, Orin. 1995. "The Revolt against the Revolution: War and Resistance in Peru's Andes." *Cultural Anthropology* 10(4): 547–580.

Stearns, Jason. 2011. *Dancing in the Glory of Monsters. The Collapse of the Congo and the Great War of Africa*. New York: PublicAffairs.

Steele, Abbey. 2009. "Seeking Safety: Avoiding Displacement and Choosing Destinations in Civil Wars." *Journal of Peace Research* 46(3): 419–429.

Steele, Abbey. 2010. *Unsettling: Displacement during Civil Wars*. PhD Dissertation, Department of Political Science, Yale University.

Stein, Rachel. 2015. "War and Revenge: Explaining Conflict Initiation by Democracies." *American Political Science Review* 109(3): 556–573.

Stein, Rachel. 2016. "Vengeful Citizens, Violent States: A Theory of War and Revenge." Manuscript presented at the IR Colloquium, Princeton University.

Stephen, Chris. 2011. "Libyan Opposition Attacks Sirte as Military Union Is Formed." Bloomberg Business. Retrieved on September 24, 2011 from: www.bloomberg.com/news/09-24/libyan-opposition-makes-attack-on-sirte

Straus, Scott. 2006. *The Order of Genocide. Race, Power and War in Rwanda.* Ithaca and London: Cornell University Press.

Straus, Scott. 2015. *Making and Unmaking Nations: The Origins and Dynamics of Genocide in Contemporary Africa.* Ithaca: Cornell University Press.

Sullivan, Christopher. 2014. "The (in)effectiveness of Torture for Combating Insurgency." *Journal of Peace Research* 51(3): 388–404.

Tavernise, Sabrina. "Survivors in Georgia Tell of Ethnic Killings." *The New York Times,* 19 August 2008: A1.

Tilly, Charles. 1978. *From Mobilization to Revolution.* London & New York: McGraw-Hill.

Tilly, Charles. 2003. *The Politics of Collective Action.* NY: Cambridge University Press.

Toft, Monica D. 2003. *The Geography of Ethnic Violence. Identity, Interests, and the Indivisibility of Territory.* Princeton: Princeton University Press.

Toft, Monica D., and Yuri M. Zhukov. 2015. "Islamists and Nationalists: Rebel Motivation and Counterinsurgency in Russia's North Caucasus." *American Political Science Review* 109(2): 222–238.

Tzu, Sun. 2010. *The Art of War* [Translated by Lionel Giles in 1919] London: Simon&Brown.

Valentino, Benjamin. 2004. *Final Solutions. Mass Killing and Genocide in the 20th Century.* Ithaca & London: Cornell University Press.

Valentino, Benjamin. 2014. "Why We Kill: The Political Science of Political Violence against Civilians." *Annual Review of Political Science* 17: 89–103.

Valentino, Benjamin A., Paul Huth, and Dylan Balch-Lindsay. 2004. "Draining the Sea: Mass Killing, Genocide, and Guerrilla Warfare." *International Organization* 58(2): 375–407.

Vargas, Gonzalo. 2009. "Urban Irregular Warfare and Violence against Civilians: Evidence From a Colombian City." *Terrorism and Political Violence* 21(1): 110–32.

Varshney, Ashutosh. 2002. *Ethnic Conflict and Civic Life: Hindus and Muslims in India.* New Haven: Yale University Press.

Verba, Sidney, Kay L. Schlozman, and Henry Brady. 1995. *Voice and Equality. Civic Voluntarism in American Politics.* Cambridge: Harvard University Press.

Vogt, Manuel. 2013. "Ethnic Mobilization, Equality and Conflict in Multi-ethnic States." PhD dissertation. ETH Zürich.

Weidmann, Nils B. 2011. "Violence 'from above' or 'from below'? The Role of Ethnicity in Bosnia's Civil War." *The Journal of Politics* 73(4): 1178–90.

Weinstein, Jeremy. 2007. *Inside Rebellion: The Political Economy of Rebel Organization.* London & New York: Cambridge University Press.

Wilkinson, Steven I. 2004. *Votes and Violence: Electoral Competition and Ethnic Riots in India.* New York: Cambridge University Press.

Wimmer, Andreas. 2012. *Waves of War: Nationalism, State Formation, and Ethnic Exclusion in the Modern World*. New York: Cambridge University Press.

Wimmer, Andreas, and Chris Miner. 2016. Looting, Loose Guns, Territorial Control, or Ethnic Cleansing? Violence against Civilians in African Civil Wars. Unpublished manuscript, Columbia University.

Wintour, Patrick. 2016. "Aleppo Ceasefire at Risk after Russia Says All Rebels Can Be Eliminated." *The Guardian*, October 21, 2016.

Wood, Elisabeth J. 2003. *Insurgent Collective Action and Civil War in El Salvador*. New York & London: Cambridge University Press.

Wood, Elisabeth J. 2006. "Variation in Sexual Violence during War." *Politics and Society* 34(3): 307–342.

Wood, Elisabeth J. 2009. "Armed Groups and Sexual Violence: When Is Wartime Rape Rare?" *Politics and Society* 37(1): 131–162.

Wood, Reed M. 2010. "Rebel Capability and Strategic Violence against Civilians." *Journal of Peace Research* 47(5): 601–614.

Wood, Reed M., Jacob Kathman, and Stephen Gent. 2012. "Armed Intervention and Insurgent Violence against Civilians in Intrastate Conflicts" *Journal of Peace Research* 49(5): 647–660.

Zeira, Yael. 2012. *Gateways to Rebellion: Organizational Membership and Participation in the Palestinian National Movement*. PhD Dissertation, Department of Politics, New York University.

# Index